San Francisco.

Gold sun and not a cloud in the blue
skies. No rain since May and none
expected before November. Soft
westerlies from the ocean.
A necklace of rooflines along the
hillsides of a city. White buildings and
blue sky making a Mediterranean
day. Road crews out repainting the
white lines. Evergreen smells down
from the Presidio.

A summer day in San Francisco.

A billet doux for the Lady by the Bay

In French, a billet doux means "sweet letter."

Billets-Doux

Fred Zackel

I was a feral child. As a five-year-old, oh, so many years ago I pushed aside a summer screen and slipped out a second story window. Grabbing the nape of a pine tree, I jumped into space and rode that tree down to the ground below my window and ran off to have fun. *Son of a gun... We'll have big fun...* After me, that pine tree was bent at the top like a fisherman's hook.

I have always wandered off. Or drifted away. I went west, mostly. Towards the ocean. I stopped when I thought I had run out of land.

My first hour in San Francisco I almost ran over Barbra Streisand, and Ryan O'Neal pulled her out of my path. They were filming *What's Up, Doc?* And I was careening down Clay Street, my first San Francisco hill.

On the Sunday night after the Loma Prieta earthquake, I drove a ferry boat captain to Treasure Island to work. I drove my taxicab. On my return I said, *what the hell,* and double-parked on the empty bridge. And all alone in the vast center lanes of the upper deck of the damaged San Francisco Bay Bridge, I danced and sang at the top of my voice for the glistening skyline until the chilly winds and vertigo said I should leave.

The city was the older woman who woke up my life. She could have treated me better, but she never broke my heart. These days she is taking a beating. Gargantuan outsider money. Homelessness. Now a pandemic. She seems to be losing her joy.

San Francisco has always been much more than a setting.

Some years after arriving out west, in January 1978 Ross Macdonald wrote, "Fred Zackel's first novel reminds me of the young Dashiell Hammett's work, not because it is an imitation, but because it is not. It is a powerful and original book made from the lives and language of the people who live in San Francisco today."

For fifty years I have been writing love letters to the Lady by the Bay.

Fifty years?! That's a lot of love letters.

The lives and language of the people who live in San Francisco today.

Let me share some billets-doux. Sweet letters to San Francisco. Read where you wish. In whatever manner you wish. For as long as you wish.

Ross Macdonald

I learned most about writing from Ross Macdonald, first through reading and then by asking specific questions. He was a very generous man. Nobody outside of my family ever treated me nicer or gave me such hope. First off, he had me call him Ken, which in light of who each of us was still amazes me. You see, he was the Literary Lion of Santa Barbara. There was no one greater in those days. He had two dozen novels under his belt, had that huge feature article about him in *Time* magazine, he had a PhD from U of Michigan, Eudora Welty praising him in *The New York Times*, two big movie studio feature length movies starring Paul Newman, all that talk about a TV series.

Me? I was a kid driving taxicab at night in San Francisco. I worked for a Chinese cab company operating out of an unmarked garage at the edge of Chinatown; my bosses were refugees from Mainland China; they were both the owners and the mechanics. I drove a fifty dollar canary yellow ex-taxicab too old and too beat to be a cab anymore.

Another thing ... He was always Ken Millar to me. He wrote letters and signed them *Ken*. He wasn't Ross Macdonald. He was Ken. The first image I remember was ... how he walked alongside me. And I know how stupid that sounds. When I was with him, we walked a lot, usually with a handful of dogs trying to run between our feet and topple us. I don't recall him ever using a leash on any of them. He truly loved dogs. His house was geared for the thundering paws of big dogs playing rough. We walked sidewalks and boardwalks and dusty creek beds and ... and ... I knew I didn't deserve that heartfelt warmth and generosity and friendship and patience, but he gave it to me without reservation.

Two very public places where I met up with Ross Macdonald was the Santa Barbara Writers Conference two summers in a row back in the mid-1970s. The second time I was there, a woman showed me a photograph from the previous summer, with Ken Millar and I walking together under the palms in Santa Barbara, lost in talking together. We looked like two college math professors debating a math problem. An odd picture in so many ways. And I saw the woman's photograph of the two of us and I clicked on Ken walking alongside of me. He listened to me and talked to me and argued with me and advised me and ... We even swapped gossip about who was sleeping with whom at the conference ... and worse. At every opportunity he was kind and he was generous and nobody outside of my family has ever been that encouraging to me.

I still have and read his letters; how he encouraged me, geez. Like nobody else has. There is other stuff, too, from him that my kids will get when I'm gone. Anyway, that woman got my address and said she'd send me the photo. I waited and waited. I asked around about her and the photo, but I never heard from her again. I never saw the picture again. About forty-five years ago now. I would dearly love to have that photograph.

Déjà vécu...

I just couldn't believe I was back in California. Six lanes of traffic in front of me as far as my eye can see. Six lanes of traffic behind me as far as my eye can see. When I look on the other side of the freeway, yep, six lanes in the opposite direction, both ways, as far as my eye can see. And nobody is moving. Yep, stuck in traffic once again.

I still miss my California, although an overnight sneak trip to the East Bay last February convinced me that everyone in the world DOES live there now. The trees seemed bigger and the streets weren't so wide. The prices were about what I expected. But I was astonished that after twenty years of my being absent, I discovered that Cal Trans had done nothing about the I-580 maze to get on the SF Bay Bridge from the East Bay.

My California. From the air I also saw the rows of houses that now housed a population that had probably doubled since my first driving license.

My San Francisco no longer exists. If it ever did.

Don't go looking for it, either. Too dangerous.

No room for me in California. I couldn't even afford to be here.

∞

Before I went for my Masters and my PhD, I drove cab at night in San Francisco for twenty years. I was a witness to the Gay Revolution. For ten years this tribe was joyously liberated. Yes, joyously. They were outrageous, silly and catty, bitchy and noisy, and brilliantly witty, and for the first time they were a collective, a tribe having the time of their lives. And out of nowhere the AIDs pandemic snuck in and crushed them. I watched a community almost die. I had written four previous San Francisco novels and never quite got it right, and when I wrote one book with AIDs as a motive, MURDER IN WAIKIKI, New York publishers were uninterested. And I couldn't figure out how to write the nightlife I had witnessed.

For all those years I took notes as I drove and what amazing things I saw and heard. But then my family and I moved east for the PhD. (After four drunk drivers nailing me, the PhD was easier.) But going back to school in my mid-forties was a different struggle. Just as demanding and just as painful. And I had to let those notes percolate for years into a story.

Gender in San Francisco was always fluid. People were and still are in transition. Pronouns would often change in mid-sentence. In mid-speech! As long as a writer listens and shows respect for that character's dignity, clarity for the reader is not a problem.

One more non-sequitur: I am doing all this all alone. I have no publisher behind me. No editor. An agent who I cannot feed or please. Years ago we all drifted apart. Once a month or so, I try self-promoting, and the blatancy always ends up tasting of cold ash. And there are so many writers' voices around me! I'd rather be writing. Being retired, my career is mostly over. Like a taxidermist, I still like puttering at my desk, sculpting my beautiful birds. Stuffed and mounted, they sit on my bookshelf.

Please enjoy!

The Golden Dragon Take-out

I left a cheery message and went home. Well, I fought the traffic and stopped first at the Golden Dragon Take-Out on Washington Street in Chinatown and for some char sui. *Hot dripping pork chunks!*
Out on the Avenues, Mary Noël had cold rice.
We picnicked.

When I started writing about San Francisco, I was fearless and naïve. The two go together. I wrote about gays and Chinatown, lesbian bars and the black neighborhoods and... Any writer who works for fifty years runs the risk of demanding his own downfall. No sense in saying that all those decades ago this casual cruelty, this racism, my stupid misogyny was how the people I knew talked. That I was copying the language I heard. For that, for every insensitive, inappropriate example, I do humbly apologize.

Anza and the Fog

I found Anza Avenue socked in by thick summer fog. It was the middle of the day, the streetlights were on, and those two rows of lights raced away down the street toward the beach and disappeared into the noon fog.

Felicity Shuang & the 38 Geary

We finally introduced ourselves. In another time we would have shook hands. In a time of contagion, no. We clunked elbows.

"Call me Felicity," she said. "Felicity Shuang. My father worked in a Chinatown restaurant in San Francisco. He would get off work after midnight and ride the last bus of the night home, the 38 Geary, after cleaning up, and he would ride that bus all the way out to the Sunset District carrying, you know, a big stainless steel bucket of soup home from the kitchen job. That was our lunch and maybe our supper the next day, while he was back at work."

The Ponytail and the Bridge

Eloise approached me in the gastropub. Reluctantly she smiled and I saw she had perfect small white teeth, except her front canine tooth on the left was chipped. I noticed her right away. She was between cute and adorable. I had already fallen all the way for the Pretty Girl with the Great Big Smile and the soft Tidewater lilt in her voice.

But after what pain I had been through in Philly, I had zero expectations. Not even fantasies. Look, I am not painful to look at, but I am ordinary. Of the things in life that are sexy, I know I am not one of them. So please let me be. I am common and clumsy, I know. The first time I got to first base in junior high, I sneezed right on her bare boobies. Oh, women never forgive you for allergies.

I said it. "You put on some weight."

She was swallowing glass. But she wouldn't leave.

I am also shallow, and I lapse into reveries and drift into self-absorption.

"I saw you on the Bridge," this woman said. She had such a soft silky drawl.

"When? Where? What bridge?"

"San Francisco," she said.

"It wasn't me," I said. Always, denial is the best foot forward. Being so big, I can seem ... clumsy and creepy, so I never make a move to flirt. I have self-esteem deficiency, too, okay?

"You saved her life."

"That wasn't me." Repeat as needed until the symptom leaves you alone.

"I'm the one who called the cops. The Highway Patrol."

Oh, damn, maybe it was her.

"You're a hero," she said. "A remarkable hero."

"It wasn't me at all. You got me mixed up with somebody else."

"After what you did? You had to be looking down!"

"I had my eyes closed the whole time," I said. It was the truth. Mostly.

"Why did you run away?"

"I got vertigo," I admitted. I gave up all pretenses. "I have agoraphobia really bad. No, I mean, acrophobia. Fear of heights. I love the Bridge. I can drive across it, I can walk it, and I can jog across it. But I can't look over the railing."

Her mouth was gaping with shock and surprise.

"What's your name?"

"Eloise. And yours?"

"I'm Nick." We shook hands.

"But you saved that woman's life!"

"If I had to do it again..." I shook my head. No way.

"You never let go!"

"Fear makes people get a death grip. They can't let go."

She backed off. "You're lying!"

"Why would I lie about something like that?"

Maybe I should say she has nice boobs, so the young woman would leave me alone. *Go away!* Well, she did have nice boobs. And a friendly face now that I noticed. And kind eyes. I get lonely.

Okay, I am a shallow person. Leave me alone!

All I wanted was to be left alone.

"I watched you save her."

"You're reading too much into it," I said.

"Are you from San Francisco?" she asked.

Get her off-guard. Keep changing the subject.

"What were you doing there?"

Flummoxed she was by my question.

"Do you mind if I join you?"

"What were you doing in San Francisco?" I said, sharp like a cop.

She blurted: "There was a Russian spy ship off Oahu. Oh, well, it's always anchored out there. But it was sending weird messages at very high speeds at irregular intervals. Very different weirder messages than usual."

"And you study very different weird messages."

"Well, sometimes I help."

By now she was sitting opposite me at my table.

"Why weren't you there?"

She was a bit forward, well, pushy.

"What? At HCC?"

"What's HCC?"

"The Hawaii Cryptologic Center near Wahiawa."

"But you weren't there that day."

"No, I was in San Francisco. I saw you on the Bridge."

"Did you take any pictures?"

"Well, no..."

"Then it wasn't me," I said. "Why weren't you there in Hawaii?"

"My brother was getting divorced."

Later I looked it up on her laptop. The HCC, which was also known as NSA Hawaii, is a U.S. National Security Agency (NSA) Central Security Service (CSS) facility located near Wahiawa on the island of Oahu, Hawaii.

That's where Edward Snowden stole all those documents from.

"Are you in San Francisco a lot?"

She was sly. "I know a restaurant in the Mission that serves authentic grasshopper tacos." When I made a face, "It's an aphrodisiac!" she claimed.

"I'm a lousy lover," I said. "I'd rather stay that way."

Eloise said, "The chapulines are free-range and gluten-free."

"What's that?"

"Sautéed grasshoppers," she said. "I know where we can get cricket tacos!"

What else happened that night?

She stayed. We talked.

Eloise was lonely and easy. Or maybe that was me.

They no sooner looked but loved.

Okay, not the solid gold truth. As the Chinese say, "chabuduo," or "close enough." Or maybe "chà bu du," depending upon who you ask. Close enough like hand grenades, horseshoes, and meat loaf at a diner.

Years later, my brother-in-law Robert Ketchum said the same Chinese word. He then said, "Safety officials use it most often to justify cutting corners or taking short cuts. A bridge was built with substandard concrete. Well, according to the contractor, substandard was close enough to being safe enough. The Chinese safety engineers said the same thing about the steel rails on a commuter train. Substandard steel is close enough! In another case, a school was warned about a wall that crushed a school girl to death during the Osaka earthquake, a substandard concrete wall. Well, the school tested it before it collapsed. The school officials hit the wall with a hammer. Safe enough!"

In the morning, Eloise said in a gangster's growl, "You're a fun date, copper." After the giggles, she said, "A naked girl will say anything to get more."

"You want more?"

Like Charles Dickens, she said, "More, please."

Nob Hill and the Fog

The City was fogged in and gorgeous. Always a spectacular view at the top of Nob Hill. Some scientists say that with global warming, San Francisco's fog will vanish and be just another climate legend.

Daddy, what's a glacier?

Taylor Street

Taylor Street in San Francisco on Nob Hill was two-way. North to Fisherman's wharf and south towards Union Square. Where it is steep, the climb gives tourists the pitter-patter heart. Where it is downhill, it is nearly breathless with dread and anticipation.

Climbing northward and uphill, the bad guys on the motorcycles whooshed around me on my left side and tried to cut in front and stop me, paralyzing me below the top of the hill.

I backed up, let the car roll backwards, saw an alley on my right behind me that I could pull into, hit reverse and speeding from the pull of gravity I entered butt-first into that alley. Slammed on the brakes. Sticking nose first out of the drive.

Being perpendicular to the street, I spun the steering wheel and shifted into drive. I drove the wrong way down the one-way street hill. The bad guys were stuck in the wrong lane above me, blocking the path for upcoming cars, and being cycles they froze in place, and then a cop car came southward over the hill from the other side, hit its lights and sirens and nailed the bad guys.

I saw Darryl Harlowe in the rear view mirror. He was shocked and stunned.

He choked out some words. "What did you just do?"

Feeling pleased with myself as we sped out and through the synchronized traffic lights of Pine Street, I told the boss, "I just saved your life."

"Yes, sir, you did! You did what? How?"

"Move your right hand uphill slowly. Use your left hand to be the motorcyclists to cut in front of my right and stop there to spray us with bullets. I backed up my right hand into a driveway and then drove downhill the wrong way. Being a motorcycle, your left hand was stuck up there and perpendicular to the hill and you could not go downhill safely quick enough. Safely is the key word. On a motorcycle, you have to ride the brake to go downhill or you spill and roll to the bottom like a trash can. Stuck with no options, you are stuck figuring it out. Being perpendicular to the street, the cops busted your ass."

Only in San Francisco, I added.

Winter among the Redwoods in Mendocino

She went stern, then sad. "I guess Christmas means nothing to you."

"It means a lot." He turned away from her. "It means I got to spend Christmas here."

Kate had taken a couple of business courses at the local junior college. She could cope with him, but she didn't need him. She decided she could finish stapling tomorrow and headed for the coffee pot.

The OK truck stop was tiny, even for Mendocino County. There were four stools at the counter and two tables on the floor. Generations of scrambled eggs had tarnished every fork, and the water glasses were plastic and discolored. But the eggs were ranch house fresh and the apple cider sparkled like California champagne. There were paper Santas on the windows, and artificial snow was swirled in Jack Frost designs on the plate glass. Opal and Kate Walker had put a lot of love in here.

The runt rubbed clean a patch on the steamed windows. I don't know what he hoped to see outside. There was nothing there. Oh, the parking lot had floodlights. Once in a while outbound semis went past us, their port and starboard running lamps like Christmas lights. The nearest town was three miles north, and redwoods went thirty miles in every direction. Even the stars weren't out.

It was raining outside, a downpour that had been pouring down for the past week. A typical Northern California winter storm—rain without lightning or thunder, just water falling from the heavens like Chinese water torture. Dull and gray.

During the Gold Rush, murderers received lighter sentences if they killed in the rain. Juries could understand how a weeklong rain could fray a man's nerves and turn his temper into a razor. The newspaper I had said this was already the coldest and wettest winter since the Gold Rush.

My mood was nearly as gray as all outdoors. A four hundred mile round trip with some second-rate presents. My youngest asking why Daddy had to drive back in the rain. Every man winches when he's being nibbled, and today had been a real bite.

Kate brought me the pot. "How was the omelet?"

"Great." I looked across. "I noticed that."

Her frown was long. "I wish he'd leave."

"Where did he come from?"

"His van broke down," she told me. "A wheel bearing I guess. He coasted this far. With the holiday, the garage can't get parts until Monday." She left to turn some bacon for tomorrow's rush.

Opal Walker came from the back room. She had stopped smiling years ago. Now she chain-smoked Pall Mall regulars. She seemed to be shrinking with the years. Her neck was bowed, she didn't move as fast as before, and her skin was tightening with wrinkles. She claimed her hearing was going fast, and her legs seemed to hurt more with every rainy season.

She saw me and came over with a fresh pot. "You got a full cup," she noticed. She pulled up a chair. "Then I'll sit down."

Opal Walker was first generation Oakie, one of the Dust Bowl babies. She and her husband had sweated and slaved and scraped to build a farm in the San Joaquin Valley. Thirty years ago, a drunk careened his pickup into a tree. Opal sold the farm, took the insurance settlement and her baby daughter, drove north from the Valley heat to these fog-bound coastal forests, and bought the first truck stop with a For Sale sign.

"How are the boys?" she asked.

"Real good," I said. "I spent most of the day cleaning up after them. They had a real good time."

"Your oldest, he comes in now and again. I always cut him an extra piece of pie."

"You shouldn't do that."

She sloughed it off. "My whole life is things I shouldn't do." She lowered her voice. "I think she's starving those boys."

"She just thinks they should be lean."

"Looks like starving to me."

"That's because you're raising granddaughters. And little girls eat more than little boys. Besides, I can't say anything. She won't listen to me."

She pursed her lips. "Since when?"

Dead Men Don't Testify

After the paperwork on his father's death, Tommy was too wired and too tired to deadhead back to his Lombard Street motel, so he stopped for coffee at the donut shop at Third and King, which according to SFPD Homicide Inspector Kristy Doyle, was a favorite rest stop for those who work all night on the streets of San Francisco.

Kristy Doyle had said, "The donut shop is canter corner from what used to be the Southern Pacific Commuter Train Station before it was moved to Fourth Street."

She then said, "Parking is tough, although there's few shops or warehouses in the neighborhood, except a bar and grill next door that goes through owners fast."

Tommy knew how to navigate San Francisco. His mother often brought him here before he could legally drive, and he drove her around the City when she was too drunk to get behind the wheel. Before he married, he brought Teresa here. They partied hard.

Like the cops, Tommy parked by the red fire hydrant. Tommy wasn't worried about a ticket.

Back at the hospital Doyle had told him, "This time of night, most cops recognize a pit stop when we see one. As long as you don't linger, it shows your respect for the next guy."

Tommy saw but didn't think twice about the shiny dark green Ford Crown Victoria that pulled up a half-block behind him and was now waiting with its headlights off. He was listening to a jet coming in for a landing at SFO to the south, wishing he was out flying elsewhere, anywhere.

He's waiting for the space to open up, Tommy thought.

Inside, Tommy ordered a pair of plain old-fashioneds and a jumbo black no sugar to go. While he waited for the order to be filled, he marveled at the cop scents that enveloped the donut shop. Tommy sensed a rainbow of scents from the dozen cops and deputies at the tables and in the booths. As far as he could tell, the scent of cops far and away overwhelmed the smells coming off the fresh donuts.

Doyle had said, "All the cops like to haunt it. Federal, state, local, private, all go there when they're in the neighborhood. It's a good Code Seven."

Sometimes Tommy's wife Teresa took Tommy into gift shops in Vegas that sold candles, and just like then, this time his nose went soaring high and not berserk.

He was okay, just barely functioning, in the donut shop. There were so many different cop scents that his psychic ability shut down in protest or maybe fatigue. Or mixed with the donuts, the scents off all these cops wasn't overwhelming. He could get in and out and that was all that mattered.

It was inside the donut shop that Tommy heard from two customers at a table for the first time that John Lennon had been killed in Manhattan outside his apartment building. By a fan of his, they said, and Tommy could make no sense of that lunacy.

Who would kill a Beatle? And why?

Confused and baffled, Tommy went back to his car and noticed neither the driver of the Crown Vic nor his passenger had come inside the donut shop. He assumed that the green Crown Vic was waiting for the fire hydrant space to open up.

Tommy noticed the other car had whitewalls. Not a cop, he thought.

The faintest hint of ... animal piss?

He got a twinge in the back of his brain, and he didn't know why.

With coffee cup in hand, Tommy drove up to Townsend, turned a left, then drove a block to Fourth and took another left and drove past the train station.

The shiny dark green Crown Vic followed him. So did that weird screwy scent.

Tommy now knew why he was worried.

Still, Tommy thought, I might be imagining situations. The green Crown Vic might be heading out Fourth Street toward the docks and the steel mills and the junk yards.

As he passed the train station, Tommy made a quick decision and made a hard right at the first street he saw. Abruptly he was in what felt like a gargantuan parking lot with no street lights.

He took King Street from Fourth to Seventh and discovered that the three blocks of King Street from Fourth to Seventh were the old trolley tracks. Two steel rails sunk in ruts in the old stone that were wide enough for an automobile to almost fit within.

His car lurched back and forth, tossing Tommy back and forth, and the chassis complained like an old leather satchel.

Tommy discovered he was alone in the dark. Nobody in his right mind drove King Street here. There wasn't a paved street here. There was no pavement, no curb, no sidewalk. No storefronts and no buildings. There were no side streets and no stop signs.

King Street was a pair of trolley tracks that cut across an empty train yard. Only ruts and chuckholes and cobblestones for three city blocks, and no streetlights to light up those ruts and chuckholes and cobblestones.

At night King Street might as well be on the dark side of the moon. For three city blocks he could only drive atop that single pair of trolley tracks with his headlights guiding him through complete darkness.

Tommy was bouncing in his seat, driving twice as fast as he should. He glanced in his mirror. The green Crown Vic still followed. His headlights wobbled, pitched, and yawled like Tommy's headlights were doing, and yet the green Crown Vic kept coming. No way he would keep coming unless Tommy was her target.

Another thing, too, troubled Tommy. If the bad guy was local, he would have known Tommy for his stupid stunt. But the driver knew now Tommy had made him.

The green Crown Vic tried closing the gap.

Tommy was then bumping across the big steel rails from the SP commuter trains. Those rails had left the station and now were curving across the old trolley tracks, crisscrossing King Street, as they headed south down the Peninsula toward San Jose.

He bounced and bounced and saw a flash in his mirror. He didn't see the bullet and it didn't shatter the windows, but he heard the gunshot and it didn't sound like a firecracker thrown by kids, and there was no one else around in the night.

He tossed his coffee out the window and punched the pedal to the floorboard. He felt sorry for his shocks. His car creaked like an old man growing older. The green Crown Vic kept coming. Another flash in the mirror, and he heard another crack! of gunfire, and the rear of his car sounded like somebody had bounced a stone off his trunk.

Tommy didn't hear the next shot.

But his rear window had a bullet hole.

Tommy, frightened, wondered where the bullet had gone and come to rest.

Another bullet blew through the rear window and thunked into the rear passenger's seat. The next one took out the passenger side headrest beside Tommy, blew it apart like a stuffed toy at the shooting range.

Terrified, Tommy punched the gas pedal.

At Seventh Street, where King Street dead-ended, he found concrete and made a hard right onto Seventh at full speed. He peeled some rubber, spat back some gravel, tore north on Seventh like a bat out of hell, and shot the green traffic light at Brannan like a coked-up cabbie, whooshing through it like a superhero on call.

The green Crown Vic went through the light on yellow, still a half-block behind him. Tommy heard a car horn when the green Crown Vic almost bought it.

He saw another flash, again heard that *crack!*

This time he heard a bullet whistle past his window.

He floored it and flew up Seventh. A block ahead the traffic light was turning red at Bryant. Tommy was still rushing north on Seventh. A fluorescent green road sign ahead said Bryant up ahead was a one-way street running west to east. In daylight, he remembered, Bryant was three lanes of fast-moving traffic coming in from the left. At night Tommy hoped the traffic was lighter, and Tommy figured if he ran the red light, being in that far right lane gave him the best chance to survive a car on Bryant crashing into his driver's side door.

Tommy had no back window. It blew out, shattered, disappeared.

Then he heard the shot that took it out.

Tommy felt his testicles ascend.

The green Crown Vic was catching up.

He took a deep breath, switched to his far right lane, and double-floored the pedal, and overdrive kicked in. With his left hand he gripped the wheel and shot across three lanes of on-coming traffic. Wide-eyed with adrenaline, he expected he'd be dying, and he prayed no innocent lives died with him.

Tommy crossed himself as he breached the intersection. Dear Lord, forgive me for my sins. *Christ, there been so many,* he thought. Bonifacio "Peaches" Larusso came first to mind. *I wish I hadn't gotten him killed.*

Tommy kept his eyes straight ahead. He heard the horns coming at him, saw in his peripheral vision their headlights looming up, heard their brakes screeching like sand-papered cats, and Tommy roared across the three lanes of Bryant without getting killed.

The green Crown Vic was closing on him, but also slowing to inch through the red traffic light at the intersection.

Tommy was under the 101 overpass. Without checking his side mirrors, he wrenched the steering wheel sideways, cut across three lanes of Seventh Street, and aimed himself like a flying dagger at Harrison Street and the Seventh Street on-ramp to the Bayshore Freeway.

The traffic light ahead was solid red. No chance for green.

Tommy crashed another red light and spun his wheels to the left. He made the ramp on two wheels, and he cut off a blue and white newspaper truck that was headed up-ramp and down-Peninsula with the morning home edition. He heard the truck driver's outraged horn and he felt sorry for cutting him off.

Tommy shot up the ramp. The green fluorescent road sign said he had a choice then. He could climb on the freeway south or he could stay in this lane. If he stayed in this lane, the Seventh Street on-ramp became the Ninth Street off-ramp. The freeway was a racetrack. Should he stay on it, or should he stop and fight?

Tommy would be helpless on the freeway. At eighty-five miles per hour, killing people gets easy. *All I have to do,* he thought, *is be more stupid than I have been so far.*

My great-grandfather's shotgun is in my trunk.

Tommy drove down the off-ramp at Ninth Street. He kept to the left and took the Eighth Street go-back-around. As he drove beneath the freeway, he stopped under the overpass. Tommy doused his lights, used his glove box button to pop his trunk, jumped out, grabbed his father's camouflage gun bag, ripped it open, yanked out his great-grandfather's shotgun, racked the slide, loving the clashing noise that metal made, and steeled himself for the green Crown Vic to come after him.

Tommy held his great-grandfather's shotgun with both hands and waited. He glanced at his trunk and saw the bullet holes above the bumper and in the trunk.

Tommy was twenty-three and terrified. Somebody wanted to kill me, he told himself. Be tough, he told himself. Shoot first, what his ma had always told him.

Tommy realized the shotgun was not loaded. He grabbed shells and tried loading as fast as he could. He lost a couple shells under his car but got his gun loaded.

No one came down the off-ramp.

Tommy waited, his eyes glued on the off-ramp, his feet spread apart, both fists clutching his great-grandfather's shotgun. He toughened up. His legs were wobbly.

No one came down the off-ramp.

Aside from the thunder of the 101 freeway above him, the world was silent. He adjusted his stance and bettered his grip on the shotgun and waited.

Tommy wondered if, when that the blue and white newspaper truck had come between him and the green Crown Vic, his pursuer never saw him take the off-ramp. Was that it? The shooter had been too busy trying to go around the newspaper truck to see Tommy's move?

He looked around at the strange catering skyline of San Francisco and realized how alone he was in the chilly night.

Nobody came down the off-ramp.

Tommy's legs gave way. He sat on the curb of the off-ramp for the freeway, shotgun in his arms, his mouth open and sucking air in and out like a bellows, his eyes wide as a newborn owl. If the green Crown Vic had missed Tommy's move, by now it was halfway to Candlestick Park, and it would never find him.

So hard to make sense of it all …

My father never knew me, Tommy thought.

I'd like to talk with him one more time, he thought.

Killing my father wasn't the goal. *Killing me was.*

I'm sorry, Dad, I got you killed.

All those people on Anza died because of me and coincidence. They were blameless mushrooms who popped up at the wrong place at the wrong time.

He remembered Laughin' Sal once talking about the slaughter of innocents:

"I knew a woman who stood between two mushroom victims. She fainted. That's what saved her. She woke up, blood splattered. Couldn't speak for three weeks. Couldn't construct sentences properly for three months." And then Sal's weird fucking barking laugh echoed like a bad divorce.

At the time Tommy had been barely paying attention.

Four dead. *My fault.* Guilty as charged.

Tommy was so drained, he couldn't get up from the curb. His body felt like a suit of tin that a tiny child was cowering inside of. Tommy was too weak with fear to fight the weight and inertia. Hard fighting back this hyperventilating.

He wondered who wanted him dead. Scary and sickening being a target--

Tommy sat alone in the cold San night air, his eyes closed, his senses roving the City. After all these years, Tommy knew most LVMPD unmarked cop cars both by sight and by scent. In a few cases, he even recognized the cop behind the wheel. He never told the Bovadiglias how good he was, what range he had, or how detailed he could sense cops.

He registered ... He was alone in the night.

What did I do to make someone want to kill me?

Sausalito on the Half-Shell

Think of an opened clam, and you've visualized the small harbor town of Sausalito.

The bottom shell is Richardson's Bay, a dogleg of San Francisco Bay north of the Golden Gateway. Richardson's Bay is filled with salt water, seagulls and sharks, buoys and yawls, dinghies and schooners, houseboats and cabin cruisers. The top shell is Wolfback Ridge, part of the California coastal range. The freeway into San Francisco is the crest of the ridge, and the slopes below it are densely wooded and dotted with expensive homes for San Francisco commuters. The hinge between the two shells is at the base of the ridge, a two-lane blacktopped road called the Bridgeway.

Downtown, the Bridgeway is lined with taverns and clothing stores, art galleries and restaurants. The drinks come watered, the seafood has been defrosted and microwaved, the clothing wears out just before the fad does, and the galleries sell watercolors of gulls and buoys.

The north end of town is further than most tourists can walk, so development there has been limited to serving the needs of residents. There are ship chandleries and marinas and yacht clubs, a couple of greasy spoons and a French laundry, a supermarket and a carryout liquor store.

The houseboats are north of downtown, too. Like all waterfront towns, Sausalito has residents whose appearances tend to frighten the tourists. Of course the houseboat dwellers say the feeling is mutual. They resent being considered tourist attractions, even if they do resemble the remark.

I drove along the Bridgeway until I found the Mohawk gas station where I had dropped Joey Crawford last week. The gravel access road alongside led down towards the boats and dead-ended at the foot of the Waldo Point boardwalk. I parked behind a weathered kiosk, rolled up my window and locked my doors, then went for a stroll on a lonely pier in the rain.

The tide was nearly gone, leaving behind a foot or so of water, and the houseboats floundered in the mud. The round-hulled crafts looked like Noah's Ark after the waters receded, and the square-hulled ones like quake victims. With thunderclouds above them and the roiled waters of a gunmetal bay beneath them, the houseboats looked like a wino's nightmare.

I stopped halfway down the boardwalk. With the tide leaving, small sea critters found themselves high and drying out, and their last gasps made the mudflats stink like rotten eggs. I didn't know which houseboat belonged to my client. I could always come back later in the day; a six-hour wait for high tide shouldn't make any difference. I retraced my steps downwind to think it over.

The kiosk had a bulletin board on its backside, flanked by a row of mailboxes. I went over each mailbox. There was no Crawford scrawled on any one, and I didn't know Dani's last name, so I set about rifling the mail inside each one. There was no mail for Joey Crawford or for any woman named Dani. Which meant I might have to wait for the afternoon delivery and repeat the whole procedure. Even that was a gamble.

The bulletin board was a good guide to the Sausalito lifestyle. There were people trying to buy houseboats, trying to sell sailboats, wanting to crew to Bora Bora.

There were rock concerts and sailing schools and organic restaurants and macramé lessons. There were psychologies and theologies, philosophies and sociologies. And a yellowed card advertising Seascape Sofas For Sale. Contact Alex Symons on board the Mal de mar.

The Mal de mar was a converted river barge jammed aft end first into a dismal little slip. The original deckhouse had been jettisoned, and a more spacious one built in its place with thick redwood beams for bracing. There was a small deck aft and a larger one forward. Large chunks of driftwood were strewn across the roof.

I went around the unpainted deckhouse and came out on the canopied forward deck. A thirtyish young man in white denims, rugby shirt and brine-soaked tennis shoes was sitting on a wood bench. His hands were spotted with grease, and he was having trouble rolling a joint, a can of Olympia was beside him. Through an opened window, I saw hanging ferns and a stereo speaker. Someone inside was frying liver and onions. A portable radio on the door stoop played an afternoon jazz concert from Berkeley.

"Alex Symons?"

He glanced up. "What can I do you for?" His face was babyish, like a fraternity boy. He had sandy hair and shaggy eyebrows and a moustache like an undercover vice cop. His hair was styled in an early Beatle, and he wore his sideburns long. His suntan came more from exposure than the sun. With his good looks, he probably did well at the fern bars and body shops on Union Street in the city.

"I saw your card on the bulletin board."

"Oh, glad to have you aboard." He set aside his makings, rubbed greasy hands on a nearby rag and offered me his hand. He had a good grip. His hands were rough and calloused, the hands of a carpenter. "How about dousing your cigarette?"

I saw the bucket of kerosene by the bench. Scattered around were tools and pistons and casings and plugs. He had been overhauling an outboard engine. I made a move towards the port side.

"Not in the bay. Use the beer can."

I did as he wished.

He saw me eyeing his joint. "I was just about to go inside." Carelessly, he tucked it into a crumpled pack of Camels. "You here about a sofa?"

"What is a seascape sofa, anyway?"

"Driftwood with legs." He pulled a tarp from a sample and told me how he built his furniture. A friend in Oregon searched for sofa-sized driftwood along the coast, then trucked the hunks down to Sausalito, where Symons would router some space for cushions, then screw legs on both ends. A girlfriend would tie-dye swatches of muslin, sew them into cushions, and then stuff with fiberfill. The price tag came last.

"How much does one run for?"

"A grand." He watched my eyes.

"Those tourists will buy anything," I marveled.

He made an effort to control himself, then threw the tarp back on. "You didn't come about a sofa."

Funeral of a US Marine

"What secrets do we learn here?" Queenie said.

"I doubt if any reveal themselves," I said.

She groused. "Should be at least one."

Queenie hated funerals. You would, too, after the AIDs epidemic tsunamied San Francisco.

Sometime after lunch on the third day Queenie, the African drag queen, and I went to the Marine's funeral in the Presidio. Although the Presidio was no longer part of the active military, its cemeteries still held the honored dead.

The funeral should have been held at midnight. More folks would have come. But there was a good crowd. More than would ever show up for my funeral. Hell, a buck says my own relatives would skip it.

I wanted to ask the mourners a thousand questions, but the local day man from *City@Nite* had that assignment. Surreptitiously he gave me the finger, but I didn't stoop that low because people were watching. I shot video though and sent it in. Maybe we could split the gig.

"I loved the man," Queenie said.

Queenie herself was a highly decorated Afghanistan War vet. She was dressed straight. Well, she could pass for straight today. Well, if you were astigmatic. She was wearing a dark blue suit and an open-necked pale blue shirt. Like all drag queens, when he was not in drag, you could walk right by him and never know what obsessed him. Or what pleasured him. Like I said, she worked as an investment banker in the Financial District.

A dozen representatives of GLMR sang "Amazing Grace." GLMR stood for the Gay and Lesbian Marine Reserve. Queenie pronounced it as "glamour."

The murdered Marine's parents came. They stood encircled by military officers and other relatives. Hopelessly lost in a crowd. Alone with grief. Merged as one in their sorrow.

At the funeral I also discovered the Marine was well-known in local gay circles. Some of San Francisco's most famous drag queens came out for the services. They wore their Sunday finest, although I doubt if many went to Sunday services. Everyone was well-behaved; the Marines and the queens could coexist for a funeral service. Although some queens panicked when the rifle volley went off.

A dozen members of a fundamentalist Baptist church group from Oklahoma and from Kansas came out to protest the military honors for a gay serviceman. They carried picket signs with hate-gay slogans. They were carrying placards and banners that condemned the military for permitting faggots to be buried in a military cemetery.

The zealous minister was out with his bullhorn, haranguing the funeral and his flock with how wicked a city San Francisco was. Yada, yada, blah, blah, blah.

Then the preacher used his bullhorn and led his congregation in various religious ballads. They sang religious songs, too, and tried passing out anti-gay pamphlets. Which meant the media was out in force. Somebody gave me a pamphlet of hate. *Wicked City!* Blah humbug.

This city's air makes one free.
Freedom and joy walk hand-in-hand here, madly in love.

Someone passed the word, and two dozen MPs from the Presidio lined up in the area in front of the cemetery section. There was a scuffle. One of the Baptists was arrested and placed in handcuffs. One of the queens was Maced in the face; her weeping distracted everyone and almost destroyed the ceremony.

I watched the day man interview the losers on both ends of the rainbow.

The Marine's father was a one-star Army general. He looked rugged, had a haircut as close-cropped as a lawn, a jaw chiseled from living granite, a spine straight as a redwood, and a face weathered and tanned by years outdoors.

The tan turned out to be a golfer's tan.

The father had retired here for the Presidio greens.

His son was home on leave, visiting his parents.

The mother kept sobbing loudly, wiping the coffin.

The father was reserved. He didn't throw himself on the coffin; his military training kept him straight; he stood back and stared at the coffin and wept without a sound.

Their surviving daughter hugged her mother's arm.

The mother fainted repeatedly. Father and daughter held her upright. Then grief opened the floodgates, and the father had no control over his emotions. His stony expression dissolved into deep gulping sobs that surprised us all.

I overheard a couple of queens describing what a wonderful guy the dead Marine was. So I filed my own story on the funeral. I hyped the jarhead a lot. If Ratzinger published it, the parents of the Marine would find a bit of comfort there.

I flipped the Finger to the Preacher.

I can't relive my old life. Those times are gone.

But I do miss those Wild Nights in this City.

Mark Twain

Mark Twain is considered the first internationally known California writer. His story about that Jumping Frog reverberated around the world. And just before that, when he was 31 years old, for instance, he tried committing suicide from despair in a cheap San Francisco hotel. (I wish I could say that suicidal loneliness no longer happens. But it does.)

When Mark Twain was seventy years old, he still wondered whether he should have committed suicide in San Francisco so long ago. Spooky, huh? And the last coherent words he spoke were about the Robert Louis Stevenson book, *Dr. Jekyll & Mister Hyde.* Spooky, huh???

Those Pagans at Lagunitas Creek

"Hell, I'm just going to stay a pagan."

"I bet you never met a pagan."

"Actually I did. Out in California when I was a young woman on the move."

He almost said, *What century was that*? But he caught himself in time.

"Yep, the closest I ever came to meeting real pagans happened back in the hippie days at Lagunitas Creek in Marin County." She smiled a wicked smile born from memory. "Look for the wooden bridge over the creek, Owen, and park as close as you can."

"They were hippies. They weren't pagans."

"They said they were pagans. They were these healthy young men who were naked and buff and skinny-dipping in the trickle from the creek, and my girlfriend Nora Lynn and I sat and talked with them as long as they would let us."

"Oh no, you didn't."

She grinned. "I like sitting and talking with naked young men on a summery day by a creek amidst the redwoods. Not that I remember much of what they said, except that they called themselves pagans, and that was about the last words they spoke that we actually listened to."

Horrified: "You stayed there!"

"We kept our clothes on the whole time."

Shameless old hussy, he thought, imagining her naked. *Eww, an old woman like her naked?*

"Something else I remember, Owen. What those naked healthy young pagan men learned about us was that our phone numbers proved to be wrong numbers when they tried calling us later. On the other hand, we may have written the phone numbers wrong."

"So you deceived them."

"Being blonde's like its own religion."

He grunted something noncommittal. She wasn't listening.

"It's a different way of life, a new way of thinking, of seeing things. People look at you different when you're a blonde.

You look at life differently when you're blonde. I was a blonde once. I liked it."

"You were a hippie once, too, so you said."

"I had fun as a blonde. I was a wild ass blonde."

Abstract calculation but no regret was in the tone of her voice.

Brenda Marie concluded, "Wild ass blondes have the most fun." She said her next words for the snoring young woman. "That's not an entitlement, like Social Security or Medicare. Just because you're blonde, or you made yourself blonde."

An underage hooker...

"When she no longer felt hunted, she came out from the shadows like a coyote comes down from the hills. Nobody noticed, or seemed to care, and quickly all was quiet and cold again. In the long hours of night, what is five minutes?

"Stiff gusts of wind began blowing in before Last Call, and those nightly breezes off the ocean turned mean-spirited. Still not a dollar or a dime to be found. Work the streets every night, and you know soon enough some nights are like that. Lonely nights, when the only thing on the streets is the wind.

"She had a long night of nothing happening. She worked to 3 AM, an hour past Last Call, until even the drunk bartenders had found their way home. Then she flagged a cab and left the streets."

El Encanto Hotel

I was walking along Geary Boulevard in San Francisco's Richmond district, or along a close approximation. A comfortable, non-threatening neighborhood filled with a wild variety of ethnicities that I knew well enough to imagine I was at home. I checked my reflection in store windows to see if I was still being followed.

I needed to cut through the block of shops on this, the south side of the street, to get to my destination, the residential homes. If I got there, I could ditch my tailgaters. Then I could go looking for my car.

A bronze sign on a wall said I could cut through El Encanto which appeared to be a small neighborhood hotel. Although I had never heard of it and thought I knew all of the hotels in San Francisco.

I found a doorway under a Spanish Colonial arch. Then I was in the lobby with thirteen-foot ceilings and more Spanish Colonial arches on various sides that lead deeper into the hotel. I felt more like I was in Santa Barbara than San Francisco.

No reception desk, per se, but a long counter with a couple of clerks in the back of the lobby at the end of a double row of display cases.

I walked to the back of the lobby. The hotel was wood-paneled in a dusky, almost swarthy Spanish style, but no lame lobby music. The lighting was all Spanish chandeliers, all traditional, all hand-forged iron.

To my left I passed a display without a glass box and I saw a curved Moorish silver knife about a foot-long that was jutting slightly from a dark Spanish leather sheath.

Around it were several Nevada dollar-sized pieces of jewelry. Lots of jewels. Not costume jewelry, antique yes, but not museum quality, either. But why display them out in the open? Sure, humans are tempted by shiny gaudy things. But what kept the thieves away?

To my right was open, the large lobby itself with leather sofas and armchairs, all low-slung and all glowing imitation Moroccan leather. A scattering of potted plants and a few coffee tables and stand-up lamps as punctuation.

The lobby to my right went deeper than I expected. Some old people sat there, all self-absorbed like vacationers. None looked at me. I filled nothing of their needs. I saw no one grinning in the shadows.

I got the clerk's attention. He was tall, very young, thin, although he might have been a gawky teenager who had mastered his awkwardness and now with a conventional grace.

He was disconcerted seeing me, but not openly perturbed,

I said, "I was told I could cut through the lobby and get outside back there."

He blanched. No, not that he knew…

He went off to look for answers. Too quickly, I thought.

Standing there, I checked out the older employees at their desks. An old man with spectacles pouring over a ledger, a salesclerk tidying a gift display case.

I waited and waited. Stiffed again.

To my right and in front of me was a small bakery shop that seemed to be selling wedding cakes, or leftover pieces of wedding cakes.

A table of samples was very close to me. I took a piece. It broke off in my fingers and the small marshmallow-sized chunks in my hand turned out not to be cake, but part of the frosting. Spun sugars, very dense, but gritty on the tongue.

Since I had moved sideways and up, I found I was close to a pretty salesclerk behind a glass counter, a row of cookie samples on a white ceramic tray beside her.

I asked if that arcade there behind her led out of the hotel.

She was confused by my words. No, it was just the area for the elevator that took guests to their hotel rooms above.

But I hadn't seen a reception desk, I said. Was this a hotel?

"The El Encanto," she said, confusing the English adjective "the" and the Spanish adjective "El." I thought about explaining that "the" and "el" had the same function in both languages, but that seemed a pointless waste of time.

"Where do you check in?"

"We rarely have walk-ins," she said.

Now I made her nervous. She looked around for some help please.

A gift shop was still behind her. New Mexican? Lots of Santa Fe turquoise, but all from five hundred years ago and the Spanish Conquest of the Southwest, but nothing new and nothing costume. All dark Spanish gold glowing like a desert sunset. The stuff that homicides were made of. Stuff to covet.

She moved back a step from me, disturbed by my presence. Or she read my thoughts.

I turned and saw the male clerk from before. He stopped moving diagonally away from me and reluctantly came next to me and the clerk.

"I'm sorry I couldn't help you," he said. "There's no way out by that way." Pointing to the elevator arcade.

Still feeling amiable, I said, "I never knew the hotel was here."

I was carrying a flat paper-wrapped package. As I set it on the glass counter, he seemed to unfreeze.

"Usually a spouse checks in by himself. And her spouse never checks in afterwards. Just goes upstairs and meets her."

"So married people alone?"

He nodded very slowly, words being precious here.

Startled, I said, "Do people ever check out?"

"They don't want to check out."

"Is this Heaven? Are they dead?"

"This is not Heaven."

"Is my wife here?" I asked.

"No one with her description has checked in."

"But I haven't described her!"

"You don't belong here," he said.

"I was just cutting through the lobby."

"You shouldn't be here."

I looked around and then more closely perused the Spanish gold, dark and swarthy, which had brought the pirates chasing after it.

"Shall I take you to your room?"

"I'm just passing through the lobby," I protested, looking back for the front doors I had entered through.

One arcade was filled with Old Mexico costumes on a rack. I wanted to go look them over, but—

"Then you should leave now," he insisted.

I took a step back, startled by his righteousness.

"If he should see you, it would be bad for all of us here."

I woke before dawn. I was on an old-fashioned Spanish Colonial-style four-poster bed with great masses of bright white bed covers. From my second-floor window facing south, a warm summer breeze came in from the desert that lay in front of me.

There was a large hole in my bathroom wall.

On the floor, a long feather, as long as my forearm. It was black in the light, then a dark blue, and then it was brilliant white as a blinding sun. Like the sheen on oil in moonlight.

The feather that cuts through steel.

I showered and then I found clothes that fit me, that were comfortable, but that I didn't recognize in the dusky wood wardrobe. I took the feather. *In Fairyland it's best to go armed.*

I walked downstairs, encountering no one, and found the lobby completely empty. I hollered several times, but no one answered. Then I walked toward the opened display and stole the curved Moorish silver knife and its dark Spanish leather sheath. *In Fairyland it's best to go armed.*

Upstairs, I made sure I had forgotten none of my belongings and then I stepped out my window and carefully inched along the red tiles on the roof and found my way down to the dirt-packed back patio. There I jumped. I ripped some skin in my right hand by landing awkwardly.

I left carrying the flat paper-wrapped package I had entered with, plus the long angel feather and the curved Moorish silver knife. There was a turquoise swimming pool on my left. It was empty at this hour, although all the loungers and chairs had been set out under extra-large Jose Cuervo umbrellas.

As I fled I saw the tall skinny man and the pretty young salesclerk standing together along the cobblestone road leading out into the desert. Neither one was smiling, but neither one was waving goodbye and good luck.

I had nothing to say.

The desert was wet with rain.

The San Francisco Aquarium

I went back through the aquarium. It was quiet and dark inside. There was a female I needed to see. My old friend Diane was three years old. Her body was scored with gouges and scars. She was a Pacific white-sided dolphin. She shared the dolphin tank with three harbor seals.

The tank was the size of a small living room. Three walls were blue concrete, and the fourth was plate glass. Salt water, moving much like the surf itself, surged through pumps and then recycled itself. A swimming pool with tidal action and one glass wall. The tank seemed very small.

I found a wooden bench spotted with graffiti. A sign on the glass wall had the dolphin feeding schedule. Today was cleaning day, and the feedings would be irregular. No workmen in sight, but every tourist in the world. A fat cormorant swam along the glass wall, fascinated by the tourists, especially the shrieking kids.

Diane could watch the tourists through the tank glass too, but she kept her back to them. She hid in the farthest corner, her muzzle away from prying eyes, her eyes focusing on the blank walls. She floated like a corpse just below the water level, motionless, as if contemplating suicide. She'd stay motionless until she had either to move or drown. Then she'd float to the surface, breathe, then sink again, and nuzzle the side of the tank, perhaps searching for a soft spot she could break through.

The three harbor seals with her were fat and sleek, like fat brown loaves of homemade bread. They had few scars on their speckled fur. They had been here since they were pups. Folks had found them on the beach and had thought they were abandoned. But their parents were only away foraging for food and had stuck the pups there for safety. So much for a good idea.

They swam effortlessly in great circling loops, continuously touring the tank, rubbing the plate glass with their bellies, rarely using their flippers. But they were crazy as loons. They always swam upside down. Crazy seals with madman eyes.

Once a seal came too close. Diane lurched and her tail smacked his muzzle. It was hard enough to stun him for an instant.

They say dolphins have a permanent smile. I saw no trace of one on her. She didn't look playful. She looked plaintive. Her eyes bothered me too. They were half-closed and red-veined, hopeless, like a weeper's eyes, or old eyes in an old-age home, or those of a panhandler back in the urban caves. And there were times when Diane swam upside down too, as if willing to be just as crazy as the seals.

Yeah. I hang around the dolphin tank.

The dolphin and man are fellow sentients. The dolphin's ancestors left the land and returned to the sea. Some scientists call that a copout. They say that return to the ocean has kept the dolphin captive to her environment. They say that man is the only animal that bends nature to live anywhere he wants.

The dolphin isn't as smart as man. And Diane is happy inside her tank. Yes, I am personalizing a dumb animal.

I recognize all those thoughts, but I choose to ignore them. The good nuns taught me that man is the only animal that sins.

See, I can feel Diane's pain. To my mind she has no reason to smile. She's serving a life sentence, confined to a madhouse. She wasn't mad, and she has no one she can turn to. She's only looking for a way out.

I felt a gun in my ribs.

Red Eyes in the Fog

She remembered driving the California coast through the morning fog. Ironically, now that she thought about it, she was then tracking down a truly frightening Caravaggio of Jesus being tempted by the devil in the desert at night. A long-lost painting now surfacing after centuries.

That night in California she was tired then, wanted to sleep, and so her guard was done. The red taillights of the truck in front of her had morphed into crimson cat's eyes staring at her through the swirling fog. Hypnotized, mesmerized, she almost flown off the road at a sharp turn.

The fog is deceptive like that.

A Girl Named Sheboygan

She said, "Sheboygan is on her deathbed and she would like to see you again."

The Devil did not wince this time, but he held himself back.

Finally he said, with his voice strained with too much emotion, "Bother a woman on her deathbed, Raf? Why make her feel worse about dying?"

"I thought she was special," Rafaela teased.

"A very sweet girl. Yes, a very sweet woman. She understood so much without me having to explain. Why have you chosen to be involved?"

"Wanted to see what it felt like," she said.

The Devil said yes. "Sometimes it is nice to be involved."

"But you are retired from all that."

"I am retired," the Devil insisted. "To my fog. To my cliffs of rugged beauty. To my bald eagles who nest over there and the orcas who sometimes come this far south in cold weather. And to my cognac. Look at the fog. The fog is bright white and sinuous. It insinuates itself through the oaks. Offshore, there is a cold current that flows down from the Bering Straits. Did you know that the vapor that escapes when the bottle is unstoppered is called the Angels' Share?"

She said, "And sometimes the Breath of Angels."

"What was she like?" Rafaela said. "Sheboygan."

"Radiant breasts. Long legs. Good teeth. Very, very smart."

"She was pregnant when you met?"

"That one she lost," the Devil said. "Apparently she had others, and they had their own." Indicating the teen frozen between them. "Once upon a time there were two humans. Adam and Eve. Now look how many there are. Over seven billion."

"Was this in San Francisco?"

"Yes, she was a hippie chick. She was from the Midwest. Smothering, Ohio, or Somnolent, Iowa. Got off the Greyhound bus at 7th and Market. I was wearing that deerskin jacket in those days. The dark chocolate one with all the fringes. Oh, and I

had that same mustache that every young man had at the time."
He laughed. "I looked like a caterpillar."

"I remember it."

"I still have it, I think. The deerskin jacket, I mean.
Somewhere in there." Gesturing over his shoulder at the white
Queen Anne Victorian house behind them. "She stepped off the
bus, one look, and she could not take her eyes off me. She made
a beeline into my arms."

The silenced teen was almost vibrating with anguish and
rage.

"And you?"

"I was enraptured. I was entranced and bewitched."

Rafaela said, "She was just passing through?"

"No, she had a boyfriend doing hard time for possession
and sales of some narcotic or another. He was in San Quentin
and she was just up for a conjugal visit."

"Did she go see him?"

"She was a couple of days late. He was worried sick about
her. Well, he was pissed soon after, especially when she said she
would never be seeing him again. By then she had moved in with
me."

∞

"What happened to him, Daniel?"

"He fell headfirst from the top of Cellblock C."

"Did he fall or was he pushed?"

"Who can remember that far back?"

She blew smoke skyward. "How long were you two
together?"

"Several years. The Summer of Love, ah. Through the
Watergate hearings. Now that was on Sutter Street. Lower Pacific
Heights at the time. A lovely two-story Victorian. It was haunted,
Raf. A century earlier it had been a Japanese bordello. Some
beautiful women died there from brutal sex and casual violence.
We would lie in bed and listen to them at night. There was one
ghost in particular …" He realized he could not tell this story. "We
used to sit on the back deck looking out over the Filmore District
laid out in front of us. Had the TV out there on a long extension
cord. Order a double pepperoni pizza and drink Anchor Steam
and marvel at the testimony coming out of Washington. The
purpose of powerful men is to stand firm for all that is wrong in
this world, to resist change for the better, and to profit from the
misadventures that ensue."

"Daniel, what did you have to do with Watergate?"

"Not I, said the Fox. Nothing at all."

"And then you two lived in the Sunset. And then she moved on?"

"She said she had never been to Seattle. Wanted to see it on her own. I gave her some money, a few thousand, I think, and a new car, and one day she drove off."

"And you never heard from her again?"

"A few postcards. She met a young man up there. An electrician, I think. An electronic engineer? He was studying computers. Software applications? She wanted to have children. Another chance at having children."

"But not yours?"

"Oh, no, not mine. Who would wish that on the world again?"

∞

He said, "How far away is Sheboygan?"

"She is in a hospice in San Luis Obispo."

The Devil was pensive. "Some lovely restaurants along the way."

"It's not tourist season," Rafaela said. "We could take the coastal highway."

"How long does she have?"

"A couple, three days at least. We could take our time coming back. Make it a week or two. Two weeks might be stretching it." Rafaela asked, "Is there any place you need to be?"

The Devil grinned. "Not for the next few millennia."

"You can give her a final kiss."

He scowled. "Do you know how many kisses I have given to dying humans?" His hand gestured violently. "Enough already!"

"You can inhale her last breath."

"She would like that, yes."

"It might give her life meaning."

"Humans value those symbolisms, yes."

"You and I could spend time in San Francisco."

"Yes, you and I, Raf, in San Francisco."

"And she was a special one, you said."

Remembering, he said, "Radiant breasts and wonderfully long legs and a warm strong heart."

"Do what's in your heart," she said.

He struggled to find and express the right words. "Love is a south wind in winter. It brings warmth and the heat of the sun onto your face."

"Who wrote that, Daniel?"

"I came up with it just now."

She blew smoke into the oncoming night. "Too bad humans never see this side of you, Daniel."

Tommy Meets the City

Teresa gave him San Francisco.

"It's my turn," she told him.

"Let me make San Francisco yours," she told him.

With phony IDs that said they weren't underage, they ran the streets open-mouthed and joyously like wolves under the moonlight.

He kept up with her. But the price was high for both of them.

Nobody can run at that speed for long.

Exhausted, they often found themselves parked on a pier under the Bay Bridge halfway between Last Call and dawn, watching the freighters churning in from the Far East.

Damn, wasn't the City romantic in the moonlight!

Even as Tommy remembered those halcyon days, he was bitch-slapped by one particular visit to the City. That night, sometime after Last Call, Tommy drove down north of the Ferry Building, to one of their favorite parking lots that overlooked the black bay. He parked there, and they drank beer from the bottle and watched the long freighters pulling in under the golden lights of the Bay Bridge and the faraway lights of the East Bay. That night was dark and cold enough for the car heater and warm enough they could keep their windows half-open.

That night he walked hand in hand with Teresa along the creosote pier. He drank in the wild, promiscuous scents of the Pacific Ocean. God, he even loved the stink of low tide.

I can live away from Vegas …

They kissed long and hard, rubbing hands against flesh, silhouettes against the skyline of the City. Then she said, Maybe we can live away from Vegas … He never answered. His hopes had just died.

What Tommy never told her was that at the same moment he sensed a LVMPD unmarked cop down there, too, further back among the shadows of the Bay Bridge. A dirty cop from Clark County, Nevada, had followed them to San Francisco. He never told the Bovadiglias, either.

Was the cop owned by the Bovadiglias, or was he a crack member of the LVMPD Investigative Bureau who just was dirty, too, Tommy could never tell. He could never pinpoint which dirty cop it was. There were too many, after all.

Back in the car, the heater blasting, they watched a San Francisco patrol car cruise through their parking lot. He didn't shine his lights on them, and they kept their beers below the dash.

Teresa grabbed his arm and stiffened.

"They're making sure we're okay," Tommy said.

"The police never bust down here?"

"Not if you're cool about it." Tommy shook his head. "They work nights, too. They understand. Just don't push it. Don't do anything stupid."

Then the SFPD drove out, gliding as silently as any black freighter on the bay.

Poor Tommy, his heart had been stoppered like a bottle.

September 1941

Alameda was warm and hazy, an Indian summer morning by the Bay. A gentle wind blew across San Francisco Bay, and the salty air was soft as velvet. The skyline of San Francisco across the bay tantalized like the Emerald City in the Oz books. Somehow seeing the Bridge in the distance meant he had more air in his chest. The clarity of the air itself, he thought.

Sullivan thought about taking the ferry to San Francisco, or even driving across the new bridge that now arched its spine over the Golden Gateway. He thought about the Chinese showgirls in their skimpy costumes showing their legs at the Forbidden City. He thought about the fifty cent martinis at the Top of the Mark. But a chevron of migrating mallards flying south over the wetlands said he had no time to dawdle. The Chinese showgirls and the fifty cent martinis would have to await his return. If he returned. He had to have hope, he told himself.

He didn't want this assignment. It was a sleeper jump, Sullivan decided, with none of the benefits. Seventy-five hundred miles of here, he thought. He would be gone for months in the South Pacific. Long enough to forget, he thought. He had a bad feeling he wasn't returning. *I must be feeling better*, he thought. *I'm not sure I want to die.*

As Sullivan boarded the Pan Am Clipper, a Boeing 314 Flying Boat, he eyed every passenger on the plane out of simple curiosity. When she glanced up, Sullivan went pale. *Oh my God!*

The tall blonde from the Reflecting Pool in Washington was onboard.

She was sitting up straight, gazing ahead.

She looked over, smiled just for him, and said, "Please join me."

She sounded imperious, a goddess at the Last Judgment. But was she the same woman from Washington? Still and slim and... But she was so much younger.

Sullivan sat beside her. She had a warm smile for him. He locked eyes with her. Her cold assassin's eyes. He felt like he was in a very frigid room with no way out.

She had the same wry smile for him, but her blonde hair was much longer than it ever could have grown since the Mall in D.C.

How fast can a woman's hair grow? Not that fast.

She ran a hand through it. Not a wig, he thought.

In the plane she had a deep suntan like nobody else had in all of Mainland America. And underneath she wore a bright yellow sundress, like you see on a hot summer's picnic. The same dress she had been wearing the other night in D.C.

The hole in her dress closed up.

She offered him a hand to shake. She said, "Emily Frost."

"Sullivan. Jack Sullivan."

As they shook hands, Sullivan noticed the pale circle where a wedding band had been on her hand. He noticed the red splotch on the web of her left hand. "Do I know you?"

"I may have known you once."

Hmm. For her, English must be a second language.

Emily Frost now had a smile that showed all her teeth, and that smile now seemed most like a shark's grin. "Slippery Jack," she said.

Sullivan's smile vanished. Few even knew that hated nickname. All he could visualize was slimy, sticky mushrooms under pine trees.

"What the hell are you?"

Was she flirting with him?

Pacific Heights

I started off downhill towards my car. It was peaceful on that shaded street. You could hear the limousines waxing in the sunlight. Wealth is a plateau above the daily grind, and in Pacific Heights the rich do look down on the poor.

Massive homes. Songbirds and trees and lawns in the city. There were no people around. They all led busy lives elsewhere. They were creative. They had taste. They hired interior decorators and subscribed to the opera. Their city park had tennis courts and flowers. The men could smile without showing their teeth, and their women could never be too lean.

Then I dead-stopped.

It felt like a steel rod. My whole spine curled up like a question mark. You can never forget the feel of a gun in your back. You swear you can feel that metal circle. Only dead men and movie stars have guts at a time like this.

I started to raise my hands slowly.

"Put your hands down, stupid." It sounded like Riki Anatole. He poked me again. "Turn around slowly."

I moved slowly. Even then I thought I moved too fast. I made a conscious effort to slow down, and still thought I moved too fast.

Riki was half in the bag and dead serious. His boozed face was drawn and angry, afraid of me. He needed sleep and his clothes looked slept in. His tie was missing, and a collar point hung over his blazer lapel. He looked like a bear leaving a cave on the first day of spring. He had a Police Special in his left hand.

"What's with the gun?" I asked.

He tightened his grip. "I don't trust you, you son of a bitch. You've been following me."

"When was I following you?"

"Yesterday." His gun hand shook. "You bastard."

"If I did, I didn't mean to."

"I don't believe you." He wet his lips. "You wanted to follow me. I told my lawyer about you."

"Is Tan Ng your lawyer?"

"So what if he is?"

I pointed to my face. "He did this to me."

"That old man?" He swayed. "I just wanted to know who hired you." He remembered his gun. He poked it my way with a cokehead's phony bravado. He waved the gun through the air. "You think you're pretty tough, don't you?"

"Tough enough to handle you," I lied.

His chin twitched, a faint and irregular pulse, just as it had yesterday with his wife at the fish company. His twitch made him an easy win at poker and a dangerous man with a gun.

People like Riki Anatole have little knowledge of guns. Amateurs with a gun were the most dangerous. They knew nothing, and that is usually more than they needed to know. What was worse, they don't understand a gun and its consequences.

"Start walking across the street."

I went slowly, deliberately. I set foot after foot ahead of me, almost counting the steps. I resisted every impulse that told me to run. Nobody runs with a gun in his hack. I found it hard to believe no one saw us.

His beige Caddy looked like a magazine ad beneath some umbrella trees. I followed his instructions and entered on the passenger side. He made me slide across the seat to the steering wheel. The big bear blundered in. He threw me the ignition keys.

I snapped the ignition. The steering wheel unlocked. Then the starter turned over. I forgot the gas pedal. The engine coughed, then died. I told Riki he needed a tune-up.

"Get on with it."

He was a bigger man than me, so the car seat was pushed back all the way. He helped me move it forward. The bear jarred me against the steering wheel when he helped the seat with his weight. That gave me an idea. I fastened my seat belt and my shoulder harness. Riki was nervous, too nervous to notice. He was left-handed, and he found it hard to hold the gun on me from the passenger side.

I started the car again.

"This time use the gas pedal."

The engine roared into life. Exhaust smoke billowed in the rearview mirror. The Caddy had a big engine.

"I suppose you're taking me to Dani."

"Why would I do that?" His laughter was coarse and laced with whiskey-courage. "You're a cocky son of a bitch. Never give up a cover story."

"What did you tell her last night?"

"I didn't say nothing," he said.

"Didn't she call you last night?"

"I wasn't home last night." He frowned. "Last night was New Year's Eve. I threw a party at the club." He started to shrink. "My wife drank too much. She was asleep before midnight." He sounded like a disappointed honeymooner. He raised his gun. "You're working for her."

"I'm not working for her," I said.

"She did hire you. Jesus H. Christ, she'll be the death of me." He looked over with bleary eyes. "You're fired. And you're gonna refund all that money."

"I'm not working for her."

"Slow down," he demanded.

We were almost going fast enough.

"My grandfather hired you, didn't he? Well, fuck him. You just tell him, I don't care if he does cut me off. I've done the best I could. Even threw a goddamn party and that didn't help none." He was lost in self-worry. "I almost lost my wife last night. She shouldn't mix pills with her booze." His knuckles went white. "That crazy bitch. I'm not going to let that happen again."

I slammed down the accelerator. The car was sluggish, almost stalled, then overdrive kicked in and all 420 cubic inches broke free.

"Hey, I'm telling you, slow down!"

I pushed down my foot. "Go fuck yourself."

"Listen, I mean it." He shook his gun in my face.

"So do I. Go fuck yourself."

He leveled the gun. Both sides were blurring.

"Shoot and we crash." I pressed it to the floor. The car shot ahead at freeway speeds. We crashed a stop sign.

He reached for the ignition key.

I slapped his hand. "You can't take the key out. The steering wheel locks." There was a Rolls Royce ahead. I knew enough to pass him. He was just cruising.

"Oh Jesus, you're gonna kill us." His face was snow white. We flew through, passing a mail truck making a left turn.

"I don't give a shit." We scared the hell out of a lady curbing her Afghan between two cars.

Sweat rode his temple. "Aw shit." He lowered the gun.

"You wanna talk this over?"

He nodded dumbly, too scared to talk.

"Throw away the gun. Out the window."

He had forgotten it. It was useless to him now. His right hand blundered down and caught the power window buttons. The vent on his side began to widen. His left hand tried cramming the pistol outside.

We hit the crest at Lyons Street. My biggest mistake.

We jumped the crest at freeway speed and Riki screamed.

The homes alongside were small castles, brick chateaus. One of the most charming streets in the city. It's not quite the steepest, but it is paved with smooth red brick. The South Gate to the Sixth Army's Presidio is at the bottom of the hill. There's a stop sign, too. An Army convoy was almost through the gate.

And I had all four wheels off the ground.

I spun the power steering sharply.

Then we bottomed. The car went whomp and the shocks gave. Riki started screaming. The tires screamed back. But slowly, ever so slowly, the car angled off to the left. I slammed down the brakes. They locked and we sluiced leftward, hurtling down towards Presidio Avenue.

But we didn't hit the convoy. We hit a mailbox.

We hit like a jetliner hailing a beer can. The noise was incredible—a planeload of plumber pipes crashing. The hinges of the box squealed and broke free from cement. The Caddy was lifted into the air. I thought we'd fly like a rock skipping over water.

But the undercarriage caught on the mailbox. When my body slammed forward, my shoulder harness kept me from the steering wheel. Riki wasn't so lucky. He slammed into the dashboard, banging his head and shoulders. His gun went off, shattering the AM-FM radio. It was quiet like eternity then.

I sat and sat and stared and stared.

Riki was slumped like a rag doll. His clothes were all bloody.

"Are you okay?"

He started swearing. His heart wasn't in it. He had a bloody nose.

"If you can bitch, you're okay." I cracked the door, hauled myself up, then stepped down.

The Caddy sat atop the mailbox like a boat on a reef, its prow dangling over a tree lawn. The mailbox was crushed. It had broken free from all four metal hinges, cracked the cement and been thrown onto the lawn. Oil was soaking into the grass. The transmission and drive train were twisted like drinking straws. The front wheels hung down like a dead man. A corpse on a rock.

The convoy had stopped. Servicemen were coming our way. The other traffic on Presidio tooted their horns, impatient. Some neighbors closed the curtains and opened their front doors.

I patted the prow and started off down Presidio.

"You're leaving me here?" Riki had crawled out.

"You don't expect me to stay."

His face changed color. "How do I explain this?"

"You were cleaning your gun and it went off and you lost control of your car."

His face changed color again. "I can't say that."

"You better say you were driving. I have no insurance, and your company won't like my version."

He realized that. "Oh my god." He was a tired man.

"Maybe Uncle Sam won't sue." I went off downhill. There was a coffeehouse down the street that sold imported beers. The walk would keep me from stiffening up until I was ready.

Susan and Her Father

Susan couldn't talk to her father about her mother. He would just look pained and nod his head in agreement, and mutter that, well, your mother means well.

Susan kept wanting to tell him that meaning well meant nothing. People who meant well were always ruining other people's lives, and ought to be stopped.

Her poor father. That quiet timid man. A comfortable man who made his daughter feel comfortable. A woodworker who lived alone in Sausalito and made custom oak furniture.

Her father was a sweetheart. He was a soft voice and rough hands, cardigan sweaters and corduroy pants. He was this skinny teddy bear that smelled of pipe tobacco and Old Spice. He hadn't gone to college as Mother had, but he could fix the chain on a bicycle, or make a great cheeseburger. He knew how to fly kites and he let her make coffee, and the School of Hard Knocks had softened him, and gentled him, and made him wiser than any high school teacher.

Daddy had always been a silent man. Words confused him. And Mother had insisted that everything be talked about and considered and discussed. And so he gave way on every decision, and so Mother lost respect for him.

Mother got it into her head that her husband would never be a success. Never mind that woodworking made him happy and he was good at it and made enough money to support his family.

Daddy would never be a success. And Mother went out of her way to make his life miserable from that minute on. She started treating him like a performing seal, and whenever he tried to stop performing, she would crack her tongue at him like she was cracking a whip. Daddy started flinching whenever Mother called his name.

Finally, Marna Cochran pushed her husband out of the house. Or rather she moved south with her daughter, and left her ex-husband behind in Sausalito, broken in spirit.

Susan never forgave her mother.

Escape to Tahiti

My apartment isn't much. Motel-thin walls and furniture returned from rental. The walls were thin enough to hear my neighbors dialing on their phones. Electric wall heaters that cost a fortune in PG&E bills. A kitchen only a robot could love. A fireplace that coughed back and carpets you could wear spiked shoes on.

Bachelors, the legal ones, not the natural ones, usually can't afford too much, so they either head toward a shared rental with other guys or grab the first studio apartment they can find. I had held out a long time and had lucked out with a one-bedroom nightmare.

My landlady says my view justifies her extortion. Her building shares a slope with Lone Mountain College. This spot is halfway across the rim of the city.

My apartment is on the third floor, a full floor higher than any building between me and the ocean. I spend much of my time counting the ships out on the water.

The view comes in pieces, like a puzzle, and the best parts lie above the streets and the rooftops. The view is spellbinding.

To the north, the Golden Gateway. The tiny white radar station atop Mount Tamalpais, in Marin County, a dozen miles farther north. The tan hills and the twin tips of the bridge. Just below that the green treetops of the Presidio, where I'd done my army time.

Below that and heading westward, the Geary corridor. A valley through the northwestern quarter of the city. Geary Boulevard was a six-lane slash along that valley, slicing through the Richmond District, ending at Sutro Heights and Ocean Beach. Sutro Park in the far west. Another patch of greenery. Beyond that, just above and beyond, a thick slab of blue water. The ocean named for peace.

And a white ship on blue water.

I grabbed my binoculars and went to the window. A gleaming white luxury ship was steaming through the Gateway like a great swan.

The ship was the Island Princess. One of the cruise ships home-ported in San Francisco. She sailed for Tahiti. Bora-Bora. The South Seas.

I have a friend in Berkeley who handles charter flights to the South Pacific. He calls it a lush paradise. I keep visualizing a drunkard on the beach.

For four hundred dollars I could get a round-trip plane ticket to Tahiti for two full weeks. That didn't include room, board, or expenses. I was fairly sure there'd be a seaman's hotel somewhere in Papeete. With the money I already had in the bank, I could have the time of my life for two weeks in Tahiti.

July was a good month to go there. The fourteenth is Bastille Day in French-speaking colonies. Bastille was the French Fourth of July. Tahiti was a French colony.

I wanted to sail to Tahiti. Live on the beach for many birthdays. Drink Hinano beer and spend months barefoot. I wanted to forget how to shave. Scare the tourists, even. Join the hermit-crab races. Be bodacious until they threatened deportation. With luck, I might be deported for having a good time.

I was daydreaming again.

Time to get back to work.

Jewelie's Place

The manager and his family sat in a darkened room. Six pale shadows of varying heights. The frightened faces of the young children. A little room with a tiny portable black-and-white television set glowing. A necklace of white shapes on a clothesline behind them. The smells from the room. Lamb mixed with curry. Drying clothes and incense and candles and patchouli.

A uniformed officer had his back to the front door of the Remington Arms. "I want you to quit smoking that shit," he told the manager. The manager didn't understand English.

"I mean it," the cop insisted. "I don't want you smoking that shit." He noticed he had witnesses. "Captain." He wondered what to say. "Everybody's upstairs."

Banagan made a noncommittal noise. He was already in the elevator. Someone had taken down the out-of-order sign.

We went upstairs. Cops in the hallway. A lot of cops who looked tall in the dim lighting. Spotlights and Polaroid flashes. Wire cutters by the door that were tough enough to buckle padlocks. The apartment door ajar.

We went into the living room. Secondhand furniture covered in batik. House-plants and Mexican vases. Record albums and plastic Tiffanies and porcelain cats. The room had Indian prints tacked to the ceiling to imitate a pasha's palace. They looked like parachutes to me.

A wall poster said "Sisterhood Is Powerful." Revolutionary reds and blacks. Women dressed like street fighters, with clenched fists and Mona Lisa smiles. They could bind your wounds or rub salt in them. They knew the Way meant Sacrifice and Dedication. The Revolution lay in front of them.

"Any prints, Dennis?" Banagan asked.

Dennis looked over. "All partials and most smeared. Some look like pecker tracks."

Banagan grunted.

The Homicide lieutenant came up. "Nobody home."

"She won't come home now," Banagan said.

"The manager's downstairs," the lieutenant said. "His name's Patel. He's a Hindu from East India."

A police inspector stood staring at nothing.

"Whatcha got for me?" the lieutenant asked.

The inspector started organizing his thoughts. "We got some dirty Polaroids. Woman on woman. In-depth interviews with vaginal orgasms and artificial penises."

"Count them now." The lieutenant looked disgusted. "I don't want no cop filching evidence."

"The girls had them," Howard said, walking up to us. "They were going into the mail-order business. Selling photos to the housewives of America."

The lieutenant shrugged. "If she had lived, we could have busted her, right?"

"She was butch, I'll bet."

Banagan smirked. "You think it's that simple."

The lieutenant spoke up. "Some of the boys think it's that simple. She was just another fruit victimized by straight punks baiting her. They think it's that simple."

The inspector said, "Maybe girls being bumped off is part of a series of mass murders."

"Like the Hillside Strangler?"

Banagan broke in. "Let's drop the mass-murderer bullshit until later. Right now it's just loose weirdos, okay?"

"What about that Mexican whore?" the inspector asked. "The one in the Loin Saturday night."

Banagan sighed. "All kinds of whores turning up dead." He was amenable though. "Maybe the killers here are the same group that hit the Mexican chick." He tried to remember. "What was it? A real funny name. Cuba, that's it. Bullshit name. Probably just for the Johns. She probably has a whole shitload of a.k.a.'s. Aw, hell, maybe she was Cuban."

I stopped breathing. "Cuba?" I said. "Saturday night?"

Banagan looked over. "You know her too."

I said, "I talked with a hooker over on Powell Street that night. Her name was Cuba. Bad teeth. Big tits." I raised my hand to my chest. "Came up to here on me."

"How does she tie in?"

"I don't know if it's the same one."

He pointed a finger. "You'll see pictures," he promised. "You got any kind of an angle on her?"

I wasn't sure. "I did see this guy hanging out on her sidewalk. A pimp. White kid. He didn't like me asking questions about his ladies."

"Does he have a name?"

"Not that I know of."

"You'll see pictures later."

I sighed. "Can I look around here?"

"Go ahead. Just don't touch it if it hasn't been dusted."

I checked out the kitchen. Houseplants and heel marks on the tile floor. Bean sprouts growing in a Mason jar. A poster that said "Fuck Housework." Mixing bowls from Mexico. An electric juicer. Cutting boards. A brass watering can for the plants. An old BB gun hole in a kitchen window. And a view of an alley littered with garbage.

The refrigerator had no meats or pastries but lots of vegetables. Ricotta cheese and a tin of tortilla chips. Herbal teas and bran cereals. Whole-wheat bread and low-fat yogurt. A quart of raw milk and eggless, imitation mayonnaise. Wheat germ and unsweetened applesauce. Wild honey and brown rice. Carrot juice.

The bedroom. A double bed with two upended melon crates as bookends. Above the bed, a large matted photograph of a fog-shrouded Golden Gate Bridge. Jane Avril posters.

I looked over the single dresser. Some snapshots of a family barbecue a million years ago. A little stuffed cat, maybe won at some carny's weight-guessing booth many summers ago. Plus the little things that only lovers collect.

Cologne bottles that looked like dildoes and dildoes that looked like cologne bottles. Stockings and panty hose, blouses and pant suits, torn and holey underwear. Lace panties in one drawer.

Then, like an inside joke, there were pictures of Jewelie's mother taken outside various Las Vegas hotels when the Beaumonts were just tourists on the Strip.

The clothes in the closet were easily divided. Hippie on one side, leathers on the others. I checked labels. Size seven on the left. Size five on the right.

There was a pizza box on a top shelf. Inside, a couple dozen record albums without covers. The albums were all horribly scratched, streaked with dried mud, their labels missing.

I peeled each apart from its neighbor. There were no secret messages, no purloined letters, and no cryptographic code sheets. Just a bunch of old record albums that had been rinsed in mud and stacked to bake in a closet. They made no sense to me.

I looked over the bookshelves. A couple paperback romances, a cookbook for lovers, a book about the signs of the zodiac, a science fiction novel written by a woman, a collection of love poems from a lesbian collective in Berkeley. Only the romances had cracked seams. They'd been read cover to cover many times.

There was a brandy snifter filled with matches on another shelf. The cops had passed it over of course. A book of matches means nothing as a clue. Matchbooks are like coat hangers. Nobody knows where they spawn, but spawn by the thousand they do.

One matchbook means nothing. But a hundred tell a story.

I dumped the snifter on the bedspread. Most promised a good future in electronics, some said high school graduates made good money, and five had on their covers a simple black-lettered name. A neighborhood bar in the 800 block of Hyde Street here in the city.

I found and opened a notebook. There is no such thing as too much love, but there is a thing about not enough love. Cherokee Sioux had written it.

I opened another notebook. The poem jumped out with its shortness. *My kiss to touch your lips. I touch cold bone.* Love poems aren't what they used to be, I guess.

I looked over the bathroom. Cosmetics and hair dryers, lady razors and tampons.

Hair curlers and hair clasps. Herbal shampoos. A little box of a room with a skinny window and a high ceiling. Towels over a stick were curtains for the window. The window overlooked a brick airshaft. Wind chimes for the vagrant winds that came through a hole in the plaster.

"Michael!" Banagan called.

I went back into the living room.

A beat cop was talking to the lieutenant. "Cherokee Sioux's rent application says she works for the Bank of America. Unlike everybody else in the building, she paid her rent on time. That young couple next door hasn't paid theirs in nine months."

"We're going to the Hall," Banagan told me.

We headed out. Soft reggae music came from one of the apartments. Jimmy Cliff and his songs. A righteous man from an island of shantytowns. Easy being righteous in a world of slums. Just don't smoke in bed.

A cop was interviewing Cherokee Sioux's neighbors. The old woman who lived across the hall. Just another senior citizen trapped in the Tenderloin. There were lots of lines in her tiny face. She had traveled far to reach this dead end. She remembered every inch she had traveled. Life was a desert now.

"She was always so friendly," the little old lady was saying." "She'd help me with my packages up the stairs. If you dropped something on the street, she'd pick it up for you. Once she kicked a man who was trying to steal my social security check. She gave me tomatoes she grew herself on her kitchen window."

I stopped to talk. "What about the other girl who lived here?"

The old woman looked worried. "Isn't she home?"

"We don't know where she is."

"At first I thought they were sisters, living together like that. It was really sad how they tried looking out for each other. Like the blind leading the blind."

"Did Sioux ever talk about her?"

"A little," the woman went on. "Susan wanted to help her, you know. She was a runaway from a broken home. Susan told me about that. Nobody wanted the poor girl. Oh, she looked so mean. And her hair, she dyed it, you know, and from the back she looked just like a parrot. Blue here and yellow here and green and red. I told Susan she had her work cut out for her."

"She wanted to help Julie? How?"

"Well, she took her in, for one thing. It's not safe for a woman on these streets, anymore, not even in daylight. They push you down and steal your money. Sometimes they kick you and hit you. Youngsters. Kids who should still be in school. They should be in school, but they're not. I see them every day out there."

We made our way downstairs.

Banagan said, "She clipped coupons and saved pennies in a jar. She entered magazine contests and read magazines about naked women. There were no fuck books, no nude studies, but she was making it with a fifteen-year-old girl. They talked sisterhood and shared the same bed and did mail-order pornography. Maybe if she had lived, I could have busted her for stat rape."

He turned to me. "Angel of mercy or a chicken hawk?"

Among the Transvestites

That night I went to the TV joint south of Market called the Dragon's Mouth. It was supposed to have a Chinese motif, but it looked like a couple of Scandinavian meth freaks had designed it. A cross between a techno club and a gay sex club, but all rainbow-hued feather boas and nipple rings. Why, yes, I carried a weapon. *Shush.*

I knew a TV who hung out there, or had hung there back in my SF days, so I went to see her. When she's wearing her three-inch heels, she's a six-foot-three black man in outrageous high heels dressed like a peroxide blonde whore with the shocking red lipstick. We were on our high school wrestling team together.

My friend Jeremy Rhett calls herself the African Queen. Like a lot of San Francisco's transvestites, her dream was to be a Las Vegas showgirl. Dreams die hard on the streets. These days she was an investment banker at the city's biggest bank. She was always tall and regal and wonderfully built. But twenty years on, he was also a bit stout.

When I arrived, the African Queen was goofy-drunk and just paying off a taxicab. "Listen, cabbie," she minced, "if you're not wearing any underwear, how about coming upstairs and we'll discuss the fare!"

The cabbie wanted only his fare.

She saw me and shrieked. "Frankie!"

I let her throw her arms around me, but when she tried to kiss me, I held her at arm's length. But I was laughing.

She mock-groaned. "Oh, I'll kill for some cock!"

"Mine's already promised, Queenie."

We walked into the joint together. Arm in arm. Proudly. Old friends.

The club seemed to have an average number of poseurs. Every game in the city is about getting attention. We all need it, I suspect. Hustle for it. Push our way through the crowd for it. We want to be noticed. Please make eye contact with me. I want to be loved.

On the other hand, the lighting encircling the dance floor was professional; flickering it off and on like that was deliberately meant to be disconcerting. But only the Space Shuttle being launched came near the bar's noise threshold.

"I haven't seen you in a while."

"Oh, I spend a lot of time on Skype in my dressing gown."

"Making any money at it?" I asked. "No, let me rephrase it. How are you doing, Queenie?"

"I'm doing very well, Frank, thank you for asking. You wouldn't think to look at me, but I've been HIV-positive for sixteen years."

"What keeps you going?"

"Well, marijuana helps."

I noticed her orange hair glowed under club lighting. We found bar stools and she preened at the mirror. "I look so pretty, I'm going to wake up in the governor's mansion!"

She fluffed her do like a vain beauty queen. "I am a true blonde," she said.

I stared at her orange hair. "Faithful and true?"

She took my hand and licked the tip of my finger. "In my own way."

She had started out her career as a male ex-porno director and now had turned artist. Now she was famous in the gay community for her realistic renderings of the male torso.

"I saw your painting at the Hairy Snake," I began. "The uncircumcised male organ."

"One of my best," she said. "I made it just for all those gold chain boys from Arabia. They love blonde boys. Do you know why they call camels 'the ships of the desert?'"

"How is Diablo? The boy with the orange hair."

"We broke it off. What is he doing now? Oh, he's buying boner pills."

"He must miss you very much," I said.

Queenie was pouting and fluffing her hair, crossing and uncrossing her phenomenally long legs. "I can give you either the décolleté or the short skirt. Not both." She was talking to the guy on the bar stool on her other side.

I interrupted her. "I heard you were behind walls at San Bruno."

"I am," she said.

"What are you out for?"

"Work furlough program. I got till nine pm Sunday."

"Do you ever see my kid Stevie in your travels?"

Who else would I ask if Stevie ever dated a transvestite? What? Do I suck it up and tell myself to get used to it? Even as I asked, I felt lower than gutter oil.

The only smart answer? Get used to it, Frank. The world was never yours. Like everybody, you got a tiny piece to live in for a very short time. Other peoples' lives are not your problem. Let it go.

"Did Stevie ever run with a transvestite?"

"He ran with a wild bunch of people last year. A couple of them could have been, I don't know. This is San Francisco. Years ago they used to call kids running wild." He tried remembering. "Oh, yeah, bohemians."

"But you never saw anything romantic going on?"

"They were kids. Kids are always fooling around. Consenting adults, right? Anyways, who cares who is fucking whom? If it's meant to be, it's meant to be, or they grow out of it. Everything is fluid in San Francisco. What could go wrong, right?"

Queenie stopped needling me. She pecked my face with a kiss and then she scurried ahead into the club's back room. But I still needed her.

I found her inside talking with a honey-streaked blond TV.

"She said you were pumped!"

"I never got pumped!" The blond TV turned and stomped off in a huff. "Where is that bitch!?"

We walked on, and she described all the queens we passed.

"Silicone shots," the Queen explained. "I happen to know one of her first implants bubbled up, and she had an extra nipple on the left side."

She looked down her nose at a drag queen holding up the bar and told me, "An anorexic with implants. There's nothing natural about her."

I said, "Who did Boy Toy get gang banged?"

"I hate silicon," she groaned.

"What are you drinking?" I said.

She waltzed up to the bar and told the bartender, "A Shirley Temple with a double back of tequila."

I bought a beer for myself and then I asked her about Boy Toy.

"Boy Toy? Oh, he's a real jerk! Have you heard? Boy Toy is dead!" She stage-whispered, "I heard his lover did it."

"Could be. Who was his lover?"

She didn't know. "But I bumped into him rollerblading in the Haight the other day. He said his lover was one in a billion. His dream come true."

I whistled. "That much?" One in a billion was a curious phrase. Even in the hyperbole of street life, one in a billion was special. "Who was saying his dream come true?"

Queenie took time out to flirt.

"So what was he doing with a U. S. Marine?"

"Love the one you're with. And he got caught. And he got killed, baby. Boy Toy, too. Freaks are so conservative, they start getting it regular, hey, regular's so hard to come by, anything threatens it, it's mine!, and I'll cut your throat!"

"Are you suggesting his lover did him in?"

"Unrequited love is noir, Frank."

"Do you know a stripper named Cherry Mary?"

"That was his steady! Oh, she is a beauty! I knew her, yes, and I was always seeing her at the clubs. We were both older than the usual clubbers. I hadn't seen her for months. At first I thought she looked heavier, but it was just gravity pulling her down."

"Know where I can find her?"

"Oh, I don't know where she lives."

"Where does she hang out?"

Victorian Row in Lower Pacific Heights

Monk lived halfway down Victorian Row, which was a rustic alley, or maybe a quaint walkway, between Pine and Bush Streets, between Webster and Fillmore Streets. It's so hidden that I expect most San Franciscans wouldn't know it was here. The owners and residents were delighted with that anonymity. As for me, Victorians are beautiful at any time, but at night under a single streetlight they are ethereal.

He told us, "I come downstairs one day, wearing just a towel from the shower, and there's a family of four, tourists from the Midwest, standing in the living room, gawking at me like I don't belong here. The front door hadn't latched right, and they thought my house was a tourist attraction so they just pushed right in."

Like most San Franciscans, he thought tourists should know their place. Like Fisherman's Wharf, for instance. Monk was that happy seeing Chad Slattery.

McGee

McGee groaned, remembering his wife.
Barking mad bitch leaving him for a woman.
Goddamn San Francisco.
The first morning of retirement he had a stroke and died.

Death in Chinatown

And then all hell broke loose.

Louis Ng forearmed his desk and threw it at the goons. Lim Song caught the brunt and went down shouting in Cantonese. Chipmunk Cheeks went sideways, around the flank. Louis had his gun up. He shot a man. I heard him die. Then whirling sticks lashed out like lightning. I heard bone crack. There was another gunshot.

The henchmen on the landing ignored me, rushed past me inside. Louis shot one of them. He had a terrible scream. The door closed from the weight of his falling.

A goon was downstairs watching the front door. He had an automatic rifle, too. He came rushing upstairs. He saw me halfway up and tried to swing his rifle around.

There were railings on either side. I grabbed one in each hand and launched myself feet first down the stairs.

The goon should have fired a burst. He swung at my legs instead and missed. I flat-footed his face and we tumbled together down the stairs. I landed on top of him and he cushioned my jump.

Then I was on my feet again. He tried to grab me, to trip me, and I kicked his face. His nose exploded with blood. I took the stairs two at a time.

A white Dodge pulled up in front of the draft board. Four Chinese guys piled out from the car, and a fifth man joined them from the shadows. I ducked back and hid in the draft board's doorway. They burst through the door, ran up the staircase and started shooting from the hip. Somebody started firing back. The plasterboard exploded with bullet holes.

I hit the bricks in a hurry. There was a phone booth across the street. I used a quarter and phoned Northern station. Speaking in Pidgin English and faking a Cantonese accent, I told the duty officer there were dead men on Jackson Street. He asked my name and I hung up. There were longer pauses between the gunshots. They were taking time to aim now. They hadn't before.

I wanted out fast. I walked downhill and found a restaurant just below Grant. The restaurant was below the streets, down a flight of stairs. It was a real Chinese restaurant, one where the yellow man eats his dollar meals in peace. You must ask for chopsticks, the tea comes in tea bags, the menu is misspelled.

I found a booth near the back and sat with my back to the wall. A middle-aged Chinese waiter came and brought me a menu. I don't remember what I ordered.

The waiter went off to the kitchen as the sirens came down Jackson. The reflection of flashing red lights wavered across the tarnished steel doors to the kitchen. They could have been Christmas tree lights. There was more gunfire. It sounded now like firecrackers. No one went outside to see the excitement.

Someone had left a morning edition behind. I read the front-page comics first. The Farallones were tomorrow's headlines. Ruth was center-page photo. She said she saved my life.

I read the lead story again. Some facts were accurate, some were off-the-wall. I understood. The cops had their games to play. The news hawks had papers to sell.

The cops were upset because I'd lucked out on a coke ring. As if my feat had anything to do with ability, talent, good detective work. I got lucky. I knew it, they knew it, even the news hawks knew it. I was grateful. Only the lucky solve cases.

But the cops like tidy investigations. There was still one loophole left to fill, and then the puzzle would fit together like a pair of lovers. It was my job to find and fill that hole before the cop shop crowd got upset with an incomplete case. I needed to get myself off the hook with them.

I needed a confession before their investigation caught up with mine. I didn't care whether it was thrown out of court by a clever attorney or a sensitive judge. Cops are like elephants. They never forget.

The red lights still flashed against the kitchen doors when the waiter brought my bill and fortune cookie. The fortune inside said my salary would soon increase. I paid my bill and left a dollar tip.

Outside a bright white light overcame the blue Chinatown night. Black-n-whites filled both ends of the street. The public servants held back the public. Two more meat wagons arrived. The Instant Eyewitness News team had their van double-parked near my restaurant. A Chinese newswoman was talking into a camera.

The Tac Squad boys came down the staircase with their helmets off. They carried their rifles like hunters after nightfall.

They went off into small groups and smoked cigarettes together. A stretcher came down the stairs. One of the boys made the Sign of the Cross.

The wind had grown brittle and cold, a popsicle taste against hands and face. The camera crew had trouble with the stiffening wind. It pushed their spots about. One shone up onto the windows above the street. They didn't want to take pictures of the frightened poor of Chinatown. Their color camera wanted blood tonight.

I found my car. I turned on the heater, then the radio to drown out the heater's whine. Some local station still played its Top One Hundred. If I wanted to hear last year again, the announcer singsonged, I should tune in tomorrow. An Instant Replay would start at noon.

I drove down Clay Street to the freeway. The streets of the Financial District were still filthy with calendar sheets. Days thrown away. One by one they fluttered away.

I had the streets to myself.

Houseboats

The houseboats came in all colors, from unpainted wood to psychedelic rainbow. Most were converted tugs or river barges, but some were covered lifeboats and floating shanties. Some were shaped like gypsy wagons and Chinese junks, while others were single-storied summer cottages over shallow hulls. Some were designed in Mineshaft Modern with redwood shingles and barbeque decks, and a few were floating mansions with stained glass windows and stone fireplaces. There was even a derelict paddle wheeler dry-docked in the mud, green slime coating her bare ribs.

Joey Crawford's houseboat was a deep water barge with a ferroconcrete hull. There were several portholes with brass fittings along the starboard side. The curtains behind the portholes were tie-dyed and drawn. A stovepipe from a fireplace looked like a misplaced nipple beside the diamond-shaped skylight.

We came single-file down the gangplank, squeezing past a ten-speed bicycle chained to the railing. The boat lurched sideways as we boarded, then settled deeper into the mudflats.

The houseboat had a single door, and there was a Yale padlock on it. I lifted the latch, checked the keyhole, then let it drop against the wood. I could open it, but I didn't need a witness to Breaking and Entering.

He was a mind reader. "Take out the screws."

"You carry a screwdriver?"

"I got one back at my boat."

What the hell. "Go get it."

A minute later he was back. Two minutes later we entered the houseboat. It was warm and stuffy inside.

Joey had left the heat on and the windows closed. But then he thought he was coming back.

The room was split level, with the lower level a small dining nook that led to the galley. The living room was done with chocolate shag carpeting and seamless burlap wallpaper. There were bamboo shutters on a bay window, and potted ferns hung from exposed beams. The plants needed watering, and a pane of skylight glass was cracked and needed replacement.

A half-cord of wood and a stack of old magazines were near the stovepipe fireplace. There was a bookcase in one corner with rows of paperbacks, empty Galliano bottles and some of Dani's college textbooks. A battered TV sat on a cable spool probably stolen from the phone company. The houseboat had a fair stereo system, and a melon crate kept the albums together. Most were hard rock, some classical, and most had Dani scrawled on the back. A hatch cover coffee table was in front of a beige sofa bed.

The galley was tight and compact—a woman or a sailor's design—with many built-in cabinets and all-electric appliances. The faucet was leaking, though, and the sink was crammed with dirty dishes. Most cupboards were bare, but one had a jar of unbleached flour and a bag of brown rice. A cookie jar held nothing but crumbs. The refrigerator held a bottle of locally produced carrot juice, a stale pack of natural cheese, a couple of cans of beer, three slices of luncheon meat, a post-dated quart of low-fat milk, a shriveled orange, several potatoes growing new eyes, and a freezing compartment of beef pot pies.

The bathroom was a man's mess, with toothpaste rotting in the sink, hair in the shower drain, a ring around the tub, dental floss on the tile floor. There was one toothbrush, no tube of toothpaste, a chewed bar of soap, a stiff washrag. The towel racks were brass, maybe from the neighboring chandleries.

There were Penthouse magazines near the toilet. It was a chemical toilet and needed flushing. Like most sailors and would-be sailors, Joey (or Dani) insisted on conserving water. I flushed it into Richardson's Bay. Behind the toilet were several fuck books. Disfigured, tattered, vulgar. I paged through a couple. Somebody had a fetish for kissing cousins. Under the Penthouse stack, I found a pink battery-operated vibrator. Maybe that was their love life. Disgusted with the tool and with my thoughts, I threw it back.

The bedroom was off the bathroom. Dani and Joey had water on the brain, for a king-size waterbed squatted in a redwood frame beneath the only window. A down-filled sleeping bag served as a bedcover. Rumpled sheets and a single pillow.

A portable heater was on in one corner. I turned it from automatic to off and the coils went from scarlet to dull gray. A secondhand dresser was nearby with a few science fiction books on top. Arranged around them were a clock radio, a calendar for the next year, a terrarium with flourishing marijuana plants, several filthy ashtrays. The two bottom drawers held men's clothes. There was a lot of empty space, very few clothes. Dani had left Joey room to spare. I found several packs of wheat-colored rolling papers in the right-hand side.

Ferrante

The new Italian restaurant Ferrante, up California Street on Nob Hill was a very fashionable restaurant; all the right people went there. Not that I'd ever be seen there. Aside from the outrageously expensive prices and the wonderfully crispy panzerotti, the marinara sauce was crap. See, I happened to know that the owner was Pakistani, the portions were small, and the cooks were Mexican.

I knew the owner by sight from Vegas. He kept his white Rolls Royce model parked outside his restaurant. He had personalized plates with his restaurant's name. I used to stare at it, and I could never understand why anybody would eat inside his restaurant. I mean, that Rolls had to get paid off somehow. Who did the customers of his restaurant think was paying for it?

This new restaurant of his was lots of chrome and mirrors, too. There were too many tables, people were crammed together, and so this restaurant was noisy, too, with everyone talking at once. Nobody noticed the bad jazz playing in the background. The restaurant was glowing golden and bright enough for a sunny Mediterranean day. The lighting was indirect or wall lights, all the lights were turned up to their brightest. Tree-like plants with Christmas lights were here and there. Closer, they were ficus saplings, but with few leaves to keep privacy at bay. After all, this was a place to be seen. Bad classic jazz was blaring in the background, and the clients were all talking loudly at once, but then this was a place to be seen. For some people, it was never the food.

There she was. Vegas Kitty. Only now she was an All-American woman. Absolutely ordinary. Nothing fancy, glossy, or glamorous. The girl next door working as a hostess. I watched Pandora at work. She was really good for a TV. She could pass for a straight chick.

California Street in the Financial District

But my super maneuver with the old man that truly got me my chauffeur's job. He was impressed by how I handled backing up through the green light and an intersection in San Francisco's Financial District.

See, Rolf Harlowe wanted me to drive him around for an hour. See how smoothly I handled curbs and cable cars and delivery trucks and the stray San Franciscan blundering about on drugs. See if what his son and granddaughter's judgment was right. If I had merit.

I was in the Financial District going east on California Street between Kearny and Sansome Streets when I saw the two riders on a single motorcycle coming up behind me at a high rate of speed in the cable car lane. Then I saw the man riding pillion was carrying an automatic assault rifle.

Up ahead, I had the green light at Sansome. Then going yellow. Then it would go...

The attack would come then.

I floored the vehicle, yelled "Get down on the floor!" to Rolf Harlowe in the back seat.

As I raced through the yellow light, the motorcycle sped up and came alongside. The passenger raised his assault rifle and I heard Rolf shouting alarm and a warning.

I slammed on the brakes and threw the car into reverse. I hit the gas and backed up through the yellow light and the intersection as fast as I could. The motorcyclist couldn't turn fast enough on the cable car tracks, but managed to turn fifty feet later and chase after me. As the two cyclists went through the intersection, the yellow light had already turned solid red and they were T-boned by all three lanes of traffic going south on Sansome Street.

Oh, the crash was loud, bloody and ugly.

By then, I had stopped, made a U-turn and went speeding up and climbing California Street Hill. Rolf Harlowe was thrown about roughly.

Rolf was gasping. "You backed up through an intersection!"

He appeared to breathe with difficulty. The right side of his scalp was bleeding.

"Would you like a hospital? An emergency room?"

Rolf Harlowe shook off my concerns.

"You drove backwards through a green light!"

"Did you want to get shot by those guys?"

Later his respiration seemed less labored.

"Confidence. You have confidence."

"I knew it was safe," I said.

"How? How could you know that?"

I told him, "Backing up, I could see through my rear window that there were no cars coming downhill and more importantly that I still had the green traffic light for going east and west. I wouldn't have done the maneuver if the green traffic light was yellow or turning red. I knew no cross traffic was started up." I was modest. "All I needed was to be fast enough to back up through a green light and an intersection."

He thanked me several more times.

Feminisima's

I took Interstate 80 across the San Francisco Bay Bridge, got off at the University Avenue exit, then headed uphill. Berkeley hadn't changed. The hippies still had community gardens in every vacant lot. But now the rows of zucchini and lettuce sprouted federal signs that called them "Urban Food Plots."

Feminisima's address was on a cross street near the fraternity houses, just above College and south of the university, half-hidden among residential homes and apartment buildings. The credit card crowd from the university lived up here. Walking uphill kept away the desperate street people.

I pulled into a parking space. A young woman with a teenage face and a nursing infant had been hitchhiking and now came running after my car. When she saw I was just parking, she flipped me the bird, then turned back to the approaching traffic.

I didn't leave the car. I thought I had the wrong place. A two-storied building with storefronts on the first floor. Camping equipment and adult comix and a pet store that rented parrots by the year. Next door some guy was testing a metal detector on his lawn.

Feminism's address was just a gated doorway. An iron gate in a door frame, and a staircase within that went upstairs. The second floor could have been an orthodontist's office, or simple apartments, or both. The windows on the second floor all had paper shades pulled down just far enough not to make the curious suspicious.

I told myself it never hurt to wait a while. Just like blackjack. Count the cards when you play against the dealer. Just sit quietly and memorize everything and consider anything that might go wrong.

A young woman sat in a chair behind the Iron Gate. She was reading a book, her chair against the wall. She wore jeans and a sweater. She could have been a student from the university.

She reminded me of the gambling houses back in San Francisco's Chinatown. Those fan-tan parlors have a "look-see" boy at their front doors who keep out the riffraff and watch for the cops. Faces that are familiar get the door buzzer.

I went to my trunk and took out my binoculars. The woman with the book was Asian. Her hair was cut short, mid-Beatle, the rice-bowl haircut that makes Asian children so charming. She had dollar bills folded around her index finger.

Aha. The joint had a cover charge.

She collected it, checked IDs, and kept out the riffraff.

A fifteen-year-old had gotten past her?

Women came and went down the street.

After a while I could decipher some of them. Most passed the gate without a second glance, but a few passed with frozen spines, their eyes straight ahead. They seemed to speed up when they passed the iron gate. More women came, and some went inside, as if it were a speakeasy. I figured they knew what kind of a joint Feminisima was. Maybe they were still nervous about leaving the closet.

I didn't want to go inside. I don't belong here. All those pretty ladies can be torture, and some in more ways than one. Once I got involved with a drunk biker chick who was looking for trouble. She had a knife, and we almost made the headlines. I spent the night in Mission Emergency. Baby-sitting in Intensive Care. Playing word games with a pair of big-city cops.

I told myself lies to get motivated. I said it would go easier than usually. I tried convincing myself that I was still curious about whatever came up next. That I might meet someone inside who wouldn't be weird, who'd have nothing to prove, nothing to hide. I told myself it was a rotten job, and what better could I expect. That if I didn't do it, I wouldn't get paid.

I left my car. I didn't bother locking it. It's a convertible. Canvas doesn't deter car thieves. If anybody wanted in—hell, they were already in.

I walked up. I even smiled. "I'd like to see the manager."

The young woman looked up. She had her baby brother's looks, but her face held no warmth for me. "This is a private club." She waited for me to leave. She knew I was no member. When I didn't leave, she set down her book in her lap. "Please go away."

"I'll pay the buck admission."

"This is private property."

"I'd like to see the manager."

"She's not here right now." She was doing something with her hands. Isometrics? She was flexing her muscles. Maybe she studied those martial arts that everybody else in the Bay area studies.

I got a stiff whiff from upstairs. Somebody was serving drinks and not sody pop. I wondered if the Alcohol and Beverage Control Bureau knew about this place. If I couldn't get in, maybe I could interest the ABC. If they let me inside, maybe this joint wouldn't be noticed.

"This is private property," she repeated.

"I'm a private investigator."

She didn't give a shit.

"I'll call the ABC."

She wavered, unsure. If she had her way, she'd slam a fist in my face and close up shop for the duration. But she was hired help. Corporate loyalty fades as paychecks approach the minimum wage.

"Wait a minute." She left me for a house phone along the wall. She called ahead, spoke a while, and then seemed dumbfounded, like any security guard kept from flexing her muscles. Finally she hung up and came over to me. She pressed the door buzzer. She didn't like me, but the boss said I could come in. "It's a good thing you called ahead."

I opened the gate. "I didn't."

"They knew you were coming."

She watched me climb the stairs. She resented me.

The second floor was a funky little tavern. It had a hewed-beam ceiling and hardwood floors. The wood paneling was tan and lightly varnished. Several interior walls had been knocked out, and several skylights had been added.

There were Samoan shutters and refectory tables. Hanging plants and small palms in stoneware. Paintings that imitated Chagall. Here and there pampas grass stuck upright from Mexican vases, their feathery plumes like gravity-defying waterfalls.

The barmaid was cutting lime wedges for the evening trade. "Take a seat. The manager will be right here."

I sat in a booth and waited. I didn't bother doing any ordering. I knew how long I'd be there.

The club manager looked like something out of a Pepsi commercial. She was young and thin and bright-eyed. Her sandy hair was waist-length and perfectly straight. She had long bangs like a sheepdog.

"Michael Brennen."

"Annie Laurec." She had an overbite that wasn't very pretty. "They told me you were coming."

I smiled. "Then you know why I'm here."

"I just called the police."

"What did they tell you to do?"

She gestured toward the bar. "Marty has a shotgun under the counter. She'll use it if you get out of hand."

I didn't bother looking at the barmaid. "Paranoid, aren't you?"

She frowned. "I'd be naive if I weren't."

"All I want is Jewelie Trinkett."

I took Interstate 80 across the San Francisco Bay Bridge, got off at the University Avenue exit, then headed uphill. Berkeley hadn't changed. The hippies still had community gardens in every vacant lot. But now the rows of zucchini and lettuce sprouted federal signs that called them "Urban Food Plots."

Feminisima's address was on a cross street near the fraternity houses, just above College and south of the university, half-hidden among residential homes and apartment buildings. The credit card crowd from the university lived up here. Walking uphill kept away the desperate street people.

I pulled into a parking space. A young woman with a teenage face and a nursing infant had been hitchhiking and now came running after my car. When she saw I was just parking, she flipped me the bird, then turned back to the approaching traffic.

I didn't leave the car. I thought I had the wrong place. A two-storied building with storefronts on the first floor. Camping equipment and adult comix and a pet store that rented parrots by the year. Next door some guy was testing a metal detector on his lawn.

Feminism's address was just a gated doorway. An iron gate in a door frame, and a staircase within that went upstairs. The second floor could have been an orthodontist's offices, or simple apartments, or both. The windows on the second floor all had paper shades pulled down just far enough not to make the curious suspicious.

I told myself it never hurt to wait a while. Just like blackjack. Count the cards when you play against the dealer. Just sit quietly and memorize everything and consider anything that might go wrong.

A young woman sat in a chair behind the Iron Gate. She was reading a book, her chair against the wall. She wore jeans and a sweater. She could have been a student from the university.

She reminded me of the gambling houses back in San Francisco's Chinatown. Those fan-tan parlors have a "look-see" boy at their front doors who keep out the riffraff and watch for the cops. Faces that are familiar get the door buzzer.

I went to my trunk and took out my binoculars. The woman with the book was Asian. Her hair was cut short, mid-Beatle, the rice-bowl haircut that makes Asian children so charming. She had dollar bills folded around her index finger.

Aha. The joint had a cover charge.

She collected it, checked IDs, and kept out the riffraff.

A fifteen-year-old had gotten past her?

Women came and went down the street.

After a while I could decipher some of them. Most passed the gate without a second glance, but a few passed with frozen spines, their eyes straight ahead. They seemed to speed up when they passed the iron gate. More women came, and some went inside, as if it were a speakeasy. I figured they knew what kind of a joint Feminisima was. Maybe they were still nervous about leaving the closet.

I didn't want to go inside. I don't belong here. All those pretty ladies can be torture, and some in more ways than one. Once I got involved with a drunk biker chick who was looking for trouble. She had a knife, and we almost made the headlines. I spent the night in Mission Emergency. Baby-sitting in Intensive Care. Playing word games with a pair of big-city cops.

I told myself lies to get motivated. I said it would go easier than usually. I tried convincing myself that I was still curious about whatever came up next. That I might meet someone inside who wouldn't be weird, who'd have nothing to prove, nothing to hide. I told myself it was a rotten job, and what better could I expect. That if I didn't do it, I wouldn't get paid.

I left my car. I didn't bother locking it. It's a convertible. Canvas doesn't deter car thieves. If anybody wanted in—hell, they were already in.

I walked up. I even smiled. "I'd like to see the manager."

The young woman looked up. She had her baby brother's looks, but her face held no warmth for me. "This is a private club." She waited for me to leave. She knew I was no member. When I didn't leave, she set down her book in her lap. "Please go away."

"I'll pay the buck admission."

"This is private property."

"I'd like to see the manager."

"She's not here right now." She was doing something with her hands. Isometrics? She was flexing her muscles. Maybe she studied those martial arts that everybody else in the Bay area studies.

I got a stiff whiff from upstairs. Somebody was serving drinks and not sody pop. I wondered if the Alcohol and Beverage Control Bureau knew about this place. If I couldn't get in, maybe I could interest the ABC. If they let me inside, maybe this joint wouldn't be noticed.

"This is private property," she repeated.

"I'm a private investigator."

She didn't give a shit.

"I'll call the ABC."

She wavered, unsure. If she had her way, she'd slam a fist in my face and close up shop for the duration. But she was hired help. Corporate loyalty fades as paychecks approach the minimum wage.

"Wait a minute." She left me for a house phone along the wall. She called ahead, spoke a while, and then seemed dumbfounded, like any security guard kept from flexing her muscles. Finally she hung up and came over to me. She pressed the door buzzer. She didn't like me, but the boss said I could come in. "It's a good thing you called ahead."

I opened the gate. "I didn't."

"They knew you were coming."

She watched me climb the stairs. She resented me.

The second floor was a funky little tavern. It had a hewed-beam ceiling and hardwood floors. The wood paneling was tan and lightly varnished. Several interior walls had been knocked out, and several skylights had been added.

There were Samoan shutters and refectory tables. Hanging plants and small palms in stoneware. Paintings that imitated Chagall. Here and there pampas grass stuck upright from Mexican vases, their feathery plumes like gravity-defying waterfalls.

The barmaid was cutting lime wedges for the evening trade. "Take a seat. The manager will be right here."

I sat in a booth and waited. I didn't bother doing any ordering. I knew how long I'd be there.

The club manager looked like something out of a Pepsi commercial. She was young and thin and bright-eyed. Her sandy hair was waist-length and perfectly straight. She had long bangs like a sheepdog.

"Michael Brennen."

"Annie Laurec." She had an overbite that wasn't very pretty. "They told me you were coming."

I smiled. "Then you know why I'm here."

"I just called the police."

"What did they tell you to do?"

She gestured toward the bar. "Marty has a shotgun under the counter. She'll use it if you get out of hand."

I didn't bother looking at the barmaid. "Paranoid, aren't you?"

She frowned. "I'd be naive if I weren't."

"All I want is Jewelie Trinkett."

The Anatole House

The house was a gray Victorian mansion stuck between two African consulates. There were many leaded glass windows, and a wreath of real holly encircled a wrought-iron door knocker. The door itself was rich mahogany, piano-width and sturdy enough to forestall the Second Coming.

The young black maid who answered the door chimes wore tie-dyed blue jeans and a Mexican peasant blouse. Dark nipples pouted like sharks against the fresh white linen. She eyed me like a doorman eyes a drunk. Maybe I was trouble. Maybe I wasn't.

I asked to see Dani Anatole.

"She don't live here."

"Then I'll wait until she does."

She pretended she hadn't heard me. "She don't live here."

I gave her a smile. "Maybe she'll visit."

"Better you go away."

I gave her my photostat. She handled it as if it might wet her hand. She didn't like the law. Not even the hint of law. I took back the card before she could spit on it.

"Dani Anatole."

She told me to wait outside. I stepped into the hallway. She gave me another deeper foul look. "Better you wait here."

"Sure. Why not?"

She turned and left me alone.

The hallway went several yards, then split into two halves. One half went level on towards the kitchen and the pantry, while the other became a staircase towards the upstairs bedrooms. The doors to the living room were closed, and white curtains hung over the leaded glass panes. The doors to the dining room had been slid back into the wall. Though dinner was hours away, there was an eight-piece setting of fine china and crystal atop a mahogany table.

I touched the wallpaper. It was real leather, and the seams were invisible. This was privacy that stretched back before the turn of the century. Security from the institutional wolves and street jackals who crave old money and the influence it can purchase. I wondered who dusted the money.

Several red tapers from the Christmas season were on a sideboard near the hall closet. They were subdued and tasteful, and their wicks hadn't seen flame yet. The morning mail was also there. I moved quickly and fanned the stack. When I saw the letterhead from the Department of Social Services, I knew my ammunition was good. Dani was still on the dole.

Then it hit me. Dani had a letter here, but there had been no mail inside the houseboat. Even though she had been gone most of December, that Mazatlán catalog in her mailbox had been addressed to her, so she hadn't applied for a change of address with the Sausalito post office. Somehow she was getting her mail.

Joey wouldn't have needed me to help him find her if he had been forwarding it to her. If he had been saving it for her, there would have been a stack of mail, even if only junk mail or Christmas cards. He wouldn't have chucked it overboard, either, because he didn't know whether she was coming back.

The maid was gone long enough to announce me, not long enough to discuss me. When she returned, her face was blank and her chin was pointed at the carpet, unhappy with the news she carried. "Miss Anatole says you should come with me."

She led me past the staircase and ushered me into a tiny library off the hallway. It was a cozy room with a ceiling a mile away. The door closed silently behind me, entombing me with Great Literature.

There were two ladderback chairs and a long flat desk with a single drawer. A nearly filled bottle of Grand Marnier on a sideboard. Some poinsettias in decorator pots by the Grand Marnier were the only concession to the Christmas spirit.

I opened the desk drawer. Inside were a ballpoint pen, a Gucci leather check binder and a .25 caliber Beretta. The Beretta wasn't much larger than a track pistol, but the little bugger was well-oiled and fully loaded. It was easy closing the drawer on trouble.

Fifteen minutes passed, and then the library door reopened. In the hallway a woman wearing tennis togs was talking with a black man in tennis whites. She wore smoke-lensed sunglasses and carried a brandy snifter with amber liquid and ice cubes. The black man, who whispered with a cultured accent, as if he had learned it overseas, fiddled with the racquet in his hand. She told him to wait for her upstairs. He glanced at me as if I were a nuisance and said something even more indistinct. She laughed and squeezed his forearm. She watched him disappear down the hallway towards the staircase. She came into the library, closed the door behind her, and stood facing me.

She came right to the point. "What do you want with Dani?"

I stood. "You're not her."

"I'm Catherine Anatole. Her sister."

Thirty-five-year-old blondes are an endangered species these days, and Dani's sister was a real palomino. A big-boned woman with long legs and a golden mane. She had a tan that bordered on fanaticism. She was a show horse bred by money and the best it can buy. Even if she hadn't been born rich, money would've still gravitated her way. She had the beauty money always finds irresistible. And you didn't have to be a woman to resent all she had.

"Where can I find her?"

"She lives in Sausalito."

"She's collecting food stamps from here."

She stared and didn't blink. Then she lifted her golden butt onto the edge of the desk. She set her sunglasses beside her. "Are you from the police?"

She gained a decade removing those glasses. Wrinkles were already showing up around her eyes. Like her kid sister, Catherine had blue eyes, but hers had a washed-out look to them, as if they'd been bleached by a bright sun.

I've never understood what makes blondes think sunlight is good for their skin. Most are fair-skinned, and they peel and blister easily. It takes time for a woman like Catherine Anatole to acquire such a rich tan. In order to keep her skin from drying, she had kept it greasy with lotions. Too much sun had dried and made brittle her hair, and her freckles were darkening like liver spots.

"This is a private investigation," I told her.

"I'm going to call my lawyer." But she didn't move. "What do you want her for?"

Chapter Twenty-Three

Ratzinger texted me: *More on Boy Toy please!*

I knew another dancing joint I could ask at. While looking for friends of Boy Toy, I bumped into my boy Stevie and his cronies in Qwerty's. The flashing neon sign just inside Qwerty's front door was a working replica of the Caltrans sign at the top of Donner Pass in the Sierras. This sign was a little different; it said, "Chains required. Whips optional."

Qwerty's was S and M. But S and M here meant sequins and mascara. Feather boas were big, too. The joint was packed for Halloween. It stunk of sweaty dancers and drunken fools. It was incredibly noisy. It was incredibly loud. The two are not the same.

I saw female impersonators and drag queens with foot-high hairdos. Most of tonight's patrons seemed to go for body paint and sparkly g-strings.

A transvestite was go-go dancing on a stage. S/he was dancing with power tools and stuffed animals. She wore a mask the same bright orange color as her underwear. Construction cone orange.

Stevie was downing shots and smoking long cigars with his best man and one of his ushers at the front bar. The boys were laughing uproariously among themselves and slamming the dice cups onto the bar. They were drunken bachelors and they were crude and randy. When they spotted a young female impersonator too good for the likes of them, they got small and mean.

"Stand her on her head by the ankles and put her on like a gas mask," one of his asshole buddies said. Even in Qwerty's he got a foul look.

They saw me coming.

"Hey, Stevie, somebody's tugging on your apron strings!"

Stevie Vashon was drunk. He saw me. "Dad?"

"Nope, I'm not your baby-sitter," I growled.

His buddy said, "Your grandmother's getting jittery again."

"She took too many valiums in the Seventies," Stevie Vashon diagnosed. "Whenever the Jaguar needs an oil change, she can't handle it."

I said, "You can tell her that yourself."

Our bartender had a chain-link fencing chain for a necklace. His one earring was even a link from a chain-link fence. He looked like a skinhead who needed a shave. "What'll you have?" he asked.

"I'm just in and out," I said, slipping him a fiver to ignore me.

I noticed, as soon as Stevie Vashon had his drink, he gulped down as much of it as he could. The others nursed their drinks.

"You going to buy me a drink?" Stevie asked.

"You have a drinking problem," I said.

"You going to buy me a drink?"

I said no. "You're too drunk."

He snarled at me. "You're cheap, too."

"Sorry, Stevie, Mom wants you sober."

He pounded his chest like Tarzan of the Apes. "I'm a man," he said. "Don't fuck with me!" He was surly, too and then he made fists and glared at me in his dice cups. "Who are you laughing at?" He might have looked tough, but his buddies giggled like tweens.

"We're going, kid. You can tell me all about it in the car."

"I don't want to go."

"Do you want another crack in your ass?"

"We should have stayed with those hookers," Stevie regretted.

His best man laughed. "That's because the hooker thought he was cute!" he told me.

"She was a nice girl!" Stevie insisted.

I looked around, saw see-through Spandex over a lace g-string, nipple rings through both nipples, a leather codpiece and silver chains through both ears and around the neck. And that was just the nearest queenie.

On the dance floor two young dancers wearing only black body stockings were nuzzling each other, going around in circles like city pigeons ready to roost. Neither was a natural blonde. On stage, a lip-synching transvestite dressed like a Klingon pimp was having the time of her life pretending she was a show-stopper.

"What brought you to this den of iniquity?"

Stevie said, "Taxicab."

His buddy said, "At first the cab driver refused to take us to Qwerty's."

Stevie scoffed at the memory. "He said he didn't know where any loose women were."

"Then, when you kept badgering him."

"He said he wasn't a pimp."

"But I gave him twenty bucks," Stevie said.

"And he brought us here."

I looked around Qwerty's. This was one of those saloons where irate cabbies dump conventioneers who pester them about helping them score a cheap piece of ass. Irate cabbies in this town could be cruel pricks, too.

Stevie whispered. "Some of the women here are men!"

I grinned. "No kidding."

"Female impersonators!" Stevie crowed. He leaned closer, got confidential. "Want to know which ones are the ringers?" he whispered.

He was as loopy as Daffy Duck.

"Can you tell which ones are which?" I asked the boys, curious to see what kind of sophisticates Pacific Heights was breeding these days.

Stevie pointed out the two women leaving the ladies Room. "Pandora's a girl. But Loraine's not."

I said, "Pandora?" But I hadn't seen either one very clearly; they disappeared in the mob. The glimpse had been a tease. I was curious now.

"Pandora Boxx," he said and then he spelled it for me.

I stopped him. "Is Pandora a stripper? Or a wise-ass?"

Stevie growled at me for being a punk. I apologized.

I asked my son, "Who is the TV you hang with? Is it her?"

He pressed another round of drinks on his buddies, and he acted as if he couldn't imagine any of them turning him down. Then he left for the restrooms. I think he wanted to be away from me.

I gave each of his best friends fifty bucks to tell me the most fucked up thing each had had heard or seen my son do.

"He fucked Pandora Boxx," Thud said.

"Yeah, he cheated on Kitty!" Trey said.

My son's best friends agreed how fucked up Stevie got over Pandora.

"Kitty is the greatest, man!"

"She's wonderful!"

"He's so lucky!"

"What do you know about Boy Toy?"

They turned on me. They knew nothing, or wouldn't talk about anybody so reprehensible. They were here having a good time and I was a downer.

As Stevie was coming back, the best they said was "Boy Toy was scum!"

Stevie pulled me away from his buddies. I was too chummy with his friends.

"What Pandora's story?" I asked Stevie.

"Poor kid," Stevie said. He looked sorrowful.

Stevie started by saying that Pandora was a prolific liar. That the woman also borrowed money that was never paid back. Then he dove deeper into her back story.

She claimed as a teenager, concerns were raised within her family about her mental health and proclivity for fabricating stories and thieving. Life under the family's roof was so bad that Pandora was given an ultimatum. Get help and be part of the family or get out.

"Have you slept with her?" I asked.

"Can you throw the first stone, Pops? He who throws the first one?"

She had recently been diagnosed with anxiety and was taking medication to keep this under control. She was taking the anti-anxiety medication Escitalopram.

"Have you been fucking her, Stevie?"

"You need a lot of lubricant for that cactus ass," he growled.

Oh, my son, my son, how far have you fallen?

The bartender faced me. "What can I do you out of?"

I gave him ten bucks and one of my *City@Nite* cards. "Do you see any of Boy Toy's ex-boyfriends or girlfriends?"

"He was seeing La Verne-who-used-to-be-Leroy."

From the way the barkeep said the name, I knew the name was always the complete name, La Verne-who-used-to-be-Leroy, and not just La Verne. The streets can be quite literal.

"How do I get in touch with La Verne-who-used-to-be-Leroy?"

"That's her on stage now."

I looked again at the go-go transvestite gyrating on the tiny stage. S/he had a thong on, and I didn't understand how s/he could wear that and still keep us in suspense. S/he was writhing up and down an imaginary pole and wobbling her gaunt buttocks in tune with the music, and in her right hand s/he had a teddy bear impaled on the tip of a power drill. The furry innards were flying out in great circles, and the audience was roaring with gusty laughter and approval and clapping crazily.

"La Verne-who-used-to-be-Leroy."

"Those tits cost her ten grand," the barkeep said, "but the governor cut the budgets before she could get the rest of the equipment below the waist."

"So she's caught between two worlds," I said.

"Or you could say she could go fuck herself."

A TV standing next to me was eavesdropping and openly, loudly, belched in my face and batted her extra-long eyelashes at me. When I faced her down, she sneered. I guess she figured I was some tourist slumming. Too drunk to flirt and not drunk enough to fall down. She had a couple of buddies in dresses who also wanted a piece of me.

I made a big project out of noticing her and then looked her face over carefully, deliberately. She almost flinched, not used to such scrutiny and then came back on-line with a haughty sullenness. She eyed me like somebody she ought to be sucking now.

I said, "Boy, I'd really like to re-do your eyebrows."

Her eyes became slits and she scowled.

"They make you look like an amateur," I finished.

She sauntered off, terribly disappointed, looking for Prince Charming.

I went back inside to see La Verne-who-used-to-be-Leroy. She had gone home. But not alone. So don't bother her. At least until tomorrow.

Stevie and his pals had also left the joint.

I went outside and saw Stevie Vashon and his pals were being verbally harassed by suburban gay-bashers outside the nightclub. The odds were mostly even. No dangerous weapons were evident, either. I left his pals to fight alone and I threw my drunken son into the back seat of my car. He flopped sideways like a murdered salmon.

"If you throw up," I said, "it'll cost you a hundred bucks."

Driving out of the Tenderloin, I used my cell phone and called Kitty Colosimo and told her I was bringing her baby home.

"Take him back to his place," she said.

She didn't want him when he was fucked up, either.

Chapter Thirty Four

Still working for Ratzinger, I went to see La Verne-who-used-to-be-Leroy. She was leaving a Tenderloin hotel in a body bag on a gurney. The EMTs had some trouble getting her down the stairs.

Her best friend was weeping.

La Verne had overdosed on fentanyl. Suicide complete with a note. The drop dead drug. She was just twenty-eight years old. She had lived several hard lives already.

TVs and trannies are said to enjoy a whole new world of sexual activity that the morally frail straights weren't even qualified to guess at. I get the straight anger. The straights got scared. They got afraid. They lashed out. They don't want people they think less of from having the same kind of life (and maybe love and happiness) that maybe they found or thought they deserved to find. I get that anger and hatred. And TVs and trannies suffered for the straight world's stubbornness and stupidity.

Most TVs I have seen in this city are dirt-poor, trapped on the streets, one step above homeless, ostracized because the straight world keeps them uppity ladies in their place. Trannies, too, because they also threaten the straights' notions of what is fuckable. Okay. Maybe that was just the ones I see. Maybe many others are doing better.

TVs live short lives, like fireflies on a hot summer night. The streets are tough. The streets will kill you. They have been that way, I will bet, since the very first cities, whenever that was. And if you don't live on the streets, or have to work on them, you don't want to hear about them.

Being a transgender or a TV is riding the razor. The cops want you in prison. Your landlord wants you dead for your security deposit. Your Johns want you dead once they discover you got a penis. The straight world takes a step back just seeing you, and they keep their kids out of your reach. Hell, they don't even tell their kids that people like you live and love and die on the streets. Your own folks back home, if you do get ID'd, might not even claim your corpse, so odds are it is Potter's Field for you.

You got to be desperate … and tough to live on the street. Backed into a corner, any animal fights tooth and nail. But odds are, you'll die young. (Chapter title of my life's story.) If you don't die weird or hard or desperate, you don't even make the back pages, and they would do anything to fill those back pages. I wouldn't want their life.

Her best friend said she had gone depressed and suicidal after somehow she heard from her siblings back in Ohio that their parents had died in a car crash a year ago. Seems none of those siblings thought to tell La Verne the news. Yeah, they looked down on her that much. And she had always harbored the idea that she and her parents could have a reconciliation someday.

Fentanyl. Death from Natural Causes, in my book. The streets will kill you.

I sat in my car and wrote a piece about the passing of La Verne-who-used-to-be-Leroy.

I couldn't remember why I wanted to see La Verne.

Later I discovered that *City@Nite* piece garnered a ton of hate mail. People said I didn't understand the street life. That I was vindictive. That I was cruel. Insensitive. And worse.

Sunday Morning San Francisco

The Devil and I were flâneuring the Embarcadero up towards Market Street on a blazingly beautiful Sunday morning, and all of San Francisco was out having fun around us.

Look for the thieves, he said. Whenever you have this many people congregate, the thieves follow. They won't be obvious. But they will look hungry. Ignore the contented people. They are the marks. Oblivious until it strikes at their bellies. Look for the hungry ones. Who in this pack has the money? Then look for who encircles them. Who flanks them? Who is coming in from that flank? Or that one? Is there anyone behind you altogether too interested in you? There may be two or more and they'll be slinking in like wild dogs. Their ears will be flattened back and their heads will be lower on their necks. They will be focused, supremely focused, like any carnivore, on you.

What kind of thieves?

Oh, always the pickpockets and the purse-snatchers, of course. But this crowd is in better shape than most of these guys and they can outrun those thieves and catch them. So there's fewer of them than you'll find in church on Sunday.

Are there worse predators than them?

Look for the loud ones and the silent ones.

Two different kinds?

Some will want to distract you while their buddies sneak in under the radar. They will have deals that you can't afford to miss out on. Or they can't stop coveting your body parts. Because it's not always your money they're after. What's the most precious thing you have right now? Scratch it or smack it or stretch against it. That's their most obvious target. Do something now to protect it. If it's your wallet, turn it sideways in your back pocket. If it's your purse, make sure it's locked and clutch it tighter. If it's flesh, get off the street. Stay within the crowd, watch for who's approaching and get off the streets.

How will I recognize they're getting closer?

Look at everyone around you as an individual. See them as separate and distinct. What makes each one identifiable? Can you describe their looks, their clothes, or maybe their attitude? Don't skip anyone. Don't let your eyes drift. Drift and you are distracted. They count on that very human habit. They'll be almost looking in your direction, but just off a touch. When your peripheral eye almost catches them, they may be gazing just apart from what they covet most from you. They'll look lost in thought, a million miles away, because most people look away rather than be nosy, and they count on you looking away. When you move to a different arena, notice they haven't disappeared from your sight. Which means you haven't disappeared from theirs. They followed you. And if you see a cop, go up to the cop and describe the person you identified. Ask the cop if he or she sees them, too. Odds are, they won't because their thief has slunk back into the shadows. Thieves don't want to lock eyes with a cop. Cops recognize them right away and automatically want to ask questions.

But they're out here? The thieves?

Oh yeah. And the hurters. Those who want to hurt you. And they never take their eyes off you. So be on the lookout for them.

Don't look like a victim in wait.

Why are you giving me advice?

I better stop, the Devil said. I better get out of here before they think I am choosing sides.

Who are they?

But I was alone in the Herd. I turned in a circle and then turned back the other way. But I didn't see the Devil anywhere. I did feel a lot of hostile eyes.

Hungry eyes.

The Bridge

He made a notation and gave me back my license. Then he threw an accident report my way, then went back into his files, making more little notes. I didn't want to wade through the thick file, but I didn't seem to have any choice.

Just after 4 a.m. this morning, when the fog hangs thickest on the Golden Gate Bridge, a black Jaguar driven by a fifty-year-old playgirl from Hillsborough stalled in the right lane around the curve from the toll booths. The drunk left her car and began hiking back to the toll plaza for help. She didn't set out reflectors or flares. She turned off her lights to spare her battery.

Before the bridge district could send a tow truck, a VW microbus came through the toll plaza doing fifty miles per hour. It struck the disabled vehicle. The microbus stopped, but the driver's body sailed forward. His head punctured the windshield, the broken glass punctured his throat, and the steering wheel crushed what was left.

A state highway patrolman doing speed-trap duty on the other approach was the first to respond. Recognizing a fatality when he saw one, he notified his supervisor who signaled the Coroner's Office in San Francisco. A two-man team of deputies was sent out. They pronounced the VW driver DOA at 4:22 a.m. An inventory of personal effects followed them and John Doe to the morgue.

The CHP patrolman and his supervisor stayed on the scene. An accident report was made, photographs were taken, receipts were signed and countersigned, and the damaged vehicles were impounded and towed to storage. The supervisor noted strong alcoholic breath on the driver of the Jaguar. He advised the drunk of her rights and asked which drunk test she wanted to take—blood, urine, or breath. The drunk became abusive and refused all three. She was arrested for Driving While Intoxicated, Resisting Arrest and Vehicular Manslaughter and taken to the women's drunk tank at the Hall of Justice.

Business as usual, as far as I could see. A lousy way to go, but business as usual. And yet the Coroner's Office wouldn't bring me down here just for an accident report. I re-read it and tried imagining I'd been there. The poor stiff had been driving an eight-year-old microbus. Those vans are death traps. The engine's in the rear, and tin foil separates the driver and the road. You hit anything in one of those—a tree, a light pole, another car, a fire hydrant—and it's all over.

When the fog hangs thick, the bridge seems more a very wide, low tunnel filled with lamb's wool. In that fog, the television scanners on the towers go bananas with conflicting shapes and images. And with every other floodlight on the bridge turned off since the energy crisis, striking a stalled Jag in the dead of night was easy.

Sure it was a goofy way to go. Too goofy not to be believable. If it weren't an accident, the CHP and the Coroner's Office were a bunch of silly-headed sorority girls. Which they aren't and never will be. They were always looking for weird details, crazy gimmicks, nutty problems. It gave them a chance to use up their cop equipment, and they're not about to let that precious junk gather dust. Not when the Feds think crime prevention means throwing money into every cop shop in the land.

I still had to ask. "It was an accident, right? It couldn't have been deliberate?"

Khoury's pencil stopped roaming paper. He twitched his nostrils, and the ends of his moustache twirled through space. I was trying his patience.

I got the message. If the lab boys found nothing suspicious, there was nothing suspicious to be found. If they were satisfied, then so was I. About the accident. Not about what I was doing here.

"So what am I doing here?"

"How well do you know John Wilmer Castman?"

"I never heard of him before. Why?"

"He's not a friend of yours?"

"He's nobody I know."

Khoury checked his file. "How about George Arthur Conroy?" He looked at me and looked back down. "Joseph Robert Crawford? James Walter Cheney?"

"Hey, I'm new to all this."

"You're a private investigator."

"I got a license, yeah, but so what?"

"Are you working on any case involving any of these men?"

"I'm not working." I raised my hand. "I swear to God."

He fished through the files, grabbing and throwing xeroxes at me. There was a fishing license made out to John

Wilmer Castman of Napa, a library card for George Arthur Conroy of Sonoma, an ATD card for Joseph Robert Crawford of San Francisco, a vehicle registration card belonging to James Walter Cheney of Los Angeles.

"Like I said, I never heard of these clowns."

"He had these in his wallet."

"John Doe?" Then I understood. "Oh, no. It's New Year's Eve. I'm not going downstairs and ID a stiff for you."

"We know who he is," Khoury said.

"No shit."

He gave me an NCII teletype. A Washington State rap sheet on Joseph Robert Crawford (aka Joey Crawford) of Spokane. It had his fingerprint classification, his FBI file number, his birth date, and his state of birth. When and where arrested, the aliases he had used, the penal code violation, and the eventual disposition of the case. Under the penal code number, somebody (probably a staff secretary) had checked the law library and translated the out-of-state code into plain English.

Joey Crawford had quite a resume. Auto theft with six months' probation. Six months in county for simple possession. Charges dropped on credit card fraud by the telephone company. Sentence waived for Aid to the Totally Disabled fraud. All in Washington State, and none for the past three years.

"What do you need me for?"

"We found this in his wallet, too." Khoury threw down a business card from Pacific-Continental Investigations. It was torn in one corner, but still crisp. "This belongs to you."

I took it. "Thanks."

"Where'd he get it?"

"How should I know? I give it out a lot. Free advertising. Good PR."

"Don't hard-nose me. How did he get it?"

Money Burns After Dark

With fresh money in my wallet, I couldn't sleep. Too much adrenaline? Or just the joy of having money in my pocket? I cruised the city like a coyote skirts a circus in the night. I was restless like a leaf in the autumn wind. I was always looking and there was always no one new. I remembered being young and when I had this much cash on me, that I would take off work until the money was spent. When twenty bucks was better than having a hundred bucks because a hundred I had to pay my bills and twenty I could blow all on me.

Where else had I planned for, instead of San Francisco?

Being as how I was hungry, being as how I always get hungry after Last Call...

I couldn't tell whether the growling I heard was fighter jets roaring through the clouds over the city or my stomach growling for hunger. I headed to Chinatown.

I bumped into my son and his drinking buddies just settling in at Louie Gooey's, a Chinatown restaurant. No women allowed, eh? The restaurant was one of my old favorite blue collar restaurants, down a flight of stairs on Jackson Street just below Grant Avenue in Chinatown. It was open twenty-four hours a day seven days a week. Moo goo gai pan on a bed of white rice primes anyone for sunrise. Forks and not chopsticks for every customer. For a guy with one hundred and sixty million bucks, Stevie slummed like me.

Stevie Vashon was still drunk. He saw me. "Dad?"

He recognized me first. But how?

We shook hands. It had been a long time.

I was surprised he recognized me. Then I started wondering if he had been checking me out on the sly. Remembering that we were strangers to each other. Then he hugged me with a drunkard's hug that creeped me out.

I would have embraced him if only I could. I held him up when his knees started to buckle. I remembered watching him learn how to walk. At the time I also remembered thinking how I hoped my son would be there to hold me on my last feeble steps. Yeah, well.

Mason between California and Pine

Cassie called me. Cranky Buddha had called her.

Chad Slattery's car had flown over the hill and crashed badly. That crash may not sound like much, but when he got shot, he was on Nob Hill, on Mason Street between California and Sacramento Streets. He hit the gas, punched the pedal to the floor boards, nicked a cable car filled with conventioneers and tourists, got airborne on Nob Hill and flew out over Mason Street to Pine Street below. He didn't go down the street-side of Mason, but rather he went down along all the cars parked sideways on Mason. One of the steepest streets in the city. In fact, you can only drive downhill. Or park sideways. It is that steep.

The driver's side window was shattered by a shotgun.

The inspector said, "Either it was closed or partially opened."

I looked straight up at the Top of the Mark at the Mark Hotel on Nob Hill at midnight. At midnight the Top of the Mark, one of San Francisco's classiest joints, is either all windows or all mirrors. It glows like Mount Olympus does when the gods are at home. If it wasn't a window looking out over the entire city, then it was a mirror reflecting everything.

His old brown Audi had blood splattered on the passenger's side glass and on the passenger's seat. The driver's side window was a spider web of shattered glass, a blasted hole in its center, and the body of Chad Slattery inside was slumped to one side, held in place by the seat belt. The EMTs were pulling him free as if he was stuck feet first in a wishing well.

His car took out twelve cars in all. Three of them were also Mercedes and two were Range Rovers. He also nailed an Audi, a Tesla, two Passats and a CRV. A good cross-section of Nob Hill, I suppose.

I could hear the cursing a block away.

Two tow trucks were trying to tow sideways on a steep hill.

Some guy with a Range Rover was hysterical. From what I could see, his Rover hadn't really been damaged. It had just received some dings from the shrapnel. From what he was screaming, he was leasing the off-road vehicle and every little ding was going to cost him a fortune at the end of his lease.

That's when the tow truck pulled his Rover from the tangle of vehicles. The Rover came free with a clashing of jagged metals. The owner shrieked, too, like a banshee being skewered. His car had just lost any resale value.

Three SFPD motorcycle cops were supervising traffic. One was on the hill itself, one at the head of Mason Street with the tow trucks, and the third was making sure no tourist on Pine Street decided to drive the wrong way uphill. Not that anyone could drive uphill. The street was too steep.

Starsh said, "Slattery got lucky because it was point blank."

"You lost me."

"The pellets went in clean. If the shooter was farther away, there'd be more damage."

"You're saying he's still alive?"

"We found him inside his car. Shot in the jaw and shoulder and neck at close range with a shotgun. He saved himself by driving off. He told us he was down at the Wharf."

"He didn't get shot up here?"

"Witnesses heard the shotgun blast at the Buena Vista."

"Then he drove up here."

I was amazed. "Hit by a shotgun, he drove up here?"

A dozen blocks? Maybe more?

I tried to visualize the drive from Fisherman's Wharf, through North Beach, up and over Nob Hill, and then down Mason Street. I saw in my mind the car climbing up the steep streets, taking the corners, crossing over cable car tracks. Shock was adrenaline sometimes.

"Then he passed out, and the paramedics took him to SF General."

Not Its Real Name

Fabulosity at Happy Hour. A San Francisco tradition. Kitty was here with some of her bridesmaids. A hen party, she called it. Bachelor girls' night on the town only in the afternoon before the cruel commute out of the city. She gestured vaguely at the dance floor. They were scattered out there somewhere. They were doing fine. She wore a wig. Her hair was lividly violet against the flickering neon strobes. She stood out, oh, she stood out.

So did the joint. On the wall behind me, above the front door so no one on the streets could see it, was a giant oil painting, maybe six feet tall and three feet wide. The sort of painting much like those of the naked ladies in the oil paintings behind the bars in the Old Wild West saloons.

The portrait was that of a naked hairy man, well, headless and only his torso, from his belly button to above his knees. Right, just his torso and hairy chest and not his face or his head or anything below his knees or his feet.

His torso was naked, and yes, his penis was centered in the painting and exposed. His penis was long and droopy and uncircumcised. The owners of *Fabulosity* didn't want clubbers to get the wrong impression of what kind of a saloon it was. *Caveat emptor* and all that, I suppose. But the joint had been in San Francisco for most of a generation.

O. Anatole's

O. Anatole Fish Company was the last building on a dead-end street down in Butchertown. Back in the Forties, when San Francisco was butcher for the West Coast, there were scores of slaughterhouses down here. The city's health department closed down a bunch, and the rest moved east to Stockton, leaving behind a rat's nest of junkyards, food processors, mills and machine shops, freight transfer warehouses, truck stops, plastic factories and beer distributorships.

The building itself was old brick and butted against the China Creek piers. It was painted a bilious aquamarine, like the inside of a health club swimming pool, and a giant dolphin in drag leered down at me.

A loading dock for long-haul semis ran the length of the north side, and there was a parking lot for employees and visitors on the south. The lot was filled with delivery vans and pickups. I drove through it, looking for Dani's Thunderbird.

A black man in black rubber boots and a red rubber apron was hosing down the loading dock. Fish innards moved sluggishly with the jet streams of water. Gulls swooped and darted around him.

As I came nearer, he turned his hose away from my path and aimed it at a large gull a few feet away. The soaked bird raked its claws and feinted at the black boots. The man tried to kick the bird, but the dingy-feathered gull scuttled away, cawing and hissing its hatred.

"Goddamn scavengers." He sprayed two others who fought over a fish head. "Flying rats. That's what they are. I wish this was a gun."

"Stop feeding them. They'll go away."

"I ain't feeding them."

"Where can I find the boss?"

"Upstairs." He gestured with the hose. "Elevator's over there."

A woman waited for the elevator. She was in her mid-thirties, a pale-cheeked housewife with average looks and not a hair out of place. Her black raincoat hung open, and she was brushing water beads from the cloth with short, choppy motions, as if they were dog hairs. Under the raincoat, she wore a black wool pantsuit with a cream-colored blouse. There was a pea-sized diamond ring on her third finger, left hand.

We entered the elevator in silence. There was no button for the second floor. She punched the third floor button, and the doors closed on us. She made a point of retreating into the corner furthest from me. I didn't think I was a carrier or contagious, but I suppose one can't be too sure nowadays.

She glanced my way and her eyes were nuggets of ice. There was no life in them, a vagueness behind them, a disinterest with the real world. I've seen that look before in downer freaks. It comes from viewing the world through a barbiturate haze. There were other explanations, too. You see those same eyes on topless dancers and starving waifs and female impersonators. Maybe she was trying too hard. Most women who wear black during the day are.

The elevator opened onto a brightly lit corridor. There were several doors on the right, and a single one on the left. The woman scooted through one on the right. I moved slower and read the letterings on each frosted window. I learned O. Anatole Fish Company was the sole occupant.

I came through the reception door. Two grizzled-faced men in mackinaws and jeans were shouting at each other. The receptionist, a middle-aged woman with short mousy hair, managed to keep them separated. She told both to sail up to the Standard pumps at Fisherman's Wharf. "Pick up your ice and five thousand gallons, then go fishing first tide tomorrow. And use those credit cards we gave you."

The sailors filed out together, grumbling and arguing over how to split up the last five hundred gallons of December's diesel fuel allotment.

She turned my way. "Can I help you?"

"I'm here to see Mr. Anatole."

"Riki's in conference right now, but if you'll just have a seat, I'll tell him as soon as I can."

"Riki? Is that his name?"

"That's his nickname. It's short for Orestes. That's what the O stands for in front of our name. He was named for Orestes Anatole, the founder."

"Was that his father?"

She shook her mousy hair. It made a rustling sound. "Great-great-grandfather. We've been in business since the Gold Rush."

"Orestes?" I didn't believe her.

"Orestes," she corrected. "Only nobody calls him Orestes. They call him Riki."

"Is Riki any relation to Dani?"

"They're first cousins," she told me.

A door opened behind us. A young man backed out of Riki Anatole's office. His long black hair was tied in a ponytail, and he had a stack of ledgers under an arm. He was all beef and solid. Fifty pounds heavier and a couple inches taller than me. When he turned and passed us. I saw he was Chinese and soft-featured. If I were a barkeep, I'd think twice about checking him against the legal drinking age.

"He's a big boy," I marveled.

She looked over. "That's our bookkeeper."

"He should be a bodyguard."

"He's a fairy." She decided to be professional and asked if I wanted some coffee. I said I'd read a magazine instead.

The magazines I found were about the fishing industry, of course. I opened one near the middle and started a technical article about tuna seining. Within a couple paragraphs, I was rooting for the dolphins.

The outer door opened again. A young woman came in. She was dressed to kill, Thirties style, completely in red. A silk flowered blouse, calf-length flaring skirt, three-inch platform shoes. Her face was as pale as any kewpie doll. Curly red hair hung over her shoulders like a rouge Niagara. Red lipstick and red fingernails. And, in the midst of all that, standing out like a fire engine, were round eyes as cool and green as jade.

I set my magazine on the end table.

She asked if she could see Riki Anatole.

"And your business?"

"It's about a job."

"I don't believe we're hiring right now, but if you want to leave an application . . ."

"We met last night. He asked me to come by today."

"Was he sober?"

"What does being sober have to do with anything?"

The receptionist didn't smile. "His wife's in the building."

The redhead's smile wavered. "He will see me, won't he?"

"Oh, I'm sure he will."

"Should I come back some other time?"

"That's up to you."

"I'll wait, I guess. I need this job."

"Whatever. And your name?"

"Gideon. Ruthann Gideon."

Ruthann Gideon came and sat beside me. She looked around for a friendly face. Finding none among the office help, she latched onto mine.

She was the kind of chick who's always cool and funky. The kind who considers Quaaludes très chic. Her closets were probably filled with Thirties trash. Sex came both male and female. Four letter words were adjectives. She probably swallowed diet pills with warm red wine. She loved dancing till dawn, and staying in would only drive her crazy.

I slumped in my chair and tried looking suicidal and disgusted. She twisted and turned so her spine faced me. I straightened and smiled to myself. I felt pretty good. Young girls with jade eyes and no job can be poison when you're carrying a thousand dollar bill.

The receptionist said Riki would see me now.

I woke from my reveries and went into his offices.

Riki Anatole rose slowly from his paper-cluttered desk to give me a hearty handshake. "Pauline said you wanted to see me." He was a big man, forty pounds heavier than me, but not athletic. He was a hulk beset by his own inertia. "Your name is . . .?"

"Brennen. Michael Brennen."

"Please have a seat, Mr. Brennen. I don't have a lot of time to talk with you. We're running a little slow today. Our trucks are waiting to go out on deliveries, and they should have been out this morning."

He was a good-looking man in his late thirties. Salt and pepper sideburns and a wavy forelock that hid a receding hairline. He wore a red blazer, dark double-knit slacks and white patent leather shoes. There was a Linde Star Sapphire on his left pinky.

Maybe it was his smile, the way he extended his hand to shake mine, or maybe just the red blazer and the white shoes. He didn't impress me as the head of a prosperous company. His type didn't run companies. They were doormen or waiters. Then I remembered his ancestors had done the hard work. They had founded this company. Riki was heir to their fortunes. That was his birthright, not anything he had earned.

"Business sounds pretty good," I said.

"This is my fifth Monday this week."

"That's a long week."

"And this is our slow season." He gave me a great big grin. "It'll pick up after the New Year's."

I smiled back, sharing his good fortune. "I bet you say that to all your creditors."

His hearty smile froze solid.

"I'm a private investigator."

"Pauline didn't mention that."

"I didn't tell her." I passed over my photostat.

He was too polite to glance at it. He gave it back immediately. Maybe the gray had always been in his face, hidden by rosy cheeks and big white teeth. Anyway, the gray was there now. Maybe he was afraid I was here to confiscate the books.

"And whose husband do you represent?"

The voice was husky and feminine and right behind me. It belonged to the woman in the black raincoat. She had been silent in the shadows until now. Now she stepped from them like a dowager queen approaching her court.

Riki's chin started twitching, a faint and irregular pulse. "It's not about me," he told her.

Her mouth made a small "oh," but no sound came. She walked around me to his side and took his forearm in a wifely gesture. The way she held it reminded me of tourniquets.

"Mr. Brennen, this is my wife Lillian."

"Pleased to meet you, Mrs. Anatole."

"Why are you here?" she asked.

"I'm trying to locate Dani Anatole,"

Her ice eyes flickered at the name. A smirk rode her tight mouth. "And whose husband do you represent?"

"This isn't a divorce case," I said. "I've got a message to relay to her, and that's all."

"You were hired to relay a message?" She was impressed. "It must be important then."

"Somebody thought so," I said.

"Have you tried Sausalito? She lives there."

"She moved out. No forwarding address."

"She must've worn him out." She smiled. "Maybe my husband knows where she is."

"I haven't seen her," he said.

"Haven't you?" she suggested.

"No, I haven't," he snapped. "Now that you've struck out, could you let us discuss this privately?"

If eyes could have thrown spears, Lillian would have been skewered on the spot. But self-righteousness is a powerful armor. She had won her point and could turn her back on us. Like a cat sometimes turns its back on a cornered mouse. She walked in a slow circle around the desk and busied herself straightening the watercolors on the walls.

Over her shoulder: "I need that money."

"What about your credit cards?"

"Magnin's won't accept them,"

"None of them?"

"If they did, would I be here?"

Riki stared at his wife's spine. "I guess we better do something about that." He spoke softly, angered with her.

She walked to the window. "I'm sure we will."

Riki's face hardened. He wanted to say something to her, but he forced himself to face me. "Let's get outa here," he growled. He left his desk slowly, like a bear coming from hibernation, fighting inertia all the way.

I had just lit a cigarette. I stubbed it out.

We left his office and Riki told the receptionist he'd be on the first floor. Without waiting for a reply, he turned and walked into Ruthann Gideon. He almost wet his pants. He mumbled something, then scooted through the door.

He stalked the corridor like a man chasing down money. Swift and purposeful. And maybe that is the mark of a successful businessman, but I knew there was more he feared behind him than anything he might face ahead of us.

"I'm sorry about Lillian," he said.

I said nothing. Who cared?

"She didn't have to insult you like that."

I hadn't felt insulted. I hadn't felt a thing. I thought she'd been insulting him. Which shows how much I know.

"She's a good woman," he told me, "but she's always watching television. All those soap operas. She thinks life's a melodrama."

We hiked the corridor to the last door. It opened onto a narrow staircase. The brick stairs were steep and slick with dampness. We started down them.

"I understand that redhead needs a job."

He shook his head. "Goddamn cunts nowadays. They're always trying to use you. You gotta hire them before they'll shack with you."

My sympathies went right to the redhead. So what if she collected cocktail napkins from the all night disco joints in the gay neighborhoods, waiting patiently for a slumming rock star to mistake her for a groupie? Anybody could get laid. Jobs are a lot scarcer than virgins.

"Why do you want Dani?" he asked. There was concern in his voice. More than I might've expected. He wanted no one interfering with her life. I felt, maybe wrongly, he could be trusted with the truth.

"She walked out on Joey Crawford," I told him. "He tried to hire me to find her for him. Try and bring her back to him. He died before I could refuse him."

"He's dead? Are you sure?"

"He gets air-freighted to Spokane tomorrow."

"He was from Spokane? I didn't know that." His mind was playing tricks on him. Doing what it could to avoid the scent of death. It lasted less than a moment. "How did it happen?"

"An auto accident on the Golden Gate Bridge."

"Dani doesn't know about it?"

"I don't see how she could. It only happened this morning. It hasn't made the newspapers, and probably won't, unless it's a dead day for news. It was a routine accident. She won't be notified because she isn't next-of-kin."

"Where do you come in?"

"I was hired to find her, bring her back. It's a little late for that now, but I hope I'm the one who tells her he's dead. I figure I owe Joey that much, and she should hear it from somebody soon."

"I wonder how she'll take it," he said to himself.

"How close was he to Dani?"

"I don't know. I didn't think too much of him, myself, but I wasn't sleeping with him."

"How long did she live with him?"

"Three or four years, I guess."

"Why'd she stay with him so long?"

"Why does anybody stay with anybody? Maybe she loved him. Maybe she got used to him. Maybe she didn't like living alone. Maybe he was the lesser of two evils."

"When was the last time you heard from her?"

"It should have been at Christmas. The family was supposed to have a little get-together, but right after Thanksgiving she called, said she couldn't make it. Which turned out to be a blessing. Lillian and I went to Hawaii. Our first vacation together in years."

"She left Joey about a month ago. Would you know where she went after she left him?"

Riki didn't know. "Have you talked with Catherine? That's Dani's sister."

"She said she doesn't know where Dani is."

"Oh. I thought she might."

"And why is that?"

"Well, she is Dani's sister."

"Are they close?"

He gave me a broad grin. "Catherine thinks they're the best of buddies. She's always talking about how close they are. But they couldn't agree on the sunrise."

"Were they rivals when they were younger?"

"Not in the usual sense. Catherine always wanted to live on a pedestal. The opera, museums, that part of Society. And Dani, well, Dani has her friends, and they're more important than any museum. In a way, she's always been the more social one. She likes to get out and meet people."

The second floor was storage space. Derelict file cabinets and outdated files and cannibalized truck engines. Spare fishing nets and surplus camping gear. Our voices had echoes among the dust.

A window looked down at the China Creek piers. Several trawlers were berthed alongside the brick building. A rusted black freighter under the Panamanian flag was being unloaded by longshoremen on the other bank. The Bayshore Freeway and the low-rent tenements of Portola Hill were background.

The mist was back, and I cursed it. I've always hated the rainy season. These coastal storms had no squalls, no noise, no lightning. They were long and monotonous. They came and sat on the city like paid weepers.

"Could she have gotten a place by herself?"

"She could've. She's done it before."

"When was this?"

"Four years ago, maybe five. She went up to Seattle. Just dropped out of college and went north. Didn't tell a soul, either."

"How'd you hear about it?"

"A postcard. 'Don't worry. I'm okay. See you around sometime.'"

"How did the family react to it?"

"Those assholes," he said. "They stuck their heads in the sand and acted like nothing happened. If you want something done, you have to do it yourself."

"What did you do?"

"I got on the phone, started calling everybody I knew up there. Friends, business associates, anyone. This buddy of mine, a salmon packer up there, he calls me back and tells me she's working as a filleter in his cannery."

"And you caught the next plane north."

"She looked like a scarecrow." The memory still horrified him. "Scabs on her legs, scabies in her hair, her face all broken up, she had lost all kinds of weight."

She sounded more like a junkie than a scarecrow, but I waited for him to go on. I hadn't seen her for myself.

"She was pissed. She wouldn't even talk to me. Like I was pulling a dirty trick on her. Like I busted in on her. Busted in, hell, I'm her cousin. I did it for her, not for me."

"That's what cousins are for," I said.

"Yeah, that's what we're here for."

"Did she come back with you?"

"She said she was staying."

"How long was she in Seattle?"

"Six, seven months. Then she came back like she had never left. But now she's got this boyfriend in tow."

Everybody kept using the same phrase. When Dani brought him home with her. It sounded like a pet following a kid home, and now her parents let the kid keep the dumb animal. Well, he was a runt. Maybe the runt of the litter.

"What did you think of Joey?" I asked.

"You shouldn't say things about the dead, but since I said them to his face, I guess I can tell you. I hated the little shit. He wouldn't shake hands with me."

"How come?"

"Because I run a fish company. Shit, there's nothing wrong with fish. People like it, and it's good for them. And that little shit had been working alongside Dani in Seattle, gutting fish the same way this family's been doing for generations."

I had to admit it made no sense. "What about the rest of the family? How did they feel about him?"

"Nobody could stand him. Nobody except my wife. She got the biggest laugh outa him. Dani the snob hanging out with a punk like him. She and Dani never hit it off."

"What about Catherine?"

"Oh, God, the way she treated him. She'd ignore him until he got nervous. As soon as he started to fidget, she'd level her eyes at him in that high society manner of hers, until he stopped. Then she'd ignore him until he got nervous again. Then she'd start all over again. God, it was cruel. But that's Catherine. She can be such a cruel-hearted bitch."

"Would Dani go back to Seattle?"

"She might go anywhere. Lake Tahoe, maybe. The family owns some property up there. She'd be close to Grandfather, too."

"When was the last time you talked with him?"

"Just after we got back from Hawaii. A couple of days before Christmas. We were coming in the door when he called. But he would've told us if she was there."

"He's the founder, right?"

"His grandfather was. My great-great-grandfather. But it's really his company more than anybody else's. He ran it the longest and built it up to where it is now. You know, he kept it going for forty years, just by himself."

"He's retired, I suppose."

"Sort of. He keeps his fingers in the business, but that's mostly to keep him busy, stave off death, so we humor him. He had a heart attack several years ago, so he sold off a lot of his holdings, set up the trust funds and moved up to Stateline."

"Trust funds? For his grandchildren?"

Riki had another hearty smile. "After the heart attack, he discovered he couldn't take it with him, and the state would grab most of it, so he decided to settle accounts before he croaked."

"So who owns the fish company?"

"Well, we all do. All the cousins, in one way or another. He divided the shares into thirds. He sold one third outright, kept a third for himself and gave us, his grandchildren, the last third in the form of trust funds. Plus, of course, the money he made from selling the first third."

"So you wouldn't have to spend the rest of your life scaling fish."

"Yes, well, that's right, I guess."

"How's Dani set for money?"

"That's hard to say. She's got some, probably not that much. A hundred grand, maybe a little more."

"You don't think that's a lot?"

"That's not much divided over the last ten years. She owns that houseboat, for one thing. A hundred grand doesn't do much nowadays. In fact, she tried borrowing from me recently. Some kind of investment, I guess. I didn't ask her about it, because I didn't have any to spare myself."

"When was this?"

"November. Sometime around then."

"Well, at least she doesn't have to work for a living."

"Oh, she had a job. She sang in a band for almost a year. More heart than talent, but she got paid for it."

"Where did she sing? Any special place?"

"She sang in a lot of places. But there was one joint she worked maybe two, three times each week. It was down near the airport. One of those cocktail lounges. Arroyo Grande. That's it."

"Does the band still play together?"

"They broke up. October? No, it was November."

"The guys in the band? Did any have names?"

"Oh, I never met them."

"Is there anybody else who might . . . ?"

"My kid brother. He might know."

"How can I meet him?"

"He works down in the smokehouse." Riki looked at me. "You've heard of smoked salmon, haven't you?"

DJ Neon

DJ Neon lived in a stucco bungalow out by Ocean Beach in the Outer Sunset. This neighborhood was one of the gloomier parts of San Francisco. And not because of the constant fog, either. Where you never see a woman. Not even in daylight. There was no safety here in sunshine. New cars fresh from the showroom look old, gray and dull.

Neon was at home working on the inventorying of his adult porno movie collection. "I have three thousand hours' worth," he said. He was an indoor creature, slightly vampiric, ferociously heterosexual.

He was rail-thin and wore those most stylish clothes that only a frail man who was rail-thin could wear. He had a posh English accent even though he was born and raised in Joplin, Missouri. He was nervous with me, uncrossing and crossing his legs, shifting position in his leather seat, and adjusting his jacket.

I tried calculating how much three thousand hours' worth of porno films was, but set it aside while I learned how much Boy Toy believed in legwork, too, as well as social media. Sure, social media was a cudgel, or maybe a battering ram, but he spent most of his daylight hours on the streets passing out promotional "invitations" all over the city. "Come to my party," he would say and then he'd press an invitation into their hands. Like a politician running for re-election, he spent long hours doing this, pressing flesh.

On the average San Francisco has three street fairs every Saturday and Sunday for eight months every year. The street fair season stretched from the Chinese New Year and the Cherry Blossom Festival in Japantown in February then all the way past the Chinese Ten-Ten Parade and Colosimo Day in North Beach during October.

According to his desk calendar, Boy Toy never missed a festival. He made it his duty to attend them all, from the Carnaval in the Mission to the Gay Pride Parade to the North Beach Photo Fair and the Cable Car Bell Ringers Contest held in Union Square. At each and every one of those festivals, he would schmooze and network, hug and kiss, and press flesh with all of his friends and their friends.

Boy Toy played hard and worked harder at playing. How long he could run at that pace was always a question. Still, he should have had glowing memories to tell his grandchildren.

"Tell me about Boy Toy," I said.

"I hated him," Neon said. "For being so sick in the head. He invited me to a gangbang once. He said come by tomorrow night and we'll put you in line with the other guys."

The gal being banged had a solid motive.

"What was her name?"

"It was a guy. Some TV named Cuddles Milligan."

"Did he say who the other guys were?"

"Freaks. That's what he called them."

The DJ named Neon knew about Cuddles' photographs. "Crop the head and auction them on the Internet. Make a fortune."

"Pornography," I said.

"Naw. Freak show shit. There's a whole subculture out there in the streets that gets off on kinky weirdo shit. As long as they're consenting adults and keep children out of it, who cares what they do?"

Neon looked down on some freaks, eh? Go figure.

According to him, Boy Toy filled his slumber parties with new acquaintances.

Did he film them? Who did?

Outside I wrote up what I heard as a sidebar feature on club promotion and sent it in to Ratface. By then I had done the math. Three thousand hours of pornography was more than four non-stop months of viewing. Oh, I quoted Neon anonymously. But I also described Neon in every possible way, especially adding the three thousand hours of adult porn. That bio of a DJ just became another side of wicked icky for Ratface. I uploaded the story to *City@Nite*, but I also sent a link to Inspector Irene Starsh at SFPD. Within thirty minutes I got a response back from Vegas. Ratzinger told the women in the office about the three thousand video hours and every one of them cringed, he said.

Blood Alley

Before Alex hung up, I slid down and hiked to my car. I threw Joey's pound of grass in my trunk, then headed off towards the freeway and the bridge.

The holiday traffic crawled across the bridge, and storm clouds and fog haloed their headlights. Red flashers on the span announced there were four south-bound lanes. They also announced CAUTION and ACCIDENT. A northbound Maverick had sail-boated into a southbound Plymouth.

I huddled in the far right lane. The Golden Gate Bridge is a lethal weapon. There is no retainer wall between the lanes of traffic, just small rubber pods every dozen feet. The newspapers call it Blood Alley.

I thought about Joey Crawford's last ride.

Then there was a clear patch in the clouds. Over the eastern railing, the beacon flashed from Alcatraz. Six seconds later it flashed again. Then the winds off the Pacific brought more fog through the Gateway.

Maybe Joey had been lucky. Maybe he had gotten off cheap.

Spyder's Tats

The tattoo artist kept looking familiar, except for the tattoos, and then I caught it. "You're the poet of the newspaper boxes," I said.

His face lit up. "You remember them?"

"Yeah, I used to see you all the time when I lived in the Haight."

He wrote and sold poetry through newspaper machines. There wasn't much market for poetry, so he devised a scheme. He printed up his poetry in broadsides, like porno newspapers, slapped a photograph of a semi-naked woman on the cover page, and sold them from newspaper machines downtown by the big hotels. Some tourist or conventioneer would step outside on their first day in San Francisco, see the row of newspaper machines in front of the hotel, and would buy the one with the semi-naked woman on the cover. Back in their rooms, they'd open it up and discover they had bought 32 pages of avant garde poetry.

"I loved your poetry. Are you still doing it?"

He said no. "Just this."

"Why did you quit the poetry?"

"I developed writer's block."

"Oh." I thought about it. "But you could still sell the old stuff. I mean, who would know? You market it for tourists and conventioneers."

He darkened. "I would."

No shit. A poet with ethics. Who woulda thunk it?

The Last Fern Bar

The last of the fern bars was along the Embarcadero. Lushly hanging plants, Tiffany lamps, gleaming brass accoutrements, bleached wooden surfaces and antiques. The stained-glass front window that overlooked the world, well, the San Francisco Bay, and the gray skyscrapers by the Bay.

Sunset District

I drove out California Street to the Sunset District. I knew the neighborhood well. Before Pearl Harbor, this area had been sand dunes and sand fleas. But the war brought people west, some to carry guns, others to make them. Many stayed on after peace to build homes and raise families.

Three decades later, their city days were almost over and retirement had come. Over the years, their homes had skyrocketed in value, and it was a seller's market for these castles in the sand.

The new buyers were happy paying hard cash. They were solitary people who had sweated and slaved and saved for their share of the American Dream. Their skin was tallow and their eyes were sloped. Like any immigrants, the Chinese wanted to move up. Like any ghetto people, they wanted to move out. Now the realtors were calling this neighborhood Chinatown West.

The address I had for Davey Huie was a dentist's office just off Clement Street. No doctor has office hours on a holiday, but I knocked on the front door anyway.

A middle-aged Chinese housewife in pink slacks and pink curlers came from her garage next door. She carried her plastic garbage bags out to the tree lawn. When she dumped them, they clattered like pent-up whiskey bottles. She saw me and came over the lawn towards me.

"He's not there on holidays," she said.

I stepped from the porch. "I'm looking for Davey Huie. They said I could find him here."

"Davey? He lives around back. A studio apartment. You have to walk around back to find it." She gave me a nervous look, the kind neighbors reserve for strangers. "What do you want with him?"

"He ripped off my stereo."

"Davey?" She was startled. "He really ripped you off?"

"Naw, I was just bullshitting."

She flushed, but I was already gone, hiking around the stucco building, dodging shrubs and small trees.

There was an enclosed porch behind the dentist's office. I found a rickety pair of steps and stepped up to the warped wood door. I knocked twice and no one came. I knocked again, and again there was no answer. I tried the door and went inside.

Davey's studio was something you'd give an overnight guest with many apologies. Or you put a washer and dryer up front and use the rest for storage. You don't rent it out. Not unless you're one helluva greedy landlord.

The room was barely fifteen by ten. Nothing more than an add-on room. The dentist, or his landlord, had enclosed a back porch with fiberfill and plasterboard, dabbed on a couple of coats of paint, and rented it to the first sucker. The room was dinky enough for warm thoughts about my own landlady.

Davey was home, but unavailable for comment. He was stretched out across a single mattress on the floor. His eyes were closed, and he was breathing slowly, regularly. He wore a terry cloth robe and his stereo earphones. Bare feet pointed in different directions. There were powdery rings around each nostril. His bandaged hands lay by his sides, and a small hand mirror lay beside the mattress. Several lines of whitish crystal sparkled on it. A razor blade and a thin-rolled dollar bill were alongside.

My shoes had an echo in the room. Even the empty streets outside were noisier. A faint whirring sound from the tape deck was the only threat to silence. I've found this same silence in other hip dwellings over the years. Davey was just another cokehead catching tunes on his stereo.

There was just the single mattress on the floor. It had no box springs or bed frame. No sheets, either, just a sleeping bag. There were no windows, either, though the room needed some desperately. A partition cut off several feet of space, and two doors were cut into the plywood. If one was the closet, the other was a bathroom. There was little else in the room. A hotplate on a ledge. A set of drums in one corner. A chair piled with last night's cowboy clothes. Turntable and tape deck and amplifier and speakers.

I punched the on button for the external speakers. A few riffs from the rhythm guitar came through the speakers. Down-home country and western music. The female vocalist was throaty, but average. Whenever she hit a flat note, the harmonica man crooned mournfully and almost covered her goofs.

I pushed the power button off. The tape deck slowed, then stopped. The music died.

Davey's eyes fluttered, but did not open. A few creases almost came to his forehead. His lips parted like a thirsty man, but nothing came forth.

I bent over him. His face was damp with sweat, but there was no fever. His pulse had weakened, and his breathing was getting shallow. Both seemed to be slowing. I lifted an eyelid. The pupil rolled like a marble on glass. It was receding fast. There were bruises below each sideburn.

I called the cops. They said they'd hurry.

Smuggler's Cove

Smuggler's Cove is a little seacoast town south of the city and west of the airport. Its name goes back fifty years, its buildings almost as far. The houses are mostly wood-frame worn by the wind and tired of the ocean. The people who live here have faces like driftwood.

Although it has a primo location along the coast, Smuggler's Cove has never developed a Gold Coast. People, like water, seek their own level, and the lowlands were subdivided and civilized a long time ago. The hills were too steep for developers, and the summer fog kept the tourists away. Headlights are no good in a fog that lasts all summer.

Smuggler's Cove had a single shopping center. It wasn't much, a couple of dozen mom-n-pops and a family-owned supermarket. There was no Sears, no Kmart, no Penney's, no Safeway, not even a Woolworth's. The mall wasn't landscaped, a capital crime in parts of California. Most people didn't bother locking their cars in the lot. The market manager probably kept coat hangers for anyone who did.

The mall was west of the coastal highway between two rugged promontories that stood a thousand feet high. A road circled those two cold rocks and the mall. Behind the mall, it skirted between sand dunes and the apartment building I wanted.

The apartment building wasn't much, either. A quarter of a century ago, someone had hollowed out a solid block of stucco, painted it like a sand castle, then partitioned it into a couple of dozen cave-like units. An outside landing had been tacked onto the second floor like an afterthought.

I took the access road between the apartments and the shopping mall. There were parking stalls on the building's backside. There were no backdoors, so the tenants had to walk around the apartment building to get inside. You could've bought any car in the wooden stalls for five hundred bucks. The majority would've gone for two hundred. Some a junker wouldn't tow for scrap. Only one stall was empty.

I parked curbside by the ocean. Every tenant had a carport, so there was plenty of street parking. The surf echoed against the rocky headlands, there was sand in the street, and the winds blew strong and constant.

A pair of seagulls flew in from the ocean, then flew up and over the roof. I looked over the blue water and white surf. There was a gold sun beyond. Surf on rock made a pleasant sound.

The building had weathered poorly. It looked tired. It faced the ocean as if it knew it was only a windbreak for a shopping center. Its walls were faded and chipped from blowing sand and salt air. There was the suggestion of a lawn, and the grass grew thin like hair on an old man's head. Nobody had plants outside their apartments. There were no hibachis, no briquettes, no bookshelf bricks, no welcome mats. You mind your own business when you live here.

The lobby was open to the public. The mailboxes said Jack Anatole lived in an end unit on the second floor. I started up the staircase, passing a ten-speed bicycle double-chained to the railing. Just another sign of the times.

There were hedges of ivy along the wall. Some leaves were gunmetal gray. Up close, they were plastic, corroded by the salt air. I looked out at the cars in the street. They all had rusted hoods, fenders, grills. The blowing sand and salt air were hell on them, too.

I rapped knuckles on his door. Hollow doors to match hollow hills. There was a decal on the kitchen window. The black horse dancing. There was no answer from inside. I tried the door again, and still no one came. I had a hunch whose carport was empty.

The door wasn't flush against the woodwork. A pushbutton lock and no deadbolt. The windows and the patio door had aluminum frames, pop-out glass and simple latches. Why should a burglar waste time with the ten-speed? From a security standpoint, the staircase was probably the toughest nut to crack.

I wondered how Jack lived. My curiosity got the better of me. After all, Jack belonged to a local Porsche club. I used an expired charge card like a knife, and the door swung free like a noose. Like the banks say, credit cards open new doors.

I had to duck my head entering. The air was stale and heavy drapes kept out the sunlight. The insides were dry and dark, like a desert cave and just like the smokehouse. The landlord had used the same paint inside, and the walls were sand, too. The surf was a pulse beat beneath my feet.

I guess I expected Dani to pop from the woodwork. When she didn't, I felt stupid. Since I was here, I went from room to room. Maybe some of her belongings were here. Maybe some clue to where she was.

I started in the living room. Furniture from rental and some cobwebs above the drapes. A portable color TV with last Sunday's TV supplement. A fairly expensive AM-FM receiver, some speakers, but no turntable and no record collection.

The kitchen was next. A six-pack and a three-dollar bottle of wine in the refrigerator. TV dinners in the freezer and ginger ale in the trash. Instant coffee and coffee cups. Some kitchenware. A few water glasses, but no eggs. A new calendar on the table, though the old one was still on the wall, stuck in the middle of last year. Lines had been drawn through the first few days of December.

I went to the bedroom. There was a king-size bed with rumpled sheets on one side only. A dresser and a nightstand and a closet. The closet had clothes neat on their hangers. A suit, sport coats, slacks, jeans, work boots. Some camping gear on the shelf.

The nightstand had a clean ashtray, a clock radio, a fuck book about the last man alive on a planet of women. There was a *Car & Driver* atop the clock radio. There was a Porsche on the cover of the magazine. I paged through the magazine, came across an 8 x 10 enlargement of Dani, a duplicate to the print I carried. Once again I found myself falling into blue eyes.

I went through the dresser. A pack of condoms. A jackknife. Some stones from the ocean. A stack of photos. I laid them out in a row. Jack or Dani standing or sitting in front of a VW microbus. No other people in any photograph. In some, a small palm tree or a cactus nearby. The Mexican coastline was background for all of them. I shuffled them and replaced them and kept digging.

And what's a bachelor pad without an address book? I paged through it. Jack Anatole was a good-looking guy, a knockout in some crowds, but he lived a cold fish life. There were four names and addresses in the book. Cousin, cousin, brother, grandfather. There were no ladies listed. He had no warm numbers to crawl to at last call.

This was the cleanest bachelor pad I'd ever seen. There were some crumbs around the toaster, some cobwebs above the drapes, but the joint was cleaner than baby teeth. No clothes or shoes or newspapers on the carpet. No dust on the receiver. Not even scratches on the imitation wood chairs.

The cleanliness bothered me. Some folks are compulsive, but the cobwebs above the drapes said Jack Anatole wasn't one of them. A man's home is his castle, and seeing how he lives shows me the man. Jack couldn't be this unimaginative.

There were no posters, no paintings, no bookshelves, no plants, no souvenirs from Vietnam and nothing a cop could call paraphernalia. None of those homey charms people use to indicate they live somewhere. There was no mail, either, not even a Christmas card. Nothing, in fact, to signify the holidays.

There was no personality to this place, as if it were swept clean daily, down to the fingerprints. There was just enough and even less. I couldn't tell if he had nothing or just didn't want to be pinned down.

I couldn't live like this. It was like being in the Army again. A transient barracks. A man getting ready to ship out, or a man waiting for his discharge. A man who hadn't expected to live here this long and hoped he didn't have to live here much longer.

Guys in prison are this neat. Killing time was important to them. Jack had spent time in the stockade. Last year's calendar had days marked off, and Jack wasn't a man to doodle. Maybe, for him, each day was the same. Maybe he had no reason to mark the days any more.

A blur in the corner of my eye banged into the side of my head. It was like being jumped by a brick wall. It knocked me flat on the floor, and I hit it hard.

I lay there for a while. I was breathing and I was alive. I couldn't remember how to stand on my own two feet again. It didn't seem that important. I told myself that if I just stayed still, somebody would find me.

I came back soon enough. Jack Anatole sat on the edge of his bed. My gun was in his hand, and it was pointed at me.

He looked me over. "You're a mess."

I saw a grocery bag with TV dinners and ginger ale. There was a battered clock radio on the bed sheets. Somebody had stepped on it with my head.

"Don't you ever get tired of this shit?"

"All the time." I had spoken too soon. My head echoed like a hall of mirrors. I wondered how my gun had been taken away from me.

He kicked my shin. "Did you have a nice time going through my apartment?"

"I was just returning the favor." I waited until I felt better before going on. "You went through mine last night."

His hand tightened, then relaxed. "Somebody's a liar."

"Where were you last night?"

He played it cool. "Celebrating New Year's Eve."

"Your Porsche." I had trouble swallowing. "Somebody saw it outside my place."

He was amused. "I wasn't driving it last night. Somebody borrowed it. Somebody from work, I think."

"On New Year's Eve?" I shook my head. It rattled. "Oh, no, you'd be in it."

"You're pretty good," he admitted.

"I know." My skin felt like a drum being tightened. My pills had fallen from my jacket. I picked them up.

He raised the gun.

"Pills." I pointed to my face. "My face." I got to my feet slowly. "Don't go away." Then I stumbled off towards the bathroom.

He watched me pour a tumbler of water. He found my guts refreshing. "You're tougher than you look."

I swallowed two tabs. "Dumber." I didn't feel brave. Listening hurt my head and talking didn't help. Right now the codeine was more important than a bullet in the back.

He sat on the pot. "You keep a messy place."

"As if you didn't mess it up more." I looked in the mirror. The stitches were where the drum skin had stretched too far. There were still green and purple bruises from my windshield, but I didn't see any new ones. There wasn't even blood on my head. I held the sink for a while to keep it from shaking.

"You got a nice face there," he said.

I couldn't think of anything obscene to say. "Why should you care?" I threw water on my face. "What did you break into my place for?" It seemed like a fair question.

"I wanted to find out who you were."

I frowned. "Who do you think I am?"

He looked down on me. "Once you were a private eye. Now you're a bum collecting unemployment. You're broke. You need dough. That's why you're playing in this shit."

"I coulda told you that," I groused. The needle was back. It echoed like the turf. It had to be my pulse. I covered my face in a towel for a while. "Are you planning on pressing charges?"

He looked around. "What were you looking for?"

"Maybe I was just looking."

"As far as I can tell, nothing's been taken."

I tried to laugh. It hurt. "You got nothing."

He raised my gun again. "You're still looking for Dani." It was an old story. The man with the gun knows all the answers.

"I almost found her yesterday."

"Oh yeah?" He wanted to hear this.

"She's been at her sister's all week." I could talk a bit better now. "But you knew that. You called her after I left the smokehouse."

"I can still talk with my relatives, can't I?"

"You told Catherine Joey Crawford's parents hired me."

He snorted. "Why not?" He looked glum. "It's truer than what you told Alex Symons."

"Why should I tell that yoyo what I want Dani for?"

He jiggled the gun like a man making up his mind. "What do you really want with Dani?"

"Did she call you last night?"

He braked to a halt. "Why was she trying to call me?"

"She needed money. She was leaving town."

"Now you tell me how you knew that."

I made a cluck-cluck sound. "You shoulda called her back."

"What makes you think I didn't? I called her right after I left your place, but there was nobody home."

"And I drove up with a chick."

He aimed the gun at me. "Now you tell me what's going on."

It seemed fair enough. "After Catherine talked with you, Dani found out about it and got scared. She took off running. What do you think she was scared of?"

"You, chump." He had a point to make. "I'm sick of you chasing her. You're worse than a guy puppy-dogging a chick."

I let that pass. "You know of any places she might've gone?"

"A million places. I'm not telling you any of them. Why should I? I don't dog people around, trying to find out what they're up to. It's none of your fucking business where she goes or what she does."

"Where would she go if she thought she were in trouble?"

"She's not here." He was matter of fact.

"If she couldn't reach you?"

"You're a clown," he told me. "How did you get suckered into this? Don't you ever investigate your own clients?"

"I told you. Joey Crawford's my client."

"A dead man for a client." He shook his head. "Bullshit."

"He wanted me to find the girl who walked out on him. Find Dani, that was his last wish."

Jack reconsidered everything. "You said, his last wish. His last wish would be to see her again." That seemed to intensify him. "I can see why they hired you."

This should be good. "Oh yeah? Why?"

"You're stupid." He talked like a probation officer trying to save some punk's life. "You don't know who you're working for. You don't know it's shit you're playing in. You don't even know what's going on."

"I don't," I agreed. "Why don't you tell me?"

He edged forward. "You're a pawn in this mess. A pawn for the muscle. Your clients aren't playing straight with you, Brennen, and they're using you to get to us. If you knew who they were, you'd sooner kiss shit."

"Okay. I give up. Who're my clients?"

"Organized crime. Or working for them."

"What would they want that you got?"

"You really don't know," he marveled.

"I don't even know why I'm talking to you."

He had a face like a fortune-teller. "They're gonna do you just like they did Joey Crawford." To him, the future was a rock so big even God couldn't budge it.

"Dead, you mean."

"Real dead." Vietnam was in his eyes. The VA hospital was filled with eyes like that. Superman could only see through walls.

"You don't think Joey's death was an accident, do you?"

He was patient. "They killed him and they'll kill you. My advice is to lay off this mess. Stay out of it."

"Is that why you called me last night?"

"I don't want you hurt. Stay out of this."

I got curious. "Are you threatening me?"

"Jesus, where do you get your lines? If you're standing in their way, they're gonna blow you away, so you better stay out of this. Tell your clients, too. They better stay away. They're muscling in where they don't belong. If they try anything, I will kill them."

"Is that why you got Davey out of Jardin's Saloon?"

He thought I was smarter. "Davey's no match for you."

"You sandbagged me, you sonovabitch."

His GI smile said sorry, Charlie. "I had no choice. I had to get him away from you. He's got a big mouth when he's drunk."

"Is that why you worked him over? To sober him up?"

He didn't understand. "When was this?"

"He had black and blue marks on his face."

"I didn't do anything to him. I'm not the Mob and I don't play by their rules. Go ask him yourself. Yeah, why don't you?" He had a better idea. "You're the private eye. Why don't you find out who did it to him?"

"Davey was a real pain, wasn't he?"

He was catching on. "Okay, Brennen, you're going to tell me what's going on." He knew my gun was a great persuader.

"He's dead. Heart failure."

He flinched and came close to pulling the trigger. "Heart failure? A heart attack? Don't bullshit me, Brennen."

"He OD'ed on coke this morning."

"I don't believe you." He almost laughed. "You don't die from doing coke."

"That's what happened."

He lost himself in thought. "I can't imagine him dead. Nobody dies from coke." He found no comfort in those truths.

"You were the last one who saw him alive."

He caught up. His face curled. "I oughta kill you for that." He sighted my gun at my heart. "Like putting you outa your misery." He sounded like a volcano finding a perfect excuse.

I figured I was dead. How do you save your life in twenty-five words or less? "You're talking just like the Mob. Don't play by their rules."

"You stupid shit." His hand dropped. "Get outa here." He wasn't even looking down at me. "Right now." He had seen too much of me.

"You got my gun."

He tossed it over. "Blow your brains out."

"Thanks for the advice," I told him. "I'll be sure to follow it someday." I stopped by the door. "By the way, where is Dani?"

"Fuck off, Brennen. She's not here."

The Neon Lady

Unlike the other clubs, the Neon Lady was run by women for women. The two women who owned and operated the nightclub only hired college girls from the School of Journalism or the Sociology Department at San Francisco State University.

Yes, these cheap colorful floozies were budding photojournalists. They entered the building's rear exit as coeds, in sweatshirts and jeans, and inside they used gaudy wigs, stage make-up, and bawdy, gaudy costumes off a rack and were transformed into costumed courtesans from the Old Barbary Coast days.

Last year I interviewed one for *City@Nite*. She had a Master's degree, btw.

"I teach college part-time," she told me. "I worked 35 class hours in the past two semesters at three Bay Area colleges, and in four months working here I made what took me eight months teaching college kids."

"What do you teach when you teach?"

"Composition," she said. "But universities and colleges can pay us adjunct instructor salaries, which are less than half what a starting instructor makes. It's a plantation system. We're just slaves that academe exploits."

"So you work here, too."

"The money's cleaner here."

Once I explained my mission, Cherry Mary was okay being interviewed by me. She was the girl with the mink tattoos who had broken ribs. "I needed the money," she said.

She too was in college. She held down two jobs to make ends meet. She did process serving as a third sidebar. Student loans were a killer. We all know that story.

We talked about her mink coat trial of fire at Danse Macabre.

She was grateful she missed out on the gunfire and murders.

"What's the latest on the shooting?" she asked.

The Breaking News, I said, was that, on the night of the shootings, the suspect in the Danse Macabre shooting was already out on the streets on $200,000 bail on an attempted murder count from a confrontation in a biker bar in May.

"A different murder? Geez."

And now, after killing two people and wounding four others, he wasn't getting out even again.

The cops also said, I added, that the name of the second person who died was being withheld pending family notification. Lastly the SFPD made no connections with the murders of Boy Toy and the US Marine. Unrelated incidents, their spokeswoman said.

Hearing that disastrous news, Cherry Mary looked around the chartreuse dressing room and counted her blessings. "This dump isn't that bad. No one touches me, and I touch no one. I'm in disguise so no one knows who I am. I'm the Lord and Master over all the men who come in here. I'm an actress playing scenes and I can turn it off or on at will. I can call it quits and disappear." She reached out and flicked off the lights in the room, and the room was without windows and blacker than a banker's heart and then she flicked the light back on. "Whenever things get weird."

Cherry Mary took me around the joint to meet the other girls. One of the girls whose name was Maddie knew Stevie Vashon. In fact, she had been dancing with him at Danse Macabre the night of the shootings.

Too Many Places to Go

I was too wired for humanity. I thought about a nap. Or a drink. I went for a drive around San Francisco. I didn't go far, just between Lombard and the Wharf and Market Street, but the driving cooled me down and mellowed me as only the city ever could.

Oh, I had a plan. I drove down Filbert Street between Hyde and Leavenworth. I drove down Taylor Street from Sacramento all the way to the Wharf. I found again that strange little cul de sac and the green grassy park around Green and Vallejo, around Jones & Taylor. I drove down Pacific Street from Van Ness to the Presidio. I parked and sat on a bench in Dog Shit Park up at Sacramento and Laguna in the sunshine.

I wanted to drive through the Presidio, park and smell the eucalyptus and redwood trees. I wanted to drive up to Julius' Castle just for the drive. I want to drive uphill past Grant and Fresno Streets and look for silly little alleys. I wanted to shop for steaks, fish and groceries at Petrini's Meats. But it was long gone.

Although I had eaten moo goo guy pan at Louie Gooey's at 3 am, now I wanted a beef brisket sandwich at Tommy's Joynt. And a pound of barbecue pork (dripping with juices) from the Golden Dragon's take-out on Washington Street in Chinatown at 3 am. I wanted a bowl of steak soup from the Original Pam Pam. Yes, I know the Pam Pam was long gone. I also wanted a chocolate milkshake at Clown Alley, which was also now gone. An ice cold beer at the bar in Rickshaw Alley (also gone.)

But I could still have a burger at Original Joe's (with half of it saved and taken home for breakfast tomorrow.) Several drinks at the No Name Bar in Sausalito. Breakfast of corned beef hash and eggs at Fred's of Sausalito. I wanted drinks with a beautiful girl at the Top of the Mark again. Drinks at the Fairmont in the tropical thunderstorm. But I did have drinks at Spec's and of course Vesuvio's. I also wanted breakfast at Mama's in North Beach, although parking was a bitch day or night.

For a start, anyways...

Oh, after twenty years gone I had a long bucket list. I wanted to drive past the Marina Safeway out to underneath the bridge, climb up the hill under the bridge, and sit on the far western side of America and gulp in the Pacific Ocean. I wanted to get on the Bay Bridge at the last Bryant Street onramp. I wanted to walk the Bridgeway in Sausalito. I wanted to sit late at night on or around Pier One and watch the big ships come in. I also wanted to drive to Bodega Bay and Point Reyes and then onto Goat Rock in Jenner. I want to drink beer in the sun down along Highway One towards Carmel.

Lord, I missed you, lady. Can a guy love a city more?

But then Sophia got knifed and time fled away like a thief.

The Iceberg Mansion

The Vashon fortune had outpaced the wildest dreams of the terminally greedy and the congenitally foolish. As a measure of the family's earliest successes, tear down six smaller, more delicate mansions and build one big enough to encircle the courtyard. Yeah, they kept the courtyard. Go figure.

I wasn't criticizing my ex-wife's family by calling it the Iceberg Mansion. Like the iceberg that slit open the Titanic, ninety percent of the mansion was underground. Two or three extra sub basements below street level.

The fad started as simply needing extra parking space. Street parking in Pacific Heights wasn't good for residents back in the Gold Rush Days. Now, with all this Silicon Valley money, unless you want your Lamborghini keyed on the street, or parked under the pooping starlings, start digging beneath your mansion. While you're down there, let's put in a swimming pool. Maybe a yoga studio. Maybe a tennis court. Why not put in a dressage stable? More importantly than all that, the sub basement had a four car garage. Imagine that. A four car garage of your own in San Francisco. Why not a cricket pitch under the lights?

I parked by Dog Shit Park. No, that's not its official name. But that's where all the neighbors encircling the city park walk their dogs. (Don't go barefoot.)

Jerry Sutton, for instance, walked the Vashon Corgis here.

I saw changes, too. The mansions next door on either side were demolished. Perfectly good mansions, too. Just too small for the Vashon family. So they planted gardens behind high hedges on either side of their main mansion. Once inside the hedges, absolute silence reigned. Oh. Garden statuary and an Olympic swimming pool inside an enclosed cabana.

But who had the dough to buy this grand acreage? Oh, I suppose Silicon Valley mucky-mucks. But would they come this far north to commute? For mongrels, they were an oddball breed.

The London Towers

The London Towers Apartments upsets some people, mostly out-of-towners until they hear that the building was named after Jack London. He was born South of the Slot, the old moniker for south of the trolleys on Market Street. He was a tough guy, even by the standards of the day. He fought the Oyster pirates and he was tougher than them. The London Tower Apartments were atop Nob Hill, within sight of the Seven Sisters, the big fancy hotels that were built before the Gold Rush. Jack London was the best-selling, most popular author in the world until he got sick and died at age forty.

∞

The night doorman at the London Towers on Nob Hill was a white guy in his early sixties. He had a ruddy face that looked like the constant westerlies off the ocean had weathered his features. But I could see the capillaries in his nose. He wore white gloves and was constantly making them fit tighter, one finger at a time.

My son said, "He sneaks vodka when nobody is looking."

∞

I gave him a twenty dollar bill. "I'm not rich like some folks, but I share the wealth."

He was sly. "Just to say hello?"

I told him what my job was. Well, I lied and said I was a babysitter. He commiserated with me.

While he debated with himself, I checked out the view from London Towers. The story goes at the end of every street in San Francisco, you see water. From here, all I saw was the red light of Alcatraz circling the bay every six seconds. *Don't hit me! Don't hit me!* I flashed on my time behind bars in the State of California. I said the same thing as the lighthouse, just not aloud. *Nothing is worth going back there.*

Mill Valley

I knocked on the front door. There was no answer. I knocked again. Still no one came. I remembered the door had a broken lock. The house might still be open.

I turned the knob. It turned easily. I went inside. Nobody home. No big deal of course. People up here in Mill Valley could leave their front doors unlocked when they went downhill for cookies and milk. Sure, burglars have cars these days, but first the burglars had to find their way up here. Winding roads that squirmed through the hills. Gingerbread houses hidden from the road. Few places to park. They all cut down on the tradespeople knocking on the back door. That's why these folks had moved up here. They didn't want to be easily found. What little crime did happen was usually local bored teenagers.

I looked around the room. The living room was timeless, like an echo.

Things didn't feel right. God knows what it was of course. I just wished He'd drop me a line and let me know. I could use any help that'd be offered.

A television like a lectern in an empty auditorium. The remote control for it sat absently on the sofa. Some magazines nearby. A whiskey bottle on the coffee table. A smudged, mostly filled glass alongside. There were many cigarette butts in the ashtray. A half pack of Virginia Slims nearby. A throwaway lighter from Safeway. Ashes on the coffee table where someone had missed when flicking a cigarette.

I went to the kitchen. There was a half-filled water tumbler on the kitchen counter. Beside it the remote unit for the electric garage-door opener. Nothing to get excited about. Some people might dump the excess water in the sink after they drank, but it was nothing worth being picky about.

I kept remembering something from growing up. A man down the street died a horrible death at the plant. A steelworker, he fell two stories into a pot of molten steel.

His wife worked downtown. When she heard the news she rushed homeward through an avalanche of tears. Somehow she got onto the wrong side of the freeway. She drove twenty miles in the wrong direction before the police could catch her and stop her.

A madwoman on the freeway. She was a heart attack coming on strong. Automobiles dodging every which way in terror. Death stalking the freeway looking for a victim.

No one collided that day. Not even a fender scraped. The cops didn't cite her, and no one complained in the dailies. People understood. Life's greatest nightmares do come true.

And then I started seeing the pattern.

Elsie Finch had had a few drinks while watching daytime television. She wasn't here now, and she had left behind her cigarettes. Elsie Finch was off and running. That had to be it.

She'd been watching TV and caught the latest news. Maybe even the Instant Eyewitness News Team. She had seen her husband blow his brains out.

Now she was on the freeway of her choice, and she didn't have to be sobbing hysterically. She could be on another planet.

I caught myself. I was getting melodramatic again. She was a modern young woman. Okay, maybe she wasn't out playing tennis with the girls. She had been watching television. Maybe she went away to debate with herself whether she should defend her husband, and missed the grand finale.

Or Banagan had called, figuring she could talk her husband into laying down his arms and coming out with his hands up. Maybe she was already on her way out to the airport.

Maybe she'd be right back.

But the booze said no. She drank, yes, but not very much. She needed something when she saw her husband die. But one swallow left a bad taste in her mouth.

The cigarettes said no. She'd have to be out of her mind to forget them at a time like this. She'd need them.

I thought about the garage-door opener. Just a remote-control unit on a kitchen counter. But it belonged in the car. Unless somebody brought it inside. If someone had brought it inside, the car keys would be its logical partner on the kitchen counter. That way you wouldn't forget either one.

Without the opener, how do you open the garage?

Her car was still in the garage.

I ran through the house. I found the back door that opened inside the enclosed garage.

Elsie's car was in the garage, motionless and idling. It was an oil burner, and white feathers of smoke came from the exhaust pipe. The carbon marks below the pipe said the car had been here a while.

Elsie Finch was in the backseat. She was in a stupor. Maybe a coma. She looked like a bird fallen from its perch. Her lips were red, like cherry bombs.

Carbon monoxide. The favorite friend of drunks, lovers, and suicides. Hemoglobin loves it two hundred times more than it loves oxygen.

I jumped in the front seat. A plastic vial was by the cushion. There were a few yellow scored tabs inside. I read the label. Percodan. A synthetic narcotic, similar to codeine, methadone, and morphine. A central-nervous-system depressant that was habit-forming. Pain pills for when the going gets tough.

Percodan and auto fumes. Oh, great.

I found myself falling under the spell.

Fuck the garage doors.

I backed her car through them. Fresh air was out there, and out there was where we both needed to be. I hoped the neighbors might notice and call the police.

I stopped the car in the drive and switched off the ignition. I left the front seat. My hand fumbled behind it for the little lever that shoves the front seat forward. I found it and pushed the seat forward.

She wasn't quite unconscious. She was finding it hard to breathe. Her heartbeat was irregular. Her pulse was growing feeble. Her skin was cooling and growing clammy.

I gave her mouth-to-mouth resuscitation. She started breathing better. I was getting panicky. Where were the neighbors?

I tried pulling her from the backseat. She was too slippery, too heavy. I grabbed her from behind and hauled her out by the armpits. She slid easily at first, then caught a sandal on the floor mat.

I picked her up like a man with bookends picks up a shelf of books. I pushed her elbows in tightly, then pulled up on them. I got her to her feet. Her feet were rubber and she kept folding on me.

She was too much to carry. She was limp and awkward. Her arms and legs were flailing weapons. I managed to tug her onto the lawn. She folded and slipped to the ground like the dead. But she was alive. Soon she'd be moving. And I was far from finished with her.

I knelt over her and shook her. She snorted once and one arm wagged empty air, then gave up. She wanted to sleep, that's all. I shook her again. I shook her the way battered kids get shaken. She sighed and mumbled that she had a headache.

I took a chance. I stuck my finger down her throat. She gagged and hawked and started upchucking. I kept her puking until the retching came up green.

She tried to get up on an elbow.

I kept her on the pine needles. "Just be quiet," I said. "Don't exert yourself. Just lie there. Are you warm enough?"

The ambulance was miles down the valley and so far away. Then the ambulance swung around a bend in the road. The flashing lights would scare the wildlife for miles around. The sirens could scare the bark off the redwoods. But the citizens of Mill Valley needed to hear their tax dollars in action.

A medic jumped from the station wagon.

"An overdose," I said.

"What did she take?"

"Percodan yellows," I said.

"Oxycodone hydrochloride," the medic called to his partner. "A combination of aspirin, caffeine and phenacetin. An opium alkaloid. Circulatory collapse, cardiac arrest, and then death. Let's go!"

They were professionals. They gave her an injection of mallophine. They used an oxygen mask and then a stomach pump. Finally they felt she was out of danger. It was safe enough to move her.

The meat wagon flicked on its sirens and began inching its way through the teenagers and the housewives in the street. The going was slow. Every few yards the ambulance driver switched off his siren and waited for the bicycles to move aside. He staggered his siren most of the block. Then he let it loose to wail like a banshee when he reached the straightaway that led downhill.

I went looking for my car.

Jardin's Saloon

From the Bayshore Freeway, which rises on steel girders above them, the San Francisco flats are just another commercially zoned district of single-storied buildings whose rooftops carry billboards for cigarettes, scotch whiskey, and economy cars.

When you leave the safety of that freeway, drop down beneath its elevated security, you've entered the place where no city has a skyline. The flats are warehouses, train sidings, loading docks. Vacant lots and dead-end streets, broken glass and peeling paint, locked doors and tow-away zones. Even the muggers steer clear of the flats. There's no business for them here.

But there is a night life under the overpass. A few neighborhood bars where night people by temperament or circumstance can find safety among their own kind and live out their fantasies. When the sun goes down, the nightcrawlers come from the long shadows to these lice-ridden firetraps. Nothing from the daylight world can threaten them there, for there is only loud music, dancing partners, chemical madness. They come to dance. The chemicals make it bearable.

Jardin's Saloon was the raunchiest roadhouse in the flats. It slouched at the intersection of Monterey and Missoula streets like a hooker on an off-night, a baby-shit brown building cater-corner to a welding supply company.

There was enough loud music coming through the walls to scare off any fire inspector dumb enough to be slumming in this part of town. And the blast of hot air that came from the swinging doors stunk of sweat and cigarettes, wet clothes and booze.

I took a deep breath and ducked inside the funhouse. The transvestite working the front door was too busy buying a handful of amyl nitrate spansules from a black man in pink pants to check me against the legal age for alcohol. Yeah, this was not the daylight world, and it made sense best on chemicals.

The band was screaming Gimme Shelter, and the bodies on the dance floor glistened and smelled. Half looked like runaways from the Vacaville mental wards, and the others like

Quentin graduates. I was the only joker in the house with a full set of teeth.

There were bikers and bearded ladies, leather boys and acidheads. Drag queens in short skirts and juice freaks getting fixed on warm red wine. Tenderloin trash and hippie nookie. Methadone junkies and panhandlers. There were six races and as many sexes drying their clothes with the dirty boogie.

I saw my quarry at the back bar. Davey Huie was half-wasted and talking to a man with two black eyes. He was dressed western-style and both hands were taped with athletic bandages. He was a little clean for this crowd. His hair wasn't that long, though it touched the nape of his shirt and covered his ears. His jeans were faded and fringed, but they didn't seem holey, and his flowery cowboy shirt had all its pearly buttons. He wore a patched Levi jacket and a powder blue Stetson. There was even a shine on his Frye boots.

I shimmied through the crowd as fast as I could. When I reached the back aisles, I scanned the back bar. Davey was still there, but his black-eyed buddy was gone. The empty stool by Davey beckoned. Maybe Davey knew where Dani had gone.

I pushed through the aisle and flopped onto the barstool, as if I'd stumbled onto a gold mine. The barkeep danced towards my end of the bar. I told him to bring me a beer.

"Anything else?"

"I can't think of anything."

"I bet you can if you try hard." He was a middle-aged leather boy, slim and wiry. He flexed his muscles with the beat of the rock band.

"Just the beer."

"Suit yourself." He pranced off.

I reached for my cigarettes, then matches. They weren't in my shirt pocket. They weren't in my jacket. I waited, cigarette in hand, for the bartender to prance back.

A pack of matches sailed through the air and landed by my hands. I lit my cigarette and then passed back the matches. "Thanks, man."

"I've seen you before," my benefactor said.

I shrugged. "Maybe you have."

"My name's Huie. Davey Huie."

I introduced myself. "But I've never seen you before."

"You useta live in Berkeley, didn't you?"

"Yeah, in Berkeley," I lied. "How'd you know that?"

"You remember me, don't you? I useta sit over on the benches in Sproul Plaza by the Student Union. I was the guy always playing the congas."

"Sure. Over by Sproul Plaza. Right by the Student Union. How come you got your hands bandaged?"

A wry grin. "Too much congas."

Davey was a lovable old mutt. His face was round as any basset's, with long black bangs over big dumb eyes, an eager-to-please mouth, and a permanently forlorn expression. Another guy trying to be everybody's pal.

I should've felt better. He had broken ice first. But he came on like a fruit trying to land another fruit. He didn't seem like a fruit, but this was San Francisco. Everybody's hungry here.

I noticed his glass was empty. It sat near mine like a tin cup from a beggar. The Chinese cowboy was another mooch, cadging drinks off the dumb. If he'd been female, he'd be a B-girl.

The bartender brought my beer.

I turned to Davey. "Whatcha drinking?"

"Tequila Marie."

I told the barkeep to get one. The barkeep gave Davey a hard, cold look—a woman's look at a rival—then went to the coolers. I felt like a nickel waiting for small change.

"So what've you been up to?" I asked.

"Oh, I was in a band for a while. It was bullshit, but a gig's a gig."

"You still doing it?"

He shook his head. "Our chick singer split on us. Everybody was fed up, anyway. I couldn't work with those people. They were all maniacs. How about yourself?"

"The same old shit. Just hanging around."

"Yeah, I know that scene. It's everywhere."

"One thing, though." I peered around, looking for someone. "I've been trying to locate this chick. She was s'pose to be here tonight, but I don't see her. That ain't saying much tonight with this crowd, but she said she'd be here. Maybe you seen her. A plain jane in her late twenties. High cheekbones, a few acne scars, an oversized nose, yellow blonde hair cut short, big blue eyes."

He cut me short. "What's her name?"

"You wouldn't know her. She's from Sausalito."

He set down his drink. "What's her name?"

"Dani Anatole. Why? You know her?"

"That's the chick who split on us."

"That singer you were talking about?"

"Yeah. That's the chick."

"I'm sorry I brought it up. I didn't know she was a bummer."

"No, it's okay. What do you want her for?"

I tried being reluctant. "I'm just looking for her, that's all."

"Hey, you can tell me, man."

I backed off, suspicious.

"I'm no cop," he told me.

"So what? Neither am I."

"So a cop can't lie to you, not if you ask him if he's a cop. If he lies and busts you, that's entrapment, and they gotta cut you loose. It's the law."

I had a hard time keeping a straight face. Davey thought cops couldn't tell a lie. Expecting undercover cops and operatives to reveal themselves on request was worse than naïve. It was downright stupid. Any lawyer could've told him that. Oh, maybe for a hooker busted for soliciting, but not in any other kind of undercover work. Undercover boys didn't have to tell the truth. They just couldn't force you against your will to break the law.

"Dani was buying a stereo receiver from me," I said.

"Oh yeah? What kind?"

"Sherwood." I thought fast. "Sixty watts per channel."

"How much are you asking for it?"

"Four bills."

He whistled. "You got more at that price?"

"Only this one. Dani's got first dibs, but if she doesn't show up, or if I can't find her . . ."

"Is it hot?"

"Nope, it's just like new. Only got a cigarette burn on the right side. That's why it's for sale. It was a demo."

"A cigarette burn?" He smiled like a co-conspirator. "What are you getting in the deal?"

"I score a little weed."

"Four bills buys a lot of weed."

"A key of regular."

"A good price," he agreed.

"Well, we're both doing okay, since there's no money changing hands. It's a trade, a little barter between friends."

"When did you set this up?"

"Last week sometime. Just before Christmas. She called me up and asked if I still had it for sale and how much I wanted. She said she had some weed, so c'mon over to her houseboat. I went and there was nobody there."

"When were you in Sausalito?"

"Last weekend and this morning. Nobody at home."

"Wasn't Joey around?"

Davey had gone with Dani to the Arroyo Grande. He knew she had split from Joey Crawford a month ago. No sense climbing out on a limb. "Who's Joey?"

"That's her old man."

"He wasn't there. Nobody's been there for days. This cat next door, he told me she split, he didn't know where."

He rubbed his jaw with a bandaged hand. "Far out," he muttered. "Maybe she left him."

"So she left her old man. So what? How do I do this deal, if I can't find her?"

"I've never known Dani to do any dealing before." He looked me over. His half-wasted eyes had smelted trouble. "Usually it's her old man, not her, who's dealing. He deals mostly in coke."

I gave him a sharp glance. "Say what?"

"Maybe you're trying to score some coke."

Suddenly a lot of things made sense.

Cocaine was rich man's dope. An ounce of coke costs as much as a pound of gold. Not many can afford a hundred dollar gram, but that doesn't stop those who believe it's magic. They'll swallow coke-filled rubbers to get it across the border. The dumb hunger for gold was nothing compared to coke fever.

Coke dealers were just as crazy. Like used car dealers or insurance salesmen, they needed a gimmick, a strong selling point to impress their suckers. Maybe flashy clothes, bleeding nostrils, a Rolls pimpmobile, a guru's smile, or maybe a thousand dollar bill for snorting.

Just the show for a guy like Joey Crawford.

I had to say something. "Maybe I am. There's nothing wrong with it."

Respect rose up in his eyes and walked away, going elsewhere, far away. "What do you want with coke?" He sounded like a social worker at the detox clinic.

"I wanna get high. That's what I want with it." I tried sounding confident in the face of adversity. "She's got the coke, I got the Sherwood. And there's this guy down in Palo Alto, he's gonna give me a good price on it."

"You're gonna resell it on the Peninsula?"

"I'm getting a good price."

"Yeah, a little easy money. Right. You gotta be on your mind. I useta do coke myself. I don't do it anymore. You know why?"

"Cos it's expensive."

"You know what coke does to you?"

"Yeah. I know what it does. It gets you off real quick."

"I grew up in China Camp. A Chinese settlement up in North Bay. When I was a kid, there was this old man next door who had a pet raccoon. Coke makes you crazy as a pet raccoon."

"That's bullshit, man."

"Don't tell me it's bullshit. You start doing coke, you start losing days."

"Now what's that mean?"

"You start and you want to do more. Pretty soon you want to do all you can. You start doing it earlier and earlier in the day."

I threw up my hands. "What's wrong with that?"

"It's so good, you don't want to slow down. You start staying up all night to do more, and nine a.m. becomes overnight. Then you start doing other shit, uppers or downers, all sorts of shit, trying to maintain your everyday style. And then you get strung out on all this shit, and you can't get your head together no more. You wake up and you got no friends. Or maybe you do, and those friendships, they're only fingernail deep. Then, what do you do?"

I stared at my drink, weighing every word.

"The devil made coke," Davey said. "And when he made it, he made it too good, almost too good to believe."

"What do you think I'm going to do? Get hooked on it? I'm gonna sell most of it, keep a few lines for myself. I just want a little freebie for myself."

"Go ahead, but be cool about it."

"I'm always cool."

"Keep your eyes open, too."

"What are you saying? You sound like somebody's gonna burn me? Nobody's gonna burn me. Dani wouldn't. Would she? I mean, she does have good coke, doesn't she?"

"If she's doing the dealing."

"Dani and me. That's it. Just us two."

"She won't burn you. If she says it's good coke, it is. But her old man would sell you shit that's been stepped on a dozen times already. It's coke, but it's also talcum powder. Or maybe sugar. He's got a sweet tooth."

"I know good coke when I see it," I bragged. "Nobody's gonna burn me."

"What about after you done a few lines of this, a few lines of that, a few more of this stuff? You won't be able to see straight."

"So I'll come back and break heads."

"And the goons'll break yours."

"What goons?"

"He's got juice," Davey cautioned. "They both do."

"City, state, or federal."

He didn't laugh. "It's bigger, and they get theirs from the top."

"The Syndicate?"

"It's got a lot of names." He stared at his glass. "They're both amateurs, not professionals like the Mob, but they got connections. If you play the Big Leagues, you gotta have connections. If you don't, you don't live."

I didn't believe him. If the Syndicate is half as powerful as half the people claim, how could it bear up with so many fourth-rate punks taking its name in vain? But I told him it was worth considering.

"You gotta consider it, if you're messing with dope. Like Dani's old man, he deals a lot of cocaine, and he . . ."

"What's he deal?"

"Mother of pearl. Rock crystal. Whatever's around."

"You know where he gets it?"

"Columbia, Peru, Bolivia."

"No, man. Where does he buy his stash?"

"Why do you want to know?"

"If I can get it wholesale . . ."

He frowned at my greed. "You're gonna end up just like him." He tried to explain. "Joey's crazy. Done too much coke. That son of a bitch tried to kill me one night. That's why I don't want to do none anymore."

"He tried to kill you? Where was this? When?"

"One of their houseboat parties. Right around Thanksgiving. The first time I'm ever on his goddamn boat, and the son of a . . ."

"They throw a lot of parties?"

"First one I ever went to. And the last, too." He tapped a matchbook to the band's music. "See, I walked into the bedroom at the wrong time. Dani, Joey, a half dozen others, all sitting around, doing one line after another. They had a mason jar filled with coke."

I gave a low whistle. "A lot of coke."

"I stuck my head closer, too, just like you would've—maybe join in, if I can. But Joey starts screaming and he jumps me." Davey gulped some tequila and went on. "He's shoving tables all around, there's chairs slamming on the floor, booze and weed flying all over, and I don't know what's happening. This was the first time I ever met the dude."

"So what did you do?"

"I started shoving tables back and forth, yelling, spilling shit on the floor. I told him to throw the first punch and make it his best one, because if he let me live, I'd kill him. Which was bullshit on my part. Shit, I'm no fighter. And that's when it got freaky. This other dude, Dani's cousin, he stands up for me, telling Joey to shut up and fuck off. Parnell does the same thing then, and he don't know me from Adam."

"Parnell." I squinted at the rafters, trying to place him. "I never met him," I admitted.

"He's this freak Dani useta know in Seattle. They're still pretty tight. He's an okay guy. That was the first time I met him, and he's coming down on Joey like Joey's done that shit before. Like it's nothing new that this guy becomes a maniac and wants to kills you."

"Maybe he knew this guy in Seattle."

"Maybe. Him and Jack Anatole got it on together, you know. Yeah, they started duking it out on each other, to see who got first punch at Joey. Joey was bug-eyed as me. I mean, somebody standing up to you is one thing. But two guys at once, and they're fighting over who gets to deck you first. Dani couldn't take it. She just freaked and started screaming. Hysteria, that's what it was. She got hysterical and took off. I can't blame her, though. That's a heavy scene. Her cousin and her old lover fighting over who's gonna deck her old man. That's insane."

"Where did Dani go?"

Davey didn't know, didn't care. "I just wanted to join her."

I had a good idea where she'd gone. She had taken off down the boardwalk, and Alex Symons had followed her. Later he had taken her over to his houseboat.

No wonder they had made beautiful music together. They had both been coked out of their minds. On cocaine, any combination of humans can make beautiful music together.

"Did you end up fighting him?"

"Oh, no. I'm just as chicken as Joey was."

"He wouldn't fight?"

"No way. He's just a show-off. A little guy with a big mouth. Scary, like any maniac big-mouth, but he's just chicken shit in front of you."

A strange story. Maybe it was believable.

"I think I appreciate this." I gave a weak grin.

"Who needs appreciation?"

I got the hint. I bought him another drink. The barkeep gave me a dirty look. I waited until he left us alone. "What am I supposed to do?" I wondered. "I still gotta find Dani."

"Maybe Symons." He hesitated.

"Who's he?" I wondered how Davey would handle this. He knew Dani was living with Symons. Since he had ignored that, it was his problem. And if you see one flaw, look for others.

"There's this guy, Alex Symons. Dani and him had this thing going. An off-and-on-thing."

"Because she had an old man?"

"Ah, yeah. Maybe he knows where she is. You can find him over in Sausalito. He lives on a houseboat near hers. It's called the Mal de mar."

"What's the name of the boat?"

He was shaken, but he repeated it.

"That's where I was. She told me to meet her there."

He was confused. "She told you she lived there?"

"When she called me. But nobody was home. The dude next door, he said she took off, and he hasn't seen anybody since."

Davey seemed genuinely puzzled. If he didn't know Dani wasn't living with Alex any more, then probably he didn't know where she was now.

"I don't know where she is," he admitted.

"What about Parnell?"

"Maybe. I don't know."

"How do I get in touch with him?"

"Who? Parnell? Oh yeah. You can try him, I guess. He lives up in Point Reyes. Inverness. Just a couple hours north of here."

A floor boy came to the stage, cleared his throat a couple times into the microphone, then called for everybody's attention. He read aloud my license number and asked the vehicle's owner to come to the front bar.

I pushed my way across the dance floor. A stuttering lunatic blocked my way and started badgering me about his gall bladder operation. I gave him a buck and told him to get me a beer. He disappeared faster than cocaine at a biker's wedding.

I asked the floor boy about my car.

He tried to remember. "Somebody sideswiped it, or somebody's stripping it for parts," His eyes looked like optical illusions. "I'm not really sure. It's not my car."

"It's my car." I grabbed his shirt. "Who told you this?"

"Just a guy." The floor boy brushed away invisible dirt. "I don't like being touched."

I took off towards the front door. I couldn't believe anybody would steal my car, but someone could have sideswiped it in the rain. I went outside. The rain came down in thick sheets. Visibility was zip. I pulled up my collar and scooted across the street.

My car was right where I had left it. It didn't look damaged, though someone might've thought so in the rain. It does have more dents than a Yellow Cab. Maybe I had been sideswiped. I couldn't tell, and it probably didn't matter. It wasn't much of a car. It had cost me as much as two Rolls Royce hubcaps. Which is what you'd expect a legal bachelor on unemployment to own.

I started back inside. My skull roared with thunder, and my eyes went pigeon-toed. I tried to kiss the wet concrete. I know I reached for it, thinking it was a good idea.

The rain went on forever. It stung my eyelids, my face, my hands. My skin went rubbery with the rain. It sounded like popcorn popping.

A raindrop ran up my nose. I woke up coughing and choking. Vertigo came like a jackhammer. I'd woken up too soon. My head felt like the silver ball in a pinball machine. The dry heaves came, had a good time, then went away.

I was in a basement doorway, beneath a wooden staircase. Dark and cold and moldy. It stunk like a toilet. A flooded drainpipe was emptying itself into my shoes. The rain coursing down the pipe sounded like popcorn popping.

When the vertigo was more manageable, I had a long talk with myself. Somebody had trashed me and stashed me here. What was I going to do about it?

At times like this, I wish I had a partner. Maybe then I wouldn't feel like such a wallflower, an old maid. Maybe a partner could keep me awake. Maybe he could lift me off my butt. With a partner, I could double my chances for standing up. Maybe even for getting out of these messes.

I gripped a beam and pulled myself upright. My arms were tougher than my legs. My legs were jello. But my arms could hold jello upright—I could stand, and that was a big step towards the future.

I had more guts, too. I wobbled up the stairs to the sidewalk. There, I tried to decide. Jardin's Saloon was two doors down, my car was across the street, my apartment was across town.

I went towards the bar, and I was proud of my reflexes. They clumped down the street like I'd walked with them before. I didn't bump anything or break anything or run over anything or crash into anything. I was real proud.

I went back inside the funhouse. The band had finished a set, but the dance floor crowd wasn't about to disperse. They had come to dance, and they waited for the jukebox. I looked them over and decided Damon Runyon had tunnel vision.

And then the jukebox started up. Suddenly the music was too loud. Suddenly there were too many people, and they all were moving blurs. Somebody asked me what time it was. I didn't know what day it was. I asked what year it was. They asked what time it was. And I wanted to die.

I headed right for the men's room. A drag queen just leaving held open the door. I stumbled through without saying thanks. Some cowboy was pissing in the sink. He looked at me, gulped part of his drink, zipped up and left me alone.

I was better off in the basement doorway. The men's room was a good shooting gallery for any junkie. Naked light bulbs and broken porcelain. Broken tiles and filthy walls. The mirror was cracked, and the paper towel machine had been ripped from its hinges. There were shreds of toilet paper everywhere, like the calendar pages in the Financial District. Puddles of water, murky and brown and algaed, like the mudflats at low tide. The smell was the same, too.

I found my reflection. My eyebrows were frowning, and my eyes were redder than the squiggle of blood trickling down my forehead. My hair was plastered like greasy leather, and there were grease streaks across my face and hands.

No worse than any wino in the Tenderloin. Maybe even better than most. But this was the night-before, not the morning-after. I didn't look like me, and I felt worse than I looked.

There was an icicle lost inside my head. It felt like an icicle, anyway, making a few stabs in the dark. Maybe it wasn't an icicle. Maybe it was a needle looking for a haystack. Maybe my head boomed with the sound of my own pulse.

It took a long time to clean up. A real long time. Finally I felt ready to face the real world. I hoped it was ready for me. I headed out to see what I could see.

I called the bartender over.

"What happened to you?"

"A mud puddle in the men's room." I didn't care what he thought. "Gimme a couple of fingers of brandy."

"The good stuff?"

"Make it rotgut." I drank down the shot glass. The cheap brandy burned like iodine on a wound. I was wider awake than anytime since breakfast. Now I was smart enough not to drink this crap. I looked around the back bar. Davey was missing. I asked the bartender if he'd seen the Chinese cowboy.

"He's not here anymore."

I wondered if I was slowing down. Of course he had split. Whoever had conked me had gotten Davey out fast. And Alex Symons had talked with that one on the telephone.

"Did you see who he left with?"

The bartender hadn't noticed. "He wasn't what you need." He had his hand on his hip, Bette Davis style, and he stared with brazen eyes at me. His thin smile was pulled tighter than his britches.

I was tired. Too tired to get upset. "I like women."

We looked over the women who sat at the back bar. They were all flat-chested, and their fat buttocks spilled over the barstools.

"Should I try and get you one?" he asked. Then he pranced away looking for his midnight love.

It was New Year's Eve. I needed someone.

I thought I knew where I could find her.

City of Colors

San Francisco is a city of colors. White buildings and green palms and blue skies and the ocean in every breath. But the city when it drizzles is a broken promise. All big cities are ugly in the rain, except maybe Paris, so I'm told, but San Francisco must be the ugliest in the rain. Everything is gray and moody and fogbound, and the clouds seem to hover around third floor windows.

The Streets of Chinatown

Like most peoples, the Chinese will celebrate any holiday they're offered. But, unlike the round-eyes, they don't sleep them away. Every day is Market Day, and, though the rest of the world might be hung over, the streets of Chinatown bustled with crowds of shoppers. Like barnyard hens, fat matrons in babushkas and slacks haggled over fresh fish and vegetables, while their husbands, weary-looking men who had forgotten how to smile, sat in their cars, practicing the ancient oriental art of double-parking.

Chinatown in Winter

Chinatown was winter quiet. There were parking spaces, and the restaurants were deserted. A rising wind rattled the glass in store windows, rattled the Christmas trees on the curbs. Tomorrow the scavenger trucks would come and swallow those trees. In some places they had already come and gone. Tinsel left behind looked like droolings from a metal monster.

A light was visible in the offices above the draft board. I figured he'd be here, not at some joss house burning prayers in an oven. That was for tourists and grievers. I found the staircase and headed up. I was lagging and needed both railings to keep my momentum.

He sat behind his uncle's desk, bent over like some ancient Chinese scribe. A pocket calculator and an IBM Selectric took the place of owl ink and the abacus. Papers on his desk rustled like the rustle of windswept leaves. He had a nice collection of paper cups and cigarette butts. He was huge.

"Brennen." He collected himself. "Come in."

"Hello, Louis." I found a seat. "How's it going?"

"I'm okay." He leaned back. "I hear you've been busy."

"I'm pretty tired," I admitted. "God, you must love your job. It's Sunday night."

He was calm. "Orestes Anatole wants the books done by tomorrow. I had to bring them up to date for him." He folded over some pages. "My uncle's reputation's at stake."

I sloughed it off. "He never had anything to sweat."

"He'll be happy to hear that." He paused, played with his pencil, started doodling on a file. "How can you be sure?"

Baytown

Baytown is a city of fifty thousand people south of the airport. A few years ago only Jesus could have walked these streets between the freeway and the bay. That's because the whole suburb is a manmade island built by developers.

They were already scarring the nearby hills with their tract homes, but what they wanted was their own island where they could sculpt in stucco and not have to deal with the law.

They bulldozed the dirt from the hills, trucked and dumped it on the marshlands below. Then prefab buildings were snapped into place atop the packed dirt. The law came to town after the last lot was sold.

Each developer left behind his own vision of the future. They clustered their tract homes together in little bulls-eyes and gave each bulls-eye poetic names like Sea Breeze and Sea Haven and Shoreview and Vista Mar.

But the pride of Baytown was Marina Riviera. Its two hundred townhouses were easily the most expensive, the most futuristic. They weren't along the shoreline, either, but at the center of the island, as if San Francisco Bay paled beside this developer's dream.

Marina Riviera was a photographer's dream, too. Each townhouse had two condos separated by four smaller ones. They were white stucco with gold tile roofs and blue awnings. Mineshaft modem with angled roofs and terracing. Manmade lagoons separated each half-dozen townhouses and each building fronted its own private marina. There were boat hampers on most back patios.

I followed a cobblestone path from the parking lot along the water's edge. The water was high and coots floated by. I wondered what the smell was like at low tide. There were only rowboats or kayaks in the hampers. Maybe the lagoons were diked in and had no access to the bay.

The Anatoles lived on a little peninsula. I suppose they needed to live near water, and I'm sure waterfront living impressed their friends. To me, they were attempting suicide by living in a prefab unit on fill dirt earthquake country, especially when the seismologists figure the Big One should come during the life of the mortgage. Fill dirt never settles evenly, and in a quake it liquefies. The Anatoles were living in a coffin on quicksand. You can get better odds on a snowball in hell.

Tahoe

A nurse answered the door. She wasn't much older than Catherine's maid, but her eyes were more placid. She had made a separate peace with her paycheck.

I gave her my photostat. "Is Mr. Anatole home?"

She told me to follow her. We went from room to room. Some rooms had paintings of trawlers and purse-seiners, and others had paintings of the ocean and the sunset. Every room had bright lights and tinted glass. There was plenty of central heating, too. The PG&E bills had to be hell.

After I had lost all sense of direction, she held open one last door and closed it behind me. I was in a solarium overlooking scrub pines and scrubland. The spotlights were on outside, and the swirling snow was confetti. A Christmas tree stood in the center of the solarium. It was decorated with tiny mirrors, strings of popcorn, candy canes, and home-made bulbs. My two boys had one just like it.

I walked around the tree and found I wasn't alone. Something like a mole sat in a wheelchair watching the snowfall and the night. It was humanoid, genderless and old. Very old. Its soda straw legs were wrapped in a thick blanket.

I went closer and found a man. His face was puffy and one eye was permanently half-closed. A phony birthmark covered a facial wart. Thick pink lips and chicken bone wrists. The jowls were thick, the chins were many, and his flesh was like chicken skin.

The mole shook himself awake. "Glacierization."

I smiled. "Right."

He looked hard at me. "Did you fall down?"

I was sick of answering. "Yeah. I fell down."

"The glaciers are coming back," he told me. "It'll be another Ice Age." Slipping dentures slurred his words.

"Take it easy," I told him. "The snow gets to everyone. You shouldn't stare at it so long."

His eyes went outside again. "When they found those mastodons in Siberia, they were flash-frozen, like breaded fish sticks." He ack-acked a few coughs.

"Don't strain yourself, old-timer." I wondered if the head nurse knew the old gray mole had tunneled from the funny farm.

"There were still buttercups in their stomachs."

"Buttercups are flowers."

"That's what I said." He was mad and his voice was shriller. He punched the power button, and the wheelchair spun half-left to face me. "You're pretty dumb, boy."

"I didn't get your name, old man."

"I am Orestes Anatole." His teeny eyes were watery and flecked with red, but there was no mistaking the Anatole birthright of blue eyes. "You wanted to see me."

No shit. "I thought I did." I needed a drink.

He looked at me as if I were a fortune being squandered. "You've been snooping around." He hushed me. "I know you have. I know you have a legal right to do it, too. I don't know what you're looking for, or who you're working for, but you saved me a trip. For that I'm grateful."

"You were coming down to see me?"

"I couldn't find your office in the phone book."

"I don't have one." I had one once. A hot little room in the basement of a bank. "How did you happen to hear about me?"

"Oh, I've gotten more phone calls . . ." He brushed it aside. "Would you like some wine?" He pushed a portable wine cart forward. "They're from my own vineyards."

I read off the labels. There was zinfandel and cabernet sauvignon, pinot chardonnay and Rhine. All were from the Mariana vineyards of Sonoma.

"Mariana sounded more Italian," he confessed.

"Sure." I poured myself a glass of white. I was still numb. I couldn't believe it. This old mole was Dani's grandfather. He looked like a mummy playing charades. I saluted him with my wine. "Here's to the Wizard of Oz."

He decided to hide his irritation. The wheelchair spun to face the snow. "I came up here for my privacy. Privacy is all I have left. I'm a harmless old man. Who cares what I do, what games I like to play?"

"Your family does," I said.

He was not amused. "They don't admit that I exist, and I try to keep it that way." But there was less thunder behind his words. He showed me wounded eyes. "I've been very successful."

I tried to think straight. This old mole was Dani's grandfather. I could see why nobody talked much about him. Then I remembered. "You must've been a helluva rum-runner."

"That was too many years ago."

"I heard you were Syndicate. Or had connections with them, back in the days when being in the Mob meant something."

"I was never in the Syndicate," he said. "Oh, I knew them. Every runner did. Maybe you don't know this, but the West Coast was never their exclusive. People like me ran the most. Amateurs. Free lancers. They tried to stop us, but even the Coast Guard couldn't catch us."

"You sold to the Chinatown bosses, right?"

"Yes, I sold them booze and why not? I sold to anybody who had the money. Does that make me Chinese? You got something against the yellow man?"

"Is that how you met Tan Ng?"

He waited before he spoke. "You're a pretty fair detective."

"Investigator's a better word."

He gave me the point. "We started out together. Back when Grant Avenue was Dupont Gai, and Dupont Gai bought Anatole fish. He ran a fan tan parlor and I sold him the booze."

"He's changed a bit."

"He's a slick old boy. Still a little fan tan, but now he's a busy lawyer. He helped me out once with the Tong people. They never did have much patience with amateurs. But you didn't come here to listen to an old man's sinful past."

I lit a cigarette. "What did you want to see me about?"

He asked me to put out my cigarette, then pointed behind him. The oxygen tanks sat like torpedoes, Bufano statues. I stubbed out my cigarette.

"We can talk better in the next room." He pressed his power button and the wheelchair scampered towards the door. "Can you hold that door for me?"

I did as he asked. He punched it and his chair surged forward and through. I wondered if he could do wheelies.

The next room was windowless and large enough for echoes. It had chocolate pile carpeting and mahogany paneling. Against the wall, a fireplace the size of my car did its best against a chunk of telephone pole. A crystal chandelier the size of the fireplace threatened the pile carpet. All chairs were leather and all tables mahogany.

"Are you married, Mr. Brennen?"

"I'm divorced."

"Why did she divorce you? No, you don't have to answer that." He pulled a file from a tabletop. "I know about you."

"You have a legal right to check me out."

"I didn't break the seal." He tossed me a pack of matches. "Would you like to burn it up?"

"Why?" I found a seat. "You have other copies."

He waited for his jowls to stop trembling. "No, Mr. Brennen, this is the only one."

"Why don't you get a refund?"

"What would you fight for, young man? What would you die for? You don't have to answer that. It's personal. Individual. But I can make a guess. Very little and certainly not for an old man like me. Not for a fish company, ever."

"I hope you're right," I said. "Dying for a fish company is stupid."

"You're very glib." He wasn't being hostile.

"Just being honest, I hope."

He wheezed his contempt. "That's my grandfather up there," he said. "He was the man who founded the fish company. He was a good businessman, too. He ran it for forty years." He glanced at me. "He came to San Francisco during the Gold Rush. He was twenty years old then."

I looked behind and above me. The founder's portrait mocked any other "founder's" portraits I've ever seen. Orestes Anatole the First was a real fisherman. He wore a fedora perched rakishly over a mop of curly hair. A wool overcoat. A stubby cigar in his mouth. He grinned as if he had just sung ten verses of a dirty sea chantey.

"A lot of ships were stranded in the Bay those days," his grandson told me. "Sturdy ships that sailed around the Horn. Their crews had deserted for the Gold Country. My grandfather and his partner bought one and started fishing."

I looked over. "What happened to his partner?"

"One day he disappeared." The old man sucked his gums. "They say he was shanghaied from a Barbary Coast saloon."

"That was convenient."

The old man went on without me. "He never lost a boat. He never lost a man. He made deals with the Chinese. He helped them sail the Bay and fish for shrimp. He bought land and held it in trust for them. He fought the oyster pirates with knives and guns. He bought land in Sonoma for vineyards when land cost ten dollars an acre. And when the Blight hit the French fields, he sold them cuttings and bought more land." He paused for air, a vital commodity at his age. "He foresaw the sardines and bought purse-seiners for the Bay. He forced us to convert to gasoline, and later to diesel. He was even the first to open a restaurant at

Fisherman's Wharf, but he lost money there. He was a decade too soon."

"He sounds like quite a man."

"He died in the bathtub," Orestes told me. "Mother and I hauled him out. He looked like a beached whale. A rather ignominious end for a fisherman, don't you think?"

I shrugged. "It happens sometimes."

He wasn't listening. "His death was the first freedom I ever had." He was talking to himself again. He noticed me. "I tried to instill that in my family."

"By setting up trust funds?"

He came close to a secret smile. "If I didn't, they'd have shot me for their inheritance already." It would take a nitro pill to make him crack a smile.

Nob Hill

I passed a cable car climbing halfway to the stars. The tracks rattled like cold teeth, and the grip man drank whiskey from a paper bag. The city had long since given up its heat to the night and ocean air.

It was windy on Nob Hill. A daisy chain of yellow cabs was outside the big hotels. Their drivers stayed inside their cabs, not outside talking among themselves. For some reason, the winds blow coldest on the most expensive real estate in town.

I passed the building before I saw it. It was hunched against the winds like an old man at a bus stop. It was stone, like the Hill itself, a symbol of eternity for the poor people of San Francisco. A mailbox watch-dogged the front while two stone lions covered the flanks. The building could have been a neighborhood branch of the public library. All it needed was a bicycle rack.

The doorman doubled as a security guard. He was reading a tenant's magazine, but he had a pump action shotgun beside him. He called ahead, then said the elevator was being sent down for me. While we waited, a Doberman came from nowhere to sniff my fingers. Money takes its own time, of course. It seemed forever before the elevator doors closed on the drooling hound.

The elevator opened at the penthouse.

I thought I was in a mountain glade. There were ferns, generations of ferns, more ferns than a redwood forest. Tall and full and overflowing. Every inch of the spacious room had something cool and green. This was a garden of delights for a midnight date.

I saw hardwood floors and tan furniture and realized this was the living room. There was indirect lighting and central heating. I looked for the F.T.D. decal that telegraphed bouquets.

Tan Ng babystepped in, sleepy-eyed. He wore a bathrobe, pajamas underneath. His robe was Chinese red and Chinese gold, while his pajamas were blue-and-white checked. Both were too big for him, something the Incredible Shrinking Man was leaving behind. With his cadaverous features, he looked like a corpse gift-wrapped with Christmas paper.

He was courteous. "You honor my house." He didn't look like he wanted to see me twice a year, let alone twice the first day.

Lim Song

Lim Song was born in Taiwan. He got his green card when he was ten. He was purse-snatching before he was twelve, joyriding before he was thirteen, mugging B-girls coming off the night shift before he was sixteen. For his sixteenth, he joined with some other kids and expanded into the stolen car racket. Their favorite haunts were the automotive garages after closing. They'd hot-wire the cars left outside, drive them behind Telegraph Hill, and strip them for parts.

If Lim Song and his boys hadn't gotten greedy one night, they might've grown wealthy. But they rolled a drunk tourist walking the wrong way back to his hotel. Some other tourists saw it and took pictures. The SFPD busted the boys in less than a week. Lim Song was sent away until he was twenty-one. He came out with a high school diploma and a barber's license.

The Sixties were a boom time for higher education. Uncle Sam wanted everybody to go, and he helped anyone with the guts to try. Lim Song's parole officer helped the boys enroll in a local junior college. Like a lot of street punks, they majored in Bonehead English and other remedial courses. And they learned it was easier filling out National Student Defense Loan forms than rolling drunks or snatching purses. They decided to stay in school.

And they were good students, too. Not the best grades maybe, but better grades than anybody ever expected. And they were good students because somebody gave a damn, or maybe because no one gave a damn. Some even took Asian studies. They read about the railroads, the vigilantes, the massacres, the Exclusion Acts and the Anti-Queue Laws.

Then graduation rolled around, and the boys found out they'd been short-changed. They had degrees but they were obsolete. Uncle Sam forgot to compute when the labor market was glutted with college kids.

But the boys had always expected the worst. They went back to the streets of Chinatown and their old ways. At least the streets were predictable. What went down went down every day.

They had changed, too. No more boosting cigarettes. No more stripping cars. They'd been politicized by Kent State, SF

State, other campus turmoil. With their heritage, they found their own reasons to become Maoists. They turned their backs on tradition and went after the Chinese Mafia. Like modern Robin Hoods, they'd hit a fan tan parlor or a Mah jongg house, shoot a few holes in the ceiling, then skedaddle with the loot. Unlike Robin Hood, they'd also shake down the hookers for protection money and freebies for everybody in the gang.

I set down my coffee. "He's Robin Hood, and I'm the Sheriff. Great."

Shoot-Out

Fog writhing in the neon. White light overcoming the blue night. A giant mermaid with big breasts and a broad tail beckoned me inside for a drink. Her slant eyes were a tourist trap, but I decided to take her up on it. Maybe she swam in the same circles as the Anatole dolphin. I could always introduce them if they didn't. Maybe they'd even let me watch.

The old cashier checked me over and went back to counting receipts. He didn't bother taking his cigar from his mouth. He made his money by the busload.

The club was smaller than a five-n-dime and darker than a banker's heart. There were dim glowing hurricane lamps above the booths and tables. The club was nautical with a hint of Polynesian. There were several life-size tiki heads, a couple of navy surplus anchors, palm plants that needed watering, even a ceiling fan.

An all-girl rock band was on stage in the back. They wore white jumpsuits with leather fringes and they sang Top Forty ballads in jagged Cantonese. There was a small dance floor in front of them, chairs and flat tables on either side.

There were a few customers down in front. Middle-aged Chinese men in casual clothes, they were slumped against their chairs, half-heartedly watching the show. Locals, they had to spend their money somewhere.

A string of Chinese b-girls sat at the bar. They were young and pretty, mostly, and they all wore cheongsams slit up the side, just like the tourists see in store windows on Grant Avenue. The bar itself wasn't very long. Nightclub owners didn't want lingering sorrow. They wanted their customers buying drinks with the ladies.

I found an empty table and took a load off my mind. The stool was an oversized capstan with padded cushions, about as comfortable as a driftwood sofa.

A waitress left the string of girls and asked what I was drinking. She'd seen round-eyes slumming in Chinatown night life before. Their money was as good as any man's.

"Anything. It doesn't matter."

"How about a house drink?"

I took the list she gave me. The house drinks were all based on rum or gin, and they came in colors prettier than a rainbow. They had cutesy names, too, like Tahitian Tumbler and Tiki TNT. My favorite was the Outrigger's Rigor Mortis.

"You get to keep the mugs," she told me.

The mugs had little tiki faces. They looked like old men in a smoke-filled room. They could keep me from drinking coffee in the morning.

"A brandy and soda," I said. "No. Make it two."

She headed right for the bar. She was a good waitress.

A tour busload of Japanese businessmen came in just then. You'd have thought they were entering a church. Their silence was sudden and reverent. Like lost children, they huddled together, finding protection in numbers. Their tour guide couldn't coax them any farther through the foyer. They weren't going to follow the leader everywhere.

The Chinese women left their barstools and came to help them inside. The businessmen liked that. Their eyes went large at the smiling ladies. The ladies steered them to an empty section far from the local trade. The local trade counted its change and drifted out and went home alone.

The waitress brought my drinks and set them in front of me, adding mermaid coasters and a couple of gratis packs of mermaid matches. I poured the first drink down my throat.

She had a smile for me. "You needed that."

"Yeah." The second wasn't much slower going down.

"Would you like another round?"

"Yeah." I remembered my duty. "Can I buy you one?"

She was agreeable. She went to the bar and had the bartender mix more drinks. She brought back my twins and a drink for herself. She said it was cognac. It was probably cold oolong tea.

She was older than the others, nearly my age. She was a nice enough woman, but she had sad eyes. There was too much of life behind them. There was too little, too.

She still stood there. "Mind if I join you?"

"Glad to have you." I started the second drink.

"My name is Suzie," she lied. "What's yours?"

"Michael. Michael Brennen."

She almost started to wait me out. "So tell me about yourself." She couldn't forget her duty. It was her paycheck, too.

"Oh, there's not too much to tell," I started.

"What do you do for a living?"

I thought it over. "I'm in the jade business." She didn't need to hear I was a private investigator, and I didn't want to be reminded of it. I remembered a cover story from work. "I'm from Paradise. It's near Chico."

She was amused. "So there is a Paradise in California."

"That's where crunchy granola comes from. It's mostly a retirement home for John Birchers. My grandmother still lives up there. She sends me apples every harvest. Jonathans and Macintoshes." How did I get into this?

She wasn't listening, anyway. She only had eyes for the Japanese. I must've looked promising to her in an empty bar, but exercising her seniority rights had blown her cut of the action. At this hour I was a frazzled case, and those businessmen were spending money like tourists.

The Japanese boys had really loosened up. They were laughing and joking and telling stories, slapping their pants with excitement. They were in Frisco and far from home.

The Chinese women sat beside them. They laughed when the men laughed. When the men ignored them, they didn't talk to each other. They sat chain-smoking and inscrutable. Like waiters in a Chinese restaurant, they were counting their tips before they got them, almost before they spent them, years after they had earned them.

I feel pity in every tourist trap. Those who work for the Yankee dollar usually get the minimum wage, but these girls made twenty-five cents less than that. Legal in some California joints if the employee receives tips.

There's nothing like the minimum wage to breed contempt. That's more than these girls had time to feel. The struggle for survival in America's most crowded ghetto leaves little time for anything else. And what another might mistake for exotic or inscrutable is usually lack of interest doing battle with hunger.

My own waitress had the same eyes. I didn't bother asking how she had gotten here. I knew her story by looking at her. She was from Hong Kong, or maybe Taiwan. Maybe she had a green card. She lived in a nearby walk-up, a building with more families than there should be tenants. Her money was pooled. There were a lot of mouths to feed. It was an old story in Chinatown.

Which reminded me. "D'you know Tan Ng?"

She wasn't impressed. "Everyone in Chinatown knows him." She remembered round eyes. She became cautious, chose her words with care. "He's a lawyer. He helps the old people move out into the Sunset."

"Sometimes he lets them sink in the sunset," I crabbed.

"I don't know him very well." She toyed with her coaster. "Is he a friend of yours?"

"We're in the jade business together."

A while before she answered. "I can't leave until after last call."

Oh Jesus. Tan Ng could get you into more than a friendly fan tan game. "What do I get for my money?"

"How much do you have?"

"How much is all night?" I countered.

"Two hundred dollars." She braced herself for the inevitable quibbling, but she was already reconciled to anything.

"What else can I get with it?"

Her smile didn't waver. "What would you like?"

"Black rice," I said. Right out of the blue.

"I don't know what that means," she confessed.

"It's an old story. Something to smoke."

Her smile was knowing. "I have some Oaxacan."

"Oh yeah? You have any to sell?"

She knew caution. "Maybe in the morning."

"How about nose powder? Tonight."

She said nothing. She waited for the pitch.

"I like staying up all night with a lady," I said. "Coke gets you up, keeps you up."

"Coke's expensive," she said. "Can you afford it?"

I showed her Joey Crawford's stash.

"That's a lot of money." She thought it over. "Lemme see." She left and went to the bar. I told her to bring another round.

The bartender had her wait until he was finished with the tour bus trade. Then he listened to her story. He gestured, it was no problem. She told him to look me over. He glanced over and saw round eyes. He started rapping hard in Cantonese, like telling her to stop being so greedy. She had started to chill off, anyway. They looked at me as if they hoped 86ing me would go easy. They were forgetting my drinks.

I threw a twenty on the table, reached over and took her drink. I tasted cold oolong tea.

She came back without the drinks. "That was my drink." She saw my empties and the twenty. "I forgot your drinks."

"Forget it. Where's the john?"

She pointed the way, then looked down at the twenty. She wanted it, but she didn't expect it. She didn't resent me, either. She was simply patient. Maybe I'd leave it behind.

"It's yours," I said. "Forget it." Yeah. I felt sorry for her. The other women were younger, and young women hustle best. A woman can make the most of it then. A hustler wears her age in her eyes. Pride was the first to leave them.

Her hand didn't move. The twenty disappeared faster than Saturday night parking. I knew Joey Crawford wouldn't mind.

The restroom wasn't built for broad-shouldered men. I was a bad case of elbows. There was graffiti on the wall. It was in Chinese. About what I deserved.

When I left the john, I started to push aside the beaded curtain, then remembered I needed cigarettes. A Chinese sugar daddy was holding up the cigarette machine, whispering sweet Cantonese nothings into his baby bean cake's ear. I counted my change. I didn't have enough, anyway.

I pushed back the curtain. I saw a Chinese male at the front register with the old man. The kid had chipmunk cheeks. I ducked back out of sight, counted to ten fast, then took another peek.

It was the goon with the nunchukas. And another goon was behind the bar. The old man had his back to them. He was scooping money from the register and putting it into a white envelope. A couple of b-girls stood by with stupid looks on their pretty faces. Two other goons by the door were warming their hands in their hooded parkas.

It was a nice quiet shakedown. No visible guns.

There was a payphone on the wall. I called Central Station and said there was a robbery in progress on lower Grant. The duty officer took down the address and told me to wait around. I said sure, hung up, then slipped out the back door.

I knew the cops would find nothing there, and I knew less than nothing. The touring businessmen didn't understand English and the old man at the register soon wouldn't be able to. The b-girls had no green cards, and the owners had hired them. It was an old story in Chinatown.

I bought the next morning's paper from the Filipino hawker around the block. He was lame from Corregidor, but he took no medicine and never complained. He had a long face made longer by a stubbly goatee.

"How's it going?"

"It's going."

Four SFPD squad cars flew around the corner, their engines close to hemorrhaging. They flew past us. Their red flashers were on, but they had no siren.

"Somebody's in trouble," the hawker said. "Whenever I see those guys, I know somebody's in trouble."

The squad cars fishtailed to the mermaid club, scaring the hell out of a poor cabbie waiting for a fare.

A brace of coppers jumped from the lead car. One leaped onto his car's hood to get closer. The front door began to open. The cop assumed Police Stance, used both hands to hold his gun, aimed it at the front door.

"Freeze!" Just as the Japanese were leaving.

They freaked. They hit the ground screaming. A couple of jokers in the rear took pictures. One drunk thought a Hollywood movie was being filmed. He started applauding.

The cops lowered their guns.

"What did I tell ya?" the hawker said. "Somebody's in trouble." His pale eyes said they hadn't seen it all, but they had seen too much.

We went on down the street together.

"How was your Christmas?"

General Assistance

Legal Aid shared a building with General Assistance and Records. It's not much of a building. Just a wedge of WPA concrete painted penitentiary yellow on the outside and piss yellow on the inside. I've always hated this building. It's bureaucratic and paper-filled and mind-numbing. The poor people of San Francisco come here to wheel and deal with their government.

The posters are the grossest obscenity. You'd expect them to be the official portraits of the HEW bigwigs in Washington, but instead they're travel posters for faraway lands. Not a soul in these halls could hope for escape.

I was surprised by the number of people in the building. Most were women. There were many minority faces. But this was the end of the month, not the beginning, and the checks were ready for mailing. Maybe the end of the month was the best time to make changes in Records.

General Assistance makes this place a madhouse. More than three thousand people were on GA in San Francisco. Every month each one received ninety-six dollars in hard cash, fifty-two dollars in food stamps, and a free pass good on any city bus. Most GA recipients are single men and women who live in the Tenderloin or along Skid Row. Without GA they'd...

Food Stamps

The Church of Saint Peter's Rock was Baptist. Stucco, vaguely shaped like a duplex and colored like pink lemonade. The first few days of every month it became a neutral ground for the poor people of San Francisco. Then, they'd forget their prejudices and hatreds long enough to queue up before its basement doors and wait as patiently as possible for their monthly quota of food stamps.

The church grounds were jammed with people. More people than I would have expected. Almost as many as bought tickets to the World Series or the Super Bowl. I wondered why so many had chosen this church. There were other food-stamp outlets in the city.

Today was a nasty day for waiting in line too. The summer fog was blowing in off the ocean. An avalanche in slow motion. Thick and heavy and woolly. The hard-driving westerlies howled between legs and across faces. Trying to be warm, the poor huddled and curled together outside the church like small furry animals, like refugees.

I went up the stairs into the church. God's house had seen better days. Even the echoes told of trials and tribulations. The church was empty of course. Today wasn't Sunday, and the real action was downstairs. Downstairs, on the other hand, paper became manna.

I went through the vestry and found the side door that led down to the basement. I opened the door at the bottom and found myself on a raised stage in the rear of the church basement. The basement was filled with poor people.

Doug Lasky was among the social workers comparing vouchers with authorization cards. For once he didn't look his usual mellow self. I whistled until I caught his attention. Absently he beckoned me forward.

The fight through the crowd wasn't as bad as I thought it might be. There were only a few times when I needed to flash my Department of Social Services ID to convince someone that I wasn't cutting into line ahead of him.

One red-faced fatso with a blond beard held me up. No one was going to squirm ahead of him, not even a private investigator with a case to solve. Luckily for him, before I blew a fuse, Doug spotted me and told the red-faced fatso to step aside. Red-faced was still reluctant and self-righteous, but rather than jeopardize his stamps, he let me pass.

I reached Doug. "How come the crowds?"

"This is a holiday weekend."

I looked over the crowded basement. Some folks were dressed in the latest styles, some in last year's durables, while most made due with whatever. Maybe some were here to rip off the government for fifty bucks' worth of food stamps, but I couldn't pick them out.

But I could read eyes. A man's pride was nothing down here, was something that worked against him, was less than a cinder in society's eye. A man earned his daily bread here by proving he was too poor to buy a loaf. And in this crowd, that made each man a tinderbox.

Doug said, "She stiffed me too."

I told him what I knew about Heather Beaumont.

Doug thought it over. "Maybe she is a high-class call girl. But maybe she was just intimidated by Legal Aid and got paranoid and panicked."

"Or she's a methadone loonie with emotional problems. Or maybe she's just discovered a new scam."

"What's her motive? What's her payoff?"

"That's the big question."

"And we won't know until you find her."

"Sad but true."

"What about her current address?"

"I called her landlady. Heather Beaumont moved in last January and moved out a month later. No forwarding address."

"What about the post office?"

"She has her mail held for her and she comes in to pick it up once a week."

"What are you going to do now?"

"Let's go get a beer."

Doug looked around the church hall and didn't like where he was at.

As we started to file out he told me I was leading him to drink.

"Okay, I'll follow you this time. Who's driving?"

He held his car keys. "I guess I am."

And the church hall behind us was a flood of shrieks and shouts. Cries and screams.

We spun as one. A hundred crowded feet away a young black man stood shaking by the basement doors. His hands were fists, cocked and clenched by his sides. The crowd had fallen back. No one wanted to be near him. He had plenty of room.

A young hippie housewife stood beside him. Both hands covered her face. Blood streamed through her fingers. The blood was bright red, impossibly red, as it always is, like liquid roses. It splattered on the floor.

She took away her hands and shook her head, as if shaking off spider webs. Blood flew out in droplets. Folks gave her more room, as if blood were poisonous to the touch. She said something to the black man. There was another flurry of fists. The woman fell to the floor, helpless, stricken.

The crowd burst at one seam and an angry, frightened, violent young man ran out toward the streets. The crowd regrouped around the helpless woman, encircling her like a band of mourners or maybe vampires, and gawked at her. A seam on the side opened and a security guard came and knelt beside her.

Someone said her nose was broken.

A man pressed against me said something.

I spun and faced him. "What did you say?"

The old derelict gulped, then tried standing tall. "Somebody should have gone and helped her."

A young blood in a green felt suit was behind him. "I'll watch your place in line." The blood's buddies smirked like guilty children.

The derelict started stammering. "Somebody should have gone and helped her."

The blood's voice thickened. "Well, I don't claim to be someone, sucker." He found some pride in that little speech, I suppose.

Doug turned his face toward mine. There was anger and violence and fright in his face too. His scowl went through me, through the plasterboard and stucco church and the city that lay beyond.

"Take it easy," I said. "I didn't do anything either."

His voice, when he found it, was a broken rosary. "You were too far away, Michael."

"So were you, Doug."

He held out his hands. They shook badly. I couldn't look at them. I pushed them downward, out of my sight. I couldn't do anything for him.

The Visible Makes You Obvious

"Let me know when you need another beer." Phillip Beaumont drained his beer, then tossed the empty can over the side of the roof. The can fell between his apartment building and its neighbor. It clunk-clunked against both walls, then clattered into a trash bin in the alley between them.

"Nice shot," I told him.

"You're from San Francisco, right?" He reached into the ice chest and plucked out another can of beer. He opened it without a problem. "You know how come I can tell? It's July and you got no tan." He drank deeply, like a thirsty man.

"It's a fog burn," I said.

Philip Beaumont looked hung over and in need of a good night's sleep. He wore tennis shoes and faded jeans. His shirt hung out and over his middle-age spread. His raspy voice grated like sandpaper.

"It's a shame about this smog." He looked over the rooftops and palm trees. "You can't see it today, but on a clear day you can see Santa Catalina Island. It's one of the Channel Islands. There's about a half dozen of them, you know. On one of them, Santa Rosa Island, they found the earliest traces of mankind in the Western Hemisphere."

I shaded my eyes and looked at the smog. "No kidding."

The rooftop philosopher winked at me. "Fire pits with mastodon bones in them. The bones were charred and gnawed. Do you know what that means? They've been barbecuing in southern California for forty-five thousand years!" He was in love with his conclusion. "Man has left his mark on the barbecue grill."

I grinned. "Sure. Throw a burger on for me."

He threw two more meat patties on his grill. "I knew you wouldn't hold back." He turned to his auburn-haired lady friend. "Sharon, how about getting that other six-pack from the refrigerator?"

She smiled, nodded, and headed for the fire escape.

We waited until she disappeared.

"Now we can talk," he told me.

I shrugged, feeling cautious. His eyes had a glint of madness behind them. A little glint was nothing out of the ordinary in Los Angeles. LA is the acting town, no matter what one does for a living. But most people show their upper teeth when they smile. His smile was all lower teeth. A perfect line of white. Unreal and making me nervous.

"What is this?" he demanded. "Some kind of hustle for child support? We got divorced years ago. There was no child support, no maintenance program, no alimony, no nothing. She got custody. I don't have to pay a penny, pal, and it's going to stay that way."

"Then where's Julie?"

The Brass Ass

I didn't like what I saw inside. A big open nightclub crowded with noisy people. Tables and chairs. The walls were mirrors. If you're a success, you like seeing what success looks like.

Black lights and strobe lights and Christmas tree lights. Just like a crash pad back in the Summer of Love. A dozen room-loud speakers hanging from the rafters pumping out the same three chords. Less cigarette smoke than I would've expected.

The waitresses were all runners. Skimpy jogging shorts and white T-shirts and Adidas. They were all beauties, but their faces looked stamped from cold plastic. A man in a glass booth suspended over the disco island played the Rolling Stones' latest disco hit. The strutters on the boards could never be mistaken for disco dancers. Most looked like they had chosen between Valium and speed.

The Brass Ass was loaded with what the society pages call the New Elegance. The rich folks who smoke a joint in the cab on their way to the opera. Some were wallflowers. Some wished they were wallflowers and wanted to go home already, while others wouldn't have missed this for the world. For a few solitary drinkers this whole show just didn't matter.

Happy faces chatting over Stolichnaya and Perrier. Men in suits. Businessmen and bankers and brokers and lawyers. Longhairs in jeans and sport coats. Matrons in pant suits. Junior Leaguers in designer fashions. Young men who wore sweaters wrapped around their necks like old women with fur stoles. Old fairies holding court over grapefruit and vodka.

I went right to the bar. One barkeep with a maniacal grin had a chalk scoreboard beside the register. Every once in a while he'd erase what was written and chalk up a higher score.

I sat near him. "Hiya, Michael."

Michael grinned. "What say, Michael?"

We solemnly shook hands. We were old buddies.

"What's with the blackboard?"

"I got this game that I play," he said. "Dogs versus wolves. I get to keep score." He whinnied like a madman, then rubbed his hands together.

Michael just makes the rest of us look healthy.

I bought myself a brandy and soda. Five bucks disappeared. "What about your boss? How does he like your keeping score?"

"Fuck him if he can't take a joke."

"Where is he?"

"As long as he ain't here, fuck him."

I almost gave up. "What's his name?" I knew the answer, but sometimes I like hearing what other people know.

"Big Moon," Michael said. "Can you believe that? He's a seven-foot ton of lard and he looks like a silo. He's dumb as grass and thinks he's cool. Big Moon."

"How did he get his name?"

"I don't know for sure," he confided. "I heard he got it back in high school." He made Groucho eyebrows, then guffawed a few times. Life is a big joke to Michael the bartender.

"What's he like?"

Michael started washing some convenient glasses. "He's the kind of a grease ball who dresses the way he figures the Mob expects. Too bad for him that the Mob in California lives out in the suburbs and drives campers on the weekend. He swears that someday he'll be a millionaire. That's when he can admit he never finished high school."

I laughed. "You're cruel."

I had busted Michael once. My first San Francisco bust, in fact. At the time he was pouring in a neighborhood joint. The owner suspected Michael was pilfering the till, so he hired Pacific-Continental Investigations, and I was sent out to get drunk for a week. My boss, in a moment of rare viciousness, asked me if I could last the full five days.

I spent that week watching Michael. I found out he was a barkeep who gave free drinks to his cronies rather than tend bar in an empty joint. A nice guy with his heart on his sleeve. On my last day we had a long talk together. I didn't turn him in, and he quit that same afternoon.

Now Michael worked downtown and gave no one free drinks, not even me. He wouldn't even play Liar's Dice. As for the neighborhood bar, well, it went belly-up because Michael's cronies stopped coming in altogether. Some new owner turned it into a gay bar last year and rumor said he was failing too. It had a terrible location.

Michael said, "The real boss of this dump is in Lompoc Federal Prison. He was convicted of perjury in a narcotics scam.

Last postcard we got, he had taken up jogging and the Jacuzzi and was palling around with convicted Koreagators in the yard."

"Where does Big Moon come in?"

"He's just the baby-sitter here. The Mob owns this dump," he told me. "Yeah, they really do." He grew semiserious. "One of their rising young stars, part of the third generation, dreamed up this idea. The old guys, they're all old men happy with their RVs and their campers, they all moved down to San Jose and Palm Springs and places like that. They're so wacked out on the pills their doctors give them that they gave that guy the go-ahead. The cost accountants figured it might work, so what the hell."

I smirked. "The Mob went disco."

"It was supposed to be a laundry. They figured nobody in their right mind would pay these prices. They even had a dress code when the joint opened. The idea was, the joint would be rocking on the books, but there wouldn't be anybody here."

"What went wrong?"

"The joint started clicking," he said. "Disco mania hit San Francisco. They dumped the dress code and raised the prices, and people still flocked in. They even changed owners, and that didn't work. Finally they just gave up. The way it stands right now, they're talking about opening a franchised chain of these places around the country." He looked down the length of the bar. A sit-down drunk needed a refill. Michael headed back to work.

I could see faces clearer now. Some faces were familiar. The new car dealer from down the Peninsula who sponsored the all-night movies was here with an entourage. His date was bright, alert, and affable. She had beautiful features. A foxy lady five years older than me. Honey-blond hair and teeth whiter than snow. Hippie flashy. Lolita glasses that were rose-colored and heart-shaped. A chocolate blouse and a blazer the color of driftwood with matching slacks. Wool or tweed. She had a gardenia on her lapel. A lot of hard work went into her beauty. Now she needed a man who could appreciate the effort, who could foot the bill for future renovations.

Heather Beaumont stared at me as if I were Atlantis rising from a watery grave. She looked guilty as hell, as if I were the landlord and she didn't have last month's rent. She panicked. She was on her feet and coming right at me.

I knew she wasn't getting past me.

Political Rally

A security guard was half-hidden by some palm plants. He was bullshitting with the black doorman. They made me sign in, then led me to an elevator. I rode up alone, listening to the Muzak being piped through the elevator. It sounded like the Beatles doing a funeral dirge.

The elevator opened at the penthouse.

I came through the doors like a sailor searching for the long-lost hooker he'd fallen in love with on his last leave in San Francisco. I mean, I was ready for anything.

She was a brunette. Long hair and round eyes. She wore a summer shift with a shawl that matched. The shift was white lace. It had butterflies and flowers. Bright red and blue ones. She was pretty as a wildflower, and she wasn't even five feet tall. Small and delicate as a little bird.

To find her here...

"C'mon in," she told me.

I looked over her head. Partygoers milling around with drinks in their hands. Small clusters huddling together in circles like covered wagons. There was a lot of noise. Some of it was laughter, but most was simple chatter. A stand-up bar was across the room, and three union bartenders were pouring drinks.

Old people and young couples. San Franciscans and commuters and a few native sons. A monsignor or two, some blacks and some Chinese, several Filipinos and a few Chicanos, and some obvious gays. There was even a bunch of people who didn't bother placing their names in the phone book. The typical mix you see at San Francisco parties.

Their dress was informal too. The men wore suits or sport coats. I saw jeans and silk, sometimes together. Some women wore girdles and some went without bras. Most of the women carried their purses, and the wealthier ones clutched them to their armpits. That meant many here didn't know each other. This was a social call.

And then somebody gave me a drink.

I tasted it. It was a vodka martini. Olive bobbing like a buoy in rough waters. Sweet baby Jesus, I was heaven-bound.

The little brunette was staring. "You look happy."

"I'm delighted," I told her. "Hell, I've been sweating torture, expecting the rack." I grinned. "This is a martini party."

She didn't quite understand me, but she gave me a friendly smile. "Well, please enjoy yourself, okay?"

"I will," I promised. "I will."

I'm great on vodka martinis. Several years ago I lived near an ailing hotel desperate for tourist dollars. The manager wanted those warm bodies enjoying themselves when the tourist buses came, so his basement lounge began advertising happy hours after office hours. Cheap drinks, after all, make people happy, and the more the merrier.

The happy-hour deal didn't last long, since the hotel was inconvenient for the secretary crowd, but for a while it was heaven. Double martinis for a buck, the bar food was all the cracked crab you could eat, and a third-rate floor show with no cover and no minimum. The black bartender spotted me as a local right off the bat. He thought I deserved triple martinis for a buck. One night I wore out the knees of my jeans crawling home. I'd spent five bucks.

A Tough Town to be a Millionaire in

Like all great cities, San Francisco has great hotels. Five are on Nob Hill, where the cable cars rest before they drop downhill.

Nicknamed the Five Sisters, these hotels are named after pirates and saints, local landmarks and old robber barons. The Wyant was one of the Five Sisters. There was some dispute over what it was named for.

The Wyant came in two sections. They actually had only two things in common. Their room rates began at twice a man's daily wages, and both had 95 percent occupancy year round, every year. Depression-proof money machines.

The old section was a half block of blond stone. It was an impressive sculpture. An old castle carved directly from a mountain. It held more prestige than any single guest. It was a museum, a memorial to the good old days before tourists. It smelled of age and wealth and power.

Presidents entertained royalty here. Corporate executives from the multinationals came here on their second honeymoons, sometimes with their first wives. Celebrities came here to be coddled and not noticed. Retired dictators brought their families and went on shopping sprees. The old section was for someone with a personal entourage or security requirements. It even offered bodyguards.

The new section was a glass-tinted tower. It started with a grand ballroom big enough to fly a kite in and ended up fifty stories later with a rotating cocktail lounge. In between, there were a thousand rooms for tourists and conventioneers.

The Wyant tower could be seen from Fisherman's Wharf. It stuck above Russian Hill like a submarine's periscope. Whenever I saw it I expected to see a giant bloodshot eye ogling me. But, then, I have a drinking problem.

Ruth Gideon and I went inside.

The lobby was marble and flowers. Sculpture in a garden. High ceilings and deep pile carpeting. Chandeliers and candelabra. Floor-length drapes that started at the ceiling. Glass-framed oil paintings and Muzak. Display cases of bone china and glassware were wedged between the coliseum columns. The chairs and sofas were leather and red velvet.

Ruth said, "I must be the youngest person here."

I looked around. She was right. She was half as old as the next-youngest person in the lobby. "You don't have to whisper. They're all deaf."

She marveled. "They must have a lot of heart attacks here."

I shushed her.

The hotel staff went about their duties quietly and professionally. Somebody delivered the mail and the daily papers. Somebody vacuumed the carpets and cleaned the ashtrays. Someone else rotated the potted plants for an even distribution of the sun's rays.

We stopped at the concierge's desk. Wyant was waiting for us in the cocktail lounge.

We rode the express elevator to the rooftop. We were jammed among tourists. There were many families. Children and teenagers. We all rode up together.

At the rooftop lounge, the tourists filed out and went off to huddle over the posted menu prices. Ruth and I went right to the bar. I ordered our favorite doubles and drank mine right down. I felt better.

Ruth gasped. "Oh, that view!"

I glanced over. "On a clear day you can see God."

Or the Sierra Nevadas." Stephen Daniel Wyant came up behind us. He took one look at Ruth and started to ooze charm. "I'm Stephen Daniel Wyant," he told her. The Wealthy always talk slow. They have all the time in the world.

She smiled. "Ruth Gideon."

"I'm here too," I said.

Wyant noticed me. "Brennen. That's right." He turned back to Ruth. "Mr. Brennen was instrumental this afternoon in saving my life. You should be very proud of him."

"That view is magnificent," Ruth said.

The lounge rotates every forty minutes," he told her. "A panorama of the San Francisco Bay area. You can sit here at the bar and watch the North Bay and the South Bay in the same hour."

She flashed her smile. "How convenient."

"I have a table over here for us."

We went to the boss's table. It was set in a private alcove. We were separated from the tourists by large plants and redwood walls. The table was set up near a prime window of course. Ruth had the best seat, Wyant took the second-best, and I made due with half girder and half view.

Ruth watched the view. "What are those two big holes below and over by the Bay Bridge?"

"That's the San Francisco Coliseum," Wyant told her. "That is, someday it will be an eighty-thousand-seat coliseum. Someday there will be rock concerts and auto shows, rodeos and athletic events there. Someday soon, I hope."

"It's very centrally located," Ruth said.

"Yes, it is." Wyant seemed to approve of her. "It's for the local trade of course. Those living within a fifty-mile radius of the city. Suburbanites and city dwellers both. It'll bring in all the Bay area. It's near the downtown hotels. Between the BART station and the Bay Bridge. It's at the end of every city bus line. And the buses to Sonoma and Marin and San Mateo counties and the East Bay communities."

"They used to call it Happy Valley," I said.

The waiter came. Ruth and I both ordered the lobster tails. Wyant settled for a small soup and dinner salad. But, then, he was buying.

Ruth was all smiles. "This is a very lovely restaurant," she told Wyant. "And such a magnificent view. I feel like I'm teetering at the top of the world."

Wyant had a sappy smile for her. "This is a precarious world," he explained. "People want security, and yet they need adventure. They need places to be human in." He gestured around at his property. "People can relax and enjoy themselves here. What could be more pleasurable than that?"

I wasn't going to say it.

"Sports?" Ruth had a secret smile. "A coliseum, maybe?"

Wyant was suddenly more respectful. "I'm at a disadvantage. I see you know all about me." He pretended to be humble. To me, he was mocking humility.

Ruth looked over at me. "That's his coliseum."

He was modest next. "I'm just the chairman of a consortium of local investors. Private citizens who choose to support this city. We've set up a corporation as the technical owner and operator of it."

I was puzzled. "I thought the city was building it."

He had a wan smile. "Most coliseums and sports arenas are built from public funds. But we've pledged that no tax money will be wasted. Not a dime will come from the pockets of the taxpayers to pay off that debt. It's a self-supporting coliseum."

I stopped him. "What debt?"

"The city issues municipal bonds, but the revenue from the events we schedule there will pay off the bonding debt. The revenues will cover both the operational costs and the retirement of that construction debt. In the vernacular, we are the renters and the city is the landlord."

"What kind of rent do you pay?"

"We're paying five thousand dollars a year per acre, starting when the coliseum is completed, to lease that land for thirty-five years. In addition, there's a special assessment of twelve hundred fifty dollars per acre per year."

Being as how I'm a renter: "What happens if you're late with the rent?"

Wyant wasn't worried. "We've promised to make up any deficiency in interest payments on those municipal bonds for the first five years. The city wanted more time on that, not just five years, but we countered by asking for a ceiling on the city's share of the revenues. We told them we would guarantee payment on those bonds for thirty-five years if we kept all the revenues, but the city turned us down of course. Naturally, they wanted those profits."

"The city gets a cut of the profits?"

He smiled over my imprecision. "It's actually revenue-sharing. Yes, we split the profits with the city. The city gets a set percent of the gross ticket sales. And the net concession revenues are split with the coliseum management. The city also gets half of the gross parking receipts. I won't mention the revenue we expect from the television and cablevision rights."

"Aren't you worried about having a bad year? Lean times?"

"Not really." Wyant was very calm. "Not with inflation. As inflation continues, fewer people are needed to attend to cover the cost of any lost revenue. The admission prices will rise. So will parking and the concessions. For the city, that translates as big profits and low risk."

I still wasn't satisfied. "A coliseum still seems risky. Couldn't the city build something else there, something that wasn't so risky?"

He didn't mind that. "True, the city might be able to make more money from hotels and apartment buildings, but this coliseum will only benefit the city. There will be more income from the city sales tax, from the city hotel tax. An increase in property-tax revenues. It'll bring more jobs to the city. Revitalize the downtown. The downtown will look better and it will be used more often. There'll be more people on the streets year round.

And that means a substantial increase in pedestrian traffic. An increase in parking tickets and meter rates. Just think of all those revenues on all those parking meters downtown. Meter maids twenty-four hours a day every day of the year."

It was a horrible thought.

Wyant went on. "That's three times what they collect now. And remember, there'll be an underground garage at the coliseum. Not just for big events, but an increase in parking spaces for all downtown businesses. A twenty-four-hour garage. This coliseum will be an investment in the future. An impetus to progress."

"When will it be done?" Ruth asked.

Wyant frowned. He didn't know. "This project was started fifteen years ago. It's been fouled up with litigation and environmental-impact statements. The wheels of justice grind exceedingly slow."

Those legal battles fed many lawyers," I pointed out. "Without them, there would have been lawyers starving on the streets of San Francisco."

He almost smiled. "I've been pushing for this project for fifteen years." He was almost threatening me.

"When does it get better?" Ruth asked.

"Next month." He faced her. "We'll have the official ground-breaking ceremonies then. We've just received the bids for excavation and shoring up the sides. The bids came in for two million dollars less than we expected."

"When do you hope to have it done?"

He clenched his coffee cup. "We could have it built by 1984."

"That was a very good year," I said.

He closed his eyes. "The coliseum might just coincide with the summer Olympics in Los Angeles. True, it won't be the summer Olympics, but maybe it will draw people who will be in the neighborhood." He opened his eyes. "After all, we are part of the Golden Triangle."

"What does that mean?"

"The West Coast is called the Golden Triangle," Wyant explained. "In the summer, Los Angeles, Honolulu, and San Francisco. In the winter it's San Francisco, Las Vegas, and Honolulu. Our researchers tell us that tourists will visit two out of the three if they come west at all. Now, we can't battle America's paradise." He looked like he wanted to be caustic. "But we can beat the pants off Los Angeles or Las Vegas. The glitter of Vegas.

The LA insanity. Freeways and crap tables." He gestured at the view. "This is San Francisco."

When I said nothing, he said, "What would you put in its place?"

I had a flash. "Low-income housing."

I had saved his life, but he didn't like me.

The waiter came and cleared the table. We all ordered coffee. Ruth excused herself and headed off toward the rest rooms.

Wyant was eyeing me. "Have you met Hayward Finch?" His eyes reminded me of a small boy enticing a wary robin under a cardboard-box trap.

I shifted uneasily. "He's the senator's adviser, right?"

Wyant nodded very slowly.

"Yeah, I met him."

"He's the senator's best friend too," Wyant told me. "They're in business together, that's all. The senator's the visible partner. Hayward's the silent partner, as best friends can be. He stutters in public, but that doesn't mean anything. He's a real smoothie on a one-to-one basis."

He leaned forward. "Forgive me this, but I checked into you. I was curious about the kind of man who'd save my life. You're a private investigator, right?"

I reluctantly admitted it.

"It seems I have a file on you in my office. Sometimes my guests have need for confidential services. It's a very informal file of course."

"What does my file say about me?"

"Your name has been in the newspapers. You and the Anatole family. You were nearly killed on a fishing boat. Your hands were tied. You were rescued by a woman. Ruth Gideon saved your life. That has been in the newspapers."

I grinned. "I just stopped taking you seriously."

"What are your rates?"

I grew very cautious. "It depends on who wants to hire me and what I think they want me to do. In my business you're grateful if your clients give you their real names. You have to guess the true reasons why they would hire you too."

"I'd like to hire you."

I blinked. "What about your own staff? I mean, you've got more here than just a house dick. You have an entire security staff. And I'm sure you already know where most of the skeletons are buried in this town. Maybe statewide, for all I know."

"I'll pay you the same amount that the senator's paying you to tell me all the things you're telling her."

"You must think I'm pretty disreputable."

"You are a private investigator," he pointed out. "I understand the state gives the pee-eye tests ten months a year every year in a dozen locations. Last year the state had to postpone those tests for the better part of a year. Do you know why?"

I sighed. "Yes, I do. Somebody swiped the answer sheets."

He was persistent. "I want to hire you to learn what the senator's up to. I want to know why she hired you. What's the real reason? What's the connection?"

"Why investigate her? As far as I know, she's an honest woman."

"What does that matter?" he snapped. "A great amount of money, power, and prestige is at stake here. A thimbleful of knowledge could be helpful."

"Slower," I said. "I'm thick."

He showed me his fist. "Money and political support. We need help and cooperation from the federal government to solve these problems. Can you imagine what it'll cost us if the United States senator from California decides not to support us? What if she opposes us, calling it just an amusement park? What if she holds a press conference to express that opposition? What if she uses her influence to kill it before it gets off the ground?"

I caught on. "It would be embarrassing without the senator's endorsement."

"Yes, it would, Mr. Brennen."

I said, "She asked me to look over her personal security. Now you want to hire me to overlook that same security."

He blinked. That wasn't what he expected.

I had my story down pat. "I used to work for the company that handles her security requirements. She wanted me to look over their work and see if it's worthwhile. She figures I hate them because they fired me. She figures if anybody can find where the fuck-ups are, this fuck-up could. That's all there is to it. To me it's a garbage gig. Now you can pay me for that information right now. If you give me a check, I'll go right downstairs and cash it at the cashier's window. Because, as far as I'm concerned, I've just told you all I know."

Stunned, he finished his coffee in silence.

Ruth came back. The lady with the red hair that tumbled in waves like the surf. The lady with the cool green eyes.

"Would you like some dessert?" I asked.

She smiled and shook her hair.

"Then I guess we'll be leaving," I told Wyant. I caught Ruth's eye, then faced Wyant again. "Thanks for the dinner."

Bong Cha?

We were buying sliced pastrami at Kroger's deli section when a scrawny middle-aged Chinese man in rimless glasses and a dark suit came up to us, spun me around, and shook my hand, breaking covid protocol before I could stop him. Then we mutually broke apart, horrified at our breach of separation.

He rushed to return my hand to me. He was in his mid-forties and wore the ugliest teal blue suit I had ever seen. He looked like a time share salesman working the Atlantic City boardwalk.

We gawked at his social faux pas. He had given me a sandpapery handshake that stupidly I returned. We could have each contaminated the other! Goddam covid!

"You saved Ling Ling! Thank you! Thank you!"

I thought he was nuts, and not just about shaking hands after lockdown.

He realized his mistake and ushered the two of us over to an Eve™ dispensing sanitizer. We both partook. Was this constant sanitizing for personal protection all part of the New Normal?

I flashed on after coitus birth control.

He told me his name. Then he said, *Ling Ling*.

"Okay," I said, "Who is Ling Ling?"

"My sister!" he exclaimed. "Ponytail, remember?"

He showed me her photograph on his phone. I didn't know her.

He told me Ling Ling still lived in San Francisco, still a graduate student in linguistics at Berkeley, and was now undergoing treatment at the Langley Porter Psychiatric Institute at UCSF.

"Even she thanks you now!"

The Ponytail on the Golden Gate Bridge.

We laughed and we almost shook hands again.

Funny thing is, I never saw Ling Ling's face. She was always facing away.

The plump old Chinese lady was impressed. "Are you a hero?"

"Never," I said. "Not me."

On the day I met her brother Robert Ketchum two years ago, Eloise began with her own reminiscence of our first meet.

"This son of a bitch of a cop saved a jumper from the Golden Gate Bridge. For ten, fifteen minutes he is holding onto this young Chinese woman by her ponytail with just one hand, holding onto the railing with his other hand to keep from pitching over the railing himself, his legs wrapped around one of the upright rods."

Her brother was impressed. "Her hair didn't rip out?"

She was still surprised, too.

"No, human hair is apparently tougher than that. Stronger than steel, when bunched up like that."

"Nick caught her by the ponytail as she was dropping?"

"He caught her at the last minute by the hair and he wouldn't let go. He was holding onto her hair with his right hand, his left hand was precariously gripping the railing, half his body was dangling over the railing himself like a teeter-totter, and oh, she's screaming, let me go, let me go, but he refuses, even while she's trying to reach up and claw his hand to let her go, ripping at his flesh with her nails, this goes on forever, the suspense a killer, and then he gives her this huge one-handed yank upwards and with his other hand manages to handcuff her one wrist to the railing, and then he lets go."

"He pulled her up to the railing?"

"Yes, and he left the woman handcuffed to the bridge flailing and screaming her outrage because she can't climb up and she can't fall down, and she is pissed and spitting because he won't let her suicide. When the California Highway Patrol arrives, Nick said, I want my cuffs back when you're done with her."

Her brother was leaning forward. "And then?"

Eloise said, "I followed him, lost him while trying to park on Union Street, I went around to all of the saloons, and found him asleep in a bar."

They were both impressed. I didn't say how sick I was at heart.

Ketchum said, "But you didn't stay there? You didn't go back to the Bridge?"

"Their jurisdiction," I said. "The California Highway Patrol had the scene in hand."

"The woman you saved," Eloise said. "When the Highway Patrol pulled her over the railing, she was angry, well, and furious. Like a little girl weeping, her fists balled up in her eyes because she wants so badly to lash out and kill something."

I wasn't surprised. Maybe even pleased.

"Women are always bellyaching," I said to get the heat off me. "They always want more." *I will be as rude or as crude as I can to get you to back off, dude. Nothing is worse than people in your face breathing on you.*

I was hooted and jeered at for that nonsense.

Today at Kroger's deli section, Ling Ling's brother and I said goodbyes. As I watched him melt into the masked crowd, Robert Ketchum came over. "How do you know that guy?"

He was already into his second change of clothes.

"Who are you now?" I said. Tried reading his lanyard.

"How do you know that guy?" he insisted.

"I saved his sister from jumping off the Golden Gate Bridge."

"He's a captain with the Ministry of State Security."

I was startled. "The Communist Party?"

"State Security, Nick! The MSS! The Ministry of State Security! Their FBI! Their CIA!"

"He seemed like a nice guy," I said lamely.

Ketchum was eyeing me like he really didn't believe I existed.

"Is that the bullshit story Eloise told me about?"

It wasn't bullshit, I told him. "Your sister held me by my pants to keep me from pitching over," I said. "She saw my naked butt before she saw my face."

He snapped his fingers. "That's the attraction!"

Why Jewelie Ran

Cherokee Sioux and Julie Beaumont were close. Girlfriends. They were like sisters. Find one and there's the other. Sure, they held hands, like lost children in the subways, so they wouldn't get lost. Like Hansel and Gretel, they needed each other. Maybe they deserved each other.

Hansel and Gretel went to the gingerbread house leaving a trail of bread crumbs behind them. I set off to follow the breadcrumbs.

I drove down into the Tenderloin. The same city block as Midge Fong's Frozen Pistol. I drove around the block several times before I found parking in a bus zone. I was in the bus stop where I'd seen Jewelie and Sioux necking in the doorway.

It was a major city bus stop. I thought about checking out the bus lines.

They could have been waiting for a cab.

I stared at the doorway I'd seen them in. The doorway to a Tenderloin hotel named the Remington Arms. Some joker with a screwy sense of humor. The really funny part about it was that down here nobody gave a damn what the dump's name was.

The Remington Arms was an old cinder-block building in a neighborhood filled with them. Fifty years ago this could have been a nice place to live. Plaster walls and hardwood floors and copper pipes. But even the landlords couldn't make it in the Tenderloin. The Loin has the highest insurance rates in the city. And most hotels have only half of a human's lifespan.

The Remington Arms was now a cheap flop. Cracked windows and plants on windowsills. Broken windows in the basement. Bad wiring and broken plaster. The kind of place where some tenants had trouble keeping cigarettes from falling from their mouths, where a down-'n-outer might hide after robbing a downtown bank, and the first place the cops would check.

Then I cursed myself for being a nitwit. Maybe Jewelie and Sioux lived inside the Remington Arms. Maybe they couldn't wait to get upstairs, or maybe they couldn't climb stairs yet.

I went up to the front door, gave it a kick, and it opened. A big sign said, "No Visitors after Ten o'clock." I saw an elevator and a staircase. The banister was missing some teeth. Maybe those staves made good weapons.

The manager watched me from his apartment door. He was a Hindu in his late thirties, thin and timid, had coffee-colored skin and needed many meals in the future. He was busy with a tenant and was quivering in his boots.

The tenant was a monstrous transvestite in an Afro wig and platform shoes. She wore a halter top and cut-offs and a Kate Jackson button on her Levi's jacket. She was fat and loathsome, and her ugliness justified suicide.

"I told you to hold my mail for me!"

The manager shook his head. "No!" The bottom panel of his apartment door looked like planking fresh from a bonfire. All charred and blackened. Maybe someone set fire to his door rather than pay rent.

"I gave you five bucks," the tenant told him. "I asked you to hold my mail, and you said you would."

"Illegal." The manager wet his nervous lips. "Wife took to post office." He was from India and in a foreign country. He didn't know why she was hassling him. Folks back home didn't look like this.

I counted the mailboxes in the lobby. There were twenty-five units on each floor in this dump, and one said J. Trinkett lived on the fourth floor. Jewelie Trinkett. The name sounded like something two stoned girls watching a Gidget movie might come up with. I wondered how many families lived in the hotel.

The tenant exploded. "Illegal, hell. That's just bullshit! I was over at Langley Porter trying to keep from losing my mind, and I gave you five bucks to hold my goddamn mail!" She kicked the wall. The fire extinguisher above rattled against the plaster.

The manager was rattled too. "Wife went to post office," he insisted. "You go to post office. Everything be okay. You see." His eyes asked me to save him from certain misfortune.

I was on my way to the elevator. A cockroach tried to drag-race me. I cheated and squashed him.

The tenant was smacking the plaster. "You goddamn drunken Indian," she shouted. "I'll break your fuckin' head and kick your fuckin' teeth down the fuckin' sewer system, you pigheaded cock-sucker!" She turned in rage and stalked off toward the street.

The manager turned my way. His eyes were wide. "She is crazy man!" he hissed.

The tenant overheard that. She spun on her heels and screamed back at the top of her lungs. "Asshole!"

The manager ducked back inside his apartment. He slammed his door closed. The echoes wandered through the first floor.

The elevator doors staggered closed with an irritating buzz. The winch began humming like a prewar aero plane. The elevator began to gurgle and fart its way up to the fourth floor.

The elevator smelled like a hot, greasy rope. A sign posted on the control board said it was out of order. The notice was six months old. I wondered why I didn't bail out.

The fourth floor was wood and whitewash. The ceiling was too low, and the light was dim and fading. The woodwork was warped, and the whitewash was chipped and peeling.

I went down the corridor. It was cold and gloomy. An old man came from the other end, blowing his nose with his fingers, and passed me. Someone had swiped the light bulb from the exit sign. Tenants coughing behind locked doors. Water marks on the walls from leaky pipes. Hand prints like primitive hex signs to ward off the evil eye.

I found a door off its hinges. It was the bathroom. No toilet paper. Just old newspapers. A broken window. A grungy sink and washbasin. Broken plaster and porcelain. Empty bottles of Rainier ale and Gallo port. The walls had holes where people had kicked them.

The door to J. Trinkett's apartment was double-locked. It even had a padlock with thick metal brackets and long, flat wood screws. The door could be kicked to splinters by a crazy man, but the padlock would last forever.

I knocked and knocked. There was no answer.

Next door a phone was being dialed. Somebody was making love in the room on the other side. I heard washers squeal when the shower was turned off across the hall. Somehow I had a hunch no one was home.

My timing was bad. It was almost sunset and no one was home. Cherokee Sioux was a nightcrawler, an overnighter by trade, and she had much to do in the evening hours. Maybe she was out making rent already.

I was suddenly very tired.

Hell, I'd done my job. I'd found Heather's kid. What else was there to do? Just call Heather and give her the address. Let her do the rest of the crap. It was time to bail out. It was all over.

I went downstairs and called Heather's apartment. No answer. I called my service. A message from Heather. Julie had called her. She was coming to her mother's apartment this evening. Heather had called my service an hour ago. I called Heather's apartment again. No answer.

I drove over to Heather's apartment building on Union Street. There was a light on inside her apartment. I figured they were back home again. I left my car and went up the porch steps. I took the stairs two at a time. I wanted to see this reunion.

The TV was on inside. Somebody on a talk show babbling about the death of the dollar. There were no other sounds. I pushed the doorbell. Nothing happened. I pushed it again. Then I knocked and knocked. Still no answer. I tried the knob. It wasn't latched. Living here on Telegraph Hill, you lock your doors without a second thought. I could always wait a week for a cop with a search warrant.

I went inside. Heather had a nice apartment.

The living room was white and green. White walls and ceiling. Green pile carpeting that went wall to wall. Wood sectional furniture. Dry bar. Chandelier made of brass and wood. Tiffany lamps and hanging ferns and wandering Jew. A stereo and some albums, mostly the Beatles. Wood-burning fireplace with gas log-lighter.

Here and there the sixties appeared. Original posters from Fillmore West and anti-war rallies. One proclaimed San Francisco "The End of Western Civilization." The posters were all matted and framed. Even a macramé peace symbol on the mantel.

A cassette deck was hooked to her stereo. A loose cassette was inside the machine. I hit the power button and pressed "Play," and the walls rumbled with the ocean.

It was a tape of the ocean. The combers thundering on a beach. The cries of the gulls. I thought I heard a foghorn. Sometimes the surf seemed to crescendo. A toggle switch on a small black box piped the sounds into the bedroom.

The master bedroom was off the dining room. It was smaller than I expected. A brass bed. Down pillows and rubber-tree plants. No lamps, just indirect lighting. A sliding door that led onto a small balcony. A wooden rocker that overlooked the city lights.

The carpeting was still green pile, and the ceiling was as white as the one in the living room. There was wallpaper this time. Green with white flowers. The quilts and comforter were white with green flowers. The pattern matched the drapes.

I checked out her closet. It took up most of the wall, and full-length mirrors covered the outer panels. The closet was large enough to be its own room. Mirrored closets. Middle-class erotica.

I looked over the woman's belongings. Flowered tops and tweed skirts. Black lingerie and pink baby-dolls. Sequined blue jeans and beautiful caftans. Blouses and halters and wool suits and pant suits. Silk robes and kimonos. Swimsuits and ski parkas. Shoes. Shoes. Shoes.

The kitchen was a small room with a luminous ceiling. Butcher-block styling and a cushioned vinyl floor. Sourdough bread in the bread box. Potatoes and avocados in a straw basket above the refrigerator. There was much glassware in the pantry. I'd be afraid of sonic booms or earthquakes.

The bathroom was spectacular. A tinted skylight above a shower big enough for four people. Twin nozzles and imitation-marble counter. Water Pik and water massager. Plants that needed little watering. Disposable razors and extra toothbrushes. Extra washcloths and towels. Supermarket shaving cream and samples of men's aftershave. A hamper for dirty laundry.

But nothing for a teenage daughter.

Where was Julie's bedroom anyway?

I found it and opened the door.

I braced my hand against the door frame, closed my eyes, and took many deep breaths. The odious aromas of urine and sweat, sex and death.

It was a nightmare inside that green-and-white room. A horror. Savage hell. I fought the dry heaves, then finally came to terms with myself. Right now nightmares were future problems. I had to see if she were still alive.

Heather Beaumont lay spread-eagled half-naked, across the brass bed. Her arms and legs were stretched out and tied to each corner of the bed. The bonds were still taut. Her limbs were broken pencils joined at the waist.

She had been raped. Bound and raped.

I went to her bedside. I touched the corner of an eye. It moved stiffly in its socket. The natural moisture was drying. Soon it would harden.

She was still warm. There was a trace of sweat, but her skin was growing clammy after the frenzy that poured from her final pains. She was meat. Dead meat carved in the shape of a woman.

She had an orange in her mouth.

Just an orange. Big and bright and colorful, like the California Dream. Just an orange crammed between her jaws. An orange that someone had used as a gag, so that Heather couldn't cry out for help when they left.

She had been forced to bite deep into that orange. There had been too much orange. Too great a bite. Too immovable a mass. Like a mountain of mush.

A fucking orange had killed her.

She must have known instantly. She must have felt her jaws pushed too far apart. Then the rattle of death calling her name, the dry heaves that began below her throat that soon became convulsions as they closed the door on her and left her alone.

She had died with her eyes open. There were streaks from them that ran across her cheeks to her ears, the hideous war paint of agony. Lines that had formed from her tears as she realized she was helpless and dying. She had died conscious.

Saliva had drooled from the edges of her mouth, had mixed and dried with the juice from the orange.

There weren't many bruises, but she had suffered enough and lingered long enough for some. Bruises from where they had grabbed her, from where they had raped her, from where she had tried not to die.

Her wrists were gouged. Bloodied skin beneath her fingernails. In panic, she had tried to claw herself free. She had clawed at her bonds and had torn flesh from her own wrists. She had thrashed her arms and her legs. She had had terrible convulsions. She had wet herself with absolute terror.

I told myself I wouldn't look at the bed again. I told myself that again and again. My stomach was still having peristaltic fits. Almost an earthquake. But I had work to do. I still needed the DOA team to arrive. Later I could barf all I wanted.

That body on the bed scared me. Fear from deep inside of me that I might someday die like this. Dead in some stinking rotten place. Dying like a fool for God knows what insanity. Broken like all life's promises. Someday it might be me there too, and knowing no reason why.

We all live in a jar of needles. There is no place to turn.

Her daughter Julie Beaumont was off and running.

Her mother was dead. She couldn't go home. And her roommate was dead. The police had been there and they had sealed off both apartments. So where did she go?

She needed some refuge.

She'd be in a daze. She'd need somewhere to think things out. Where she could make plans for the immediate future, which stalked her like a hungry tiger. Maybe she'd look for comforting voices, security, companionship, and solace. Or she'd want to be alone somewhere. Whichever made her feel comfortable.

I didn't think she had much money on her.

Where would I go, in her shoes?

I'd need a drink. Maybe a bar.

I remembered she was fifteen and a lesbian.

Maybe a women's bar.

A woman chooses her bar for the same reason a man does, only more so and more cautiously. A women's bar reflects her life-style, her self-image, her economic situation.

A women's bar is like a lingerie shop or any other specialty shop. You'll find several downtown, of course, for downtowners and those who often come downtown. You'll find them in the local neighborhoods too, though never more than one per district. Some of the ones downtown were near the Loin.

I remembered the matchbooks in Julie's apartment.

The 800 block of Hyde Street.

The fringes of downtown. Mostly residence clubs and apartment houses. Working single people. Five blocks uphill to the nearest cable-car line. Ten blocks down and west to the nearest freeway on-ramp. Halfway between Nob Hill and the Tenderloin. Near the gay men of Polk Street, yet not among them.

Fresson's. That was the name.

Fresson's. Hyde and Sutter.

I parked midway in the next block and walked back. Both cross streets were one-way, and there was a brown residence club on one corner. Fresson's was in the basement of the residence club, with its entrance around the corner and halfway uphill, a concrete staircase that led down and inside.

Fresson's was just another downtown bar. The front door was always open. The jukebox wasn't loud enough to drown out the city buses. The place reeked of cigarettes and booze. It was kept dark enough to make you squint both when you came and when you left.

Fresson's was just a little harder to reach than most downtown bars. Word of mouth brought people here. Like most of its neighbors, it wanted nothing more than to be left out of the limelight.

A working-class bar. I expected to see day laborers here, refugees from the residence clubs, some visitors from the laundry mat across the street, an off-duty cab driver or two, maybe even a cowboy or a middle-aged Chinese. That's pretty much the people I found at the booths and on the barstools. Lovely ladies, all of them.

The barkeep watched me walk inside. I must've been the first man she'd seen in a week and the last thing she expected today. I was a big surprise, and her face said she hoped I wasn't trouble. I didn't know what she was worried about. I knew I didn't belong here. The last thing I wanted was to get eighty-sixed.

I found myself a barstool.

The barkeep had a cute face and a great shape. She wore jeans and a Softball shirt. She'd been listening to some magenta-haired butch who wanted to borrow plane fare to fly back to Montana after having blown all her money on some Chinese chick who had turned out to be straight. The way the butch spoke, it was almost a touching story.

The barkeep came over. "Yeah?"

"Whatcha got in imported?" I asked.

"The ones on the shelf," she said, indicating dusty bottles above the register. She knew today was going to be one of those days.

I said, "The third from the end."

She went to the cooler and drew a cold bottle. Her street shoes clattered atop wooden slats. I set a buck on the bar. She brought my beer, picked up the dollar, then rang up my purchase on the register, all without saying a word. She knew she had to serve me, but she wasn't going to like it. She'd be damned before she broke her silence.

"I'd like to ask you something." I slid one of Waldo's photographs across the counter. "Do you know the young girl in this photo? Her hair's a lot shorter now. She wears a shaggy crew cut and she looks like a furry parrot from the back. She's got it all painted up in different colors. Blue and green and red and yellow. She's been hanging around this neighborhood."

The barkeep grinned. "What did she do? Walk out on you?"

I grinned back. "Yeah, she left me for another woman."

The magenta-haired butch laughed like people do after a roller coaster ride. The barkeep suddenly wasn't very happy.

I let both of them read my investigator's license from the Bureau of Consumer Affairs. Then I gave them my business card that had Legal Services printed below my name and phone number. "You can keep this one."

"Who is she?" the butch said.

"Her real name is confidential," I explained. "She's been calling herself Jewelie Trinkett." I spelled the name for the ladies. "Maybe she's been in with a girl named Cherokee Sioux."

The butch was disgusted. "What a name."

"She doesn't belong on the streets," I said.

The barkeep smirked. "And you want to take her off them." She could have been mocking a daytime soap opera.

"She looks young," the magenta-haired butch said. Her tone was a bit different now. Maybe she knew what it meant being young and alone on the streets could mean.

I said, "Fifteen, going on sixteen. She's already done things she shouldn't have heard about yet."

"Underage," the keep muttered. It was illegal serving booze to minors. She grew suspicious. I might be from the Alcoholic and Beverage Control. "What do you want with her?"

I drank some beer. "The police want her. Her mother's dead. She was murdered last night." I polished off my beer and started to hike back toward the rest rooms. "The men's room's back here, right?"

"I want to talk with you," the keep said. Then she went mute on me. She had a weighty problem. There was only one way to say it. "I don't like minors hanging around the joint."

"Understandable."

"The one you're looking for, do you think she's in trouble?"

I liked her suspicious nature. "Her mother got offed last night. She's got to be in trouble. Has she been in here before?"

"Maybe she has," the keep admitted.

"How often did she come in?"

"I can't say," the keep lied. "I'm not here all the time. I trade off with my partner. Three days on and three days off." She had a problem. "What if you're the killer and ..."

"So call the cops. I don't care who finds her. I just want her found, okay?"

"You say, call the cops?"

"Look, lady, I have to put up with a whole lot of shit in my job, but I'm not going to put up with a fifteen-year-old."

"What's that mean?"

"Let me put it this way," I said. "I'll stop at nothing to get her off the streets. She doesn't belong there. Nobody does, maybe. Not you. Not me. Not a fifteen-year-old, especially." I pretended to consider my words. "If dust comes to dust, I'll be the ABC and get you closed down on suspension. I'll hound your regulars to get someone to ID that chick in this joint. I get one page of testimony, I get it notarized, and you're shut down for thirty days."

The keep understood. "She was here yesterday twice. Yeah, she came in twice yesterday. First time she came in with Sioux. That was around noon, I guess."

"Sioux's dead too," I said. "She got murdered too. Might even make the dailies. What were they doing here?"

The keep was stunned. "She's dead too?"

"What were they doing here?"

"Sioux was thirsty, I guess. She bought a drink, bourbon and seven, I think. Jewelie bought orange juice. They talked a while in a back booth and then they left."

"What about the second time?"

"Late. Almost midnight. She was alone then." The keep hesitated. "She was in bad shape. She was looking for a place to crash. She said her apartment was all smoked out. A mattress fire down the hall or something." The woman reconsidered. "She was lying about the fire. I could tell. You know, she needed help last night."

"What happened next?"

"I couldn't help her." She shrugged.

"So where did she go?"

"Berkeley," she said. "That's where I told her to go. There's a place for women over there. She could find a place to crash over there, that's for sure."

"What's the name of this place?"

"Feminisima," she told me.

"A feminist club?"

She rolled her eyes. "A place where women can go when they want to be with other women. They can talk to one another there without men hassling them."

"Do you have an address to go with that name?"

She knew the address without checking the phone book. "Just above College Avenue and south of the fraternity houses."

Valdemar

Valdemar Road was a dead-end street below the coastal highway. It wasn't much of a street. Just a dirt alley that paralleled the road and the highway until it petered out.

Hummingbird House was the last house on the street. It may have been the last house in the village. It was certainly the farthest one north. From the gravel drive I could read the city-limit signs on the coastal highway. Valdemar was 437 people and squatted twelve feet above sea level.

Hummingbird House was late-Victorian. Huge and rambling. Four stories and at least a dozen bedrooms. Part mansion and part farmhouse. And painted in four bright colors. The same colors as the cable cars back in the city.

The house was engulfed in bougainvillea. It was all funky and postcard perfect. If it were any closer to the coastal highway, tourists would be stopping to take photographs.

There was no real backyard. Just a vegetable garden fenced against deer and a field of golden poppies. The poppies stretched out and faded into rolling rangeland and a horizon dotted with dairy cows.

I had almost been here once before. Somewhere off there, off toward the north, there was a giant house that overlooked a tidal lagoon. And a pregnant girl who sometimes went barefoot.

"Can I help you?" A woman's voice.

I turned around. "Is this Hummingbird House?"

The woman said it was. She was in her seventies. A little old lady in a double-knit pant suit the color of a pink flamingo, like something found glowing in the dark in Orange County. She had a shape like a silo. "Are you with us or against us?"

"Which would you prefer?"

She laughed like a gull. She still had her real teeth. "Oh, that's rich!" She had a round face and a pixie haircut. Snow-white hair and a face full of wrinkles. "My name's Brennen. Michael Brennen." She gave her hand. "Marissa Duncan."

"What is Hummingbird House?"

"A senior citizens' rights group. We advise the pre-retirees on their rights. Things like: Don't sell your home until after retirement. Or if they shoot for early retirement, in some cases they can collect unemployment before they need apply for social security. We're trying to get legislation for mandatory prison sentences for anybody convicted of a felony against people sixty-five years and older or the disabled. We try to lobby against things too. Like those dog-food commercials aimed at Granny's food stamps."

"Do you run this place yourself?"

"Oh, no, I'm just today's spokesperson. Nobody runs Hummingbird House. We all do. Participatory democracy. We all vote every weekend, whether we need to or not."

"Vote on what?"

"Chores, for example," Marissa Duncan said. "Think of this as an old-age commune. Yes, we live like hippies." She gestured back at the house. "A dormitory of shared rentals. Each one of us has a scrumptious room, and the rents that we pay cover the mortgage. It's no secret. It isn't even news nowadays either. It's another viable alternative for older Americans."

"Hippies in a mansion by the sea."

"We've very lucky. We can afford this."

I felt better about my job. A hippie house, only with grandmothers sharing the cooking. My job still had its moments. We started toward the back door. "I'm looking for Donald Finch."

She was sharp. "Are you a relative?"

"His son asked me to see him."

"Karl, right?"

"His other son," I said. "Hayward."

She became angry. "Why couldn't he come?" She stopped me. "Tell him to come visit his old man. At night he lights a candle in his window. This house has drafts. They blow out his candle. He just relights it."

"Why does he do that?"

"It's for his wife."

"Is she dead?"

"Twenty years now."

I thought that was a beautiful gesture.

She wasn't so sure. "He told me once all he had is gone. All he has left is worthless. He said, if he didn't remember his wife, no one would."

I wasn't so sure. "He's got something to hold. I know people who wouldn't mind memories like that." Maybe I meant myself. I held the back door for her. "What kind of shape is Donald Finch in?"

"He gets grouchy, and he's awfully suspicious. But he brightens up for visitors. Oh, he'll talk your head off. He'll tell you how much he hates everybody here. Everybody here is too religious."

"At least he's well enough to complain."

Her expression said that was important. "Before I retired," she confided, "I was a charge nurse in a nursing home. It was more like a slaughterhouse than a nursing home. Old folks getting jammed with Mellaril until they're incontinent. And it was always the in-laws. They always said the same thing." She mimicked an in-law. "'Oh, I'll never put you in a nursing home.'" She was too disgusted to continue. "Thank God there's Hummingbird House."

We came into the common kitchen. It looked like a hippie kitchen, only cleaner. Giant kettles for all the mouths to feed. A full array of spices and salts. The long table where everyone ate together. The hash-house stacks of clean dishes. Coffee cups drying on a sideboard. Posters on the walls. One said, "Together We Have Clout." Travel posters about Mazatlán, perhaps because social security checks went further down there.

An old man was huddled over a cup of coffee and the morning paper. He wore red pants and a blue jacket and a brown tie. He had coffee stains on his shirt and two types of buttons. He looked like he was trying to remember why people ever laughed.

"Donald Finch?"

He looked up. "That's my name." He was a very old man. A forties matinee idol who'd aged hard. A strong profile gone gaunt. Bloodless lips and bulging veins in his neck. His mustache was razor-thin with little waxed ends that curled up. He seemed to have a lot of knuckles.

"You're Hayward's father, right?"

He nodded slowly. "Did Hayward send you?" He talked as if he had all the time in the world. A clock behind his head belied every syllable.

I almost hesitated. "Yes, he did."

"Were you paid to come here?"

I paused. "Yes, I was."

"He's Karl's brother," Donald Finch told Marissa Duncan. "Hayward's five years older than Karl." Maybe he remembered his older son best that way. Marissa Duncan had a mother's wistful smile.

Donald Finch wasn't smiling. His lips were tight and crisp. His eyes were unshockable, unflappable. He reminded me of a beat cop I once knew who worked in the Tenderloin. The cop hated his beat, and that hatred kept him going. His spine had turned to steel through hatred.

"He asked me to talk with you."

Finch looked up. "Patricia too?"

I said, "If it's the same Patricia I'm thinking of."

Donald Finch faced Marissa Duncan again. "Do you know how come Hayward never married? Patricia Cardine, that's why. That's his vision of a wife and three kids. Hayward's a workaholic. If you could get him away from his surveys and reports and polls, you'd find him a regular guy. You'd even see him pinching the stews on the butt."

Marissa Duncan had a faint smile for him. "I think Mr. Brennen wants to talk to you alone." She patted his shoulder. "I'll see you later, Donald." We watched her leave.

Donald Finch looked up. "What do you want?"

I went and made some coffee for myself, then came and sat beside him. "You were the personal adviser to Joe Cardine."

The old man soured more. His brow furrowed, like a time traveler choosing between old calendars. "If Joseph Cardine were alive today"—he spoke slowly— "he'd be sixty-three years old. Last month was his birthday."

I was impressed. "You still remember."

"He was the high point of my career. Thirty years in California politics. Fuck Joe Cardine. He died a happy man."

"What's wrong with that?"

"He didn't deserve it. He was the happiest man I ever knew. Happy as a postmaster. Life gave him more than he ever wanted. He used to say he was one of the lucky ones. He was lucky, I guess. An aneurism in his sleep. Never woke up."

"He was a state senator, right?"

Donald Finch snickered. "You know, there're forty men in the state senate. Some from the cities. Some from the woods. Some are rich and most are lawyers. The two biggest reasons men go into politics is power and money. Some even find it in the senate."

"How was Joe Cardine different?"

"He was the life of the party. Being a state senator kept him on the hometown front page and on the government payroll. It kept him supplied with booze and people who liked smiling a lot. Yes, he was a boozer. One of the best. He was always half-smashed."

"How does a drunk like that stay in office?"

"Joe Cardine was the perfect politician," Donald Finch told me. "He used to say he had the perfect temperament for the perfect job. One of the few who could handle it and not let the bullshit get to him. Oh, he was very successful. He didn't do jack shit for twenty-five years. He used to say the only thing softer than a city job was a state job."

"What were his politics?"

"He had none. He was photogenic, not political. He liked getting his picture taken. He liked smiling a lot. I mean, all you ever saw of him, if you ever shared a cab with him, was his teeth. He had a great smile. Just sometimes when he'd get up to talk, he wouldn't have anything to say unless it was written in front of him. He memorized his speeches in case he'd forget how to read halfway through a paragraph. But he looked great."

"How did he ever get elected in the first place?"

The old man thought I knew. "Joe got his senate seat from his father. Yes, he was state senator before Joe was. Same district too. The wine country. His father spearheaded the state legislature's drive back in December 1933 to repeal the Eighteenth Amendment."

"Prohibition, right?"

"Repeal was a personal triumph for Mario Cardine. Yeah, he plotted the state vote for repeal. Repeal ended the Depression up there in the wine country. After that everybody figured he had done enough. His last three, four terms were a gift."

"What was his son up to at the time?"

"He was in school mostly. He got married the day after Utah became the thirty-sixth state to ratify the Twenty-first Amendment. Joe was twenty years old then. He came home from Annapolis to get married. Patricia was born two years later. God, she's such a sad girl. I think she was born disappointed in him. She never understood where he stood in life."

*Joe Cardine went to Annapolis?"

"His father got him in there. He didn't do jack shit in the navy. Come Pearl Harbor, his old man got him a captaincy and a soft post in San Francisco processing hotel billeting."

"So when did he run for office?"

"After the war. In '46 it was. He never would've run except his father died, and the party wanted to keep it a safe district. Joe won the election hands down. He stayed in the senate until his death in 1970."

"How'd he keep getting reelected?"

"Because he got so many dams and highways built for the people up there. He ran unopposed every time. Even when they found somebody to run against him, he ran unopposed. See, when he campaigned, he mostly talked about bunk beds and deer hunting and sugar content. That's important up in the wine country."

"How do you know he was a good politician? A good representative? The voters never had anybody to compare him with."

"He did the three things his constituents paid him to do. They wanted him to vote party lines, and they wanted to be left alone by the state government, and they didn't want to be embarrassed by their state senator. He was a natural at all three."

"Because he didn't do jack shit."

"Oh, well, he introduced bills and fought for them too if the boys back home wanted him to. Mostly he kept his mouth shut and did what his party leader told him. He never made waves. And the party faithful voted for his bills as debts repaid."

"What about the committees he was on?"

"He voted with the chairman every time. He never voted against him. And he never had enough seniority on any committee to become a chairman."

"How was he at making money?"

"Oh, he got rich, but not too rich. He inherited some from his father of course. He made most of it from his Chevy dealership. He sold pickup trucks. His father sold them before him. Nobody owned him. There was no big-money machine in the wine country then. People up there were naturally independent. They didn't want any part of big government. The big wine combines weren't there yet, not like they are now. When he was state senator, the biggest power in the valley was a vintner's co-op."`

"You're saying he was always clean?"

Donald Finch frowned. "I don't think he was ever approached by anyone. He was never charged with conflict of interest, and nobody ever suggested he could be bought. He always voted with the party, never a waiver, and loyalty like that is useless to anybody trying to buy votes or influence. He was never power hungry either. He had all he ever wanted."

"And he never embarrassed the voters?"

"He came close a couple, maybe three times, but nothing serious. Once, in one of those lumber towns up in the Sierra foothills, he was drunk and dancing naked, chasing some woman down Main Street at midnight. But something like that, even the sheriff wanted it covered up. I mean, the sheriff was throwing that party."

"I heard Joe Cardine had a girlfriend."

"Why should that matter nowadays?"

"Heather Beaumont, right?"

He rumbled. "I know her name."

"I heard she was a whore."

"I won't slander her." Finch sighed. "I'd forgotten about her. God, she was the one bright spot in an otherwise foul profession. She was a really nice girl."

"I heard she was a whore."

"At first she was, I suppose."

I hesitated. "Love at first sight?"

"Pretty damn close."

"Was she tricking him?"

"I never did find out. I know he paid all her bills for eight years. I know he saw her every day for the first four years. I don't know if that makes her out a whore. The old man in the room next to mine, he lives with his wife. They got divorced many years ago, and now they're living in sin for social security. Halves the room rent too."

"How'd you find out about Heather?"

Donald Finch thought back. "He met Heather in 1962. I don't know where or how. He traveled alone and knew a lot of people. He went to parties alone. He drank whiskey-overs in every cocktail lounge between Mexico and Oregon, between the Sierras and the ocean. Back then, state senators had a lot less work to do. I mean, he started office before anybody was calling it 'big government.' He had no bodyguard, none of that shit. He met her somewhere though. She was nineteen. He was forty-nine. Not only was there a thirty-year age difference but he had a daughter who was twenty-seven."

"How did you meet her?"

"Down in San Francisco. Some convention was in the city that week. Some statewide or regional outfit. Auto dealers or something. He was there to introduce the guest speakers. Afterward we went to this bar on the top floor of the hotel, and she was at the back bar by a window in the sun, with the whole skyline of the city right behind her."

"When was this?"

He thought back. "In 1967. He left me standing in the doorway. In the time it took me to turn my head, he was across the room and breathing heavy. By the time I ordered a round of drinks they were holding hands and leaving through the back door. I needed a phone number to call him later so I blocked him from going. She gave me her phone number. After that, whenever I needed him, I called her. She always knew where he was."

"How did he treat her?"

"Like his wife. She got a monthly allowance, and so did his wife. His wife got enough to maintain a house, and so did Heather. Her home wasn't lavish, but it wasn't any worse than his wife's. He took her to Pebble Beach and Palm Springs and New York as often as he took his wife. She was like his second wife."

"How about in private?"

"I went over to her house once. It was after eleven at night. I had to see Joe about something or other. She was popping popcorn in the kitchen, pouring out the melted butter. He was in bed catching the eleven o'clock news. He sent me away before Johnny Carson began his monologue."

"What about his first wife?"

"She had a great smile," he considered. "That's all anybody ever expected from her. Nobody really cared about her. So long as she could stand up without cracking. She was always fascinated by cameras and lights. That was her secret. But those lights, those cameras, they did something to her."

I got curious. "What did they do?"

His long fingers were restless. "I don't know. Some kind of cumulative poison. They leeched her mind out of her head. Toward the end, every time she met the press she'd get all glazed. Smile at the pretty lights, that's all she could do."

"Did she know about Heather?"

"She had to know. But he was always devoted to her. He was the perfect husband. He was devoted to both of them. Those last years he managed two different households. He never got them confused. Never had a slip-up."

"How could he pull it off so long?"

"Politics, maybe," the old man guessed. "I don't think either one of them knew where he really stood. Maybe he convinced them he was devoted to politics."

"I don't understand."

"I mean, a man keeps part of himself divorced from his woman. Just another side to him, you understand, that his woman never sees. Just as every woman has a part of herself hidden from her man. The way I see it, Joe Cardine convinced them both that his hidden passion was party politics. That he had all this pressure on him, being a politician and all. How could they know he didn't do jack shit for twenty-five years?"

"And it never came out into the open?"

"Oh, it did. Joe brought it out."

"He brought it up himself?"

"Yes." The old man tried remembering. "In 1966, I guess. He had broken up with Heather just before that. The first of their growing number of tiffs and walkouts. He was down in the city. A fact-finding mission was what everybody said. Hell, they were drinking, that's what it was. Everybody was talking about hippies. Most of the boys had never seen one. This was back in 1966, and a lot of the boys in the state House came from farm towns. Everybody was fascinated of course."

"Even Joe Cardine?"

"Oh, God, yes. Absolutely fascinated. You know, he was the first politician in the state to call them the counterculture. He said they reminded him of stories his grandfather told about the Indian tribes when the Cardines first came west. Just like the Indians, he used to say."

"This was back in 1966, right?"

"They all went down to the Haight that day. Went to gawk at the hippies. He ran into Heather on the street. Hell, I recognized her. But he went off with her. Next thing I hear, they're out in public together."

"What did his old buddies say about it?"

"Nothing much. They were jealous."

"What was she like back then?"

"Heather? She was a hippie chick in San Francisco. All cleaned up though, not like most of them. She looked great without makeup anyway. And on her, long hair was sensational. She wore flowers in her hair and long white dresses and no underwear. Paid cash and smiled like a dope. She could go anywhere on her looks alone."

"Were they in love?"

He didn't know. "They always acted like it."

"Is Julie Beaumont his kid?"

Donald Finch took his time before answering. "I honestly don't know. He treated Julie like she was, treated her better in fact than he treated his own daughter, but he always refused to discuss it. Maybe he didn't know for sure. I don't think Heather knew either, but, well, she always acted like it didn't seem to matter."

"Why tell me all this?"

"You asked."

"What if I were a journalist?"

"It wouldn't matter." He looked smug.

"You could be hurting Patricia Cardine."

"Fuck her!" He trembled until his anger subsided. "I'm getting senile. I can't think so fast anymore. Sometimes I got to take notes so I remember. Three weeks ago ..." He swiveled his head. "She's screwing us."

"How is she doing that?"

"You know who owns this place?" he demanded. "You guessed it. She does. This hippie house for old people. We pay the rent, and she pays off the mortgage. All this public service builds up her equity. And she gets this place when we all die. By then, of course, we'll have it paid for outright. And she's already a millionaire."

"She keeps it fixed up."

"She got federal loans to pay for renovation. If she didn't do that, she'd be no better than a slumlord in the Tenderloin."

"How long has she owned this?"

"Her father before her," he told me. "Yes, Joe Cardine."

"When did he buy it?"

"Ten years ago, I guess. Something like that." He didn't bother figuring it out. "Joe made the down payment on this mansion. She just inherited it. You know what's funny? Heather gave Joe the idea for this place. It shows her scheme of things. There were hippies living here before he made it into an old-age home. He claimed that made him the state senator who understood the needs of older Americans. But do you know why he did it? Because he was having trouble with the hippies he had living here, that's why."

"So what's the big screw?"

He grew nastier than before. "Patricia delivered a rent increase at four in the afternoon on June 6. That was right on Election Day. Right while Proposition 13 was being approved by the voters."

I stopped. "She's raising the rents?"

"Saturday last was the first of the month. That was the day we got a 6 1/2 percent increase in our social security checks. Every six months rents go up like clockwork. Whenever social security goes up, our rents go up too. Young man, don't you ever grow old."

I grinned. "How do I do that?"

"I don't know," he admitted. "I wrote my congressman about that. He couldn't do anything either." But joking tired him. "Old folks ..." He started over. "Only fools joke about old age and death. You get it in your throat. Then in your heart. You know how old you are. Soon you're dead. I've watched my whole life dribble away like old peoples' slobber. Yes, I'm still political. And

I'm bored stiff. I want to make waves." He stared cold-eyed. "And you work for the landlord."

"I guess I'll be going now." I wasn't mean enough to linger. "Take care of yourself, okay?"

He called after me. "What did you come here for?"

I stopped at the back door. "Hayward wants me to tell you to expect the press."

He sank. "How bad is it?" He looked like a card player at sunrise dreading the last hand of the game.

"Heather's been murdered, Julie's on the run, and Patricia's being blackmailed about her half-sister Julie."

He was taken aback. "All that?"

"That's just the highlights."

He sucked his gums. "What does Hayward want me to do?"

"Whatever's in your heart."

His long fingers couldn't relax.

The Road back to Valdemar

Ruth came from the bathroom wearing jeans and a flowered blouse and leather sandals. She carried a tote bag, and her red hair was held back by a woven headband. Indian jewelry by the ton. She was back in disguise again.

She threw me my car keys. "Do you know where Valdemar is?"

I slipped on a jacket. "It's on the coast, north of the city. Rustics and attempted rustics. Is that where Jerome Johnson hides from the city lights?"

"Hidden Valley Road," she said. "North of town."

Outside we had sunshine, so we put the top down on my old Chevy and crossed the Golden Gate Bridge. There the fog was thick as wool on the span. For warmth we cranked the heater up all the way and huddled together and played the radio loud.

On the other side of the bridge, Marin was having a summer day. The coastal range had held back the fogbank, and it was sunny on the other side. Perfect top-down weather.

The bridge was bright red and just fitted between the city and Marin County. The bay was bright blue. The sky beyond the fogbank was bright blue. The tiny white specks on the bay were forty-foot sailboats.

Over our shoulders the city was a skyline of white buildings butting against the bright green of the Presidio trees. Ahead, Sausalito. Houseboats and boathouses. Richardson's Bay. Raccoon Straits. Mill Valley and sleepy Mount Tamalpais.

The road to Valdemar went westward from the freeway over the coastal range, snaking through eucalyptus groves and golden hills and watersheds of tall redwoods. Suburban tracks became more and more vacant lots. Soon wildflowers filled the fields and houses became rarer than virtue.

We reached the coastal highway and swung north. The fog joined up with us again. It was thick as surf. Fog piled up here, unable to cross the coastal range. The ocean was slate, maybe dark marble. Sea spray and alfalfa. Golden grasses in the westerlies.

I raised the top on the Chevy. The coast was lonely as telephone poles. The road shimmered with little mirages. Soon there were beaches and hiking trails. We were slowed by campers and RVs with out-of-state plates.

We passed Valdemar and kept going north, following the dotted yellow line that rocks and rolls along the California coast.

Hidden Valley Road was between the sea and the coastal highway, just before the river and the next rest stop. The road led west of the headlands, until asphalt became dirt.

We took the dirt road. After a while it circled a wedge of alders and drifted along a ridge above the high-tide mark. The road dead-ended in a small canyon. A road barrier stood before us. The hillside was red shale and clay, sprinkled with conifers and California poppies. The evergreens were fifty feet tall. I could see the Pacific through the pines. It was a good place to strip and ditch a car.

There was a house below us in a shaded cul-de-sac overlooking a tidal lagoon. A giant A-frame with a huge deck out back. There were bird feeders everywhere. The windows were filled with driftwood art. A telescope in an upstairs window. Book-shelves behind another window. The house was not quite on the shoreline, and tall pines blocked its view of the ocean.

A woman waited by the front porch.

Ruth went forward. "Mrs. Johnson?"

The woman almost nodded. She was younger than Ruth. A pixie haircut that hadn't been combed in days. A long dress like a nightshirt from the pioneer days.

"My name is Ruth Gideon. Legal Services, hired by Winston Bradley. He's the lawyer who'll be defending your husband. He was hired by the radio station."

The woman almost nodded. Her face was pale as the fog, and serious. She was barefoot and pregnant. She wouldn't look at me. I was a man. She couldn't stand the sight of another man now.

Ruth went on slowly. "Mr. Bradley sent me here to get your statement, if you're ready. If you're not, there are some other papers you should see."

The woman forced a smile. Her face froze, like rictus on a corpse.

"May we come in now?" Ruth asked.

The woman was terrified. She turned back toward the door and had trouble opening it: as if a whole raft of horrors might float in with us. "Can you leave us alone?" Ruth asked me.

"I'll go for a walk," I said. "An hour?"

"That's a good idea," Ruth said.

I left them there. I went out back behind the house. There was a hedge, a windbreak against the westerlies. There was a break in it. A trail that wound uphill.

I found myself heading south along the ridge above the lagoon. A black cormorant with a long neck gawked at me like a teenager at a strip show. A great blue heron prowled through the mud, followed by a family of white cranes. A sign near the lagoon said the waters were polluted and eating shellfish would poison anyone.

I hopped a wood fence and found myself on the coastal highlands. Wild wheat and oats and alfalfa. Tall grasses and tan hills disappeared inside heavy fog.

I started hiking. The range was empty, like a lonely pier at midnight. Dairy cows in the fog. Holsteins and white-faced Herefords. I wondered if there were many broken fences.

I stopped on a bluff and looked down at the beach. Fog and distant foghorns. California poppies among the rocks. Brown pelicans in single file against the fogbank. It was a great fog. Fog that was real and tangible. Bone-cold and sinister. Wet against my face and cold inside my lungs. It had body and shape and texture.

I went down to the beach.

The ocean was black and moody. Swifts flying past like white porcelain. White-caps and white surf. Sand dunes sometimes green with ground cover. I had the beach to myself. Nobody comes down here without a good reason. Abalone poachers, maybe.

The wind had risen sharply and the westerlies rattled the wild grasses. It was colder than bat shit in a cave. I climbed the bluff and headed back.

Ruth was waiting in my ragtop. She said nothing when I got behind the wheel. She was quiet. She looked like she was ready to bail out of life altogether.

She frowned. "She's living here all alone," she told me. "Her husband killed her brother. Her husband's in jail and her brother's in the morgue." She looked beyond the windshield. "And this is summer. Nothing but fog. This place feels like Wuthering Heights."

"I gather we're going."

"Yeah, we're going."

I twisted the key. The Chevy whinnied like a foal and then the engine roared with life. We started back down Hidden Valley Road.

"You think she should be left alone?"

"She won't leave," Ruth told me. "I asked three times. The poor woman's afraid to do anything." Absently she crushed a fistful of hair. "She hears voices."

"She should come back to the city."

Ruth looked over. "She says they've always heard voices. Strange and pitiful cries in the night. Poor woman. She says the house is haunted."

"It isn't very cheerful," I admitted. "They say haunted houses get their reputations because they're old and built near the sea. Underground rivers and tides and ocean currents and old wood shifting in the night and thick fog like this. Sounds travel funny in the fog."

Ruth was skeptical. "Underground rivers?"

"Haven't I ever told you about the Polk Gulch ghost? Oh, yeah, there's an underground river beneath Polk Street." I looked over. "Do we turn back?"

"She told me not to stay," Ruth said. She shook her fabulous hair and stopped paying attention to the road. "The lawyer's trying to hire a live-in nurse. And there are neighbors who drop in twice a day."

"Who lives out here?"

"There's a hippie commune down the road. Religious freaks. Ex-speeders who found God. She told me they come over all the time with help."

"I'll bet," I grumbled. "Bringing quilts and homemade preserves." I realized what I had said. "Just what she needs." I watched the road. "She shouldn't be out there alone."

Ruth crushed another handful of hair. "I'll talk to Bradley." She sighed again. "But you know how lawyers are."

"Why do you do this to yourself?"

She was startled for an instant. "You think I should quit, or let myself get fired, like you did. But you haven't quit, Michael. You're still doing it."

"I never said I was smart."

She had a wry grin. "At least I've got benefits."

"You've been there too long," I told her. "Just look at what it's doing to you."

"Let's go to bed when we get back."

I agreed. "I'm ready right now."

She said, "Look for a place to pull over."

"You're kidding me."

"Of course I am, Michael."

The Mark Twain Trail

Cherokee Sioux died in Mark Twain Alley.

A liquor store was across the street from the alley. Just another mom-'n-pop store downtown among the skyline. A plastic sign in the window said the store was open every night until midnight. No reason for the management to stick around any later. Downtown is empty streets after midnight.

I went inside. The store could hold seven people at any one time. Sandwiches in clear plastic wrappers. Sunflower seeds and playing cards and tampons. A concave mirror above every aisle. Wine and beer coolers against a wall. A produce box with oranges and other fresh fruit. The register was in a small alcove near the rear wall.

The store was crammed with stock easily bought with small change. Cigarettes and aspirin. Cookies and sourdough bread. Soda pop and mixed drinks in a can. Disposable razors and candy bars. Shampoo in tiny bottles. Everything came economy size, yet the prices were no bargains.

The night manager watched me. He was Persian. A young man, nearly my age, with a young mustache that showed little promise. No shoulders, no sideburns, little hair. His chocolate eyes were wide open. He didn't seem to like blinking. He didn't want to take his eyes off any customer that long.

He leaned against a stool behind the counter, a commander in chief of a legion of liquor bottles lined up behind him. He closed his cash drawer as I approached, but his hands stayed beneath the counter. Perhaps his gun was there.

"Can I help you?"

"This is an official visit." I hauled out my Department of Social Services ID card. "I'm an investigator for the Department of Social Services." I let him read every word on the card.

"What is this?"

"Food stamps," I said.

"Yes. We accept food stamps." He was a foreigner dealing with the Heat. He knew simple truths. Read their lips as officials talked. It made the Heat easier to deal with.

"Do you get a lot of them?"

"Yes. Sometimes."

"We're checking to see if any winos have been coming in lately using their food stamps to buy alcoholic beverages."

He knew what that meant. "That is against the law." He understood the law. There was a lot of law in America. The law was something he was nice to. The law could take him away.

"Oh, we know it's done."

"Not here," he said. "That is against the law."

"That's your side of the story."

He grew bold. "Why are you here?" He knew we had no proof.

I threw the next curve. "That dead woman last night."

He saddened. "Bad business."

I took out my notebook. "A wino found the body in the alley." I read a blank page. "His name is Zero."

He nodded. "Zero. Police took him away."

I leaned on the night manager. "Zero bought booze here last night. Maybe he was using food stamps to pay for it. Our office felt we should check into it."

He knew simple truths. "That is against the law."

"How many bottles did he buy?"

"He always pay money."

"How many bottles?"

"Four. But he pay money. No food stamps."

"Has he been in here before?"

"Sometimes. We get many bums in here." And he had stared at each and every one of them. "They all pay money. No food stamps."

"What time did he buy those four bottles?"

"Closing time. He come in, pay money, no food stamps. When he go, I lock up, go home. He find body. I don't see body. I go home already."

A long shot. "What about his buddy?"

"Him too. They all pay money. No food stamps."

"They came in together, right?"

"Many bums come here. Last night. Every night."

"They both found the body, right?"

"I work inside. I lock up. I go home. I don't see body."

"What's his name?"

He stopped. "Name?"

"What's his name? Zero's buddy."

He was positive I was nuts. Only the law would give a damn about a wino's name.

"Don't you know his name?"

The night manager squirmed. He was helpless. "I don't know name. But he always come in with Zero. They buddy-buddy all the time. I don't know name."

"Was he in here today?"

He would admit nothing. He didn't know. He was behind his counter. He couldn't tell me who came in. He was busy, always busy. He had to watch for thieves and robbers.

"Where do Zero and his buddy live?"

That he knew. "Down the street. Yes. Down the street." He gestured east-southeast, across the street and beyond the alley, toward the approach to the San Francisco Bay bridge. "The holes down there. The holes."

"Where the coliseum's going in?"

The Holes of Happy Valley

"Down the street. Down below the street."

There are two holes in Happy Valley. Two excavation sites between First and Third, between Mission and Folsom. Holes left behind by Redevelopment Agency razings. The modern ruins that only urban renewal makes.

Fifteen years ago there were office buildings and warehouses and cheap hotels down here. Liquor stores and gospel missions. Parking lots for commuters and union headquarters and places to sell blood. TV repairmen and watch cleaners. Tall-people stores and public parking garages and some apartment buildings. They'd all been condemned and razed.

Two city blocks gone. Eighty-seven acres of nothing surrounded by an eight-foot windbreak of wooden planks and a wire fence. Twin rubble pits that shelter pigeons and rats and slow-spinning spiders.

I shimmied through a rip in the fence and found myself on a jagged ledge of concrete held up by steel girders. It was the lip of the sidewalk, and a pile of dirt lay several yards below me. A makeshift ladder was several yards down the lip. The ladder was rickety, but it held my weight.

I wandered across the excavation. Dirt and yellow weeds. Broken glass and broken brick. Clumps of plastic. Cracked boards and asphalt chips. Piles of trash. Cigarette butts and empty bottles.

Someday Wyant's coliseum would be here.

These days there were caves along the perimeter and beneath the lip of the sidewalk. Natural caves formed when buildings were yanked out by the roots. Basements that extended beneath the sidewalk. Storerooms left behind by the wreckers. Concrete cubicles formed by the broken bracings. Most held leaky water lines and puddles of black water. Some smelled of piss and shit and stale wine.

Cave dwellers had set up homes in some of these 12 x 20 caves. Bums and winos and derelicts. Men of all races and creeds had homes beneath the sidewalks. Men who could survive on next to nothing. Nomadic men too proud for welfare. They'd rather panhandle. They all lived a floor below the streets and one rung above the doorways.

I could see the smoke from their fire pits. Country and western music coming from somewhere. Each cave kept plenty of space between it and its neighbors. Maybe some of the boys were sleeping in.

Mattresses on dirt floors. Laundry hanging on exposed nails and spikes. Broken chairs from garbage trucks. Tables from old planks. Shelves made from throwaway wood. Cardboard partitions to cut the wind. Even graffiti. Somebody had spray-painted Fuck Rats!

I walked along the caves and found only a few people. A bum was asleep between two pieces of cardboard in one cave. I let him sleep. A city block away a wino was stomping beer cans and dumping them into a large cardboard box. He was my goal.

An old man in coal-black rags was stretched out on a throw rug in the sunshine. I'd seen him before, begging on Market Street, squatting on blankets in a four-wheeled box, in front of the department stores. Those times one leg had been a stump. Now he had both legs.

I went over. "How's it going?"

He shaded his eyes with one hand. "How are you doing, young man?" His nose was a mass of broken blood vessels. The booze had palsied his movements, had dulled his mind, and had made him forget why he had started drinking. His face was ancient enough never to give a damn again.

"Cops bother you down here?"

He had a cheery grin and a raspy voice. "They don't bother us down here." He was missing some teeth. The ones he had left were discolored with yellow crud. "Cops only bother us on the street. We're underneath. We got space here. Privacy. Safe too. The police decoy team works down here."

"Where does Zero live?"

He perked up. "You looking for Zero?" He looked dirty and he smelled like he had shit in his pants.

"Do you know where he lives?"

The bum went sly. "We're just like organized charities," he prattled to the sunshine. "People always talk about how they don't trust giving to charities 'cause so many people live off the money before it gets down to this level. Hell, they ought to just give it to us, just like that, but they don't."

I took a five-dollar bill from my wallet.

He could almost taste it. "You got any spare change, Mr.?

"Where does Zero live?"

The bum pointed. "Over there. That third one."

I gave him the five bucks.

His pant legs were rolled up. Pale, skinny legs that hadn't seen daylight for months. There were sores above his ankles. Small, but at least a dozen. Some were raw, some had scabs, but all were inflamed from scratching.

"What happened to your legs?"

"Fleas." The beggar sat bolt upright, wagged a ghost-pale arm out at the yellow weeds. "All over." He scampered to his feet. "Drink some port with me, Mr.?"

"I'll pass."

He scurried off, stiff-kneed. His world began and ended five feet in front of him. From the back he looked like a walking pile of dirty laundry.

I went and checked out Zero's living arrangements. Four stained mattresses. Sleeping bags and old blankets. A table made of old planks. A crate of water-soaked paperbacks. Westerns, fuck books, the daily papers. Time magazine and The Wall Street Journal. Empty packs of Kools and old hats.

There was filth in most cubicles, but Zero's cave was almost clean. Plastic jugs of fresh water. Stacks of beer cans and pop bottles aimed for recycling centers. Shirts and socks neat on a clothesline. Jackets up on nails. Even a frazzled old broom.

The fire pit was bricks topped with a barbecue grill. Chunks of bricks that had been chopped from the retaining walls. The grill was crusty and rusted. Kindling had been torn from the wooden fence that surrounded the excavation site.

I looked over his food stores. A tin of pepper. Instant coffee. Powdered eggs and powdered potatoes. Mustard and salt. A half loaf of Wonder Bread. A tin of Vienna sausages. Paper plates and Styrofoam cups. A mechanical can opener. Eating utensils.

Zero's belongings were hidden behind a pile of newspapers and chunks of broken plasterboard. A knapsack and a sleeping bag. A khaki jacket with a ripped sleeve covered a cardboard box. Underneath, his personal belongings. A comb and Bugler tobacco. Tiny bars of hotel soap. A deck of cards and a jar of skin cream. A religious medallion. A shoelace run through the eyehole and both ends tied together. Saint Francis of Assisi. This town had been named after that gentle brother. I wondered how soon Zero's comrades would strip his stuff. Maybe they wouldn't.

"You just hold it, Mister."

I turned around.

A worn-out bum in his late thirties. Watery eyes and long blond hair. The usual wino's beard. He carried a hunting knife. He held it like an Indian fighter. And the point was aimed at my guts. He growled like a sick animal cornered.

"I know how to use this, Mr.," he told me. "I was in the Marines. Now, you get away from his things."

I backed off. "Sure."

"They're his things. They ain't yours."

"I've got some identification in my wallet."

He sneered. "Well, I ain't."

A dog wandered by.

"Can I take it out?"

The bum squinted in thought. "Okay. Slowly." He wore a green sweater with the sleeves rolled up, a brown shirt underneath. He couldn't button his fatigue jacket. It was too small. Black sneakers and baggy jeans. A burnout for sure.

I let him read my DSS ID card.

He lowered his knife. "What do you want here?"

"I'm looking for Zero."

The man with the knife faltered. "He ain't here."

I hauled over and sat on a stump of wood. "Last night Zero was out buying booze, probably for you and your buddies. In fact, he had already bought four bottles when he stumbled over a dead woman in Mark Twain Alley."

"He called the cops," the bum pointed out.

"And now he's in detox."

He was cautious. "Laguna Honda, right?" The bum brought down a tin can. Inside there were many half-smoked cigarettes. He straightened one out, shook loose some ash, and then lit it with old matches. "If he's there, what are you doing here?"

"How come Zero went for the booze?"

"He's the bank," the bum told me. "He takes care of all the money for us. That's why he's called Zero. He's never lost a dime since 1972, and that was when they threw him in Langley Porter and that male nurse clipped him sixty-five bucks."

"He's always been the bank?"

He squinted at his cigarette. "We all got chores. All four of us here. Chores each and every day. Somebody goes out to panhandle. Somebody gets firewood and fresh water. I stomp the beer cans for the recycling center. Zero buys the morning and evening bottles."

"The other night did Zero go alone?"

"Oh, no. Zero ain't right in the head."

"Who went with him?"

"Cody did." The bum's cigarette was nearly out. He looked around, grabbed an empty wine bottle, and stuffed his butt down its neck. There were other butts in the bottle already. I guess, after the wine is finished, the bottles become ashtrays.

"Is that his real name?"

"He just calls himself Cody."

"Do you know where Cody is right now?"

"He went to the movies."

Bingo!

The bingo movie house on Market Street was crowded for the Fourth of July. Three full-length features for a buck and a bingo game between features. A community center for the lowlifes and the dispossessed. Where a derelict could sleep safe and reasonably warm for a few hours every afternoon. The movies weren't that old or that bad either. Today they had a kung-fu action-adventure, a Spanish Western, and Rancho Deluxe.

The theater was between movies. A PA system crackled.

The house lights were on. There were winos scattered around here and there, every few seats, and always several seats from the next guy. There were a few couples, but less than a handful. Most people left everyone else alone, and everyone else was expected to do the same. The losers always want to be alone.

The theater manager was onstage with a microphone. A huge bingo wheel flanked one side, a blackboard flanked the other. The audience stirred and yawned, shifted in their seats, and stretched, stood up, and rubbed sore muscles, put out cigarettes and reached for fresh ones, or slept through it all.

The MC started again. "You all got your bingo cards."

A female wino down in front spoke up.

The MC was patient. "You got it when you bought your ticket." He listened to her complaint. "Look under your seat," he told her. "Maybe you dropped it." There was a moment of silence. "Too bad, lady." The MC spun the wheel. "N-42."

The audience grumbled. Hackers coughing and tuberculars wheezing. It was like looking over next season's victims. The ones marked for death by the streets.

I found Cody where he always sat, his back to the stone column nearest the men's room. He looked like he had shaved with a dull rock. He had a face frazzled like a scarecrow after a long winter. His fair hair was thinner than virtue and dirtier than vice. It was gathered in clumps, like spider webs, around his face.

"Cody?" I took the seat next to him.

Startled: "Who the fuck are you?"

"Cody, listen, Zero sent me."

He needed proof. "Zero sends nobody."

I let him read my DSS ID card. "I'm with Legal Aid, Department of Social Services, City and County of San Francisco."

He growled like a sick animal cornered. "What do you want?" He had the whitest teeth I'd ever seen, but I wondered how often food passed between them. His eyes were dull and lifeless, tired of everything, including trying. Like black stones, his eyes plugged his sockets and kept blood from falling out.

"This is for you." I gave him the Cub Scout manual I had found at the used-book store up the street. "I figured you and the other guys could use it down in the holes."

He was impressed. "Thanks." He paged through it. "Thanks a lot. This'll come in handy." He was too busy paging through his gift to wonder much where and how it had reached his hands.

"Why do they call you Cody?"

He snickered. "Because I got my name in Cody, Wyoming. Cos I burned down a liquor store when they wouldn't serve me." He tried being sly. "I got me the better part though. I ain't never been in Wyoming, 'cepting Laramie once."

The PA crackled. "B-4."

Somebody yelled "Bingo!"

"You can't have bingo yet," the MC explained. "There's no way you can have bingo because I haven't called any G's yet."

Somebody somewhere in the audience suddenly started laughing like a hyena. Nobody paid any attention to the shrill screams. Nobody even woke up.

The MC spun the wheel. "B-10."

"I've never met Zero," I confessed.

"How'd you know him, then?"

I grinned. "A computer sent me."

"A computer? Don't that beat shit. That's the fuckin' government, ain't it? The computer won't let him go free, and it send you. Him and his crazy insurance policies."

I caught it. "Insurance?"

He caught himself. "Aw, forget it."

"He got involved in that thing the other night. Is that what you mean?"

Cody had ants in his pants. "I ain't saying he shouldn't. It's just ... Him and his damn insurance. He gets crazy in the head sometimes. Does stupid things that always come back on him like a bucket of shit falling over his head."

"Are you and Zero old buddies?"

"Yeah. We panhandle together all the time."

"You can get ten days in jail for that."

"Shit, that ain't bad," he told me. "They let you out, don't they? And at least you get to take a shower. That's what's nice about jails. Showers. Rest of it sucks."

"Both of you were out buying booze last night."

He figured his odds. "We already bought it."

"You both found her, didn't you?"

He figured his odds. "Yeah."

"But he stayed behind."

"Because he's dependable. Hell, I ain't. Hell, it was only a dime. He thinks he's a Good Samaritan, you know. Figures someday somebody will do the same for him. He calls it his insurance policy. It's just a harmless thing, you know."

"But you came back alone."

"Yeah. I had to take the bottles back. Guys have to have their wine, you know. Shit, yeah, you have to get the wine home. People were waiting around. Why should I want to stick around a dead body for, anyway?"

"How come you didn't wait with him?"

Cody got frustrated. "You know why. A fuckin' dead body. No bottle. It makes sense, don't it? Shit, neither one of us wanted to. Not only 'cause the body was there but 'cause of the cops too. Who wants to stick around a dead body waiting for the cops? Shit, I needed a drink myself. Jesus, you know how slow the cops are when you need them. Shit, Zero was ..." He looked at me. "Is that how come they won't let him go?"

"He clawed a cop's shirt right off his back."

"He did that? Where is he?"

"He's at Laguna Honda."

"How come?" Cody was slow.

"The cops say he freaked out."

Cody relaxed. "They got clean sheets there every day. He likes that. And he can use the B-12 they'll give him."

"Is that what they use?"

"Yeah. And big fuckin' needles too."

"G-52," went the PA.

"Did you see anybody else on the streets?"

He was startled. "I seen the body. I wasn't looking much for anything else after I seen the body. Aw, shit, man, that's enough to look at."

"Were there any cars around?"

He gave it up as hopeless. "Maybe Zero saw something. I didn't see nothing. You ought to speak with him. Maybe he seen something." He was watching the stage closely now. "You know, I only won one thing once. I was fourteen years old. I won this cast-iron lawn mower at the store. Some kind of summer raffle, I guess."

"B-II."

"I almost didn't get it," he went on. "You was supposed to be sixteen to win, and some kid down the block started bitching 'because I was only fourteen, you see. Well, the store manager, he didn't like the kid, because the kid had a big mouth, and he liked me better, so he got all nervous and quiet when he gave me the lawn mower."

"What did you do with it?" I asked.

He couldn't remember. "But it was the only thing I ever won."

The MC had stopped the game. "Okay, bring up your card," he told the microphone.

A wino brought up his card.

The MC scanned it. "You don't get the ten bucks," he told the wino. "No, you don't. You don't have the winning holes. You just punched holes wherever you wanted, not the numbers I called out."

The wino started protesting. This time there was laughter from the audience. The audience could see there was nothing to fear from the wino on the stage. If competence was a rock, the wino couldn't bash his head in.

"Just go back to your seat," the MC said. He waited until the wino was marching down the steps. Then he started calling out numbers again. "G-55."

Cody was concentrating on his bingo card.

"What's the matter?" I said.

He showed me his card. "You look at it."

I looked at it, then at the blackboard.

He concentrated. "I think I won."

"Yep. You won."

"I won?" He tried harder.

"Go on up and get your prize."

"What did I win?"

"I guess you won ten bucks."

"No shit!" He realized he had won. "Shit, yeah." He galvanized himself and jumped from his seat. He started running down the aisle. "Bingo! Bingo!"

Mill Valley, California

Mount Tamalpais is the only mountain in Marin County, no matter what the park rangers may claim. It stands out, huge and green and tall, like a two-thousand-foot rumple in a big green quilt. Most of the county can see it on a clear day from some window.

Mount Tarn is woodsy. Almost a wilderness and only twenty minutes from the city. The top half has a couple of curvy peaks close together, the twin white nipples of the radar station, a necklace of dirt trails for the fire patrol, strawberry patches, bishop pines and bay trees, redwood groves and alders and poison oak.

It is alive with animals. Mountain beaver and black-tailed deer and raccoons, foxes and bobcats, coyotes and red-tailed hawks and quail. Even a mountain lion or two. And of course joggers and backpackers and hikers.

There is an Indian legend about Mount Tarn that stretches back centuries before the first white man came to rip everything off. The Tamal Indians believed that the long eastward slope was a sleeping woman. The human bride of the Sun god. She fell from his arms as he tried carrying her away to heaven. The summer fog was her blanket, made by the Sun-god from his tears.

The Tamal Indians would stand on the western slopes of Mount Tamalpais and watch the early European sailing ships exploring the California coastline. Then, hoping to postpone their destiny, they'd call upon the Sun god to send down the fog and hide the entrance to the San Francisco Bay. It was a good feat for two centuries, but destiny has a mind of her own. In 1769 the Bay was discovered by the white man.

The white man brought civilization.

The Tamal Indians are extinct now.

Karl Finch lived in the ridges above Mill Valley, the town that is between the sleeping woman's thighs. There are few big cars in Mill Valley. These mountain roads work against big cars. People here had four-wheel drive or foreign compacts.

I drove uphill in my big car and listened to my tappets. The road had two lanes, but it wandered and doubled back like a cat's cradle. There were no curbs, just slopes, and few parking spots. The woods were dense and made canopies over the road.

The Finch residence was a gingerbread house cantilevered over the valley. Redwood shingles and shanks. Split-beam fences. Gravel parking beneath eucalyptus trees. The house lights made the house glow like a Christmas candle wreathed in evergreen. A cabin in the woods twenty minutes from the city. Very pretty in the fog.

I pulled onto the wide gravel apron and parked behind a seven-year-old Volvo. The Volvo had a bumper sticker that said "Redwoods Do It Longest." The house blared with the latest disco sounds. The walls echoed like speakers in a jukebox. I'd bet there wasn't a mountain lion within miles of here tonight.

I pressed the doorbell several times. Nothing happened. I didn't even hear the doorbell. Disco was drowning out the bell. I rapped knuckles on the door, waited a minute, and then rapped again. Still nothing. And the beat went on. Disco madness.

The door wasn't locked. I went inside. I paused on the threshold and rang the bell again. It must have been out of order. I got scared of what I'd find.

The living room had indirect lighting and skylights. Denim chairs and sofa. Rough wood bookcases. A chandelier made of crystal. Lots of plants. The stereo was vibrating on a shelf, but not a soul around.

I tried the kitchen. Blue tablecloth on a hardwood table. Hardwood chairs with cane seats. French turn-of-the-century posters lined the wall above the sink. A vase of dried wildflowers sat on a windowsill beside several framed pieces of stained glass. Still no one.

I headed for the bedroom.

Elsie Finch didn't know there was another soul within fifty miles. She had her eyes closed, and she was naked except for a pair of leopard-spotted bikini panties.

She was lost in ecstasy, a sweet little rock-'n-roller dancing as fast as she had done a decade ago. She was dancing in front of a full-length mirror. Snapping her fingers and shaking her tail feathers. Singing along with the disco albums on the stereo. She had a hot little dumper and a question mark for a spine.

A thin blue cloud was chest-high in the room. That old familiar smell again. And a roach clip smoldering in an ashtray.

Elsie Finch was deep inside her dancing. She did an elegant three-sixty, snapping her shoulders in tempo, her eyes still closed, still lost in ecstasy. She didn't see me. She was working out, deep in the beat, and dancing was sweet and delicious. She was a thirty-year-old woman getting dressed for a night on the town.

She stopped in place, her back to me, primped and preened for an instant. She put her hands on her hips and grinned at her reflection. She laughed aloud.

"Fantastic," I said.

Her head snapped around. She saw a stranger in her bedroom. She went wide-eyed. Startled, she flew back backward and grabbed for a housecoat. "Who are you?"

"Michael Brennen. Hayward made a—"

"Get out of my room!"

The bedroom door had a hell of a slam.

"I'll be in the living room."

I waited in the living room. I wondered if she were already calling the police on me. I made myself a drink and tried remembering Hayward's 800 toll-free number.

Elsie Finch came from the bedroom. She was dressed in a bright red hip-hugging dress. She looked like the wrath of God. "What the hell are you doing here?"

"We met at the senator's party."

"Just how did you get in?"

"I heard the music, and the front door wasn't locked, and your doorbell doesn't ring."

She stared. "It wasn't locked? And the doorbell?" She was disgusted. She'd draw and quarter her handyman when she saw him next. But she wasn't finished with me yet. "What are you doing here?"

"Hayward—"

She cut me off. "That dirty ..." She looked up at me. "He's not here. He went off somewhere with my husband."

"Do you know where they went?"

She didn't know or care. "Call his service. Go ahead. Call him. I want to talk to him myself. This is my home, and my home isn't political."

I called Hayward's answering service. The woman told me to leave a message. I said I was at his kid brother's house in Mill Valley and that Mrs. Finch wanted to talk to him personally. This was an emergency. The woman said she'd give him the message. She'd have him call as soon as he checked in.

I hung up the telephone and turned to Elsie Finch. "Are they coming back soon?"

She stiffened. "Not tonight."

I felt real lame. "I'm very sorry about barging in like that. You see, I'm a private investigator—"

"I know." She was livid. "And private eyes are always finding dead bodies in the bedroom."

I said nothing. The truth wouldn't set me free here.

She stared at me, wishing I was dead, and I was silent with remorse.

"It's okay," she relented. "It's not your fault. Just never do it again, okay?"

I agreed. "It looks like you're going out."

She decided to brazen it. "I've got a date tonight. And it's not with my husband." She smirked like a schoolgirl with a secret love.

"What about your husband?"

"Fuck him. That's what I'm doing, and I don't care what he thinks." She tossed back her long brown hair. "This is the first time in years I've felt really free."

I broke into a grin. "What I meant was, you don't think your husband or Hayward will be home tonight."

Laughter broke free. "Oh, God, no, they won't be back here tonight." She laughed like a schoolgirl comparing lovers. "And I've got you to thank for that."

I was curious. "How so?"

"That party." Her pixie smile widened. "That's when it all happened for me. For once somebody was telling me that I didn't have to put up with his shit anymore. I was having a good time. Karl didn't like that. He gets jealous. He doesn't like you. You should have heard what he said about you."

"Was he watching us at the party?"

"Karl is an asshole and a turkey."

I grinned. "You know him better than I do."

"That asshole." She shook her head in disbelief. "He's been taking me for granted too long. I'm tired of it." She ran out of words and breath at the same time. "Well, fuck him."

I prompted her.

"That asshole is always leaving me alone. He gets to go out there, playing around with the bigwigs and the hot shots while I'm just staying in, standing around, in the background like some fool." She tensed her arms with fury. "Since he goes out with other women, I'm going out with other men. I'm going to have other men too."

"That he's messing around is easy to say and hard to prove."

She didn't need any proof. She said politics was simple. "Men have a wife and then they go whoring around."

"Have you checked his bankbook?"

"Why should I do that?"

"You aren't living high enough on the hog that he can buy pussy with pocket money. If there are big chunks of money missing, then maybe he's not sleeping just with you."

"I never thought of that." She whirlwinded across the living room to an imitation-wood desk. She had his checkbook from the drawer in an instant. She leaned against the desk and started scanning the pages. She paged forward, stopped, paged backward, and then forward again. She looked puzzled.

"Well?"

She stared at the book like an archaeologist with the wrong set of hieroglyphics. "Dammit. I can't figure it out. Oh, there's something wrong, but ..." She threw back the book. "Fuck it. I know." She tapped her heart. "I know."

The phone rang.

She answered it. "Hayward? Yes, it's me. Look, my house isn't political, remember? You promised. Hayward, fuck off. Don't you ever do it again!" Then she slammed the phone back on its cradle.

"He'll be calling back."

She remembered. "You wanted to talk to him too."

Hayward called back. I answered it.

He was apologetic. "We missed connections. Sorry about the heat. How was my old man?"

"All piss and vinegar." I laughed. "He's great."

"Is he coming down on us?"

"Not if he has to slander Heather's good name."

Hayward was silent for a moment. "Then the rest of your report can wait until morning." His voice had gone flinty. "Just come over here in the morning. First thing, okay?" He knew his father was just another bite. He hung up.

"Be seeing you," I told the phone.

As I hung it up, it rang again.

I answered it. "Yes?"

A man's voice. "Is Elsie there?"

I gave it to Elsie Finch. Her cheery disposition faded as she listened. When she hung up she looked over at me. She looked minutes away from a breakdown. "What's wrong?"

"Tonight's off." She pushed herself, as if skirting the rim of exhaustion. "His Mercedes is fucked up." She looked like she had been in a cage too long.

"How about dinner with me?"

She turned, surprised.

I grinned. "After all, your husband won't be home tonight."

She blinked. She remembered. She appraised me. Her mouth found its secret smile. A smile like the Mona Lisa's. That's what that smile is all about. "Where?"

"I know a place in Mill Valley."

She went to find her coat. "Let's fly."

A restaurant that was down a winding path. It was near the bus depot and the town's movie theater. A cheery little path. Old bricks and tile roofs. Spanish-style buildings. Trees and plants. Moss and gaslight and moonlight.

The restaurant was warm and toasty. It sat perhaps a dozen couples. The owners were Viennese. Small tables and tall candles. Old-brick walls. Rough wooden shelves and bottle racks for the wine. Red table linens and huge crystal goblets. Filet mignon in tarragon sauce. Veal cordon bleu. Strawberries Martinique. Johannesburg Riesling.

She had a child's delight in the restaurant. She asked me how she looked. She looked frantic and vulnerable, a tiny woman trying to assert herself.

"You look great," I said.

She had a pixie grin. "I feel like a slut."

"You wear red very well." Her face was framed in candlelight. "Why did you marry Karl?"

"It was good at the start. Isn't that what they always say? He was easy to live with in those days. He became ... different. Now ... Now he has more moods than the ocean."

"Which two come most often?"

She smiled. "That's a good question. Frustration mostly. Guilt and frustration. My parents made the down payment on the house. He resented that. He still can't pay them back for it."

"But he works. Doesn't he?"

She sighed. "Without his brother he's unemployable." She rummaged through her thoughts. "People treat him like shit. They forget he was in law school."

"I didn't know that either."

"He flunked the bar exam last summer. He has to wait until this August to take it again. But only one in every three pass it the first time. Even the governor had to take it twice before he passed it."

"How much does he make at the office?"

"A thousand a month. Not much, is it?"

"How can you afford to live in Mill Valley?"

"Well, I work too. I'm successful, too."

"I never meant to suggest you weren't."

"I teach elementary school here in town. You should come by and see me sometimes. Laurel Woods School. We can go to class together and do some finger painting with my children. That is, if I still have my job in the fall."

I had a hunch. "Prop 13?"

She didn't smile. "Summer school was canceled, statewide. I was laid off with everybody else. And I don't get unemployment either, because summer school is considered extra money."

"Do you think you'll have a job?"

She didn't know. "If I don't, in the fall I can get unemployment. That's something. Not much, maybe. Karl's been worried about that too. How we're going to survive in the fall."

When we left the restaurant I kissed her.

She quit too soon.

I backed off. "Okay. I overstepped."

She shook herself from my arms. "I've been married a long time." She was nervous. "I have to go slow. I have to. Damn!" She shook her hair. She had been in a cage too long.

"Where do we go from here?"

"I don't know," she said.

"Let's go dancing."

She had a better idea. "There's a hot tub back at my house."

The Financial District

Montgomery Street is San Francisco's financial district. Wall Street West. I've heard that San Francisco rates second only to New York among the financial giants. London has more money on deposit, but our volume of transactions is greater. I have no way of judging the truth.

I know rush hour is always in progress in the financial district. A rush hour that comes before sunrise and ends long after sundown. The stockbrokers come before dawn to keep New York hours. After sunset, legal secretaries scurry down empty streets.

Daytime: bankers keeping bankers' hours. Cabs to the airport. Cable cars and corporate jaywalkers. Briefcases. Working girls in tan raincoats. Courier vans and mail trucks. Armored cars and must-turn lanes. Tow away zones and trees in planter boxes. Newspaper vendors and night deposits and no parking anywhere. Buses and their paralyzing fumes. The late-morning edition and the early-evening edition.

"Where would you like to go?"

I hesitated. "Wherever you want to go."

"Then we'll simply circle the block until our business is concluded," the businessman said. He tapped on the center divider for his chauffeur's attention. He made circular motions with his index finger.

He was a white man in a wool suit. A businessman about fifty years old. Six foot three, two hundred pounds. He had a good profile, silver hair, and a sturdy frame. His voice had no accent and he spoke like an American, but he wasn't American.

"What do you want with me?" I asked.

"I represent some corporations."

I marveled. "More than one?"

He was a cocky son of a bitch. "I wish I were a corporation instead of a human being," he told me. He stopped and reconsidered. "I amend that. I'm delighted to be allied with the boards of several corporations. A king's power without his responsibilities." He was drunk as a skunk and as smug as any drunk can be.

"I'm the one with the DT's," I decided.

I had him pegged. He was one of the New Conquistadors. The men on the jet planes with briefcases and three-piece suits. They lived in global villages of Concordes and satellite calls. They carried stamped visas and air-travel cards and Telex forms, and their secretaries renewed their passports automatically every six months. There aren't that many of them in this world, but they get around.

He noticed me. "Have you ever seen the world from a satellite? The world is a most majestic planet. I'm sure you've seen those satellite pictures."

I caught on. "The world is our market." I almost added, "And profit is our most important product."

"I don't represent Oppon International."

"But you do represent more than one corporation."

"Yes."

"Do they pool their resources to rent you?"

"Do you know what an interlocking directorship is? Either primary or secondary? Board members. Executive directors and chief executive officers. Presidents and salaried executives. They make a phone call to a friend."

I smiled. "And you're a friend, right?"

The drunk ignored me. "Maybe it's a satellite call." He noticed me. "In a few years, with the space shuttle in operation, they'll have their own satellites."

"Where do you come in?"

"Tell us all about Senator Patricia Cardine and Stephen Daniel Wyant."

"That's all?" I marveled.

He frowned with impatience. "You've been sequestered all day with the senator."

"And that upsets you?"

He knew I was a stupid twit. "We're concerned. We want to know what going on. Who killed Heather Beaumont? Why? What's the senator's connection with you? What's Wyant's, for that matter?"

"Gee, I'm afraid I can't help you there."

He patted my kneecap. "You have plenty of time to make your decision. You don't have to make it here with me. There will be others after me who'll ask you for it." He had a thought. "Others will even help you with the paperwork. I'm just the first stop along the journey through the land of bribery."

I tried an end run. "Look, she's a United States senator. What if I tell her what you're up to?"

He chuckled. "What can she do? She can't prove that I exist, that this limousine exists, that today exists. We're all electrons floating in some computer bank, and scientists can't define electricity. They know what it does, not what it is. Pedestrians in a skyscraper world. Apples and oranges."

"Are you talking straight cash?"

He stared like a drunk, too. "We don't work that way. It's too difficult keeping a man bribed with cash. We like having proof that you were bought. That way we all hang together, so to speak."

I looked around the limousine, as if he'd dropped something. "What'll the money look like?" Can I help it if I get curious?

"It'll be a corporate check from some division in some corporation or other. I don't even know which one they'll choose. But you will sign a contract, and the money will be ticketed off and mailed to you. The money will be as clean as money laundered by the Mob or the CIA." He smirked at my expression. "Can't the good guys use it too?"

"Oh, you're one of the good guys." I grinned. "Just shows you how much I know."

He sighed like an old whoopee cushion. "I'm not the Mob, the Mafia, the Mafiosi, whatever they call it. Oh, I'll admit that for a while I had guilt feelings. I felt like I was working for the Mob or the CIA. I got over it, and so will you."

"How much for me?"

"Any price that is reasonable. You sit down and draw up a simple budget. You name the amount by your purchasing power. Our boys in Accounting will red-line any obvious excess."

"You'll give me five minutes free shopping in your supermarket."

"Ten." But he was smiling. "Actually, duration is conditional upon the information you have or can acquire."

I said, "Give me some parameters."

"An apartment without rent," he guessed. "A bank card without 18 percent interest. A home loan for a new house that's never repaid. Maybe a new car yearly for the next ten years. Maybe you want a job. How about being on permanent retainer to study security problems in some South Pacific operation?"

"What if I say no?"

He shrugged. "I'll ruin your credit rating for life."

"Aw, I've done that already," I boasted.

"Excuse me," he said. "Forever."

"So I declare bankruptcy and start again. One cancels out the other, doesn't it? I know how the system works. I'll be back charging again inside of a year."

"Not with a glitch in your record. A gremlin. They're like trolls, elves, Maxwell's Demons. They hide in foxholes in every single computer program. They only come out once in a blue moon, but they bite with malice. They could say you're a registered sex offender, and they're simply computer error. Do you want to spend your life in court battles with a credit card company computer to get yourself a telephone or keep your car insurance?"

"How do I know you're for real?"

"How about your FBI file?"

I said nothing. He was a fool.

"Direct from the FBI."

"What is it? The CIC files?"

"The FBI," he insisted.

I shook my head. "Any phone phreak can build a black box for the CIC network. You got into the CIC files, not the FBI files."

"If we can build a satellite, we can surely hire someone better than a phone phreak."

I made a noise. "Okay, so maybe you bought yourself a sheriff somewhere and you can get into the CIC network. People think they're the FBI files, but compared to the real ones, they're publicity handouts."

"This would be the FBI files," he persisted.

"Don't try to con me with that crap. The FBI won't let you or anybody tie into their in-house network. Too much of their history could compromise their future."

He pointed between the limousine seats. "You see that, don't you? It's like a Telex into their microfilm files."

A video screen was built in where the liquor cabinet should have been. There was a keyboard beneath it, with a phone attached to one side like an oversized ear.

I made another rude noise.

He took out a plastic card, then stuck it into the card slot beside the screen. A fast stream of musical tones riding up and down the musical scale. The card seemed to have activated the commercial phone lines. They sounded like phone tones, but there were too many tones, one right after another.

The screen darkened, then lightened. Print began a slow Australian crawl up the screen. Entire lines of print at a time.

Quotrons in a stockbroker's office print stock market quotations in much the same way.

My fingerprints came on the screen.

I read the copy. My fingerprints had been entered into the FBI in-house network during the Truman presidency. But that was impossible. I was only five or six at the time.

I remembered the two FBI men who had visited my first-grade classroom. The good nuns had said this was just like a field trip, only we didn't have to go outside.

The two FBI men had spent most of their time praising the Old Man and telling us how the Bad Guys had been machine-gunned to death. They had brought some cop equipment. Silhouette targets and shackles and handcuffs and caliber charts.

They told us what our fingerprints were. They dusted the radiators to show how prints were lifted. And then they let all of us in the class ink our fingers and press them down on real FBI ID cards. We thought it was a lot of fun.

My next entry was during junior high school. I rode a school bus to a football game in the next state. The bus was vandalized after we won. The FBI had gotten involved because the team had crossed state lines.

"Most recently," I asked.

He punched a keyboard button, the screen seemed to shimmy for an instant, and then the most recent entries on me began crawling from the bottom upward. Most recently, the FBI files said, the bureau had grown interested in me as of: *July 1, 1978.*

"Go slower," I said.

He punched another button.

San Francisco Police Officers Curtain and Howard had memoed the SFPD public relations desk concerning a private investigator's presence at the summer office picnic for United States Senator Patricia Cardine.

Oho. A leak in the SFPD.

I stopped. Maybe there was no leak. This might be info pooling, standard operating procedure.

Within hours an eight-man agent team had been assigned to me for round-the-clock surveillance. A simple two-man backup that changed every four hours. A floater squad of wheelmen was made available at the same time for routine freeway surveillance.

Freeway? Saturday?

Oho. The FBI were the guys in the suits in the yellow pickup on the way to the airport.

"This is a phony," I said. "You made this all up." My throat was dry.

A footnote came up on the screen. The floater squad was cross-charged to Accounting as per man-hours-on-duty. Then a cross-reference, again to Accounting, concerning billing practices and account numbers and payroll statistics and individual agent personnel files. That was footnoted too. Some supervisor complaining that the agents assigned from the Sacramento offices may have overstated the cab fare from the airport on their expense sheets.

"You can stop it," I said.

He switched off the video screen.

My mind went elsewhere. That goddamn Yankee know-how. The Big Business of Big Government. A world of paperwork. The computer mind at work. A toilet choking with its nonnegotiable demands on us poor pitiable hostages.

Once I believed that Big Government was so overwhelmed with busywork that she had little time for the likes of me. Thank God, I thought at the time. But I had been wrong. Her busywork was keeping track of people like me.

South of the Slot

South of Market is a general term for the area between China Basin, the Central Freeway, Thirteenth Street and Market Street. It's the moat for this city of Oz.

Rush hour is like the tide. Twice a day it comes between the big buildings and the Bay. The streets are wide here, with five full lanes to help relieve the pressures.

Most people leave San Francisco from this side of town. Down here you have the train depot, every bus station, two freeways, even a bridge approach.

The two freeways run parallel down here. There are one-way streets between those off-ramps that either leave or enter the downtown districts.

The Hall of Justice is down here. Also leather boy bars and dental supplies and welding shops. Sheet workers and printers and mill-machine shops. Sweatshops for Chinese garment workers and legal-help offices if you're the wrong color.

An automotive garage like a thousand others in this city. Two stories and a drive-up ramp on one side. The ramp upstairs from the street was blocked off by roll-down metal doors. The huge windows on both floors were frosted with cracks and filthy with dust and spider webs.

Downstairs they fixed engines and did body work. Upstairs they stored the tough problems and the overnight trade and the slow payers. There was no basement.

The garage was between an auto-parts supply and a scuba shop. The rest of the block was warehouses and tool machine shops. All single-story buildings, concrete or cinderblock, all beige and windowless. There was a tannery downwind. The noxious fumes from the curing calfskins made my stomach twist and turn.

An Olds Cutlass was on fire in the street. A black-'n-white squad car was crushing it against a telephone pole.

A man was lying in blood in the street. He looked like he had fallen asleep while walking and this was where he had landed. There was an automatic pistol near an oddly twisted ankle. There was blood all over.

The front door to the garage had been shot off its hinges and it swung on the last screw left.

The cops had the street blocked off. They were hiding behind the doors of their squad cars. I wished them luck. I wasn't getting any closer than this. Even a .22 shell can go through a car door. The only thing a cop car door can stop is a shotgun's blast.

Howard nudged me. "C'mon, let's go."

We ran hunched over past the police barriers.

I kept my head down. I made sure I kept an engine block between me and the upstairs windows. It wasn't much protection, but it was a damn sight better than an aluminum door or a car seat.

"What's happening?" Howard asked.

The nearest cop spoke. "We got a hostage situation." He gestured at the dead man in the street. "We got him before they got inside."

"How many inside?" somebody asked.

"Two men plus a woman hostage. Maybe more, but I doubt it."

"Are they upstairs or downstairs?"

The loudspeaker came on. "Police officers. Come outside with your hands up. Do yourself a favor. Be cool. We want you to very nicely put your hands on your head and come outside, if you would, please."

A gun cracked and a bullet went wild.

Everybody ducked.

"'Have you ever thought about doing something serious, like detective fiction?'"

I met Ken Millar in the summer of 1975 at the Santa Barbara Writers Conference, the event that author Barnaby Conrad has so wondrously run for all these years. I went to the conference not to meet Millar (a.k.a. Ross Macdonald), but to quit writing.

I was 29 years old and was giving up. Oh, I had set off five years earlier, determined like every other writer that I was going to produce those words everyone had always been itching to read, only they didn't know it yet.

In truth, I had sold nothing and I no longer believed anything would sell. But I wanted to quit on a high note, not feel like I had failed. After all, being a writer is like swimming up a waterfall. Nobody is surprised that so many can't do it; we are only surprised that some do succeed.

I chose the Santa Barbara Writers Conference because it was advertised as being held on the beach at Santa Barbara, at the Miramar Hotel. The Miramar had two bars, two pools, and security guards on little golf carts that went around the bungalows at last call to make sure the drunks got back safely.

If you're going to quit writing, why not at the Miramar? Why not at the Santa Barbara Writers Conference, with its annual crowd of real writers to hobnob with? Ray Bradbury was there, as was Alex Haley, who was then finishing up Roots, and Irwin Shaw, who was now a Rich Man and not a Poor Man, and Maya Angelou and Gay Talese and Charles Schultz and... and Ross Macdonald.

I had admired Ross Macdonald for his work for years. I can remember the day a college roommate gave me his copy of The Chill and dared me to read a mystery. I read it in a single sitting and was blown away by the intellect that could conceive such a lucid pathway through the maze of human deviousness.

I was a fan. That was enough.

And I saw him there at the conference. Ross Macdonald was tall and stately, stoic and gentlemanly. He wore a straw hat; Santa Barbara was hot that summer. He had buttoned the top button of his short-sleeve shirt; he was elderly. He walked deliberately. He looked unapproachable. Until I saw him with other people. His smile was open and flashing; he was generous with his smiles.

I didn't try to approach him. He was a published novelist. I was from the other side of the universe. The unknown side of that side. Whatever thoughts I had ever had about being a writer -- hell, I was there because I was quitting writing. That anguish was for other people. I didn't feel bad that I wasn't cut out to be a writer, that I had wasted a few years of my life. Hey, I was a child of the 1960s. No loss there.

One or two days before the conference ended, I got the word from Barnaby Conrad's people that every "student" at the conference was supposed to submit some work they had done. Well, I had nothing substantial with me. Certainly nothing I wanted to show anyone. I hadn't brought any completed stories, any polished poems, anything. What I had were pages of dead-ends, cul-de-sacs of unfinished stories: Evidence I might need to keep my resolve if I lost my courage and thought about giving the writing life another try.

For some reason -- maybe my latent fear of authority figures -- I looked in the small notebook I always carried to see if there were any miracles I had mislaid. The notebook wasn't much. Inside were a bunch of observations about the nightlife in San Francisco, where I was then living. I had a job as a cab driver; I saw things I never wanted to see. What was written in there were things I didn't want to forget. But no prose pieces. Not even a plot. Not enough for a character sketch. Just a bunch of one-liners about the streets of San Francisco after midnight.

I could remember my college professor whispering, "If you call it a poem, it's a poem." So I took two dozen of these one-liners and stretched them into a free-form poem, borrowed somebody's typewriter, submitted the poem, and promptly forgot about it.

The next morning, someone -- I still don't know who -- telephoned my bungalow and said I had to get up, it was 8 a.m., and I had to get over to the convention center. Well, if you wake me up by screaming at me, I get up and never wonder why. Especially when I'd been present at last call the night before, and looked it.

Everybody was in the convention center. Somebody was announcing the winner of the "poetry contest." And it was me!

Somebody said I had to come up on stage and read my poem. Somehow I did it. The only face I saw was Ross Macdonald's, and he was staring so intently, I got scared and wished I were elsewhere. I didn't figure he was buffaloed by my poem. I figured I won the poetry prize because everybody else there wrote fiction.

By 8:30, I was on a stool in the Miramar bar. I was alone.

Ross Macdonald looked in the bar. I was impressed. This was the closest I had gotten to him in six, seven days. I toasted him with my draft beer, and he came over. He stuck out his hand and I shook it, and he said, "That was a very nice poem you wrote." I was stunned. When I'm stunned, I get as charming as I can be. "Can I buy you a drink?" He scowled and said, "I don't drink before sundown." Oh.

Then he left.

While I didn't think I had blown it, I didn't think I had made a very good impression on the writer I most looked up to. But I knew I was just a fan, and he would forget me quickly enough. There's always salvation in anonymity.

Twenty-four hours later, on the last morning of the conference, I was in the bar again, nursing another of those a.m. drafts, and Ross Macdonald stuck his head in the bar again. He saw me and came over.

"You look down in the dumps," he said.

"I have to fly back to San Francisco. My plane leaves in four hours. I have no place to go before then, so I'm just sitting here in the bar at the Miramar."

He frowned, almost said something, then made up his mind. "Do you need a ride to the airport?"

"Thank you, sir, but not for four hours."

Ross Macdonald said, "Why don't you come up to my house for the next four hours, and then I'll give you a ride to the airport?"

I think I said yes.

I know I followed him out of the Miramar bar, my suitcase in hand. We walked about a hundred yards to the parking spaces on the road into the Miramar. Two elderly women were there, standing by a compact car.

Ross Macdonald announced to them, "This is Fred Zackel, who wrote that poem about San Francisco. His flight there leaves in four hours, and he's having difficulty getting out to the airport."

Then he introduced me to his wife, the mystery writer Margaret Millar and the other woman with her. "He's on the same flight you are," he told the other woman.

He told them I could hang with them, and we could all go to the airport together. The two women weren't happy with his generosity, but we all piled into the car. His wife sat behind the wheel, while Ross Macdonald sat beside her. I sat in the back seat. Next to author Eudora Welty.

Margaret Millar drove like a bat out of hell.

She drove a tiny Japanese car, one of those early models that barely held four adults. And she went around curves like the chase at the end of a thriller, and more often than not jumped the curb doing so. She never slowed, either. She went full-bore and flat out.

She scared me the most when we swung by the Santa Barbara fairgrounds. Honest to God, I didn't think she'd be able to pass a truck changing lanes on the inside before he, too, filled the lane she wanted. But she did it, squeezing through like a teenager in a crowd.

Ross Macdonald sat beside her. I sat behind him, and Eudora Welty sat on my left. I felt so sorry for her. Every time Margaret Millar took a turn, either Eudora Welty smashed into my shoulder, or I would crash into hers.

Eudora Welty was not a small woman, but she did appear delicate and fragile. Banging into me must have jarred her as much as getting smacked with a swinging door. And every time I flew into her, I nearly squashed her like a bug.

We had no seatbelts in those days.

And nobody said a word the entire way.

The trip to Santa Barbara's exclusive Hope Ranch neighborhood was over quicker than it should have been.

We all went inside the Millars' ranch-style house on Esperanza Avenue, the one they had bought with movie money.

The Millars had dogs -- great German shepherds, for the most part -- and like all true dog lovers, they kept the house safe for galloping hounds. After the handful of dogs told us all how grateful they were to see us, Margaret Millar let them out.

Over instant coffee I was quizzed about my past, present, and future.

Being quizzed was a terrifying experience. These three writers were brilliant, famous, and successful. I was not. I felt very much out of my league.

I tugged out a cigarette. "Do you mind if I smoke?"

All three faces lit up with disapproval.

"No one smokes inside the house," Ross Macdonald said.

"Mind if I smoke outside?"

I went poolside and lit a cigarette.

I stayed outside longer than I should have. I felt defiant. I had nothing to lose, I thought.

Back inside, the quizzing began again.

"I came to the writers' conference to quit being a writer," I explained. "In the past five years, I have sold nothing, and I don't believe anything will ever sell."

The three looked at me as if I was a talking dolphin.

"Why go to a writers' conference to quit writing?"

"I wanted to go out with no regrets. The Miramar Hotel is on the beach in Santa Barbara, has two pools and two bars, and the security guards drive around after last call in golf carts to pick up the drunks and make sure they get back to their cottages."

"Read your poem for us," Ross Macdonald said.

I took it from my binder and read it aloud.

All three leaned back and contemplated the cosmos.

When I was done, all three looked at each other and frowned.

"What kind of writing have you been doing?" Macdonald asked me.

I said I had been trying to write literary fiction about Midwest farm towns. About people as gray as a winter's sky and hearts as cold as a coffin's touch. About being a stranger in my native land. You know, tedious crap.

"May we see some of it?"

I went to my suitcase and unpacked the chunks of paper.

Each writer took a swatch and read. Then they passed the papers around. I drank black coffee and watched them read. When they were done, all three gave me back my manuscripts, stared at the floor and frowned.

Finally, Ross Macdonald spoke.

"Have you ever thought about doing something serious, like detective fiction?"

I said, "No." In a panic, I said, "I don't know how."

He said, "I will help you."

Three of us stared at him.

That first meet changed my life's direction. Over the next few years I had Ross Macdonald as my mentor.

We swapped letters back and forth -- "Although," he wrote once, "you shouldn't spend writing like that on a letter. Save everything for the book, especially yourself."

When I could, I showed up at his house on Esperanza Street ("Street of Hope," in Spanish). Sometimes he knew I was coming and he was ready for me, and sometimes I came unannounced, too afraid of being turned down over the telephone, and so I would wake his wife and him up. He was always generous with his time.

He showed me his office, his shelves of books, and his notebooks, one for each novel, some that had been started decades before. He had stacks of notebooks, and each one was written in as meticulously as a bookkeeper's ledger. I couldn't imagine how he could begin with a single metaphor, and yet it would grow almost miraculously into a novel.

He had his leather recliner and the wooden board he used as a writing table. He would lay that board across the arms, and that chair was a transporter worthy of anything the Starship Enterprise ever carried. That chair carried him -- and all his readers -- to great adventures.

We went for long walks with his dogs on dry riverbeds, and I would ask him every question I could imagine. He was always generous with his answers.

He said, "The detective isn't your main character, and neither is your villain. The main character is the corpse. The detective's job is to seek justice for the corpse. It's the corpse's story, first and foremost."

He said, "You don't need to describe your detective. He describes himself by the questions he asks and by how he reacts to other people's answers. Your readers will visualize him in their own minds."

My fears were the usual, although I never knew it.

I asked, "What do you do when everything you wrote is completely wrong?"

He said, "You start again."

He was always supportive. "This is very promising material," he wrote me once. "Guard it with your life. And give it a good, strong, not too complicated storyline."

And when my first book, *Cocaine and Blue Eyes*, was done, he read it and said, "You have written a large, good, contemporary novel with a style which seems to me very much your own, composed out of the daytime speech and nighttime visions of your characters."

Later, he wrote a blurb for *Cocaine and Blue Eyes*: "Fred Zackel's first novel reminds me of the young Dashiell Hammett's work, not because it is an imitation, but because it is not. It is a powerful and original book made from the lives and languages of the people who live in San Francisco today."

Well, that was unbelievable. Almost unthinkable. Hell, nobody could live up to that blurb, although I do know a dozen truly more deserving P.I. writers who should have had something like that attached to their names and reputations. But Ken was a sweetheart of a guy who went out of his way for me and transformed my image of myself.

He did more, and said more to me, and all of that is more personal than I wish to be here. But because of him, I wrote and published two novels. In both hardcover and paperback. In not only English, but also French and Spanish. My first novel was reviewed by Time magazine, and that became a special moment I still cherish. The book went on to become a TV movie.

I, too, went on. I earned a master's degree and a Ph.D., and I taught creative writing and contemporary fiction on both the graduate and undergraduate levels. I even taught an honors course I created myself. "The Detective in Literature" was its title. And my mentor had a special place within the pantheon.

Then last October, almost 25 years after all this started, I received a note from author/critic Tom Nolan, saying that my name would be appearing in his new biography of Ross Macdonald. He wanted my permission to use some lines I had written to Macdonald in a letter.

Nolan sent me three or four manuscript pages, and I discovered again why *Rashomon* is my favorite movie: Each of us thinks we know what's real, but reality has more sides than a disco ball.

In his biography, Nolan quotes Eudora Welty: "It seems that Margaret [Millar] had said she didn't ever want anybody to come to their house. This should just be their house."

There was more. Some of it was painful.

I never knew the bond between husband and wife. The value they put on their privacy. That their home was their sacred shelter.

I never knew how much she despised anybody who came acallin'.

I never knew the price Macdonald paid to help me and others like me.

All that he did for me comprised such a tiny part of his life, but it was a turning point for me.

A quarter of a century later, I am even more grateful.

Mario and Cheryse

After midnight the foggy streets of San Francisco were like a foreign country. The night was so dead quiet that the hookers had spread out from the Tenderloin and into the decent people's worlds and now were promenading across from the Cliff Hotel. And still no johns were striking at the bait. Last time I'd seen San Francisco night life this quiet was the last time an Alcoholic Anonymous convention hit town.

A beat cop who quit the streets to become a junior high school teacher once told me what hooking is. He said the word "prostitute" comes from a Latin word that means "to stare," and hookers stare for hours. Time passes slowly when you stare for a living. When you're new to it, the hours go by like years, and then you grow used to it, and the years go by like hours, until one day you realize that what you're staring for is what's long gone.

I did a stake-out at Hooker Heaven, the corner of O'Farrell and Leavenworth. I parked behind a Volvo with an old bumper sticker on the rear fender that read, "Die, Yuppie Scum!" He was another individual unclear on the concept.

Time dragged like a legless dog. Now and again vice cops cruised by in their unmarked cars that everybody who works the streets instantly recognizes, and every-so-often beat cops came by, swapped lies and bullshit with old regulars, and memorized new faces for next time. The streets went on and on as they always have. Seventy minutes into the stake-out I watched a homeless man fight his shadow. He fought dirty. It still came out a draw.

Two hours into the stake-out, I saw the girl again.

She was holding up a building, just one of the many hookers scattered like fireplugs around the neighborhood. She had changed clothes. Now she wore a red skin-tight dress and red high heels and a thin parka. From my vantage point, her fourteen year old eyes were cold-blooded and ruthless.

I watched her work the street. I watched a homeless man give a calculating look at a woman he couldn't afford. I watched her flip him off when his back was turned. I watched her get into a purple Camaro. The purple Camaro drove a hundred yards, then parked in an alley. Ah, the old hand job in an alley.

Don't ask me the going rate. Just because I work on the streets doesn't mean I live on them. The last time I was curious, I was new to the streets, and spending money that way struck me as foolish and deadly.

But it was hand job interruptus when a San Francisco garbage truck came down the alley the wrong way. Like all garbage trucks in the City and County of San Francisco, after dark he drove like he had the right-of-way over all but emergency vehicles. He was determined to go the wrong way down the alley, and no out-of-towner scoring a hand job was going to slow him down or keep him from his appointed rounds.

The garbage truck leaned on its horn, and the sound was like a locomotive blowing through a cloistered nunnery. He had a route, a schedule, and zero sympathy for anyone parked in his path. He blasted his horn and hit his high beams, and his high beams lit up the purple Camaro's interior like klieg lights at a Hollywood premiere. He blared his horn, he sat on his horn until all the apartment dwellers above the alley on either side were screaming for the purple Camaro to back out and let the garbage truck through so they could go back to sleep, goddammit! The purple Camaro had no choice but to back out of the alley. Once he pulled backwards into the street, and the garbage truck had swung around him, loudly cursing him all the way, the driver of the purple Camaro kicked Cheryse Geneva's skinny ass out.

Cheryse Geneva stood on the street again, staring at the long shadows that were everywhere. She looked as desperate and lonely as the country & western music sounded that was coming from the deserted laundry mat behind her.

Time passed like a gallstone. I watched two transvestites kiss. I watched pigeons pecking at road kill. I watched a drunk in a wheelchair cruising down the middle lane of O'Farrell Street.

The night got colder. Hotel flags were snapping to attention from the winds off the ocean. The winds pressed her parka against her dress. She stood at the bus stop like a victim waiting for a villain. She held hot coffee from a fast food outlet and sipped it as if it were the Holiest Sacrament.

An empty bus after midnight came down the street and stopped in front of her. The bus had a placard on its flank that said Use Condoms. She walked from the bus stop, huddled in her whore's dress, her thin parka.

A drunk got off the bus, looked around and licked his lips at the sight of her, and tried to hustle her. He looked twenty-two years old. He was apple-cheeked and had blonde hair. Had the California surfer look down pat. He probably lived in blue jeans and T-shirts. And he tried to hustle her. But something was wrong, and he wasn't right, and she tried brushing him off. He tried copping a feel, and she pushed him aside and off her. Snarling and growling, the drunk came at her with hatred and blood-lust. He didn't see her whip out her stun gun and zap him.

She stunned him good. He lay on the sidewalk, clutching his face, and howled with the misery and the pain of a wounded animal. She zapped him again, just a quickie, to scatter his brains, then left him quivering alone on the cold concrete.

She walked uphill, into the shadowy recesses of a residence hotel, and watched him drag his maimed body downhill. She stayed long after he was gone.

When she no longer felt hunted, she came out from the shadows like a coyote comes down from the hills. Nobody noticed, or seemed to care, and quickly all was quiet and cold again. In the long hours of night, what is five minutes?

Stiff gusts of wind began blowing in before Last Call, and those nightly breezes off the ocean turned mean-spirited. Still not a dollar or a dime to be found. Work the streets every night, and you know soon enough some nights are like that. Lonely nights, when the only thing on the streets is the wind.

She had a long night of nothing happening. She worked to 3 AM, an hour past Last Call, until even the drunk bartenders had found their way home. Then she flagged a cab and left the streets.

The cab took Jones to Golden Gate Avenue, then crossed Market, and took 6th to Harrison. Then the cab climbed onto the 101 freeway south at 7th Street. Only a handful of cars were up there at this hour. The cab and I rode awhile through a sleeping city, then we both left the 101 freeway south at the Candlestick exit.

But we didn't hang left and cross over 101 to reach the 'Stick or Hunter's Point. Instead we bore right and took Old Bayshore Boulevard and the Cow Palace turn-off that led down into the housing projects that were Vivisection Valley. We wound down the long curving road until Old Bayshore Boulevard was jabbed in the side by San Bruno Boulevard. The cab didn't have the green light, but goosed itself through the yellow light, and I caught the red light in all her car-stopping glory. I gritted my teeth and watched the cab turn onto Visitacion Avenue and disappear.

Once I got on Visitacion, the empty cab came from a street four blocks up, and he passed me going the other way like a bat out of hell; he was deadheading back downtown, I guessed, or maybe out to the airport. Sure, a cab is like a hooker; it only makes money when it's on the streets. But answering a radio call down here was downright dangerous, and the fastest way to die in San Francisco was to pick up somebody here off the streets who was flagging you down.

The fourth city block led directly to Vivisection Towers. The front doors were locked and chained, but a service entrance on one side gaped like an open sore. I looked all around, I saw no signs of life anywhere, but that was no comfort.

I guess I was both amazed and depressed. Mario Rosales's last best place to hide was Vivisection Towers. He and his girlfriend were squatters in a derelict housing project. Boy, had they hit rock-bottom.

The service entrance door moved with the wind. I couldn't imagine anyone in his right mind walking through that door. Behind that door death waits.

Any cop will show you dozens, maybe hundreds, in the City. The dispatcher gives them a call at this address, that address, any one of those addresses, and the cops drive up, stop, stare, lock their doors and wonder why they should go open that door, why they should step inside, wonder why they should hear that door clang! shut behind them.

They think about their families, try to remember when they last kissed their babies good-bye, wonder if that was too long ago to count, and wonder if they should take this final fatal stroll.

They know the chance they take. They have done it before, swallowed their pride and their fright, and walked that lonely walk through those long shadows on a deserted street on a moonless night and walked through that door.

They didn't die then. They might not now.

They might not now.

I looked around to see if any of the long shadows had sprouted arms or legs or handguns. This was the heart of Vivisection Valley, if it had a heart. And what was on these streets at this time of night was no different than those punks who killed Old Pete and tried killing his son.

I should go home, I thought. I could have a couple beers, watch Movies 'Til Dawn, I'd be fine and dandy.

I felt I stood out. Hell, I thought, I wouldn't stand out more if I were buck-naked blindfolded holding a handful of hundred dollar bills. Christ, I was about as subtle as a blowtorch lighting a bowl of rock cocaine.

I didn't look like a potential crack customer. No, I looked like a sucker. A dumb jerk saying, steal my car and dump my body in an alley kind of sucker. These jokers here could kill me and never remember me in the morning.

I should just drive off and forget everything. I reached down and twisted the ignition key, and my car started right up. I should throw 'er in gear and get the hell outa here. Then I had another thought. If I leave my car here, it might not be here when I come out. If I came out. A C note says you won't, I told myself.

I remembered the last time I had been here. A red Eldorado had been parked in front of those front doors to hell. It had a busted right taillight. I stared at the memory of that Eldorado and saw again the two bodies thrown inside its trunk like golf bags.

Why should I enter Visitacion Towers?

I shouldn't. It would be like walking into a dragon's mouth. But I kept thinking about how Mario Rosales was the only eyewitness to whatever had happened here five nights ago.

Suppose I did go inside the Towers. Whatever happened in there was final. There was no way out. I could expect no help. Paramedics wouldn't go in there. The Fire Department would let it burn. The cops left their cruisers locked and wore bullet-proof vests when they swept the building with their riot guns and their pepper sprays. The crews on the city garbage trucks wore bullet-proof vests until even they refused to come down here.

Together, my Browning 9 and I went in Visitacion Towers. Smashed and ravaged and charred and splintered and gutted and burned out and looted. Doesn't even matter when all this was done here, I suppose. That this housing project from Hell would end ruined like this was a foregone conclusion the day the cornerstone was set in concrete.

I don't know why the electricity was still on; maybe some squatter had reconnected the disconnected. There were still electric lights in a few hallways, though most hallways were dark from stolen bulbs and broken fixtures. Gang graffiti was scrawled on every surface. Plaster hung in shreds from the ceiling.

The elevator was out, of course, and it stank like somebody had recently taken a dump in there. I took the stairs as quietly as I could. I went up slowly, checking out each floor, one at a time, and made my way up toward the penthouse suites.

Broken glass and garbage were littered in every corridor and entirely filled some rooms. In some corridors there was a foot of rubbish, and I had to kick my way from one end to the other. Target practice with automatic weapon fire had put bullet holes in many of the walls and doors.

As I walked, I saw my breath coming out in front of me in little icy clouds. This hell on earth was ice-cold. There was a natural break in the coastal range here, and the same icy summer winds that made Candlestick Park world famous blew through these broken windows first. Fog was actually visibly curling in some corridors like wraiths from the netherworld left behind to haunt the living.

On the third floor I heard a woman's low voice. She was wheeling and dealing with a dealer. She had a hand gun to trade for a rock of cocaine. She told him she had found it behind an after-hours bar twenty minutes ago. The dealer wanted to know how hot the gun was. When she couldn't tell him, he told her to dump it in a storm drain. I kept prowling onward because these two weren't my prey.

More signs of squatters on the fourth floor, on the side away from the street. The toilets had long been smashed or stolen, and now people shit where they could here. I was careful where I walked.

On the seventh floor I heard a woman's shrill voice. She was angry. I crept close and saw a mother berating her mentally retarded daughter for wasting all the mayonnaise. The mother must have weighed a hundred pounds. Her daughter was in her late forties, was weeping, and must have weighed three hundred.

I reached the ninth floor. Down at the end of the hallway a luminous glow came from a Coleman camp light. A shadowy figure was lighting candles. I saw a cooler near the window. Beside it was a stained foam pad big enough for two sleeping bags. On the other side of the pad, a small microwave oven sat on an overturned cantaloupe crate.

I saw Mario Rosales. I came closer, and I saw the fresh stitches on the ugly red wound on his neck from the bullet that had narrowly missed his jugular vein. He was wearing a T-shirt under an oversized flannel shirt, and baggy pants he could hide a litter of puppies in. I see kids like him hanging out in the malls and movie theaters all over California. Good kids, all of them, or almost all of them. Restless and eager, they had wants and hopes. And I hesitated.

I reminded myself that Mario Rosales was all punk. That he was a fugitive and the cops wanted him for murder. That he had no conscience and was all trouble. I tightened my grip on my Browning, took a deep breath, and steeled myself for trouble.

I saw Cheryse Geneva up close. Her blue zombie eyes and her corn-silk hair were in my face, breathing hard on me, and my Browning was useless with my wrist grabbed like this and stretched out away from her.

"Que pasa, hombre?" she said. She was pale and tight-lipped. She smelled of fresh strawberries.

I made no move against her. She held a stun gun inches from my face. She punched it for several seconds, and a blue arc of electricity streaked out of the dark.

"You're the boss," I said.

She took my Browning. She held it like a brick and smashed me in the side of the face, and when I jumped for her throat, she zapped me down to the concrete. I stayed down because for the longest time I couldn't breathe. I told myself I'd pitch her out an open window given half a chance. We were nine floors up. That was high enough.

Once I was okay again, she held the gun in one hand and the zapper in the other, and I rose to my feet like a ballerina amid broken glass. She pushed me into the camp light's glow. Mario Rosales heard us coming. Startled, he jumped to his feet.

Mario hissed. "What's he doing here?"

Cheryse frisked me, picked my pockets, field-stripped my wallet, and stole nearly two hundred dollars of my money. "He saw me downtown working," she said. "He must of followed me."

He was bigger than I had remembered. His shoulders were broader and his chest was deeper than I had remembered. Lots of red meat and vitamins keep making the next generations bigger. Hell, he was fourteen, but he looked seventeen, maybe eighteen. Maybe he just had a growth spurt.

Mario Rosales swallowed hard and steeled himself to do harm. He stuck a shiny new Glock 17 in my face. "I should blow you away," he said. That's when he actually thought about what he was saying. "I didn't want to blow away nobody," he regretted. And his voice cracked. Nothing like puberty in a gunman to make me tread more cautiously.

And yet . . . And yet I thought I saw him differently, with new eyes. The kid was standing in front of me, but his eyes were huddled in a corner, like a pile of dirty laundry that missed the hamper toss, like a homeless woman huddling in a sleeping bag to stay warm.

No one who has ever known me has ever accused me of being a pollyanna. I've worked the streets long enough to know pollyannas on the streets die quicker than first lieutenants on the battlefield. And yet . . .

He was still a kid. He still had the wide eyes of a young boy who was now neck-deep in more trouble than he had ever been in before. He was scared shitless.

I'm the father of two boys. I looked at him--into him--and I saw my boys. In both cases, I saw boys growing up without a father in the house. I pushed aside my own regrets and pushed aside my own better judgment and concentrated on the boy at hand.

"What's the real story, Mario? What happened outside here?"

"We gotta blow, Mario, 'fore someone else finds us," she said.

I got bold and up-front with him. "I came to help you, Mario. Help you see why you gotta turn yourself in, before some nasty cop with a hard-on for you blows away you or Cheryse."

She banged me across the back of my head. I think she wanted to bang some sense into my head. Thank God she didn't have the same upper body strength as Mario. She could have killed me if she had the strength to do what she wanted done.

"We got to take care of you, Mario," I said, not daring to slow down the jive.

"Your grandmother made me promise to get hold of you and save your ass."

"My grandmother," he said. His eyes said he didn't trust me.

"She loves you and wants you home."

"I ain't going home to her!"

"Don't you want to think for a moment about going back home?"

He thought I was nuts. "Fuck Rehab," he said. "I been there three times."

"What do you got here that's so much better than home?" I dared.

Cheryse rolled her eyes. She knew I was a fool. A growl came from her throat. She wanted me circumcised with a chainsaw.

His jawline went stubborn and set. "It's okay here."

"I talked with your grandmother," I said. "She loves you." Watching his disbelief grow, I felt my spirits sink further. But I pressed on. "She doesn't want you dead, Mario. She wants you alive and smiling and healthy and sitting beside her even if it's just Visiting Hours. She doesn't care if you're wearing a red jump suit and shackles. She loves you and wants you alive and wants to fight for you. You stay here, you get cremated by Welfare money and your ashes get dumped in Potter's Field and all she gets is a lousy photograph on top of the TV set to remember you by, and she wants more than that, Mario. She loves you."

He flinched. For an instant he was a kid in pain getting chewed out by an adult, and he blinked fast, and the kid in pain was gone, replaced by an android's smooth features, the kind I saw all the time in Juvenile Court.

"What about his mom?" Cheryse Geneva asked.

"His mom's in jail for a two year old burglary charge for which she failed to appear."

Mario didn't seem to care about that. "You don't know my grandmother."

"You live by Point Avisadero. On a clear day you got a view of downtown. You got a rusty bike with two flat tires chained to her front porch, and your grandmother's got a plastic leg that screws on and off."

Cheryse was taken aback. "Gross!"

They didn't exactly release me. More like, they stopped holding me so tightly. I had a chance to take a closer look around their scatter. They were camped out in a squatter's apartment. I thought about what it must be like coming down from a drug-high and finding yourself here. Being straight here was like living in the House of Usher on a bad day.

"Why here?" I asked.

He gestured behind him. "That toilet still flushes."

I was sympathetic. Mario Rosales was a fourteen year old who had lived too hard and seen too much. Ambushed by drug dealers. Patched up and then snuck out of the hospital. On top of all that, now he was a cornered fugitive living on Vienna sausage from a can and cold PopTarts while his girlfriend had to go out hooking. Ask him what he was most afraid of. A gang out to get him? The cops who wanted him? T'aint easy being Mario Rosales today. No wonder he had holed up here, exhausted.

I looked at his lady love Cheryse. Like most teenagers, she acted sullen, and she reminded me of a gargoyle on a ledge above a cathedral. I had no problem with that. Teenagers are small children with big hormones.

"Do you get coked up here?" I asked her.

"Can't get it," Cheryse said. "No money."

I didn't bother asking if they'd get cracked up if they could buy some. Crack would make anybody forget how ugly and short their life looked here.

I was suspicious. "Why did you shoot those two white guys?"

I saw the flesh whiten on Mario Rosales's throat wound.

"He didn't kill nobody!" Cheryse said.

"I was set-up."

Yeah, you and everybody else.

"Who hired you to shoot 'em?" I asked.

"Nobody," Mario said.

"Who hired you to shake down the old man and his kid?"

"Nobody!"

"Who was the boss?"

"You talk about Mad Dog," Cheryse told him.

He wet his lips. "He's dead. I saw him buy it."

"Who was Mad Dog?" I asked.

Cheryse told me, "Mad Dog was a bastard man. He killed a man with a runny nose for snorting his powder. Let that fucker die forever!"

"He sold rock all over the City," Mario said.

"But he bought it here at the Towers," I said.

"Yeah." His eyes backed away from me.

I surprised him. "I don't give a shit who sold it to him, or who he turned around and sold it to." I gave pause, to start another angle. "What went down outside here?"

"What went down . . ." He swallowed hard, not wanting to confess more than what he needed, but wanting desperately to get it all out. The effort to both spill his guts and keep his yap shut left him speechless and frustrated.

"--was a carjacking?" I asked

"The car was free to us, man, so we took it!"

"You were just out scoring rock," I disbelieved.

"Yeah!"

"You're not straight with me," I threatened.

"I swear, yes."

"Why did you kill the old dude in the trunk?" I asked.

"Never knew he was in the trunk, man."

"Who hired you?"

"I got no job," Mario Rosales said. "I wasn't doing nothing!" he insisted. "I was following Mad Dog. I was there to look big, look tough. I wanted to sit in the car, play with the buttons on the dashboard. He made me come upstairs here and watch him buy rock."

"You were s'posed to look like back-up muscle?"

"Yeah! Everything inside goes down cool. We make the buy, they're all friends, high-fives and see ya soon, bro. We get outside, and the air lights up with bullets flying at us. I got shot, he gets killed, I go to SF General."

"What was Mad Dog's real name?"

"I don't know. He liked being called Mad Dog."

What can you say about anybody who likes calling himself Mad Dog? The dumb fuck defames himself. Just asking to be shot down in the streets.

"Who drove the Eldorado to the Towers?"

"I did," the boy said.

"Is that how you got involved?"

"I'm the one that parked it there."

I grinned. "Wrong spot, right?"

"I didn't know the space was reserved," Mario Rosales swore. "I would never park there, 'cept it was empty."

"How come you drove?"

"I was the designated driver."

"Fourteen years old, right?"

He had a lopsided grin. "I don't do rock when I drive. Mad Dog and the guys can get fucked up and still get home okay. Somebody gotta make sure we get home okay."

"Where did you start off from?"

"From the Sunshine Apartments."

I kept cool. "Mad Dog lived there?"

"That's one place where he sells. He got a place there, another one on Rose Alley, and another on Dolores."

"How did you get the Eldorado?"

"We found it. It was double-parked in front of Mad Dog's car with its windows down, the key was still in the ignition, the engine running. There was a raggedy twenty dollar bill on the floor mat. We check it out, shit, we took it for a ride."

The equation was simple, in his mind. "Free car. Free ride."

"Did you know the old white dude who owned it?"

"I seen him at Sunshine Apartments. Old white dude."

"Did he ever talk to you?"

"Never."

"What did you think when you saw his Caddy there?"

He puzzled over that. Finally: "Free car. Free ride."

"Did you check the trunk before you drove it?"

He scowled like I was crazy, but he spoke wistfully. "You always check your trunk before you drive a car?"

"Did you shoot him?"

"Never!"

"Do you know who did?"

"No."

I thought back to the first time I came down here, the scene of the crime that it was, walking through it with Captain Banagan. The red Eldorado with the two bodies in the trunk. I kept seeing that busted taillight in my mind. Let the cops pull it over. And I saw how the deal went down. It was all slicker than ice on glass.

"You were set up," I said.

He agreed. "I was set up."

Why did I believe they were set up?

The busted taillight.

Cops love busted taillights. A busted taillight legitimizes stopping John Q. Public and checking him out. Ted Bundy got caught because cops stopped him for his taillight. The busted taillight is probably the most cost effective piece of cop equipment cops got in the never-ending fight against crime.

The rock hounds were just patsies. Too stupid for words and therefore dumb enough to take a fall. They went joyriding in a stolen car. They were supposed to get stopped by the police. Did you know you had a taillight busted? May we see your registration please? Please step out of the car. Pop that trunk, son. And then they would go away to prison forever. A deaf, dumb and blind DA could put those fools away. Who would believe them? Even the Public Defender's Office wouldn't.

"Why did you run from San Francisco General Hospital?"

"The electric chair," Mario said.

"It's the gas chamber in this state."

He knew it was something evil. "I'm sitting there, and nobody told me nothing. They told me who I was, and I was in trouble. A million dollars bail! I told them they was wrong. They said I was lying. I was causing trouble. They know what I done. They wasn't listening when I said I didn't do nothing."

Cheryse was watching him, her chin trembling, fighting back the tears, having a cigarette.

"Who set you up?" I asked.

"I don't know who."

I snickered. Who wouldn't want to get rid of Mad Dog? Everybody wants to get rid of the rock man. Cops. Other dealers. Scammers. Bangers. Rock heads looking for free rock. Straights.

"Did he have any face-to-face enemies?"

"One he talked about. Some chump he fucked from South Bay, San Jose maybe. Mad Dog got him busted because he owed the chump money and didn't want to pay him."

"He framed the guy?"

"Yeah. The guy got San Bruno time, not hard time, but he was gone six, seven months. That's something."

I called bullshit on that. "Misdemeanor time anybody can do standing on their heads. Snitching on anything less than felony time is stupid."

Mario glowered, a habit he probably didn't know he had. "The dude was s'pose to do long time, be a three time loser and never get parole, but the DA dropped it down in plea bargaining, 'cause the jail's too full with three-time losers."

"So Mad Dog's snitch didn't hold."

"Man, it snapped."

"What was the chump's name?"

"Mad Dog called him the Spaniard. He wasn't Spanish, just another Mexican that got some money, so now he called himself Spanish, not Mexican. Don't know his name. One tough dude, I heard. Mad Dog was scared of him."

"What did he look like?"

"Mean." Mario was glum. "I never seen him."

"Where does Cheryse come into it?"

I saw how they looked at each other, and I saw hopeless love that was doomed from the start.

She spoke up. "Yo te quiero mucho," she told him.

I swallowed hard. "La mona, aunque se vista de seda," I quoted. I broke off seeing Mario's face in obvious pain. "Where'd you two lovebirds meet?"

"We was in Juvie together. Then I seen him a prisoner over at Mad Dog's."

Surprised, I looked at Cheryse again. "Why were you there?"

Mario talked for her. "Mad Dog made women have sex with him to score rock. He never gave no free drugs. Her pimp wanted some rock, so him and Mad Dog made Cheryse have sex with me, and they watch us. She help me 'scape once, but I still got caught and had to go back."

"How did you help him escape?"

She was proud of herself. "Broke a window."

According to her, Mario was held captive by Mad Dog, allowed a single meal a day, and had to sleep in a room whose windows were boarded up and whose door was often nailed shut.

"How long were you a prisoner? Three months, right?"

He nodded. "If I 'scaped again, Mad Dog said he knew where my mother lived. Where could I go? I don't try no more."

"Your mom and the cops say you sold crack," I said to the boy.

"He sold crack so his mom can keep her house and not be homeless."

"I liked the dough," he admitted. "But if I don't sell rock, I don't get food."

They waited for me to answer.

I caught on. I was an adult, a grown-up, and the children were waiting for me to answer them. We all knew they wouldn't listen to me and my words. They knew an adult's answer was no solution to their problems. They knew adult answers involved too much up-front pain, and they were children who still believed good things can come true, if you just wish it hard enough. If you close your eyes real tight and click your heels three times and say, "There's no place like home," you could go home again. But childhood is a jockey who rides on a paper horse. Nobody rides the paper horse for long; there's too much rain.

We locked eyes, Mario and me. I wanted him to turn himself in to the police. I recognized the look in his eyes, and I knew from all my experiences on the street he never would. He was doomed and both of us knew it. I wondered if Cheryse knew it, but then she was a fourteen year old hooker, and she was more doomed than he was.

"What do you want, Mario?" I asked. I talked like a big brother, not a father. "No bullshit. No preaching, no sermons. What do you want?"

He looked at Cheryse, and she looked back. He licked his dry lips and looked at me. "Me and Cheryse go to Mexico, my family's village. In Mexico I don't live like this."

"You're fourteen years old."

"In Mexico I'm fourteen years old. In San Francisco I'm gone be tried as an adult for nothing I did."

"Don't you worry about those Vivisection shooters here?"

"They don't live here now," he said. "The cops want them so bad, they cleared out and won't come back."

"That means this place is up for grabs," I told him. "Soon somebody is going to want this turf, and there will be gunfire and the air will be filled with stray bullets and innocent people will die."

"We can leave now," he said. "Got nothing holding us."

"You can stay and get your name cleared."

He scoffed at that nonsense. "I can't defend myself here. If I win, I still go to jail forever. In Mexico we get a new start."

"You need cash to blow town. So who you gonna call?"

"We gonna be all right."

"Right." I thought of the American Dream: a fresh start in a new land. "If you went to Mexico, you can never come back to the states."

"I never want to come back here."

"You can never come back!"

He truly understood this time. "Por tola vida!"

I agreed. "Until the end of time."

He gave me a kid's goofy grin. "Going this way I don't got to sneak across the border in the dead of night."

"Are you going to steal a car to get to Mexico?"

He did not look at me.

"You'll have cops every step of the way."

"I die if I stay here."

The night outside our window erupted with the sound of gunfire, random shots fired into the darkness. Automatic weapons fire shattered the window and punctured the walls and the ceiling. A second swarm of bullets burst through the windows and chewed up the ceiling and the walls, and plaster chips fell like hailstones on us.

Cheryse grabbed up the stun gun. She touched my arm and jolted me. The touch lasted forever, only a fraction of a minute, and I thought I was having a heart attack. I bellowed and screamed, and as I fell to the floor, echoes ricocheted throughout the cavernous hall.

Cheryse Geneva zapped me again. While I lay writhing, Mario Rosales and Cheryse then grabbed what they could-- including my two hundred dollars--and took off running. They could have killed me easily enough, but they didn't. Nowadays that makes them the good guys.

When I could stand, I climbed to my feet. I went to the window. I thought I saw the two running from the building toward the far shadows behind the other tower. They disappeared into Vivisection Valley. Romeo and Juliet on the run. I wished them good luck. I knew they had none coming.

I searched their love nest and found they had left most of their belongings behind them, along with several piles of garbage. Those belongings included all her trick outfits and a sawed-off .12 gauge Remington 870 shotgun.

I wrapped the shotgun in a whore's chemise, careful not to smudge any fingerprints. I couldn't leave the shotgun here. It would be gone before I reached my car.

Two days later at Molly's Donuts I read in The San Francisco Examiner that a teenager was shot and killed by a San

Diego police officer during a struggle as the officer attempted to arrest him and a teenage girl for allegedly stealing a car.

The two teenagers, both fourteen, were stopped at 3:30 a.m. when the officer noticed them driving with a busted taillight. The officer's computer reported the car had been stolen. While he tried to handcuff the driver, the girl attacked the officer with a stun gun.

During the struggle, the officer's gun discharged once, striking the boy in the head. The boy was taken to San Diego Medical Center and pronounced dead on arrival. The girl was booked at the San Diego Juvenile Hall for auto theft. The San Diego police did not identify the youths or the officer to the newspaper.

Polk Street

Polk Street was bright and gay. A street fair. Sidewalk vendors with pottery and leather, stained glass, and wood planters. Gays walking hand in hand. Curious straights. Crowds and laughter and balloons. Jugglers and mimes and fire-eaters performing for one and all. Police sawhorses kept away the traffic, and folks mingled for seven blocks.

A leather boutique was having a fashion show on the street. The chichi models struck poses like Joan of Arc and strutted like poodles past the plate-glass store windows, hoping to cast just the right reflection.

A jazz club with a Sunday matinee had its front windows open wide, and the curious were lined up along the sidewalk. A record promoter wandered through the crowd passing out hand-sized Frisbees. The small black discs flew up from the crowd like shooting stars going home.

Waldo Burl had his executive suite in a two-story office building across from the Catholic Church. The storefront downstairs was a barbershop filled with old men who smoked cigars. They spent a lot of time watching the Polk Street parade.

Waldo Burl had moved here three or four months ago, shortly after Larry Flynt, the Hustler publisher, had been shot while leaving a Georgia courthouse. The shooting had left Flynt paralyzed from the waist down. An ironic twist for a pornographer.

Waldo Burl was a pornographer and a worrier. He worried about organized crime and religious foundations, the law and former employees, women's groups and competitors. He refused to take any more chances. He took all his calls here now. His secretaries transferred them from his Off Broadway address, just as they kept track of his appointments, most of which were just a quick cab ride away.

Paranoia, it seems, is a social disease.

I jiggled the doorknob. It was locked with a dead bolt, but a razor-tipped ice pick blade from my wallet opened it. I went inside.

There was little furniture in his two-room apartment. A couple of soft chairs. His refectory table with telephones, pads of paper, files and time sheets, and a clock radio. There was a long sofa against one wall, a wormy roll-top desk against another. There were a few Woolworth nudes and some old-time cinema posters. There was no one around.

"Anybody home?"

The rooms were silent. Maybe Burl's paranoia again.

And then I heard the unmistakable click of an automatic pistol being cocked. It came from the bathroom in the other room. "It's Michael Brennen," I called.

The bathroom door opened slightly.

Waldo stuck his head out. "I'll be out in a minute."

I sat at his desk. It was covered with his private papers. I started reading them.

Waldo closed the door and a toilet flushed.

In his own words, Waldo was an over-the-hill fruit. Two dozen years in the Bay Area had made him practically a native Californian. He drove Porsches and skied Bear Valley, neither very well. He was obnoxious with charm, and he made three hundred grand a year from his beaver features.

Waldo was about my height, maybe two decades older than me, and about half my weight. He would never make it as a tough guy, except with small children frightened by his cadaverous features and his fanatical seriousness. He was sallow and anemic, and there were gaunt hollows below his cheeks. His eyes were always red and Watery. His limbs were long and bony, without flesh or muscle. The only gaiety left was his sexual preference.

He'd been dieting for years, just trying to keep his ghoulish figure. So long, in fact, to retain his youthful slenderness, that he wasn't aware he'd look like a vulture any day now. Already people asked if he were trying to starve to death.

His hair was pompadoured and waxy. A dull tangerine from too much coloring, processing, dyeing, and bleaching. It was phony-looking, but it was real. His friends wished it were a toupee. He had a few good years left, as long as the money chase and the young male hookers treated him gently.

Waldo Burl knew all about runaways. Once upon a time he'd been a bounty hunter for their parents. He had opened up shop during the Summer of Love, a one-man agency that specialized in runaways.

Most private investigators back then started hunting runaways by calling the drug clinics and the hospitals, the morgue, and the mental wards. Waldo worked the Haight exclusively.

He'd smoke joints with young runaways, rap with them, run through their activities and their life-styles, find out their past histories, and then track back to their parents. He'd call up "back home" and say their kid had asked him to tell the folks how he or she was doing. Often enough he'd get a commission from the parents to send their little child home.

Waldo had a phenomenal success rate. He made good money during those years too, until he was hounded out of business by the SFPD, who misinterpreted his motives. He always claimed he was just maximizing survivors, saving all that he could, and just bringing out the wounded. Most pee eyes in the city criticized him, but I never did. He had a high survivor rate. He'd saved enough lives to justify his pipsqueak claims.

But the years had taken their toll on Waldo. Times changed and fads grew rough-Waldo had problems maintaining his cover. Dope razored his morals. He slipped up several times, then found he had a terrible downer habit. Too much dope had also made him sleazy.

Five years ago Waldo turned to writing fuck books for five hundred bucks a manuscript. Then he became a publisher of nudie magazines. They cost him seventy cents each and retailed for ten bucks.

His distributor told him that two million people go to porno films every week and that he could double his investment in eighteen months. Waldo invested and tripled his within the first year.

Waldo turned to the production of beaver features. He started with seven-minutes loops and mail order. Some folks might've expected him to specialize in hard core chicken movies, but he never filmed man and boy unless girl and woman were included. His actors and actresses received thirty bucks a day and a share of the profits. Gradually he went Super-8 and color. His films grew longer.

Now he shot full length in 35 millimeter and Dolby sound. His budgets often approached a hundred thousand dollars. He made three versions of each film-Hard-core, soft-porn, and some with an R rating for the overseas audiences. He even supplied versions in video cassettes for folks at home.

Waldo finally came from the bathroom.

I was reading his time sheets.

He had a devilish grin. "Michael, it's been years. So good to see you." He wasn't bothered that I was behind his desk. He sat on his sofa and set his pistol beside him.

"Push it farther away," I said.

He did so. Then, for a moment, he admired me. "I heard you opened up your own shop."

I looked up. "I heard that myself."

"Do you really want all that competition?"

"Are you going to trip over my feet again?"

"Now, Michael, you know I wasn't tripping over you. Just some cases get out of hand now and then. And of course I don't do pee-eye work anymore, but then one doesn't know, does one, what the future will bring."

"I'm here to bribe you." I threw the pound of weed on his desk.

He glared at me, but he wouldn't touch the dope. "How much is there?"

"About a pound," I said. "I haven't weighed it. No PCP. No paraquat. Just good old-fashioned Mexican regular."

He was flabbergasted and speechless.

I said nothing. The pound has been an albatross on me for too long. Just getting rid of it might be absolution.

He stiffened. "It's hot," he guessed.

"I've had it for months now. Evidence that was never needed. Nobody knew I had it."

"It's not hot? Why give it to me?"

I leaned back in his chair. "I want to keep it above board with us. I'm here on business."

"You don't want to get personal," he guessed.

I threw him the dope. "You got it."

"Michael, why do you always talk to me this way?"

"You're a snitch," I said. "I always talk to snitches like this." I shrugged. It made sense to me.

"I'm not a snitch!"

"Waldo, you've compromised people."

He drew back. "That's an insult."

"You compromised your own lover. What was his name again? The one who said he wanted to marry you. The one who was willing to sign a premarital contract so you'd never have to pay him alimony."

Waldo looked remorseful. "His name was Harry."

I grinned. "An apache dancer from a gay cabaret. You thought Harry was a dream come true. Until you caught him selling your Valium. And what did you do? Setting him up like that in the post office."

"He was a thief," Waldo insisted. "There's a difference between being a witness to the commission of a crime and being a snitch."

"Yes, there is," I said. "And you're a snitch."

He paused. "Open your jacket."

"I'm not wired," I said. "And it's not from the Mob, so you don't have to worry about poison. And I don't think the CIA's after you, so you can forget about them, too."

Waldo didn't get hostile. He opened the plastic Baggie and took a deep whiff. Satisfied, he leafed through the weed. He nibbled part of a bud. Satisfied, he resealed the Baggie and looked up. "What do you want to know?"

"It's about one of your films."

He was amused. "Which one?"

"A Rock Star's Honeymoon."

His forehead wrinkled. "A Super-8, right? God, I almost forgot that one. I made it last February, March, maybe. Only spent a day on it. I had cash-flow problems at the time."

"Tell me about Cherokee Sioux."

Waldo stared at me. "She's been in many films for me. Shit, she's so shallow, Michael, you couldn't wet your baby toe on her."

"What's her real name?"

Waldo claimed he didn't know. "Her social security card says Cherokee Sioux. Maybe she got another social security card, and maybe she didn't want to be traced by Welfare."

"How did she get her name?"

"I suppose she made it up herself. She was from West Virginia, or maybe Kentucky. Maybe she's got some Cherokee blood in her. Or her first name is Susan."

"Waldo, what's her name?"

He realized how serious I was. "Susan Hubbard." He was curious. He chewed on his lower lip. "Why her? C'mon, Michael, tell me."

"Where does she work when she doesn't work for you?"

"Some stroke joint down in the Loin."

"Do you remember the name of the massage parlor?"

He shook his head. "She never told me."

"Tell me everything she ever said to you."

Waldo had a great memory. "It was just a job. A steady job. The men are either pathetic or absurd. She doesn't mind it. It's her body, after all—she can do with it what she wants. Mostly she gets by, but she's had five-hundred-dollar weeks. She doesn't get emotionally involved with it. She said she'll stop doing it someday."

"What've they got her doing down there?"

"Sucking and stroking, she said. A power trip, she told me. She's always in control. She gets the money and watches them squirm. She said men look ridiculous lying on a table just about to come."

"What kind of shape is she in?"

He considered. "She's a very well-adjusted woman these days," he said. "She's very casual. Amused at making money this way. She said she feels all middle class."

"How long have you known her?"

"Eight, nine years, I guess." He counted the years in his mind. "Oh, no, more than that. It was back in the Haight. The Summer of Love. Her parents hired me to track her down. She had dropped out of junior college and come west to San Francisco."

I said nothing. Heather had lived in the Haight too. Maybe there was a connection. Two kids from the Haight. Maybe it was just a coincidence. A lot of people passed through the Haight in its heyday.

"I found her too late," Waldo went on. "She was already a burnout. She wouldn't come home." He looked expectant.

"That's not worth a pound of weed. Give me the details."

He thought back. "She must have moved out here in '66, I guess. She was living in some crash pad on Stanyan Street. You know what they were like. A dozen transients spreading sleeping bags around like VD. She was living on thirty cents a day. Thirty cents went a lot further then than it does now. A head of lettuce and a loaf of white bread. Chicken necks and cornbread. Lettuce sandwiches to stay alive. Her brains were fried. Brains like a kitten. Pleasant chick, Michael, but she needed help wiping her nose. Another lost child. That was the sixties."

I remembered the sixties. Half my clients at Pac Con were parents desperately trying to decipher their children. Why did my kid drop out and run off with the sixties circus? I never knew any polite answers. They were all salt in their wounds. How do you answer when they wonder how their kid could become a hairy savage?

"Was she simpleminded?"

"Oh, God, yes. She thought acid was way out. She got fucked up on it. For a time she was as smart as a vegetable. A real spaced chick. Everywhere except on the streets of course.

Even a pea brain like her could see how tough they were. But then she just disappeared for a few years. I heard somewhere she went back to Kentucky, West Virginia, wherever she was from."

"When did you see her next?"

He considered that. "About five years later. She was dancing topless up on Broadway. She was a good dancer. She could have been great, but she didn't care. She danced like a robot most of the time. It was calisthenics. She was fired from the job because she was so sluggish. A couple of months later I got a phone call from her. She had committed herself for psychiatric observation at Presbyterian Hospital." Waldo pursed his lips for a moment, then shrugged. "She fell down hard. All the way down. She was trying to stay out of jail. She was there four, five weeks. When she came out she came to see me. She needed money, and I gave her some of course."

"Of course," I said.

He knew a punch line too. "She told me she had fallen in love with somebody she met inside there. Somebody from the women's wards."

We stared at each other. "Was she a lesbian?"

He assumed she was. "She tried being bi. Sometimes it worked out. I saw her once in county jail. She was crying, very suicidal. Some butches had played macho rape games with her. Women made her cry just as much as men did."

I snuck it in. "Her girlfriend?"

He brightened. "I was glad when she met Jewelie." He spelled the name out for me. "I think they met at some rock concert up in the wine country. Jewelie kept Sioux from suicide. Oh, yes, Sioux thought she was a failure as a sex object."

"What's Jewelie's full name?"

"Jewelie Trinkett." He spelled it out for me. "I don't think she was ever a virgin. Sexually she's a gymnast. While the cameras were being readied, she'd be reading the letters in Penthouse, looking for new gimmicks. The two of them had this joke about short-lived millionaires. That's Jewelie's goal. She'd get Sioux to lie down on her back, then she'd get up on top, like they were fucking, and then she'd rear back like a stallion, whap-whap, like she was slapping an old man. 'Once before you die,' she'd scream, and then they'd both fall down laughing like seagulls."

"Do you know how old Jewelie is?"

"She had a valid ID. That's all I know."

"She's fifteen, going on sixteen."

He looked surprised. "Well, I thought she was older. The way she shepherded Sioux around." He said nothing for a moment. "Michael, there are ten thousand other cock-suckers on the streets of this city who are fifteen, going on sixteen. I don't ask them their age. The law prohibits asking people how old they are. Discrimination and all that."

"Waldo, you're full of shit."

"You can call me any name in the book, but my employees get regular paychecks, disability, unemployment insurance, and social security, percentages on the gross, and Christmas bonuses. My books are always open. Do you have any idea how rare that is in this town?"

"Don't blame the town for the way you make your living," I told him. "Some scams just last longer than others. A fifteen-year-old making fuck films. That's a no-no, Waldo. Kiddie porn is a felony in this state, pal."

He had nothing to say.

"What are their addresses?"

"I don't know where they live."

"You better find out damn fast." I grabbed and held on to my temper. "Now, not only is there a juvenile at stake, but I'm stuck in this shit, too. If you don't give me the addresses, I'll go tell the SFPD you wouldn't give them to me, and you know how they act around you. Just think of a kiddie porn trial blazoned across the headlines. A fifteen-year-old girl making fuck films. How many times have you been arrested?"

Waldo was gray as stone and stiff as a spinster. Everybody thinks about his name in the headlines. Some people more often than others. He held the Baggie in his lap as if it were a sleeping kitten.

"What are their addresses?"

His voice snapped like celery. "I don't know." He started sweating. "They live together. Sioux just moved. She wouldn't tell me where. She was always afraid of this. She didn't want the police to know where she was. She wanted payments under the table. She said the government always wants to know everything. She wanted to be invisible so she could live her life in peace and quiet."

"So you paid her under the table," I said. "You were giving her a break. You let her think that, didn't you? Of course that was a tax break for you too. Unemployment insurance, disability, social security, employee taxes. I'll bet you saved plenty under the table." I fisted his desk. "Dammit, don't you have any address at all?"

He waved a helpless arm. "They live around the Loin somewhere. I don't know where to tell you to start. She could be anywhere down there." He fell silent, lost in his worries.

I was tired and irritated. "Do you have any photos?"

He blinked twice, then went and opened a closet on the far side of the room. There were file cabinets inside. He pulled out a drawer, pawed through some files, and extracted two 8x10 glossies. When he came back my way he dropped them on his desk.

Cherokee Sioux and Jewelie Trinkett.

Close-ups. Full facials taken in front of the movie lights.

Sioux. Blond hair. A dopey smile. Eyes like Johnny Belinda's. She was dressed Chinese style, a blouse maybe.

Jewelie's face. Gaunt like a fashion model's. Her skin flawless like a teenage android. Bored. Resigned to talking to trash. Short-cropped hair and butch as hell.

The City Without People

I came up Third Street, driving with the window open and the heater on. This late, I am the only car on the dark streets in any direction. I see where the sweatshops have let their employees out for the night, and a flock of three dozen Chinese women are running for the last bus to Chinatown. An empty bus is suddenly full. It waddles off like a fattened animal.

I hang back, preferring the silence. We humans are a noisy lot. But after midnight the City is astonishingly quiet. Silence hangs like a low fog. It's so quiet, I could stare at every other car that passes me. But I am alone.

I travel at my own speed. I can synchronize myself to each and every traffic light. I can double-park at a stop sign.

I can park in the middle of the street, stretch my limbs, walk around my car, sit on a fender, and ponder like The Thinker.

If I want, I can drive the wrong way up a one-way street. There are no car horns behind me at night. No one knows. If no one knows, no one cares.

Most traffic lights are busy flashing yellow; good thing they don't get tired of their job.

I cruise slow enough to catch some lights, and silence is the norm, except for the mumble of my engine and the traffic lights ticking off their metronome ways. Those traffic lights are synchronized, perpetual motion machines, and I could hear them clicking through their changes.

I drive one-handed, my arm out the window, slouched against the door. I drive city-style, a foot on the gas, the other poised above the brake, my eyes checking the sidewalks, the shadows, for any animal movement. Shit happens quickly in the City, especially after midnight. Be prepared. Stay alive.

I am a night owl, a night crawler. I am a night person. I couldn't tell you the name, address or location of any grade school in the City. But I know the massage parlors. I don't frequent them, but I frequent some of the people who do. I even know the only honest massage parlor in town.

I love the City without people. It becomes a special place when humans have deserted it. Being out and alone at this hour is delicious. My senses are all on full alert, and I feel fully alive.

The streets are quiet tonight. Even the cops are gone to roost at their favorite donut shops. And you know it's real quiet when the cops are off the streets, not cruising like alley cats.

The City is deserted more often than most people would believe. Come downtown on a Sunday morning. Or any time after midnight and before dawn.

After Last Call the City relaxes, takes several deep breaths, stretches like a languid predator, and waits for people and the day. The pulse rate of the City becomes languid, mellow, *smooth*.

In daytime people befuddle and foul the City. They give off energy. We all get caught up in other people's lives. Be around people, and we assume part of their energy. Like osmosis, we suck in a third of the energy around us. We feed like vampires off the energy we feel around us.

In daylight City life is immediate, spontaneous, now and in our face, and we become caught up with it, and make it our own, and think this is the only way it can be.

But be ground zero with the skyline of the city after midnight. The great columns of concrete and glass thrust their defiance up to the heavens, and it is an empty gesture. The buildings are deserted. The endless beehive of lights have only the janitorial staff behind them. On the street the winds moving briskly along the empty quiet sidewalks; the sidewalks are as deserted as the streets themselves.

In the hours after Last Call your eyes widen like the owl's, and you can see more. You can see farther.

You can see better at night. The streets glow in the night. Visibility is no longer limited to the back of the head of the pedestrian in front of you, the tail lights of the car ahead of you, the pack of people around you, or the jam of traffic you have become a part of.

The City is a vaster place at night. A street is three empty lanes wide; there is so much room. At night, what with no cars in those parking spaces, the streets are two lanes wider. Look to your left, to your right. You can see every doorway.

The rear view mirror is as empty as the road ahead.

In daytime you follow the car ahead of you. In the middle of the night your eyes sweep the street looking for any movement, but for entire blocks ahead there is no one. Your eyes are on the horizon, the spot where streetlights come together.

At night you are no longer concerned with what is front of you or what is behind you. Now you focus on what goes down two blocks away; it may be the only action in the night. Visibility is determined--limited--only by topography.

You can see completely across a parking lot to its farthest corner. The commuters are gone. They are home, asleep, dreaming or grinding their teeth, however they bid their time until the daily grind begins again.

After last call the streets are smooth sailing. There's no need for jackrabbit starts or slamming down the brakes. Green lights last longer. You're not hemmed in by other cars. Where's the stress? Anxiety disappears without people. No one slows you down. You have no appointments to keep. Not even the rush to sleep anymore. Whatever claims to be important can wait for daylight. No need to concentrate, to focus in. Now you widen your focus, open yourself up to the night and the air.

Daylight is harsh. The night is less demanding. It is softer than daylight.

There is less light, so imagination stirs at this hour, perks up its ears, listens for that trigger that says go ahead! Anything can happen at night. The unknown surrounds you.

For those like me who love the night, the fear of the dark is delicious, to be relished, to be savored. There are all possibilities out there beyond the light. Yes, savor the fear. Relish it. Let your skin tingle with your fear until goose bumps come.

Be aware. Always be aware. Taunting the dark is dangerous fun. There are predators and dangers in the shadows.

The night is filled with possibilities.

With four wheels off the ground, you're not living on the streets, only cruising them. You can drive fast. You can get away.

Parking lots have horizons. Trash stands out more, looks more transient, more foreign against the relative permanence of stone and concrete and brick and asphalt. At night you can notice a piece of litter on the street, watch it flutter and fly off into the shadows. See the tall weeds under the freeway.

After last call the streets are timeless.

In daylight all is in transit and the City is a destination. Everyone is going somewhere. The goal is arrival.

But at night the City is a presence. It does not brood, nor does it bustle. The City is. It exists, inanimate, larger than life. For a being without consciousness, it overwhelms.

The City without people is real; it's alive; it feels.

"the streets of san francisco"

the streets
is locked doors & tow-away zones
an empty bus after midnight
broken glass & peeling paint

the streets
is far removed from cafe society

the streets
is the only place
where no city has a skyline

the streets
is where you couldn't make a living
even if they let you

the streets
is filled with dog shit
paper cups & gravel
alley cats & newsboys
cigarette butts

the streets
is fear
crowding you from the curb
& the streetlights
into the shadows
& dim-lit recesses

the streets
is where streetlights point you out
make you visible
a target

the streets
is where the fear of the known
outweighs

the fear of the unknown

the streets
is where curiosity
is groping the bottom of a garbage can
is where warmth
is dirty newspapers tucked into dirty pant legs
for underwear

the streets
is where cops travel in pairs
is where winos are randomly littered
in doorways
dying soused disheveled
in disgusting disfigured pride
celebrating after selling blood

in a vacant lot
an infant & his head
crushed by a rock
on a dead end street
a yellow cabbie with a machete
on his back
in a pool of his own blood
the taxi's engine rumbling
the meter clicking away
faithfully

the streets
is where the action is
& if you're smart
you'll leave the action
to the streets & someone else

the streets
is cruel.

Sunday School

The taxi rolled down the California Street hill.

"Shame you gotta work on Sunday afternoon," Naomi Lewandowski said, letting the hill do her work for her.

The passenger, a businessman in a three piece suit, stifled a yawn. "No choice. It's the only time the Hong Kong market and the London office are both open." God, do I hate Sundays, he thought.

A cable car was stopped in the intersection ahead, and tourists from both sides of Chinatown were ready to surge and board the cable car. Naomi Lewandowski left the left lane, entered the right lane.

"You'll blow the red light," the passenger warned.

Naomi said no. "The Don't Walk sign starts flashing a full fifteen seconds before the light turns red."

The taxi entered the intersection of California and Grant Streets as the light turned red and the tourists all stepped off the curb.

She squeezed through the tourists. The grip man angrily rang his bell twice at her, but she ignored it. The feud between cabbies and cable cars was as old as the City itself.

The passenger was wide awake now. "That was close!"

"Vaseline on both sides of the cab," Naomi said.

"You really know your lights," the passenger said, impressed.

"You gotta, in my business." Naomi started braking. "Just like there's no way I'm gonna get the green light down at Kearny."

She pulled ahead of the cable car and slipped back into the left lane. She hit her horn and startled the hell out of a tourist with a camcorder in the middle of the street. She eased around him, took her foot off the gas and coasted downhill.

There she could forget about parked cars pulling out in front of her and concentrate on the beautiful day in front of her. Sunday afternoon in San Francisco. Sunny blue skies, and a crisp wind off the ocean. A shame she had to work, but a good day to go for a drive.

The light turned red at Kearny. She stopped gently. She looked both ways. She had no pedestrians. She took the opportunity to check her mirrors. No one behind her, no one in her blind spot. The cable car was still a block back up the hill behind her, still loading up, and no one was passing it on the inside, heading her way downhill.

She looked ahead. The Financial District was deserted. A few cars were parked in front of the tall buildings. Except for a lone BMW coming up the street, Naomi could've shot a cannon down California Street and never scared a business suit.

She looked right on Kearny. The traffic coming up Keary was light, a half-dozen cars maybe. She knew the big blob of traffic was stuck down near Post Street, a full five blocks away, held back by synchronized lights.

The Beamer was jet black, had the sunroof open, was sitting in its left lane across the intersection from her. The Beamer was brand new, a forty grand investment, and it had flipped on its left turn signal.

"See the Beamer over there?" she asked the passenger. "He's going to cut me off when he makes his left turn."

The passenger scuttled forward, peered over the edge of the front seat. "He's going to turn in front of you?"

"Yep." She goosed the gas just enough to move the cab over the crosswalk lines.

The BMW inched closer into the turn.

"He is!"

"Not if I can help it." She looked over her shoulder at the passenger. "The Law says through traffic has the right-of way over vehicles making left turns." The BMW had its wheels cocked and had moved another inch forward and to the left.

"He is going for it!"

"As soon as the light changes." She gestured at the Beamer. "He's going to cut that corner as close as he can, as fast as he can, and flip me off when he does it."

The passenger looked down, then up Kearny. "You're going to warn him, aren't you?"

"Oh, yeah," she said. She flickered her turn signals and flashed her headlights several times at the BMW, who moved another inch left and forward.

"I don't like the Beamers," Naomi said. "Not a cabbie in town does. Those arrogant yuppie pups think just because they can buy a high performance car they know how to drive one."

The BMW moved another inch.

"He's gonna cut me off, blow past me faster than sin, and flip me off while he does it."

"He'll flip you off?"

"Guaranteed. Hey, just 'cos you got a fifty inch dick doesn't mean you haveta use it on people. But hey, try and tell the Beamer people that."

The passenger had no idea what she was talking about.

"You shouldn't own a high performance car in San Francisco, anyway. Where you gonna drive it? I mean, you get two green lights in a row, it's a miracle. Now a car like that, it's a wonderful car, but you gotta live back east somewhere to enjoy it, Nevada, Utah, maybe Montana, where you got an open road and you can open 'er up!"

She kept her left foot on the brake, and her right held the gas pedal down. The cab rumbled with power.

The passenger grew nervous, wondering what his driver was going to do.

Naomi couldn't see the Beamer driver's face, but she could see his fender throbbing, and she knew by that he was riding the brakes and goosing the gas, too.

"Is this a new cab?"

"It's a month old, a Crown Vic with the biggest V-eight Ford makes, with a double overhead cam shaft. It can carry six adults up the steepest hill in the City, and it can leave rubber at a green light."

She checked her mirrors. Still no one. As far as California Street was concerned, she and the Beamer were the only cars in the world. Out of the corner of her eye, she watched the traffic light flash the cautionary yellow for the Kearny-through traffic.

"Really embarrassing if when the light changes, he throttles down, cuts me off, then stalls in mid-curve. He knows I'll lay on the horn and make him feel like a jerk."

"Maybe he'll wait and go around you."

"He's got a BMW," she scoffed. "Beamer babies figure they can get away with murder." She started snickering, a most godawfully sinister sound in her passenger's ear.

More nervously: "Do you have to cut him off?"

She grinned. "It's my civic duty. It's the least I can do, and I always do the least I can do." She realized his concerns. "Hey, what's the point of living if you don't try to make people live by the rules?"

"God, this is a long light!"

She agreed. "But it has to let the Kearny traffic through." She looked down Kearny. No traffic coming.

The BMW cut his wheels far left; he could go no farther till the traffic light changed.

Naomi Lewandowski was getting edgy. She gripped the steering wheel with her right hand, and poised her right thumb above the horn. Her left hand was on her turn signal lever, ready to flipper it for the flashing headlights. Her left foot held down the brakes, and her right foot was juicing the gas. The cab rumbled and thundered.

"As soon as the light turns green," she mumbled.

She massaged the gas. The passenger could feel the cab pulsing and throbbing with her gas pedal. He gripped the top of the front seat in anticipation.

She backed off the gas and the brakes.

The light turned green.

She slammed the gas pedal to the floor. The cab lunged forward, left a patch of rubber.

The Beamer popped his clutch, squealed left, leaving rubber and smoke where his tires had been.

She went at the BMW to T-bone it to hell. She went thumbs-down on the horn and held it down, laid on it like she could push it through the firewall. She flippered the turn signal lever, flashing her headlights non-stop and frenzied.

The little German car spun its butt around, its tires caught fire, and the car jumped ahead like a pouncing kitten and tore off up Kearny Street.

Naomi saw fleetingly the driver inside, youthful and tanned, goofy sunglasses hiding his eyes. He flipped her off, contempt on his face, and he was gone in the blur of his own making.

As soon as he had passed her, as soon as he had committed himself irrevocably to Kearny Street, she backed off the gas, gave up on the headlights and backed off from the horn. Effortlessly she flowed around the tail of the BMW and cruised down towards the foot of California Street, unpressured.

The BMW was now committed to Kearny, going the wrong-way up a one-way street, with three lanes of traffic coming right at him.

She felt good. It was a bright sunny day. A shame she had to work, but, hey, she thought, we all have things we don't like doing. She thought warm thoughts for all poor unfortunates who had to work Sundays.

"By any chance," she asked over her shoulder, "didja hear how the Niners are doing?"

"Fog, Fog @ Nite, Rain, and Sunny Days"

Fog

Some days the fog is eggshell gray.
Some days the sun burns through the fog onto the city streets, beams down a patch of bright gold, and suddenly people and buildings have shadows.
Some days the fog never burns off completely.
Sometimes it drizzled.

Fog so thick, the golden hills around the Golden Gate Bridge were purple bruises.

This fog was giving us weather like we get 'round Christmas; we were all stressed and depressed, but there were no lights on the trees.

Fog in the fir trees, like a Japanese lithograph.

San Francisco was a windy city, and the flags in front of City Hall were all standing erect on their poles. But then flags are always erect in San Francisco. It's those constant westerlies off the ocean that keep them snapping in the breeze.

I watched long enough for the heavy rain to change to a light mist, then back again to heavy.

She was freezing from summer fog and the westerly winds, all bundled up, standing on a street corner. A jogger ran past, covered in sweat, wearing only running trunks and a t-shirt. She stared after him, disgusted.
"They're going to inherit the earth, just you wait and see," she said.

A tourist was taking pictures of the fog.

The fog hadn't burned off, and the sky was cloudy, like just before the rain starts.

August means coastal fog, with the awesome regularity that only God could create.

A stormy sky that looked pistol-whipped.

Seagulls soaring the slope, riding the updrafts along the cliffs, hovering in mid-air, on the beachside.

Offshore, a cold current that flows down from the Bering Straits.

A seagull flying through the fog down a city street.

The sky was ghost. A lobster-faced sky.
The weatherman on the car radio said lots of prevailing winds meant another storm on the heels of this one.

He lived in a pink pastel-painted duplex apartment on Dawnview Street off Burnett and Portola. But in the fog the pastels were muted, faded, and the duplex looked shabby. In this part of Twin Peaks, the fog was ground-level.

From Tiburon, the skyline was serrating the fog, and the buildings stuck up like rocks in the surf.

Hard to guess how tall buildings are in the fog.

The fog was ground-level.

The fog was thick. I couldn't see the billboard-size signs on the freeway.
The night was rainy cold and still. The fog was so thick, the Richmond Bridge was all I saw, and the only reason I saw it was because I happened to be driving across it.
Most summer mornings the fog ends two blocks east of my apartment and almost right above the old Sears store on Masonic. From there eastward is good old California sunshine, never-ending sunshine in a sky that is never-endingly blue.
How bright the fog was. I realized this still was summer. Fog that made me squint. But San Franciscans eschew sunglasses. Sunglasses were affectations of Angelinos.

It was noon, and visibility was four blocks.

Nobody sweats in San Francisco.

During the summer the weathermen xerox a week's worth of their weather forecasts and phone them in. "Coastal fog extending inland. Temperatures will range from sixties along the coast to the nineties inland."

The fog begins as cold breezes from the constant westerlies that spread out from the Golden Gateway to ease the insane heat in the Valley.

The heat in the San Joaquin Valley sucks in the cool Pacific air. Fog forms from the hot air inland meeting the cold air off the ocean. Drive up or down the inland highways, and you will see "the fingers of God" curling over the coastal range.

San Francisco is the only major break in the coastal range from San Luis Obispo to Oregon. Sometimes the fog comes in at water level, below the Golden Gate Bridge. Sometimes it tumbles like a fluffy avalanche over the Bridge.

In the summer San Francisco usually averages three days of fog, three days of sun, then three days of fog again, all the way through until Labor Day.

The fog never disappears during August. Only waits a dozen miles offshore for the Valley to heat up again. Then the hot air rises and sucks the cold air in under it.

Fog at the end of the alley. Fog that came in rivers of oyster sauce and salt sea air. Foghorns, like songbirds, fewer each year.

Blue as the summer fog at twilight, as blue as twilight itself and thicker than lamb's wool.

I looked up at the bland fog-colored sky.

Foggy streets like a foreign country.

Sometimes the fog is so thick that it becomes a wet cold mist for windshield wipers. Sometimes the mist is thick enough to convince the tourists it's raining. But the natives refuse to call it rain. It's just heavy dew, they proclaim.

Fog at noon. All day had been grey overcast, and I wondered again what had happened to summer. Christ, this is supposed to be August. Meter maids in down parkas had their scooter headlights on at noon.

Sometimes the fog doesn't burn off all day.

"Why is there fog?"

"I think because the dew point and the condensation point met."

A sea breeze came through the alleyway, rattled the brittle ivy on the brick walls. The ivy was multi-colored, had died with last autumn.

Three walls of the lot were fenced. The chain-link fence was threaded by ivy. The ivy was multi-colored, brittle and dry, having died the last season.

Golden Gate Park was dripping with fog.

I could see my breath in the cold air. Even my piss steamed.

Flags were snapping to attention from the winds off the ocean. The winds pressed her dress against her body.

See from Marin the tips of the skyscrapers above the white fog bank.

A fog advisory had been issued on the Golden Gate Bridge. The fog looked like some mad scientist movie, looked like foam spilling over the rim.

Brutal wind and rain on the bridge.

The daily sea breeze on the Bridge was an icy draught that gave me goose bumps.

The fog had come in. I couldn't see the top of the hill. It was ice-cold.

Something sinister about the fog.

Fog and wind blowing up skirts.

Fog = cold smoke-filled town.

I found sprinkles on the windshield.

One location has patchy fog and bright blue sky. On the other hand, another place has grey low clouds, and some airplane flies through the patch.

The fog in San Francisco contrasted with the hot sunshine of Orinda, Santa Rosa, Palo Alto, and the other suburbs of the City. The temperature rose a degree for every mile driven east of the Golden Gate Bridge, until Sacramento was reached, and the 100 degrees Fahrenheit mark was topped.

Fog, like another season altogether.

The City had a killer fog. The stop signs were silhouetted in the white out. The weatherman on the radio said this blizzard of cold clouds was clocked at 40 miles per hour.

Bayside fog.

On the ridge side, under fog I could see the blue sky of SF bay.

A gray car in the fog.

Tourists were frantic to find the sun.

"I need a beach," she moaned.

It was Getaway Weekend in August.

She loved the fog, she said. "I couldn't stand a regular summer. All that bright light for days and days. I couldn't take it."

Fog like a snow bank. Fog like a first snowdrift. Fog thick with raindrops, alive and growling, a wind that buffets the blue tourists.

"I always wear a hat in San Francisco. You lose a third of your body heat from your head."

Fog like a horizontal waterfall across the Golden Gate Bridge ...

Morning had brought fog and drizzle.

Rain

The day was gloomy with approaching rain.

A cyclone of scrap paper and leaves, like a butterfly in a cyclone.

Rain. At first big drops like the paw prints of a cat on the car hood. Then furious rain bounced. Raindrops that could crack the windshield. Wipers were worthless.

San Franciscans are tolerant of almost everything except long rain storms. They still drive at 75 miles per hour in the slanting rain. According to KCBS, there had been a twenty car pile-up in the South Bay and that the resultant mess would take time to clear up.

A pickup truck passed me at eighty-plus miles per hour at that exact point where a truck identical to his has moments before gone off the road into a water-filled ditch.

The best part of San Francisco is after the rain. All the cars are off the wet streets, and empty streets glisten under the streetlights. The lights of the city shine brighter. I could see across the bay, and Oakland actually sparkles like the jewel it'll never be. Even Berkeley looks cheery.

Sunny Days

San Francisco weather.

Same as yesterday. Same as tomorrow.

The TV weatherman said the radar satellite says there were no clouds in California today.

California's never-ending blue skies. The kind of day cabbies hate. Blue skies. A good day for walking.

Backing down the On-ramp

Twilight was just a darker shade of fog. I turned my car lights on and drove six blocks to the other side of Masonic and parked. I ate a burger and a shake at the Cable Car Diner on Geary between Presidio and Baker. I read the afternoon paper as a way of not thinking about Terry Danvers. Instead I thought about my marriage and the dusty "X" that marked the spot. But I didn't linger over that old news. I don't like looking back. My ex-wife hooked up with a chiropractor making a hundred grand a year in the Wine County. She had everything she ever wanted in a place God Himself always wanted to live. Me, I missed my kids.

I reached my apartment building after sundown. Truth be told, I didn't see the sun go down, but the fog had blackened. I opened my door, saw all was dark inside. I reached for the light switch.

The jolt unnerved me, sent me flying. My body slammed into the doorframe and I crashed to the carpet. The blast of pain was unnamable and awesomely intense, and I could make no sense of what I was feeling. I was sprawled on the floor, terror the only thought in my head. How'd I get here? I hadn't touched the light switch.

Another jolt slammed through me. My jaw clamped shut, and my teeth tried grinding themselves to shards. My senses were scattered. All that my brain registered were the hairs and fibers on the carpet and the smell of commercial rug shampoo. If the jolt had lasted longer, I would have lost control of my bowels.

After glaring at eternity, I tried to stand. I was jolted again and my fingers clawed the carpet. The shag was long enough, I pulled out two clumps from it. My limbs convulsed violently, uncontrollably. The tears in my eyes made the world unseeable. I was too weakened to do more than shudder and shake without reason.

A large hand grabbed me by the throat and shook me like a puppy being punished. I swear by god my eyes bounced around in my skull like loose marbles in a goblet.

I was pulled to my feet and thrown out of my own apartment. I was shoved down the flight of stairs, and when I reached the bottom, I was kicked in the ribs at least twice. I saw him then. He was wearing the kind of deer hunter's face mask that costs ten bucks at K-Mart or Wal-Mart. The stun gun was in his left hand.

I was shoved outside my building and zapped when I moved too slowly, and I could feel the spittle flying out of my mouth as I convulsed again in agony. He hauled me to my feet and made me reach my car. He pushed me inside, knocked me across the front seat until I was behind the wheel of my own car. While I was desperately trying to catch my wits, the thug climbed into the back seat behind me. With both hands, he reached around over my shoulder and grabbed the shoulder harness of my seat belt. He pulled it up to my neck, making sure the seat belt was pulled horizontally against the soft flesh of my throat.

I didn't recognize the voice when he spoke. I know I'll never forget it. There was a trace of a Latino accent, but he sounded young and overdosed on movie bravado. Which did nothing to lessen my fears.

"Listen, asshole, I'm just grazing you with this zapper. This a Taser, you'd be dead. But if I hold it on you, you won't move or think for five full minutes. You might even die. Do you want to die?" He yanked the seat belt tighter.

I thought he was killing me, but he only wanted my undivided attention. After forever came and went, he eased up. Took me a while to think, find words, and speak.

"I...want...kill...you." I sounded like a palooka.

Could be I might have fought him, but I was yanked into submission with that hangman's noose of a seat belt.

"Where is Peter Staples?"

"Witness Protection Program," I lied.

"Bullshit! You had him this afternoon. Start the car!"

I took a deep breath and willed myself to survive. I dug for my car keys, found them, then started my car. My hands were shaking.

"Head for Masonic," he told me.

I wanted a weapon. I wanted to fight back. I remembered my tire iron wasn't in the trunk, but was draped across the seat lever of the driver's seat. I dropped my left hand and my fingertips started moving for it.

"Where's Peter Staples?"

"The cops took him downtown for questioning."

"You brought him here."

"And they took him out the back door thirty minutes later."

"Take a left. Where is he going next?"

We drove south on Masonic. Masonic was enveloped in night and fog. The streetlights were looking like some connect-the-dots puzzle. There were few cars out: a cab double-parked by the blood bank, an empty city bus, a motorcyclist throwing himself down the street, an RV with Ohio plates slowing down for green lights.

I drove down toward the Panhandle and I could feel the belt's edge digging into my fleshy throat. "I told you, he's in the Witness Protection Program, and I swear to god I honestly don't know where he is or where he's going next."

I was jolted again. I convulsed so hard, I ripped at and tore the genuine leather cover from my steering wheel. I almost lost control and took out the tiny Geo Metro next to me. I couldn't blame the Metro for being so heavy-handed on its horn. He had to hop across the double yellow line to dodge me.

But the asshole believed me.

"If he testifies, he's dead," he said.

"Yes, sir, I will tell him that."

"You're getting off the case."

"I'm off, I'm off," I said.

"Turn on Fell Street," the asshole said.

I turned onto Fell Street and joined three lanes of one-way traffic headed downtown. I looked around for help from the other drivers. The woman in the Volvo beside me had her visor down and was putting on her make-up as she drove, while the man in the BMW on my other side was picking his ear wax and singing along with his car radio. The synchronized traffic lights kept us steady at just under thirty, and neither the Volvo nor the BMW looked my way once.

The asshole leaned in, hissed into my ear. "I'm not the one starting this," the asshole wanted me to believe. "But I be the one finishing it." He was bitter, even desperate. I wondered what he meant.

We were approaching the Fell Street on-ramp to the freeway, one of the busiest on-ramps in the Bay Area. Within two blocks I would have to shit or get off the pot.

"Want me to change lanes or climb up onto the freeway?"

He sharply pulled back on the seat belt again, then slowly, cautiously, eased up. "You're going to slow down as you go through the intersection of Fell and Laguna and then you're going to stop at the foot of the on-ramp.

"I'll be rear-ended by a thousand cars!"

He smacked me in the head. "You will do it."

With my heart in my throat, I did it.

As I slowed, I angled my body and this time my fingertips reached and then touched the tire iron--

He yanked brutally hard on the seat belt, choking me, and the tire iron slipped from my fingers.

"Stop the car now!"

I slammed on the brakes, and we fishtailed out of my lane and into the left one. The car behind me had squealing brakes, but missed striking me. Car horns started going off all around me.

The asshole let go of the seat belt and then he was gone. The back door smacked shut behind him. I heard the blare of a car horn dopplering around me as the asshole ran off the ramp.

I had no choice. I was on the on-ramp. I couldn't back down. I could only go forward. The cars and trucks behind me wouldn't let me do anything else.

In the rear view mirror--

A semi barreling straight for me!

I floored it, peeled rubber and was on the ramp. The semi was still coming! I heard no horn blowing. Silence was out to kill me. I punched the pedal twice, and the fuel injection cut in, pushing me back in my seat. The car lunged forward. I said every prayer I had ever heard. I watched in my rear view mirror him coming at me, growing larger, looming over me. I heard his air brakes squealing; he was trying to slow for me.

The semi smacked into my rear end. My body went to slam into the steering wheel. My car banged the rear end of the Volvo in front of me. My airbag blew. I went face-down into it. I lost control of my car and careened off the concrete guard rail on my right. The semi barreled past me, my front fender was clipped by one of his rear tires, then my car ricocheted and flew off across the left two lanes of traffic, narrowly missing a Buick, and I hit the barrier on my left. Scraping the concrete, I still took the curve, listening to the car horns behind me, and then found myself on the freeway headed out. The freeway widened out, opened up, and there was gravel on my side of the freeway.

I managed to pull over and park without dying.

I sat and trembled as the cars and trucks rushed around me. My palms were red and raw from grasping the wheel so tightly. Screwy enough, all I could think about was my auto insurance. Boy, was I screwed now.

I caught my wind, but the horns never stopped blaring. As the cars and trucks rushed around me, I realized none of the cars or the semi had pulled over or were coming back. Figuring out why not took the longest time. Why should they come back?

Reporting this would increase their auto insurance, and what California driver could afford that grief? That I had been dead-stopped on the on-ramp didn't matter. According to California law, all rear-enders are always the rear-ender's fault. How come you couldn't stop in time? And whose fault was it that you were tailgating in the fast lane?

Some teenagers barreled past and freaked me out of my wits by throwing a paper cup of soda and ice over me and my windshield. My nerves were shot, and I screamed epithets after them, until I realized they weren't there to listen.

I was gasping, coughing, couldn't see for the tears in my eyes. My heart was racing, and I had a splitting headache. The soda and ice dribbled down my windshield. I held my hands out in front of me, and they shook like a dying wino's. I grasped the wheel and held on until I was back in control. I got mad then. I decided to go after the asshole. I decided to back up and then back down the on-ramp and go after him until I found him.

I'd never get him.

Fuck it! I was going for it.

Except my ribs ached.

And I was exhausted.

A drop of something thick and dark went into my right eye, blurred my vision. I wiped at it, discovered it was my blood. I looked at myself in the vanity mirror and I had a gash halfway across the forehead. I must have banged into something when the airbag blew. I looked around the dash and the steering wheel, saw nothing with any blood on it, gave up.

Yeah, I was going to back around the freeway curve, ignoring several hundred cars and trucks, back down and off one of San Francisco's busiest on-ramps backwards, then go chase after a lunatic asshole on foot who had a dozen different directions he could go and every advantage on his side.

I sat on the gravel longer. I counted to twenty, then counted another twenty, until going after the bastard was not feasible. My nerves were too shot for me to be slick.

I glared at my eyes in the rear view mirror and wondered how the asshole had found out Peter Staples had been released from the hospital. Simple tail-job, I suppose. And then he came back after dark.

After I smooshed down my popped airbag, I climbed back on the freeway without being killed or crushed and rode it around the city until I reached the next off-ramp, which was at Fourth Street. I left the freeway, circled the block and climbed back on the Fourth Street on-ramp going west and dead-headed back to Anza Street and my apartment.

Foggy, foggy night on Anza Street. No one walking and no one driving. Damp enough to curl my hair. The streetlights had halos.

After I parked under the brightest streetlight I could find on Anza, I checked out the damage done to my car. The driver's door opened okay, but the driver's side looked like a mountain after a rockslide. I yanked off the chrome that had been ripped and stored it in the back seat. My trunk looked punched in by a giant fist.

But it could still open. I dug out my Browning 9-millemeter automatic from storage in my trunk. I chambered a round, grabbed a couple spare magazines and a halogen flashlight, then trudged toward my building. After my on-ramp adventure, how could a 13-shot clip hurt?

I went upstairs and found how the door lock had been jimmied. I had missed it earlier. I racked the slide on my Browning and took comfort from the sound of metal clashing against metal.

I flicked on the lights and went in slowly, wondering what I'd find, hoping that Dr. Staples was still gone and not dead in a corner. Browning in hand, I hunted from room to room. Every shadow had ominous eyes, and I was ready to blast the first shadow that blinked. I even looked under the bed. I found the place empty and a message on my answering machine.

Before I played the message back, I took stock of my apartment. The asshole had gotten inside. My place had been searched, but thankfully it hadn't been trashed. Vandalism, it seemed, wasn't his game. Nor was theft; everything I owned was where I had left it. Cleaning up took me less than an hour. I was not moving fast. And I kept my Browning close to my hand as I cleaned.

Then I relaxed and had a shot of my best cognac. Then I sat and had another. With loaded Browning in hand, I glared at the cold television like a couch potato after Thanksgiving dinner. After a while, I went into my bathroom and soaked my face with cold wash cloths until my face was chilly and pink. I put hydrogen peroxide on that gash on my forehead, saw it wasn't half as bad as I'd thought in the car, then slapped on gauze and a bandage over the nastiest part. I took off my shirt and glared at the two-pronged bruises from where the stun gun bit me. Ugly suckers were already black and blue.

Outside Danse Macabre

At the Oakland Airport I flagged a cab. He pulled over. The cab was one of the oldest on the streets. The kind the drivers call "widow makers" because the company owners call the drivers "self-employee contractors" because they don't give a shit about their welfare.

"I'll buy your tire iron," I said. "Not the one that came with the cab, but the old L-shaped one you keep hanging over the front seat adjustment lever." Something I had learned about cabbies in my Vegas travels

The cabbie didn't want to sell. "How much?"

"I'll give you twenty bucks."

"Twenty bucks!" He was scandalized. "You know how much one of them costs?"

"Twenty bucks, and you'll take the tire iron out of the old wrecked cab that's parked next to yours in the cab company lot after you check in tonight."

"Twenty-five."

"Twenty bucks." I bought the tire iron. Gave him forty.

I was inside Kitty's mirror now.

That night I drove to Rincon Hill and under the San Francisco Bay Bridge. Where I stopped for a red light, water was dripping down from the freeway above me. Thirty thousand people a day pass overhead. The noise is continuous and deafening.

And below the bridge an old guy in a suit was writhing on the ground in the parking lot across from the gay nightclub. Three punks were stomping on him. He jerked violently with every kick and blow.

Against my own best judgment, I jumped the curb, went full-throttle through the parking lot, blaring my horn and flashing my high beams because the coyotes were mauling a drunk in the back of that parking lot. He was crouched, or maybe on his haunches, his hands over his head trying to protect himself. The victim wore a white shirt and a dark suit. A buck said he was ambushed, caught off-guard while outside his car.

I drove into the lot, my hand pressing my car horn down. I thought about hitting one or the other, or even all three, but the way they were grouped around their victim made it too dangerous a stunt to pull off.

Even as I roared through the parking lot, I saw one of the transvestites punch the victim in the head. The victim collapsed on the ground, and the other two TVs kicked him again and again.

I flippered the horn and my high beams and sideswiped some trash cans to make more noise.

By daylight, I was in a fenced-in commuter lot. But the night was still in diapers; later all these spaces would disappear and the overflow for the clubs would start hitting the lots.

I slammed on the brakes, smacked the gear shift lever into park, pulled out my emergency flashers, and made sure my high beams were lighting up the crime scene.

As I climbed out of my car, I left my high beams on and turned off the ignition. As I stepped out, I had the tire iron in my right hand and my cell phone in my left.

I was punching out 911 on my cell phone while I hefted the iron.

If I thought the lights or the horn was enough, I would never have left my car. First Law of the Streets: don't EVER get out of the car. A corollary is: never go back inside the bar again.

Cabbies carry tire irons because the cops won't let them carry guns. Both are considered lethal weapons, but cabbies think cops will give them a break for defending themselves with one. They think wrong, but when you are on the streets night after night, the better part of wisdom is protecting yourself. Draped over the front seat adjustment lever, cabbies can grab them in an instant.

I heard the victim yelling that he had no money, that he had nothing valuable, and then he curled up in a fetal position and tried to cover his head.

One of the TVs stomped on his head. Then she took time out to spit in his face. Then she hit him in the head with a stick.

I saw the black limousine off to one side, its engines running, its lights off, and I figured the scene out. The limo driver needed to take a piss. He pulled off the line, found this parking lot, probably ducked into the alley to take a piss--and the coyotes decided the herd needed thinning.

The three were coyotes. Homeless street dwellers, they were street trash, street dogs, Tenderloin trash. A mouthful of meth, and they'd kill. More than a mouthful was just gravy.

They wore costumes, like sinister clowns. One of them wore raggedy petticoats—no longer fluffy and no longer white--

and it had their victim's blood stains on it. She growled at me, showing her teeth.

The TVs were a gang for their own self-protection. Scavengers of the night, scrawny with hunger, filthy and crafty, filled with animal cunning. Young predators. Carnivores. Mean as a pack of wild dogs. There were worse predators out there than them. But not many, thank God.

One of them hit him over the head with a beer bottle. A side swipe that splashed out bright red blood. The second one stabbed him in the back again and again. A short-bladed knife, I figured, because he wasn't going down dead.

I punched 911 on the cell phone as one of the TVs moved out of the high beam and saw I was alone.

The third of the transvestites stopped to stare at me from beyond the glare of my high beams.

"Officer down, officer down," I told the 911 dispatcher. "Police officer is down in a parking lot across Folsom Street from the Danse Macabre."

The TV called out, "What are you looking at, mister?"

Another one said, "Get out of here, mister!"

"Ladies, ladies, ladies," I said. "You shouldn't gang up on a guy like this."

I had my old tire iron in hand. You have to be careful with a tire iron. Don't aim at the head, for instance. One blow that connects is enough to change your destiny. One solid hit, and the perp is facing a lifetime of either speech or physical therapy. Too good a hit gets you charged with assault with a deadly weapon, or even attempted murder.

How dirty, exhausted and underfed they look.

Life on the streets is a son of a bitch. As I swung the tire iron...

Only one way to fight a street fight. You fight to win. You fight hard and fast and dirty to get it over as fast as possible. A tire iron is the fastest way to break arms or legs. I never try for a headshot. I don't want to kill anybody.

But fight like you're going to die.

I know I broke a hand that pulled a knife on me. I heard the hand break. It went crack, like a celery stalk bitten into. The transvestite howled like a cat being sodomized and fled with raggedy petticoats flying.

I swung the tire iron like a swashbuckler. A second TV fell to her knees gasping and choking and holding her guts with both hands. I sucker-punched her in the kidneys with the tire iron.

I feinted with the third one. She fell for it. I grabbed the front of her blouse and gave her a short jab in the face and then I gave her a straight punch to the side of her head that sent her reeling. Followed by a tire iron in the crotch. One more punch in the face and she went down.

I grappled with the second one again. She was maybe twenty years old and wild. I was twice his age and half his strength. But I was game. I was once a street fighter.

I was blindsided and took a punch above my ear, and suddenly my eyes watered. I kicked out, and she went backward, fell on her butt, and her feet went high in the air, and I brought the tire iron down like a guillotine, but she dodged out of my way. I kicked her in the chest. But God she could scramble to her feet so fast!

Twice as old and out of shape.

What the hell was I doing?

I punched one of them in the throat. She fell, landed hard, where she began gagging. I reached down and pulled her earring from her ear. She screamed with pain.

The one I had punched in the throat was still on the ground, still choking, and both hands were holding her throat.

I gave her buddy an uppercut and I heard her teeth click together loudly. I rammed my knuckles low and into her stomach and then I punched the side of her jaw and sent her reeling.

I punched one in the face, and her lip split. I grabbed her wrists. She tried pushing me off-balance. I could feel her breath on me. I resisted her and then abruptly gave ground. When she pressed forward, I let her own weight throw her off-balance and then I gave her an elbow in the nose.

Our bodies thudded together. I lost air.

We made noises when we crashed together.

Things got a little vague then.

She hauled up her petticoats and ran like ten thousand devils were chasing her. She was a real high stepper. And I was bleeding. My left hand had taken a hit. I hadn't felt the cut, but now it hurt like hell. They all took off running.

I looked around for help or even an eye witness, but we were still alone under the freeway. I saw the bright purple neon sign for Danse Macabre across the street. First came the club's name Danse Macabre and then under the purple neon in flaming yellow neon came the club's slogan: Until You Drop.

The neon sign had a pair of dancing skeletons doing the dirty boogie together. If you paid close enough attention, you would be scandalized.

The old guy was standing up. He staggered forward. I might have thought he was drunk until I saw he was drenched in his own blood. He left a trail of blood behind him. He fell down on one knee several times and then he collapsed and lay flat on his back. His face and his hands were covered with blood.

I went back to my car, replaced the tire iron where I keep it, draped over the driver's seat lever, and then I called 911 again. I didn't want the cops seeing I had one handy.

The old guy looked at me. I saw the broken blood vessels in his left eye from where he had taken a headshot. He was bleeding from that ear.

He had been smacked hard in the head more than once. The left side of his face was already swelling. He had bruises on his face and his jaw.

His nose was bleeding from the beating. He tried to cup his nose, keep the blood from pouring out. He was spitting blood.

He was bleeding, too, on his left side. He had a five inch slash under his arm and another long one by his neck. Oh, the knife wounds.

His pack of cigarettes, splashed with his blood, started to fall from his shirt pocket. I went to catch them. His bloody hand grabbed my wrist and tried tightening on me. He looked me in the eye and tried glaring at me. But he had no strength and had to give up. The look on his face was the look of a man giving away his family jewels. I shoved the bloody cigarettes back in his pocket.

I said, "What's your name? What's your last name?"

"Jerry," the man said. "Sutton."

"Jerry Sutton?" Had I heard right?

"Yeah."

I said, "What did you say your name was? What's your last name again?"

"Jerry," the man said. "Sutton."

"Jerry Sutton?"

"Yeah."

"Are you Jerry Sutton?"

I realized I knew Jerry Sutton. Well, I didn't know him, but I had seen him hundreds of times. He was the chauffeur who walked the family dog every day outside the Vashon family mansion by Dog Shit Park. Brown suit and brown chauffeur's cap.

Leave him alone! Walk away! Let him die!

I applied pressure on the worst of the wounds. Blood was pooling everywhere. This poor guy must have been stabbed four or five times to generate this much blood flow.

I looked to see if the attackers were returning. Then I looked at his black limousine. His limousine had its hood chained down to keep the thieves at bay. It was also waxed so thoroughly that I could see the reflection of the moon in the hood. The real moon was full and blonde and high enough over the Oakland horizon to illuminate the lot. Those few spooky shadows that fought the moonlight only made the lot more sinister.

An EMS ambulance came to our rescue.

The driver was chewing gum; he blew a blue bubble gum bubble.

I pointed out the victim. He wasn't drunk, I said.

He had fainted from loss of blood.

The paramedic looked at me. "How are you doing?" He pointed.

I had some cuts on my forearm. "I'm okay."

He said bullshit. I had a deep wound in my right hand from trying to defend myself.

"I'll do it later," I said.

He did me then.

The paramedic said, "What's your name? What's your last name?"

"Jerry," the man said. "Sutton."

"Jerry Sutton?"

"Yeah."

"Tell me, Jerry Sutton, what happened to you?"

I decided it was time for me to leave.

The cops caught me before I reached my car.

"Excuse me, sir? Can I see your driver's license?

I turned my attention to the police officer.

"Yes, sir," I said. I handed it over.

He grunted. "Las Vegas? Why'd you come across this parking lot?"

I blinked. "I had to. He was being attacked."

"What were you doing here?"

"I was driving down the street, looking for a parking space, and I saw this going down."

"Did you know him?"

"No."

"You're just a good Samaritan?"

"Oh, no. The Good Samaritan took the guy who got mugged to a hotel, paid the hotel bill and for the doctor and then checked in later to see how the guy was doing. Me, I just shooed away the hyenas and called the paramedics."

He tilted his head. "Who are the hyenas?"

"What do you call muggers who attack from the shadows?"

"What are you doing here, South of Market?"

I pointed across the street at Danse Macabre. "I'm supposed to meet a guy inside there."

The older cop gestured towards the ambulance. "It wasn't this guy you were meeting?"

"I never saw him before in my life."

The cop asked me for and I gave him detailed descriptions of each mugger.

"Weren't you scared going up against three of them?"

"I never gave it any thought. I just saw them jacking him and I went in to chase them away."

"How come they didn't go after you?"

"They were like wild animals scared of the headlights. Besides, by the time I stepped out of the car, I had already dialed 911 and was giving out my location. They must not have seen me."

"What if they had stuck around?"

I blinked twice, acted like I hadn't thought about it beforehand, and went wide-eyed. "Oh geez." Then I put a look on my face like I was trying to remember where I had lost a set of car keys, or maybe trying to decide why I had acted so recklessly.

The cop didn't buy the look.

"Did you get out of your car?"

"To help him, yes."

"Did you face them down?"

"Oh, god, no! They were running off as soon as I got close."

"Do you carry a gun?"

"No, I do not."

He looked around my trunk and then walked and looked in my car windows. But I once lived in this city, and I learned long ago to keep my seats as clean as a whistle and keep anything valuable in the trunk or out of sight.

"Three men with three knives," the cop mused.

"They were transvestites," I said.

The younger inspector noticed I had said the word transvestite. "You know how come San Francisco hookers don't wear short shorts?" he asked his partner very loudly. "They'd freeze their balls off!" He was the only one who thought his wisecrack was funny.

I knew what he was joking about. Only a slim majority of the hookers in San Francisco are females. The rest are male hookers. Half of those are transvestites. I got nothing against them. A gal has to make a living in this world.

I couldn't resist. "Is that why you guys like to stop and strip-search them?"

He turned to stone. Cops strip-searching transvestites for no good reason--without probable cause--had cost the City a small fortune in law suits.

The older inspector said, "Did you hit any of them?"

"Oh god no!" I said.

He grunted. "That's good. You assault someone with a deadly weapon--even a mugger--they can sue you for all you got."

"It's a fucked-up world," I said.

He stared at me; I knew how he categorized me.

His partner called him away to confer together.

Since there was no easy way out of here, I walked over to the paramedics and listened to them quizzing the injured man as they worked on him. "Tell me your name," they asked. "What's your last name? What happened to you? Tell me your name."

They would keep asking those questions until either he died or they reached the hospital.

The victim was covered with his own blood.

The paramedic raised his voice. "No, Jerry, you don't need them."

Jerry--the victim--pulled at the paramedic.

"He didn't want to give up his cigarettes."

"He refuses to give up his cigarettes."

The paramedic took the cigarettes away from him.

The victim lunged and almost grabbed his cigarettes back. He would have broken the restraints on the gurney to reach his cigarettes.

"Goddamn smokers," the other paramedic said.

Just before the paramedics took the bloody man to the hospital, one of them called me over and gave me a pack of cigarettes.

"He wants you to take care of them for him."

I looked them over; an unopened pack of cigarettes. Blood-splashed.

"They'll get lost in the hospital," he said.

I gave him my card.

The cop said, "Probably they came to party, spent too much money inside the club, saw you and figured you were buying them breakfast."

Poor Jerry Sutton was having trouble saying his name. He was in shock. His one eye was swollen shut from the force of that blow.

A police photographer came and took photographs of the crime scene.

"Attempted murder and assault with a deadly weapon," the cop predicted.

I couldn't believe all the yellow markers that indicated fresh puddles of blood.

The two uniforms told me that I would probably be called downtown tomorrow for the six-packs, aka, the photo ID of suspects; mug shots. I made sure he returned my driver's license.

When I got back to my car, I looked at the smokes I still held in my hand. I threw the unopened pack on my dashboard. I don't smoke.

As the ambulance hit its sirens and lights, I checked my watch. Time to take my medicine. Time to throw myself under the Wheels of Life. As the ambulance took off, I walked across the street. I had a gig at that crowded gay dance club across the street.

"The Most Valuable Thing in the World"

"The most valuable thing in the world," Naomi Lewandowski mused. "That's something I gotta think about for a moment."

I thought, more than everyone else in the world, you might have some thoughts about what's the most valuable thing in the world.

"I had this guy in the cab a while ago," Naomi started, "right after the Loma Prieta earthquake, and we're talking earthquake stories."

Like everyone does.

"Oh, sure. You gotta have an earthquake story to tell. Otherwise you're not one of us. Where were you when the last big one came? Oh, you missed it? Aw, you poor thing."

Naomi made a cluck-cluck noise. "The worst calamity that can happen to a California native is to miss out on a big earthquake. Imagine having nothing to talk about the rest of your life."

Oh, the loneliness, the desperation, the horror.

"Right. And this dude tells me, the biggest fault he's got is he's fastidious."

You mean . . . ?

"A guy who's always cleaning up after himself. He can't let an ashtray get a dead butt before he's up and washing it."

He smokes cigarettes? Oh, horrors!

Naomi grinned. "Yeah. Right. Oh, horrors."

You didn't let him smoke in the cab, did you?

Naomi was horrified. "And risk second-hand pollution?"

Good for you.

Naomi gave me a funny look. "Don't you non-smokers sometimes think you're being a bit too intransigent?"

But smoking is a foul and dirty social disease.

"I suppose that's how everybody sees it now. But, hey, this guy, for instance, he told me he had quit smoking for twenty years and then started up again against his own better judgment. You can't cut the guy any slack?"

C'mon, Naomi, what about the most valuable thing in the world?

"You on a treasure hunt or something?"

Naomi!

"All right, all right. Anyway, the guy works downtown, but it's the World Series between Oakland and San Francisco, and he's taken off work early, and he's down in his new apartment off Divisadero in the Marina waiting for the game to start when--"

The earth moves under his feet.

"Precisely. And his apartment's got this gigantic bookcase arrangement directly across from his leather chair. You know, combination TV set, wine rack, stereo CD system, genuine leaded crystal Pilsner glasses, the works."

The quake brings it all down on him.

Naomi glanced over the back seat. "Don't get too far ahead of me, okay?"

Sorry.

"Like I said, he's the fastidious type, right? He has to clean up the mess. Which he does. Takes him thirty minutes to clean it. But he finally gets the crib in order. All the broken glass thrown away. All the CDs back in their stacks. Club soda on the spilled wine."

Then what happens?

"He's gotta use the bathroom. Now, in the bathroom, there's a window right above the toilet tank, and outside the window there's a brick wall. But there's been an earthquake. And the brick wall's not there anymore."

Oh no.

"And the apartment building that stood beyond the brick wall is also gone. There're flames rising up from the rubble."

Oh no.

"So he goes outside to see what's going on. Outside he finds out, not just the apartment building next to his is on fire, but so is his own building on fire."

He didn't know it?

"He was busy. Cleaning up the mess."

Aw, the poor man.

"The cops are there now, and they won't let him back inside his building. So he's gotta stand outside his building and watch it burn up and crumble to the ground."

If only he hadn't been so fastidious.

Naomi agreed. "He wouldn't have lost everything he had in the world."

He must've been kicking himself.

"I don't think you or I could kick him harder."

He could save nothing?

"Not a thing. Not his wine rack or his stereo CD system, not his high school football trophies, not even his Porsche in the garage on the first floor of his building."

His car too!

"He was down to the clothes on his back and the three shirts he had at the French laundry around the corner."

Completely wiped out.

"See, that's how come he started smoking again. He walked down to the neighborhood sports bar, sat at a barstool and watched his apartment building burning down to the ground. He turned to the guy beside him and asked for a smoke. He hadn't smoked a cigarette in twenty years."

And took up the filthy habit again. Poor man!

"By the time I talked to him, he was getting over the loss, mostly. He got a loan from his company to tide him over. He slept on a buddy's couch until he got a new place. The insurance company paid him off on his Porsche fair and squarely."

He came out okay then?

"But the most interesting thing he said was that of all the things he lost in the earthquake, what he missed the most was his family photograph album."

All his family pictures!

"He said his parents were dead, he was an only child, and almost all of the photos were one of a kind. Oh, he got some replaced from relatives and friends, but all he had left were mostly just memories."

So family photos are the most valuable things in the world.

"As far as he was concerned, they were irreplaceable. He said, if he could do it all over again, he would have kept them in a safe deposit box and thrown away all the rest of the junk."

My Story

I got into academe by accident. And I mean, by accident. After I was given my Bachelor's degree several presidents ago, I went west with the hippies to California. By the time I made it to the Golden State, all the good jobs had been taken by the high school dropouts.

So I worked all kinds of lousy jobs. I shoveled the grapes from the vats in a winery, collected shopping carts at a suburban mall, was a shipping clerk at a fish company, became a Kelly Girl and used a comptometer. Mostly, I drove taxicab at night in San Francisco.

And I read whenever I could. At the hotel stands and while waiting on radio calls and at the holding lot in the basement of San Francisco International. That was my favorite place to read. I read *The Decameron* down there while waiting. Only took eight months, a chapter at a time.

I went back to academe after eighteen years away because the fourth drunk driver in the past five years rear-ended me on a dark street on a Sunday night in the City. My wife said I was better off inside those books than on the streets.

If You're Going to San Francisco... ?

Be sure to visit Burris Alley ....

An ex-student writes:
"I am not sure if you had written back or met with this student already but I would say to DEFINITELY have them take a look at the Haight-Ashbury area. Although kind of normal today it was a pretty interesting place if you have some background on it. When I was there it was pretty hard to believe that it was nearly impossible to find a place to live in the 60's because of the strong hippie movement there haha.

"Also I would recommend checking out Napa if he/she has a chance to do so. It's about 60 miles but definitely a cool place to check out. I am sure you covered a lot of this when you met with them, just thought I might want to give my insight. If this student has any questions tell him/her to feel free to email me with any questions."
Another ex-student writes:
"I am currently a grad student at UT and have had the pleasure of taking three classes with you while at BG. I understand that you are a busy professor, but was wondering if you would mind giving me some advice about what I MUST see while in San Francisco because I will be making my first trip out next month during spring break. If you want to get coffee with (who is currently taking your online California literature class) and me, or just simply email me back it would be greatly appreciated. I was interested in hearing about some of your favorite spots!
Thank You..."
I am honored and delighted to do so. I will try to get it done by this weekend, and I will share the news with everyone. One of the pleasures of teaching this class is that so many students take the class because they have been to California or are planning to go there.
A student went off to visit San Francisco:
"I returned from the city yesterday, but as for now-my heart is still in San Francisco. I learned that you really don't have to spend much money-just pay attention to receive real

entertainment in this wonderful city. I didn't feel a hustle and bustle that I experience when in Chicago, New York, or London.(Maybe it's just where I decided to go).

"North Beach was wonderful. The energy in city lights bookstore was amazing. . I sat upstairs and read about the great minds who once congregated there. I ate too much food-See's candy, gelato-you name it. I took your advice when you said the bad guys don't just exist in stories when having an uncomfortable encounter with a man at about 5:30 in the morning on the way to Yosemite (No harm done-just a scary encounter).

"There seemed to be great artists and musicians everywhere. This city just seems to resemble open-mindedness and I love it! We did check out a few places on your list. I think I have to go back next year to even get through half of the list. Thank you for sharing your recommendations. Watch your mailbox. We didn't forget about our teacher when in the city! :-)

"Thanks again! :-)

Another ex-student writes:

"Thank you so much Dr. Zackel we will be sure to print off this helpful travel guide to help with the navigating of our Flaneuring. I don't really connect with the idea of being a "tourist" so we will definitely be checking out some of these small local joints that will truly make our experience authentic. We will also be spending a few days in Yosemite which is what I was most excited for but it will definitely be a week of extremes and I look forward to sending you an update of how everything played out. Thanks again I really do appreciate the fact that you took time out to help us out and give us a bit of a bearing for our travels."

You are going to San Francisco. Fantastic! Everybody's Favorite City. No, that's not just a marketing slogan. In fact, a few years ago the top 500 global movers & shakers were asked where they wanted to have their annual get-together, and everybody's first choice was their usual vacation spot. But San Francisco was everybody's number 2 spot. Oh, yeah, San Francisco, great!

This list is not a complete one. But it'll give you some places to get started. Dump the list when you start having fun. Oh, and I assume you are old enough to drink. In California the legal age is 21. OTOH, every joint listed will let you in for a good cup of coffee.

San Francisco is a great walking city. *Be a flaneur!* The term flâneur comes from the French masculine noun flâneur—which has the basic meanings of "stroller," "lounger," "saunterer," and "loafer"—which itself comes from the French verb flâner, which means "to stroll."

The naughty French poet Charles Baudelaire developed a derived meaning of flâneur—that of "a person who walks the city in order to experience it."

On the other hand, go ride a cable car. If the grip man (the guy in front) is named Randy, ask him how the Grateful Dead are doing. Then say hi for me. Do not go anywhere with him after he gets off work.

If you are surrounded by crowds, watch for pickpockets. Locals bust them when they see them, but a few do slip through. Watch your wallets and your purses.

If you are downtown in Union Square, walk uphill along the cable car line to Bush Street. Turn right and walk down to Burris Alley, above the Stockton Street Tunnel. Sam Spade's partner died there. A, large metal plaque celebrates his death here. Notice the plaque is bolted into the wall; people kept trying to steal it. Notice the plaque says whodunit.

Across Bush Street is a doorway with another plaque: Robert Louis Stevenson stayed there. Just for yourself, you should also check out & read "The Silverado Squatters." I didn't know that the fine Scottish writer Robert Louis Stevenson spent his honeymoon living for a few months as a squatter at an abandoned mine above Calistoga in Sonoma County, California. (I went hang-gliding in Calistoga. Cool!) The Wine Country, folks.

Climb some more of the hill, up to California Street. (You'll see the cable car line.) At the top of Nob Hill are the big hotels: the Fairmont, the Stanford Court, and the Mark Hopkins. Yes, the hotels are named after the Big Four railroad guys. Go to the Top of the Mark in the Mark Hopkins for a drink at twilight. Lovely.

Because of the term's usage and theorization by Baudelaire and numerous thinkers in economic, cultural, literary and historical fields, the idea of the flâneur has accumulated significant meaning as a referent for understanding urban phenomena and modernity.

Go to North Beach. Visit Lawrence Ferlingetti's City Lights Bookstore. Across the alley is Vesuvio's. Go have a beer in a great beatnik joint. Directly across Columbus Street is Spec's in the Alley. A lovely bar. Go play dominos over a beer. Look for Jack London Alley.

Across Broadway and uphill from there is North Beach, the Italian section. Take Fresno Street for the Fresno Street Saloon, which has a very distinguished reputation as one of the wildest saloons in San Francisco history. Weekends are nuts. North Beach has fabulous restaurants and great bars. It has fortune cookie factories and Old Country bakeries. This is a great hangout. It is busy day and night.

Stop and eat wherever you are. Trust your instincts.

If you see a gelato store … go buy an ice cream cone now. Also, while you are there, get a loaf of sourdough bread, some Gallo salami, or maybe See's Candy.

Drive up through Pacific Heights and Presidio Heights. See the grand mansions. Eat at the Filmore Grill. Is Jack's Jazz Club at Geary & Filmore still there? Since Pacific Heights is one of the ritziest neighborhoods in California – hit the Goodwill store and the other consignment stores ast the top of the Filmore Hill. Wow. What rich people donate and you can get for pennies on the dollar!! On a Saturday walk the residential streets looking for garage sales. One place my wife found had a $2400 side table from Louis XVI. What a deal!

Drive through the Presidio, by the way. Go to the end of Pacific Street and turn right. You cannot miss it. Once this was an army base. The most beautiful army base in the world.

Once you get into the Presidio, look for the signs to Crissy Field. They will help you discover how to get underneath the Golden Gate Bridge. Go there when the weather is nasty. Bring all your cameras. Oh, and stop at the little trading store / coffee shop run by the National Park Service under the bridge. Nice stuff!

On your way back from the bridge, go to Union Street. A great neighborhood to shop. At Perry's, all the bartenders' names are Michael. (Tradition.) The front bar is known as Divorce Row. On Union Street, shop until you drop. The Balboa Café is wonderful. The Mauna Loa at Union and Filmore has a slick pool table. Watch out for hustlers.

College nightlife in San Francisco happens at a couple, three spots. South of Market is the biggest area. SoMa is huge. Look for Slim's as a starter. (It is Boz Scaggs' nightclub; great music almost every night.) The Hotel Utah is forever changing; check it out. If the bartender at Dave's between Mission and Market on Third has a beard and is built like a bear, it might be Dave himself. Give him my very best. The Stud may have the weirdest bar crowd you have ever seen. Don't say I didn't warn you! But it is safe and it thrives!

More nightlife is in the Haight-Ashbury and in the Castro and a few other spots. Minnie's Can Do is an old haunt of mine back when she was up in the Filmore. If you see Minnie, who is one of the beautiful black women in this world, give her my best. She won't remember me.

Downtown and tired of shopping at the great stores?

John's Grill is at 63 Ellis at Powell Street, where the cable cars turn around. Have the Sam Spade Special (pork chops & tomatoes) or try the scallops (my favorite.) Kuleto's is around the corner, if you don't want a sit-down place.

By the way, there are speakeasies under hotels on the streets around here, yes, left over from Prohibition. Now the bartenders on the first floor use these basement rooms to store the hotel liquor. (Don't ask me how I know.)

Check out the Garden Court at the Sheraton Palace Hotel, 2 New Montgomery St. President Harding of Ohio died upstairs. He may have been murdered.

Chinatown is special after midnight. Oh, go there first in the daytime, too. Go walk Grant Avenue, which is the touristy spot. But walk uphill from Grant Avenue to Stockton Street and the neighborhood markets. See the real daytime Chinatown scene. The Chinese culture demands absolutely fresh food daily. This includes ... live fish ... and live duck ... and live pigeon. (Minced squab is a Chinese delicacy, by the way.)

Buy something cheap and kitschy on Grant Avenue. It's okay. Everybody does.

Go eat at Sam Wo's which is uphill at 813 Washington between Grant and Stockton, a classic, a real San Francisco treat. The food at Sam Wo's is not great, but the ambience is. Going right through the kitchen to get to the stairs to the upstairs dining room, ah, that's SF!

But Chinatown after midnight is open all night, and after the bars close everybody goes to Chinatown for its all-night restaurants. Jackson Street and Washington Street are your best bets. The Far East has clams in black bean sauce, while the Golden Dragon is more sit-down. Speaking of the Golden Dragon, across Washington from its main restaurant is its take-out store. Char sui bow is barbecue beef. Delicious. Oh, and try the duck.

Good food outside of Chinatown? Tommy's Joint on Van Ness & O'Farrell or try Original Joe's downhill from the Hilton. There, order the house burger and the steak fries, but save half of it for later, once you get home.

Check out the Castro; it's the gay neighborhood and unlike anything you will ever see in Ohio. Great stores, great restaurants, and great saloons. And the street scene is perfect safe for anybody. Do not let your preconceptions sabotage a great time. The people there are fine wonderful people.

At Fisherman's Wharf, do try the crab from the sidewalk vendors. Take a sweatshirt or hoodie with you before you go there; it's cold on the water!

You might want to skip the touristy restaurants and have more reasonably priced San Francisco seafood at ...

Any bar & grill in the city. A bar & grill caters to business lunches, mostly, so each place has to have great steaks, salads, seafood, pasta, everything, because so much of their business is done on expense account for clients. A secret tip? The best steak on the menu is the loss leader in almost every bar and grill. The restaurant has to have it on the menu, but never can price it what it realistically should be priced.

Best bar & grills? I do like Tadich's on California Street. And I do like their Wild Pacific Salmon ... which comes with their fabulous steak fries. The Financial District or near the big hotels by Union Square. Union Street (which is not the same as Union Square) which is also called Cow Hollow and is in the Marina District.

Take the Hyde Street cable cars from downtown up and over the hills towards Fisherman's Wharf. Get off at Lombard Street, the crookedest street in the world. It was constructed that way so that horse-drawn wagons could get down off the hills. Notice the sidewalks are ... stairs. Walk down Lombard Street. Then do downhill into North Beach, north to the wharf, or go climb a street back toward downtown.

Do not ... I repeat ... do not walk two blocks south from Lombard and Hyde Street to the Steepest Street in San Francisco. You cannot drive down Filbert Street. Notice at the bottom of the street is ... a stop sign. Ask somebody like me to drive you down it. Yes, I LOVE driving down it with no hands on the steering wheel. True.

If you have time, and do take the time, take the Sausalito ferry (the terminal is by the Ferry Bldg at the foot of Market Street) across the bay, passing the Rock (aka Alcatraz) and go have a sexy drink at the No Name Bar at 757 Bridgeway in Sausalito. The sign hanging out on the Bridgeway has nothing written on it. Hence, the No Name Bar. Try the Anchor Steam Beer or the Ramos Fizz. And on Bridgeway, buy a souvenir for yourself.

In Sausalito, go visit the houseboats. Yes, the houseboats. I lived on one for three years and I still miss the sound of seagulls pacing up and down on the roof, the smell of low tide, the great house parties where everybody on the pier ….

I recommend the sushi at Sushi Ran at 107 Caledonia. You can read the menu online at … sushiran.com. And because the restaurant is just up the Bridgeway and just around the corner from the Sausalito Police station, you'll find free street parking. Really!! Back on the Bridgeway, maybe 100 yards towards the bay, look for Cibo on the Bridgeway, a great place for snacks and organic ginger ale.

If you're in the East Bay, say, in Berkeley, have the burger at 900 Grayson Street, which is also its online url. (www.900grayson.com.) I have relatives who swear by their "chicken and waffles," but I like the Grayson Burger. If the line in front is too long, try uphill – which is to the east of the bay – at La Note, a restaurant Provencal in the 2300 block of Shattuck. Technically the French don't eat breakfast – an apple and coffee is enough – but this lovely little place can give you a great humungous Americanized French Breakfast or brunch. I like the raspberry oatmeal pancakes. OTOH, the cinnamon brioche is to die for!

Both 900 Grayson & La Note will have very long lines on the weekends. So, unless you can get there before the religious get out of services or the non-religious roll out of bed – try either on a weekday.

Getting back to the city by the bay …

A word about the homeless. Ignore them. Do not give them money. Do not stop and talk. Do not share with them either yours or their life stories. You can do nothing to change their situations; even the City & County of SF is most often powerless. Statistically, half of them are mentally ill drug or alcohol abusers.

Use common sense. If it's late at night on a street deserted except for the homeless, get the heck out of there as fast as possible. If you find yourself in a questionable environment, go inside the nearest bar – whatever kind of bar it is – and ask the bartender to call you a cab.

Cabs are the secret treasure in San Francisco. Be careful, be cautious, and realize you are in a very big city, and bad guys are not just in the novels we read.

Most of all, enjoy.

Stonewell

The rhino Stonewell was mourned at the San Francisco Zoo when he died some years ago. He was the oldest living black rhinoceros in captivity and lived to his thirty-seventh year. He sired ten offspring and was a grandfather many times over, according to his keeper.

After his death, while describing Stonewall's fertility, keeper Jane Tollini told *The San Francisco Chronicle*, "He didn't have a tooth in his head these past few years, but he still managed to put a bun in the oven every season." He never failed to mate with his longtime companion Ellie, but then he needed his alfalfa pre-chopped.

Progeny is our immortality.

Chuck Cody

I bought him brandy at Enrico's in San Francisco, and so he talked:

My name is Chuck Cody, I'm a fisherman, and I'm 59 years old, but I look ten years younger with all my black wavy hair. I have spent three years growing my beard and I like drinking brandy.

I have epilepsy because I drink. My hair hides the scars from epilepsy. My hands have large scars, too. The scars there come from stingrays. I got eight stitches here, five here, one there.

That stingray, he slapped me, so I slapped him back with my other hand. He got me again.

That sound -- that paddy wagon sound makes me nervous. You know how Indians gets treated.

I am a Sioux Indian. I was born in Texoma. Grew up on the Delta in Louisiana. Grew up fishing for catfish.

Before I came here to San Francisco, I was in the Florida Keys. The sand fleas left me scarred on the knees. See?

When I fish for white bass, I make $45 a day.

I still fish for shrimp. Fat shrimp, that is. I won't tell you my bait. But I go out to the mudflats. Two hours later I got boxes. I caught 180 pounds yesterday.

I know how to cadge a meal. I know where to get loaves of bread free or free steaks, too. A hundred years ago I would have been a pioneer. Instead I was a saddle tramp and a bum.

I drove taxicab in Chicago. Yellow Cab.

I was driving along Lake Shore Drive, got two little old ladies in the back seat. I seen this jetty sticking out. Hell, I did it. I drove off the jetty into eight feet of water.

I didn't get fired. My boss, he couldn't fire me. I owed him a hundred bucks. Boss ain't gonna fire you if you owe him money.

My wife-- I was married for thirty-seven years. We worked the cotton fields together. She's dead now. She was riding her horse and my dog ran between the horse's legs. She fell off and started spitting blood.

She and my dog-- When she steps on his tail, she would cuss him in Indian and then in Italian. I don't know where the Italian came from.

She likes drinking brandy, too. She'd come on to you, then say, Can you give me a ride to the bus terminal? Then she'd borrow five bucks, but then she would buy you a drink.

My dog was part wolf. Lemme tell you, you treat women like your dog. Not as some souvenir, not as a pet. You treat her as a companion.

I get misty. I'm still repeating myself. I reach out in bed. Aw, forget it. She was gone. I went out and looked at the full moon instead. Yeah, I get lonesome.

I went to a funeral in Diego. Indian funeral. Real rare Indian he was. He was going bald. Going bald for an Indian's like losing your manhood.

He sliced his own throat just for going bald.

No guts to do that.

Bury me standing up and facing east. I want the largest processional of Caddys they can find.

I want an Indian burial. It's in my will that I'll be facing east. It's insured. Eight feet down and two feet from the bottom.

Can you give me a ride to the East Bay Terminal?

He borrowed five bucks, then he bought me a drink.

I gotta get home. I'm supposed to show up at Al's Liquors in Oakland at 5 am. I'll be on the boat by 6 am.

Want to know my secret?

Come by the Lorraine by DiMaggio's at Fisherman's Wharf. It's the third boat, the one with LA plates. LA is Louisiana.

My bait is a sardine can slightly opened up. Sardine oil, that's what brings the shrimp.

Come by and I'll buy you a brandy.

Today I learned how to wiggle my ears

Today I learned how to wiggle my ears. I was parked out on the scenic highway in the Presidio, at one of those vista points on the green bluffs on the coast side of San Francisco. I was in my car watching a slow freighter aimed at the Golden Gateway. I was watching the tin cans of commuters driving on the bridge to and from Marin County. I was watching the tourists standing at the edge of the cliffs filming their memories with Pentax, Instamatic and Nikon.

The tide has so much to do with a ship's speed. A freighter from Oakland steams out from under the bridge, while the inward-bound one struggles against the current. One churns, and the other plods. The eager young adventurer versus the tired old sea tramp.

Perspective is Einsteinian relativity. If a balloon flies from Sausalito to Berkeley, what time does Berkeley reach the balloon?

Water is a fluid. It is viscous and porous. It fills and bends itself to its container, assuming the shape of its container. And the displacement of water is equal in weight and volume to the object displacing it. Archimedes discovered the latter in a Grecian steam bath. I forgot who discovered the former. Another wily old Greek, probably.

What is remarkable is a ship's motion in the water. Its passage is, of course, quickly invisible, like a snake's path on a warm rock or a planet's orbit around the sun. The wake falls back upon itself, filling instantly the vacuum of its passage. And a ship is the opposite of an airplane, though both are based on the same theory. The propeller on the bow pushes water backwards. The propeller on the nose pushes air backwards. More relativity. Depends on how you look at it.

I thought it was a nervous spasm, a twitch. I hoped that it was not a warning sign of some imminent nervous disorder. Pain is a defense mechanism. It warns your body that something is interfering with its normal functions. It demands that your body do something to relieve the pressure, the tension, or the lesion.

An exobiologist once essayed that there were three commandments in the animal world. Thou shalt not let anything injure or destroy your teeth, break your skin, or harm your genitals.

Your teeth maintain proper food ingestion. Your skin protects you from disease and / or the loss of precious bodily fluids. And your genitals protect your future progeny. All is not fair in love or war. Don't injure me or my children's children. Protection of the Individual and of the Species.

I was worried by the nervous sensation. I set my pint of chocolate milk on the dashboard, extinguished my cigarette in the ashtray, and slipped my sunglasses into the side pocket of my windbreaker. I peered into the rear view mirror for confirmation of my fear, for denial of my diagnosis. Curiosity compels man to investigate his own decline. Such is the stuff of journals and essays.

To my relief, the involuntary twitch was simply an involuntary twitch. Most probably brought on by lack of sleep, inadequate diet, and failure to exercise. For I have been overworking myself lately.

Curious, I tried flexing my forehead again. This time I could reproduce that same twitch voluntarily. Man has always sought to adapt himself to new specialties. Man is a generalist; he wants to do all things under all conditions. Man is mimicking nature.

That forehead flex -- that involuntary twitch -- makes my ears wiggle. Something I could never learn to do at that elementary school I once attended.

"Margaret Mead Was Wrong" *

* *Bumper sticker seen in Samoa.*

A trio of transvestites were eating outside the fish-n-chips store on Geary Boulevard at Polk. To me, they looked like the three witches from Macbeth at a costume party. But I live in this San Francisco. To my friends from Ohio, they were stranger than the Man in the Moon.

Annette stared at them. "They really do look like prostitutes."

"They are men," I told her.

"Ugly men," Walter said.

Annette indicated one TV wolfing down fast food, sitting slouched on a fireplug, legs demurely crossed. "What about that one?"

"She's a boy," I said. "San Francisco has lots of TVs working the streets. In fact, one old joke the cops tell is how come the hookers don't wear short shorts in the summer."

"Why is that?" Walter asked.

"They'd freeze their balls off."

Annette was looking around the street corner, surprised. "There are some awfully good-looking men out here!"

I said, "Yes, there are."

"How do they get their legs so good?"

She shouldn't have said anything. The transvestite busy wolfing down fish-n-chips noticed her staring at him and commenting about him to her passengers. He stopped chewing his fish and started stalking us.

Annette made a second mistake. She fumbled for the electric window switch. The window began humming up. The transvestite came close enough to stick his nose in the window. The window just barely closed in time.

"Weirdos don't think they're weirdos," I said. "They think they're as normal as everybody else, only just not so boring."

The transvestite howled like a mad dog at Annette. She panicked and power-locked the doors. The TV smashed both palms on the window and screamed at her. Surprised, Annette screamed back. The transvestite smeared his vinegar-soaked fish on the glass. Then he spat on the window.

Annette slammed down the door locks for a second time. The transvestite broke the window. Glass showered us, covered us.

Annette spun and faced me, her eyes as wide and terrified as an alley cat caught off-guard.

Walter, startled, came alive, went for his door handle, started to go after the maniac TV. I grabbed his shoulder, squeezed until he gasped in pain.

"You stay inside!" I insisted.

Horrified, Walter faced me. "Aren't you going to do something?"

"She got a green light," I said. I nudged Annette's shoulder. "You have a green light, Annette," I indicated.

Annette punched the gas pedal and the red Rover shot forward, roared off, leaving behind the teeniest patch of rubber and the teeniest squeal of tire.

I looked back. The transvestite stood in the street, giving us the finger and grabbing at her crotch, giving us a hideous eyeful of her underpants. She was screaming obscenities at us, her face contorted and ugly like a monkey choking on poison.

Annette roared down Geary Boulevard in first gear.

"Second gear!" Walter called out.

Annette hit second gear like a born Indy racer. The red Rover gasped, thought about stalling, then whooshed forward.

"You got a red light at Van Ness!" I called.

She hit the brakes, and we slid home--safe!--our front wheels just touching the crosswalk. Most of us breathed a sigh of relief.

Some jogger banged the hood as he jogged through the intersection. "Back up, asshole!" he shouted over his shoulder.

Annette gasped for air.

"They can be vicious," I agreed.

Naomi Now Loves Strawberries

"Strawberries," Naomi told me. "That's how you measure true success in this life."

Naomi Lewandowski is the wisest person in all of San Francisco. She may not have met everyone in this city, but she's met most of us. She may not have seen it all, but she has seen too much. Naomi is a San Francisco cab driver.

How can strawberries be true success? I asked.

"This guy gets in the cab down by the B of A building, salt and pepper hair, a nice suit, a clean look, and tells me to take him home to Nob Hill."

A rich guy, eh?

"This dude had gold dust dripping off his collar!"

And Nob Hill is where he lives?

"One of those tall apartment buildings by Grace Cathedral where the butler dusts the money all day."

The rich don't live like you and I.

"I do a U-ie across four lanes of rush hour on California Street, and we're going uphill before the tow trucks can blink at us, and he asks me what kind of car this is."

This cab we're in now?

She rubbed the dashboard as if rubbing her favorite puppy.

"This baby here."

One thing about Naomi, she always had one of the newest (and cleanest) cabs on the street, and she shamelessly babied it. Always a pleasure riding with Naomi.

"I'd just gotten her from the bosses. A brand new Ford Crown Vic with everything on her. Fast and gutsy, too. She still can carry six adults up California Street with no problem."

To prove this, Naomi hit the gas pedal and we whooshed around a cable car reloading at Grant Avenue. Scattering tourists, of course, but then Naomi always drove like a cab driver.

"The rich dude's leaning over the front seat, just like you are, and he's asking me what kind of a car is it, whether I like driving it, how much does it cost, stuff like that."

And you told him what you thought of it?

"Ford makes a wonderful car nowadays. I think people should buy American these days. Hey, call me a cock-eyed optimist!"

So he was thinking about buying a new car?

"He said he's not sure if he should. Said he had a car in his garage on Nob Hill, but he only puts four thousand miles on it a year . . ."

Four thousand miles a year isn't very much driving.

"I asked him what kind of car he had, and he tells me a Rolls Royce!"

Wow! Lucky man.

"Yeah. He says he really loves it, but he worries he's not getting his money's worth."

I suppose they must be expensive to maintain.

"I asked him about that. I said, just between you and me and the meter, how much auto insurance do you pay in a year."

And he told you?

"He said he didn't know."

He didn't know? How could that happen?

"He said his personal secretary paid it."

He never asked how much?

"Right. He said it was like the strawberries."

Strawberries?

"Strawberries."

I leaned back and laughed. Okay, Naomi, you got me hooked.

"He said he wasn't always rich. Said he made it the hardest way a guy could make it. Said he was dirt poor growing up. His family had nothing. He and his brothers and sisters ate gruel and mush every day growing up."

A rags to riches story.

"Exactly. But he also said once a year his mother would treat 'em all with a box of Kellogg's Corn Flakes for breakfast."

They were poor!

"He'd eat the Kellogg's Corn Flakes and look at the box they came in and dream about being rich enough to have corn flakes every morning."

Some people's dreams . . .

"Have you ever looked at a box of Kellogg's Corn Flakes? There's a bowl of flakes on the cover, right, and along with the corn flakes, in the bowl there's strawberries."

That's right! Strawberries!

Naomi nodded. "And this little kid would dream about being rich enough someday to have strawberries and corn flakes every morning."

And now that he's rich enough . . . ?

"Now that he's rich enough, every morning he now has strawberries with his Kellogg's Corn Flakes."

What's that got to do with his Rolls Royce?

"Just like he never asks his personal secretary how much his Rolls Royce costs him each year, he never asks his personal cook how much the strawberries cost him every day. Because then all he'd think about is how much they cost him. Not how much they mean to him."

And he wouldn't want them anymore.

"Maybe he would. But for all the wrong reasons."

A Writer's Gratitude

Geez, I know I'm just grateful I am here in academia; it's a job with medical benefits and maybe a pension, something I never dreamed about getting at the cab company. Oh, at the cab company I used to sit across from the bulletin board, waiting for the day driver to bring it in, and stare at the notices about medical benefits, and dream about having medical coverage for me, my wife & two babies. Never could afford it. Lived in absolute paranoid fear that I was imminently moments away from total flame-out. One drunk driver away from making my family homeless.

∞

One night, right about twilight, driving cab down Sansome Street in the city, Sutter street being the cross street, I saw a mother in a doorway of a big bank reading a Little Golden Book to her two babies. They were in a sleeping bag at twilight in the doorway of a global bank, and the kids hung on her every word. She was smiling at them; they were her babies. What got me then and still knifes my belly is my family had that same Little Golden Book and at that same twilight minute up in Santa Rosa, my wife was reading our copy to my little babies.

∞

I think the first guy who I got in shock & awe about was Lawrence Durrell and his *Alexandrian Quartet* (*Justine*, etc.) In about 1957, Life magazine ran a section of his first novel, and it was all about sex. Being a newspaper boy who delivered the Cleveland Press to the deviant residents (hookers, railroad guys, and other transients) of the Canterbury Hotel on East 185th street, I knew all about sex and wanted to know more. I read his stuff through the library, thought it was pretty heavy stuff, although I understood one word in ten. Durrell was full of literary shit, of course. "The great winepress of love," for example, sounded erotic as hell; I had no fucking idea what a winepress was. Decades later I had a shit job at Nasty Asti Winery outside

Cloverdale, California, and found out what winepresses really were. Big whoop. Durrell was full of shit, talking about 1930s Alexandria, Egypt, as having five sexes; I found out later driving cab that so does San Francisco's night life. But he was a British poet, which meant no American can write that stuff without sounding like a "poof," to quote the Brits.

The Doorman and Me

One of those dead nights when everybody goes home early, and the streets were left pretty much to their own. I mean, so dead, even most of the other cabbies have gone home, except maybe for some of the Yellows and the Veterans who gotta work their ten hours whether there's anybody on the streets or not, and maybe a couple other independents like me, who really feel just too good to deadhead in and head for home.

Not many people to talk to, when the going gets slow, so I was pulled off on Clay Street over by Earthquake McGoon's, talking with the doorman from the Playboy Club. The Playboy Club was closed down for remodeling, and the doorman had switched to McGoon's for the duration.

The real reason behind the shut-down, he claimed, was cockroaches, not remodeling, and the Club was so depressed, he didn't figure on going back there, once it reopened. He liked McGoon's, he said. It was just as busy, which meant it was really just as quiet as the Playboy Club, because the Playboy Club hasn't been making money for a long time, what with only the tourists and conventioneers making any money for the club. Real slow, he said.

We were talking about that. That and the fact that since the car dealers had left town after their convention, the town had dried up again, like it had for a week or so after Labor Day. I told him the word was the town would be staying quiet till after the first of March, a full six weeks away. That I was planning on half-shifts and plenty of television to get me through the dry period. He wasn't so sure, said he had word that another convention was due in soon, and he hated to spend February in the rain, what with his arthritis and all.

He had arthritis, all right, probably worse that most thirty-eight year olds I knew. He was strange like that. Thirty-eight years old and suffering from arthritis. He had other problems, too. He looked like a twenty-eight year old hippie, not a doorman, what with his sea captain's hat and his faded raincoat. Big beard and small height. A gentle guy, probably burned too much by LSD in the Eighties. Normal, though, with a gentle manner. He had some small charms. Only, don't get him excited, because the acid burns made his brain a little like Jerry Lewis's nutty professor. He would get giddy and flaky and make the tourists a little scared of him, with loud laughter and giggling sounds. And talking too loud.

He had more problems than a rush hour cop. He had a bulbous nose that came from a deviated septum, he said, and the doctors had operated a couple times on his beak, breaking it, healing it, then breaking it again, just trying to let him breathe right. There was something wrong with his spinal column, too, that prevented him from parking cars and retrieving them, prevented him from being a valet.

He was pissed at the Playboy Club, he told me. He had played Santa Claus for the bunnies at the Christmas party, and the manager wouldn't pay him the forty bucks for his being Santa Claus. He had done it twice before, on other Christmases, but the new manager claimed he didn't know what the manager before him had done, so he couldn't stick his neck out and give the doorman forty dollars.

The Club was losing money so fast, he told me, whispering like it was a big secret, even though we were the only two people on Clay Street at twelve-thirty in the morning. He had heard that, when the Club reopened, you wouldn't need a key to get in. And a key club without a key, he told me, means the Club was losing money.

We were just jawing, when McGoon's front door opened, and three dizzy blondes came running out. They were all good-lookers, not a fat or an ugly one in the bunch, which is not to say they were great-looking, just a touch better than average, which is pretty good at twelve-thirty at night on a Tuesday. They're scurrying and giggling and rushing about, until they see me. Oh, it's a taxicab, one blondie cried, as if that meant something extraordinary. And they bustle into the cab, faster than the doorman can open the doors for them. One climbs in on my other side, and the two fill up the back seat.

The doorman stuck his head in to say something to me, but I lost him in all the excitement and confusion. All the dizzies are hollering at me to step on it, get moving, don't stop, get going, real quick like, because we're leaving this joint right now.

I start up and make the accelerator earn its keep, but fishtailing away from the curb doesn't cool the chicks and their giggling excitement. Quick, go around the corner, I'm told, so I spin south at Montgomery and make the turn from Clay. I'm interested now, so I immediately make the turn from

Montgomery onto Sacramento Street, heading down the one-way street back towards Kearny Street, planning on circling the block.

But one of the dizzies is petrified of circling the block. They'll see us, they'll see us!

Which is crazy, I tell her, nobody looks up the one-way street. They look down. Where to?

The Buena Vista at the Wharf, one says in my ear.

But that's where we said we were going, one countered.

But they won't believe us, another said.

They won't look for us?

Sure, they will.

Not after what they spent on us.

They won't show at the BV, the one insisted. They'll look for us on Union Street before they'll think of the BV.

Besides, I said, playing the game, maybe you can get your giggles looking at the guys you left behind.

How did you know that?

Just by listening to you, is all.

We passed Clay and Kearny Streets, and we all craned our necks down the one-way street towards McGoon's. Where the doorman was helping three businessmen from the saloon's front door.

There they are!

I hope they don't see us!

They didn't, one crowed.

Oh, they were so old, another marveled.

It was all so funny, I really cracked up, started laughing so loud, my hat flew off the back of my head. One of the dizzies in the backseat caught it and passed it over the seat. Do you think it's funny? she asked.

Sure, it's funny, I said.

You wouldn't think it was so funny if you were us.

Aw, you'd think it's funny, too, I said.

By this time they were relaxing, unwinding, and a couple of them got their chuckles, too. Oh, they were so old, the one in the front seat repeated, mimicking her girlfriend in the back.

Well, they were.

They weren't that old.

The one I was with, he was old. He was so old, his fingers shook when they brought out the cake.

Maybe it's arthritis, one said.

Maybe senility, another said.

Jesus, what losers!

Conventioneers? I wondered.

Uhn-uh, just on a business trip.

Where'd you meet them?

At Trader Vic's.

How'd you get over here? I wondered.

We took a cab.

What's the story? I asked. C'mon, you can tell me.

Well, it was her birthday.

You wanted the drinks at Trader Vic's.

Well, it was your birthday.

We couldn't afford much, one broke in, telling me the story. We're just working girls, but it's her birthday, so we figured we could afford one or two drinks at someplace fancy, like Trader Vic's, so we went there after work and started drinking those rum things with the cherries and the fizzle on top . . .

And these guys, one in the backseat interrupted, they asked us is they could buy us dinner.

They sent the waiter over to us.

So we had dinner!

A free meal's a free meal, I agreed.

And then they brought out a cake.

What for? I asked.

For her birthday!

And they bought us so many drinks, and everything.

Why'd you come to McGoons?

We just had to get out of Trader Vic's.

It was so embarrassing.

You're just helping some old farts get their kicks, I told them.

Old farts is right.

I don't want to be their kicks.

So we ran away from them, one told me. We ran outside while they were getting their topcoats, and there you were.

You're cute.

He is, you know.

I almost blushed.

By the time we reached the Buena Vista, their plight had made up for the slowest of evenings. The fare came to a little over four bucks. They were gripping about how fast the fare had been rising. I told them I'd settle for two bucks. They managed to scrape that up, part of it in pennies. Wishing them good luck, I left, finding a fare headed back to a hotel on my way down Columbus Street.

It was a while before I got back to McGoon's.

I told the doorman the story.
He didn't laugh. They do it every night, he said.
Every night?
Different guys, but . . .
He shrugged it off.

Vivisection Valley

Nothing good happens after three a.m.

Semi-awake, I drove down the street I didn't want. Ahead, the police had it blocked off with sawhorses, and red flares like brilliant rubies were burning at their necks. I couldn't see what lay beyond the sawhorses, for there was a crowd of poor people from the Projects between me and the barriers.

I parked as close as I could. I could hear a police siren, a non-stop banshee's wail in the night, but it neither moved far away nor came closer to us, and I wondered why no one had shut it off. I smelled smoke. Then I heard the bark of gunfire. Automatic and semi-automatic weapons. Everyone perked up at that, went up on tiptoes, tried peering over the people ahead of them. Many were taking photos with their cell phones.

After midnight on a cold foggy night in San Francisco, and all these folks were congregating outside in their bathrobes freezing their butts, hoping for more excitement than the infomercials that their cable TV were offering at this hour. They had gathered here because they hoped to see gun smoke in city air, hoped to hear gunshots echoing through their backyards, wanted to see flashing lights reflecting like disco lights off their windows.

From all the red, white, and blue flashing lights ricocheting off the houses, trees and faces, there could have been a rave party going on beyond the barriers. The lights were on in every house on the block, and more neighbors were streaming out of their houses and coming this way. Still, this was a couple hours before dawn.

I was bull's-eye in Vivisection Valley. On San Francisco city maps, it's named Visitacion Valley, after the Virgin Mary's visit to her pregnant cousin Elizabeth. It absorbs the southeastern edge of the City and County, and its southern-most flats lie in San Mateo County. The streets all run east-west or north-south. Most houses were two-storied single-family dwellings of stucco and pastel paints.

Vivisection Valley might be the cheapest place to live in San Francisco. Once it used to be a blue collar neighborhood filled with decent, hard-working people, but over time they have been surrounded and out-numbered by those who pay for public housing with government vouchers and by those night-time carnivores who prey on the poor people of the Projects. Now it was one of the most dangerous areas in San Francisco.

I waded through the spectators at the police scene, and their laughing chatter reminded me of seagulls flocking to the city dump. Beyond the gawkers and the sawhorses, uniformed officers were stretching out the yellow crime scene tape. Straddling the street behind them were the baby blues and the black-n-whites, all with their flashers on. The coroner's blue van had pulled up ahead of me, and the police cruisers were pulling back to let it through.

Then I saw the black-n-white police cruiser on fire, and the scarlet flames leaping up into the night were impressive, like the annual bonfire at Stanford before the big game with Cal Berkeley. The fire department had two units here trying to put out the flames. This was the source of the wailing siren. The sirens go off when a police car gets torched.

Up closer, the street looked like the police were holding a convention. My rough guess said every other cop car on duty in San Francisco had been pulled off-line and dispatched here. Add in all the ancillary units from the fire department and the coroner's office, and the City and County would be dishing out the overtime tonight.

The media vultures were having their vigil between the barricades and the yellow crime scene tape. I suspected there were snipers in the neighborhood when I saw a newsman holding a flashlight on his face while he talked into a camera's lens; both of them were hunkered down behind a police car. Still, a few feet away from him a news hen with strangely arched eyebrows stood combing her peroxide flip before she went on the air. She looked familiar, attractive even, but not interesting enough to risk putting up with her neuroses.

A ruddy-faced uniformed officer with his thumbs in his gun belt stopped me at the police barricades. He tried to tower over me, but we were the same height. "Can't let you go past here without some identification."

"Frank Pasnow, Legal Investigations." He eyed me like a hooker eyes a cop car, and then gave me back my business card. "Get back in your car, pal, and drive away home. There's no road kill down here for you." He got edgy when I stayed. "I suggest you move along, pal."

"Captain Thomas Harrison," I said, "Captain of Detectives for the San Francisco Police Department, called me and asked me to come down here."

He soured. "He's by the Towers."

I walked around the barricades, ignoring the hoots and catcalls from the brothers who wanted to know who the hell I was, and what I saw suggested another big budget movie maker was on location in San Francisco. I watched cops jotting down every available license plate number, and I watched other cops interviewing on-lookers for possible witnesses. I watched two dozen men and women, all experts in their various fields, all called out in the middle of the night to witness Death in the City. There were also a dozen officials walking around aimlessly, talking into cellular phones, and I knew they were useless appendages on the body politic.

I walked through the crime scene as slow as a cop car after lunch. I grew anxious when I noticed every uniformed officer carried his Beretta .40 semi-automatic sidearm loose in its holster. Some of the boys in blue had out their six shot semi-automatic shotguns. I noticed everyone official had their bullet-proof vests on, and I wished I had one. But I also saw no one giving any out.

I moved deeper into the crime scene, into where the real action was going down, and all the weapons specialists in their body armor began checking me out, their high powered .223 semi-automatic assault rifles cradled like babes in their arms. I passed their inspection and found the City and County's orange and white EMS vans and saw the yellow plastic tarps over two bodies in the street. I passed paramedics with latex gloves and detectives, and they all had vests on. I passed a dead body spread-eagle in the street, a young white male, his head in a pool of blood that was as big as him. His face was uncovered. He didn't look like anybody I knew. He didn't have a vest on, either.

Captain Harrison was wearing a bullet-proof vest. He was a short lean man. Over the years his freckles had darkened into liver spots, and his red hair was thinning faster than it grayed.

I watched the captain watching the fire department try to deal with the flaming police cruiser. He was the toughest cop in San Francisco, the cop who spits icicles, with all the compassion of a motorcycle cop with hemorrhoids. After my parents got killed by a rogue cop on meth, Harrison always treated me as an insider, which was something denied me by most everyone else in the San Francisco legal system. I was grateful to him for that, but it was not something I was comfortable with. Being around

Harrison made me as nervous as a sparrow in the mall. Being called down here in the middle of the night made no sense at all.

Captain Harrison saw me coming, walked over and shook my hand. "Frank, good seeing you." Behind him, the police cruiser exploded, and we could feel the heat flashing over us. The flames had reached the gas tank. The city workers ducked and covered themselves, while the poor people oohed and ahhed and some applauded.

"How are you, Captain?"

"Good, Frank, good." He stretched, stuck his hands back in his pockets, and then smiled like he was my favorite Dutch uncle. "How are your boys?"

"Fine, fine," I said. "Saw them this past weekend."

"A shame you don't have custody."

Because I didn't want him more involved in my life, I made a point of gesturing over his shoulder at the police activity. "Looks like a war zone."

"Welcome to Sarajevo Towers." Harrison shivered, probably from the fog. "It is a war zone. Complete with snipers."

We both looked at the Towers, checking out each window, the rags dangling from balconies, the curtains flapping from broken windows, the eerie play of lights on the walls and windows, the sound of distant gunfire echoing down from McLaren Park and the projects on the hill.

I wished again for a bullet-proof vest. "Was it sniping that started this off?"

"The sniper's an opportunist. He didn't get started until all this was in place."

Vivisection Towers were two nineteen-story buildings, two concrete hells that rose up instead of dropping down. They were lit by searchlights from every police cruiser looking for snipers. Racial epithets and gangland graffiti were written even on their sheer walls. The Towers was a derelict housing project HUD had recently taken over after the San Francisco Housing and Redevelopment gave up. Uncle Sam had moved everyone out and was getting ready to tear the whole mess down. Now most of the windows were blocked by plywood, and the pigeons had the patios to themselves. Back when the Towers were open, it was little more than a city block of pain and sorrow. According to last Sunday's paper, a handful of squatters still called it home.

A fireman came around and warned us to move back, saying the tires on the burning cop car could explode from the intense heat. The acrid stench from burning tires and the thick plumes of black oily smoke made him easy to obey.

Harrison gave me a tour, or rather walked me through the Crime Scene. We stepped over writhing fire hoses, and I felt like I was walking through a temple of snakes. That's when I saw the chalk circles around the bullet casings. This area had been a field of fire.

"This incident began with an ambush," Harrison told me. "One-sided, of course, as most ambushes are." He could have been dictating a rough draft of his incident report. "Four white males, possibly Latino, came out from the Towers' main door and walked into a crossfire from five, maybe six, black males, possibly from the Vivisection projects on the hills up there. One assailant was killed instantly. Another managed to stave off death for almost a minute, until they shot off the back of his head. The third one was peppered with a half-dozen shots, was gut-shot and left for dead. The ambushers stood over him and confettied him with bullets, just to watch him die in the street. The fourth one was seriously wounded and he crawled behind some bushes." Harrison stopped, scanned the perimeter once more and then scowled at the picture in his mind, as if struggling to remember the precise choreography of violence that had erupted out here. "One of the killers stood over him, shot him four times. A witness said he finally stopped when he heard the gun clicking on empty chambers."

"It's all this hot weather," I mused. "People's tempers flare up."

A helicopter flew over the crime scene, slashing through the fog like a suicide bomber racing towards hell, and a powerful searchlight lit us from above. It was KVIP-TV's News Chopper, and at least a dozen cops gave it the fully extended middle finger. The silver chopper circled once and flew off toward the other projects up the slopes.

Harrison waited for the chopper's noise to doppler off. "The rest of it went down the way it always goes down. The SFPD came as fast as they could. The first unit on the scene called for immediate back-up. There was a brief shoot-out. Our officers traded shots with the Vivisection ambushers and killed two of them without sustaining any injuries." He pointed out the two corpses. "But then our officers have been to the pistol range." He smiled with pride. "Training pays off, Frank."

Harrison went on composing his report aloud. "An unknown number of the Vivisection gangsters managed to escape police capture by running up the hillside toward McLaren Park. Two patrolmen went after them, firing when they could. The other two patrolmen left their car and went on a foot chase inside the Towers after one or two suspects. When the patrolmen came back, they found their patrol car torched and blazing."

The poor people were now grousing how the fire was being extinguished. A few were hollering how they wanted the flames to burn every cop and fireman in town. A lot of them had open quarts of malt liquor. A few made pig noises at the officers.

Surrounded by cops, I still didn't feel safe.

"About that time, the rest of us arrived here."

"And the bad guys are either dead or gone."

He watched his step. "The wounded man in the bushes was taken into custody and then shipped to San Francisco General Hospital. He'll live, but he won't enjoy it."

"A shoot-out over drug turf," I concluded, and wondered again where I came in.

"Could be, could be."

"And that brings you to me," I guessed.

"Stop them!" he scolded the nearest uniform. "Those bystanders there, they're picking up bullet casings. Stop them!" He shoved the uniformed officer forward. "They're taking evidence as souvenirs." Once the uniform was in hot pursuit, Harrison turned back to me, and then gestured toward some parked cars. "See this red Eldorado?"

We were standing in front of the Towers' main entrance. The cherry-red Eldorado was parked in the handicapped parking slot. It wasn't the only Cadillac in the lot, but it was the only one that was both cherry-red and brand-new. It had no handicap plaque on its dashboard.

"It's beautiful," I said.

"The patrolmen noticed the Eldorado right away. Eldorados parked around housing projects usually belong to dope dealers."

"Safe assumption to make," I guessed.

"The Eldorado was not shot up," Harrison added.

"You're right. I don't see any bullet holes."

But a bullet had pierced the car window of the one parked beside it. And another had drilled the radiator of the car beside that one.

"Frank, when we approached the vehicle, we found blood on the rear bumper and a hunk of shirt caught by the trunk lid. When we searched the trunk, we found two bodies."

A cold sickness plopped down in the pit of my stomach and started squirming like a bucket of black eels.

"Anybody I know?"

"Black Pete Staples, for one," Harrison said.

I was shocked. "Who would kill him? How come him?"

"The other body in the trunk was his son Peter, Junior. Their hands, feet and mouth were bound with duct tape. Black Pete had been shot in the back of his head twice. Maybe with a .38 caliber."

Once upon a time Peter Staples, Senior, and I had both worked as investigators for the same corporation, Kaste and Sammons Investigations. His son I knew through the father, and not well at that. I grieved for both of them. Black Pete and his son were an odd couple. Black Pete was old enough to be his son's grandfather. The younger man was first generation San Franciscan, while the older man was born in Bristol, England, and a naturalized citizen. Their generation gap was two generations wide. But --

Something the Captain said . . . or hadn't said.

"Was Peter shot, too?"

"Just once. Smaller caliber. Maybe a .22 or a .25. His head wasn't blown apart like his father's was." Harrison smiled like a man with a secret. "Which is why he is still alive, or was twenty minutes ago. He was just taken over to SF General."

I had my second shock. He lives?

My next thought was all the medical bills that were accruing. You were better off dead than lingering in the hospital.

Harrison said duct tape.

"Was it a carjacking?"

"We don't know yet."

This bloody spectacle smelled like a classic carjacking to me. Except for the duct tape. Street criminals usually don't bother taping their victims. Just shoot 'em and leave them lying where they fall.

"How'd you ID them so fast?"

"Their wallets were there, and so was their money."

"They weren't robbed?"

"Both still had their ATM cards, too. Let me ask you some questions, Frank." Captain Harrison searched my face. "What's Black Pete been up to lately?"

"You think he might've called this down upon himself?" I tried to remember. "I worked with Black Pete at Kaste and Sammons in Los Angeles." I tried to clarify it. "If there was anybody who taught me the dark side of the game, it was Black Pete."

"Did he cut corners?"

"With a chain saw," I said.

"Was he retired?"

"He told me he was never going to retire. Said he was going to die on the job." What I said gave me pause. "He went into business for himself some time ago."

"What kind of jobs was he getting?"

"Watching salesgirls ring up purchases. Watching bartenders pour freebies for their good buddies. Nothing special. Not like the old days when the lawyers said, Get me Pete Staples."

Gunfire drifted down from the projects. Harrison and I looked up at the Towers again, checking for snipers. I saw no one. But wasn't that the whole point of bushwhacking?

"Why do you suspect Black Pete was up to his old tricks again?"

"What about his son Peter?"

"He's a resident at the UC Med Center on Judah Street. Fourth or fifth year. There's nobody else, no other next-of-kin that I know of."

Even as I said it, I thought of Annie Harker. How do I tell her? What do I tell her? She would take the news hard.

"His wallet says Black Pete was living down at Sunshine Apartments on the Wharf. Does that match what you know, Frank?"

"I didn't know he was there," I admitted. "I know money's been hard for him to come by the last couple years."

The San Francisco Fire Department started foaming down the burning police cruiser. The clowns on the nearest lawns, windows and balconies found this activity disgusting. They hooted and howled and cried catcalls.

The AAA tow truck arrived from Captain Hook's Garage. He had bubble-gum flashers on his roof. His flashers were syncopated yellow, a new distraction in the darkness. The driver stuck his head out the window and looked around with eyes as wide as a kid on Christmas morning.

Harrison flagged him over. "The cherry red Eldorado," he indicated. "Yeah, the only one there. The one with the busted taillight. That's right. That one." Harrison noticed me. "Come by the Hall after breakfast. We need somebody to ID Black Pete."

I went back to my car and sat watching the surreal scene for a few minutes, struggling to make sense out of these events. And I used my cell and called Annie Harker at home and told her the bad news.

"I'll meet you at the hospital," she said.

Sunrise in San Francisco

Sunrise and Annie Harker arrived as Peter Staples, Junior, reached step-down. Well, it would have been sunrise, except this was the summer the streetlights stayed on all day. San Francisco always has a cool, gray summer. Plenty of fog, too. Figure three days of fog followed by three days of sun in this City Air-Conditioned by God. Usually the fog clears by midday. But this summer was the coldest in a hundred years. In fact, San Francisco had forty-five straight days of thick, cold summer fog shrouding the city. And now it was August in San Francisco, the coldest August in history, and all the pretty girls on the beach were wearing down parkas.

Sausalito Houseboat

Once upon a time I was Lieutenant Christopher Doyle, Chief of Homicide for the San Francisco Police Department. I changed my name when I went in the Witness Protection Program.

Until my wife died, we lived on a houseboat on Sausalito. Then I lived here alone. Was I lonely?

The day I snapped, the one-arm woman who lived on the houseboat next door was tossing saltines to a flock of whirling, screaming seagulls. The gulls would chase the saltines like jet fighters. She flirted with me, which alarmed me. I didn't remember the next step to take in flirtation. She had a pet among the flock of seagulls, a one-legged seagull.

I was lost in myself when he flirted. Somewhere someone was gotten away with murder. My wife's murder. I was stuck between heaven and hell.

Once I chased after perpetrators.

Now I was the victim of a crime.

At that moment I was acutely aware that I, being stuck from rising up the career ladder by the glass ceiling above me, was the stopper holding back itchy male and female detectives, all of whom saw me as holding them back in their climb up the ladder of success. They all wanted me to retire. The blue code of silence was only in the movies.

As I approached compassionate retirement, I knew everyone below me knew how many months I had left.

I sat alone in a dark room aboard my houseboat, listening to Japanese jazz. My supper, ice-cold strips of crisp bacon on rye toast, sat untouched on the coffee table in front of me. An opened bottle of Chablis and a full wineglass sat beside me supper. I couldn't drink my wine, couldn't get drunk.

I was a lonely man. I was at home and I missed my Susanne. I missed not having her around. Susanne had filled so many days for me. Now my wife was a hollowness in my life.

How I missed Susanne. Often I turned to her, and she wasn't there. Last night, for instance, after all these months, I called her name in my sleep, then reached out to him across the queen-sized waterbed. Susanne wasn't there. She would never be there again.

Not that our marriage had been such a great success. We both knew better than that. Each of us had stopped feeling sexy around the other years before. But when two people meet in a narrow hallway, they still make way for each other. There was still respect.

I was still making way for Susanne in the hallway. I was still brewing too much coffee every morning, still buying too much food every week, still making too much rice in the rice cooker, still buying too much toilet paper. Only she was not here.

And I had all this room to myself. And all these things.

I looked around my houseboat. It had been our houseboat. Now it was a floating museum, a tribute to her. It was filled with her things, her touch and taste, her smells. All were memories that burned like thorns pressed into flesh.

My wife's photograph sat atop a television set I no longer watched. The liquor cabinet I had tired of months before it had managed to get its claws into me. The shelves with their best sellers and their hand-carved ipu gourds from Hawaiian vacations. The koa rocker by the bay window and the koa sea chest against one wall. The hibachi on the deck and the ti plants here and here. The throw rugs on the hardwood floor. The floral prints Susanne had bought from Maui because she knew the local artist personally. The pair of Baccarat dolphins I had bought Susanne on a trip to New York City. The Nepalese wind chimes she had the audacity to fasten above their waterbed.

I looked around my houseboat and told myself I shouldn't hang onto it too much. Hanging around an empty house isn't good for you, I thought. Makes you tend to thinking too much when you should be out there doing something to keep your mind off your losses.

I should get out and about, I thought.

But I had just arrived here, had only been here an hour, hadn't even spent an hour per day during the past seven months. And the only reason I had come home now was because I was too tired to stay away.

I had been broken by my wife's death. Now I wanted to be inured to any more deaths, to any future deaths. I wanted to be prepared for them, and be spared their terrible sting. I wanted to be excused from Death. Save my own, of course. I was okay with dying.

Dying now solved things I couldn't solve.

Even then I suspected I was being foolish, that no one can beat or cheat Death, and that Death made its own whimsical demands regardless of whatever Man or Woman tried.

Still, just that morning, I had caught myself picturing everyone I knew, each of those people dead and in some coffin in some church. Trying the scene on for size, so to speak. To take the sting out before it happened. I was whirling around in a black hole I would never get out of.

I unlocked and opened the sliding door and went out onto the deck. I watched a pickup truck pulling into a parking space at the marina's gate. One of those trucks with an extra set of wheels on the rear axle. I had always thought of them as trainer wheels. Until one of them struck my wife. Susanne had been crossing Sutter Street and Laguna in the City, and the impact sent one of her tennis shoes to a second floor balcony canter-corner to the accident.

I had been on duty that evening. When I arrived at the scene of the accident, an off-duty detective slowed me down and handed me Susanne's wallet.

These days I was a workaholic. It kept me from thoughts of my wife. It warded off grief. Chasing the madmen and outlaws was a never-ending task. I needed a never-ending task, some perpetual motion machine that always needed tending to keep me mind off my dead wife.

I made up my mind. I went and put on my shoulder holster again. Then I phoned in. "I'll be back on duty in a half-hour," I told Dispatch.

After a while the CD player reached the end, and the CD player turned itself off. Outside the rain started up. After a while it stopped. Soon the sidewalks were dry.

The Hall of InJustice

San Francisco's Hall of InJustice is the only major government building that wasn't in the Civic Center area of the City. It's an easy dozen blocks away. No one would ever call it a pretty building. Like the cops it sheltered, it was all business and no nonsense, a column of poured concrete that didn't care what anybody thought about it. Even the 101 freeway curves around it, avoiding it.

I parked around back in the lot under the freeway. Then I came up the back walk, brushing shoulders with the Monday morning dayshift coming in to work. A panhandler in a "Les Miz" T-shirt held the morgue door open for me, so I gave him a buck for his initiative.

The San Francisco Morgue is behind the Hall of InJustice, in a separate building. Somehow going past justice to reach the morgue makes sense to me. The priorities were right. First comes Justice, and then the Morgue.

I was done in the morgue after five minutes. I identified the body of Peter Staples, Senior. He was dead. I pitied the dead man because I could see myself in his place. Worse, I was afraid of the dead man because I could see myself in his place.

Homicide has its offices on the fourth floor of the Hall of InJustice. It was a hot little room with poor quality fluorescent lighting, government-issued tile floors, desks shoved together to make room for more battered and abused cardboard file cabinets, and enough unfiled paperwork to frighten a clerk-typist into permanent disability.

I walked in on a battle royal in Homicide. Three fat senior detectives stood in the center of the room, arguing over who was going to get the last slice of cold pizza. Their voices were raised, fingers were poking each other's beer belly or jabbing in each other's jowly faces, and they were one step away from bouncing bellies off each other or throwing fists. What really frightened me was all three were armed.

I asked around, was put on hold, and then got to meet the two detectives Harrison had assigned to the case.

The Kids in the ICU

We thought we stood alone, but then the drapes of the slot we stood in front of were pulled back, revealing the slot held a teenage boy who was having his gunshot wounds re-bandaged by a nurse. Even while he was being poked by some wicked-looking needles, the teenager couldn't take his eyes off us, looking us up and down like any junkie scoping out his next target. I noticed him because I noticed he was handcuffed to his gurney and a police guard stood watch beside him.

An old San Francisco proverb says that if they look weird, they are weird, and this boy looked weird. The boy looked sixteen, maybe seventeen, Latino, broad-shouldered and muscular. He had the face of a future murder victim. He wore a poker-face, a gang tattoo on his forearm, and his neck had a fresh gash from a gunshot wound that had narrowly missed his jugular vein. I saw the red eyes of a cracker. A cracker with burnt fingertips from red-hot bowls of rock cocaine.

His girlfriend was hovering beside him, eyeing the nurse's machinations as if the hospital was administering poisons. She was maybe fourteen, had high cheekbones, a long body and hard flesh. Her face had thick make-up slapped on like spackle. She wore a sleeveless T-shirt, cut-off jeans and a baseball cap with the bill turned backwards. When she took the hat off, I saw she wore her corn-silk hair like the teenage Lauren Bacall. The girl had hollow eyes, bad skin, and scabs. Her eyes were right out of The Night of the Living Dead. Zombie Eyes. Crack eyes.

They were kids. They were both too young for their hardened stance, their flinty-eyes, defiant chins, the bravado. But they were throwaways, as far as the rest of America was concerned no better than soda pop cans and candy bar wrappers. They both were streetwise. Their cagey eyes were counting exits, looking everywhere for a way out. But they were dead in my book. Crack is the quickest way to hit hell's basement.

Ignoring America's future, I scooped up Annie by the elbow and managed to steer her to an elevator and down to the basement. We rode the elevator with a mother and her child screaming insanely at each other. If you want to die, go to a hospital.

The elevator took forever. Like everything else public in the State of California, it had been deserted by the voters, was still being asked to do too much, and so now it was overworked and exhausted. It went from floor to floor like a wizened old man without his walker.

The Sunshine Apartments

The next morning I drove across town to Fisherman's Wharf and cruised Bay Street for a parking space. August of course is peak tourist season. Fifty thousand tourists with blue flesh from the cold fog were busy snapping photographs of nationally franchised chain restaurants they had back home. Meanwhile T-shirt shops and sidewalk hawkers, taking advantage of the cold, sold over-priced San Francisco sweatshirts to the blue-hued tourists who hadn't dressed for a San Francisco summer.

The Sunshine Apartments used to be the Sunshine Projects. What had started out as temporary housing after World War II for those demobbed servicemen on the GI Bill gradually became a low-income housing project in the mid-Sixties. The projects had been languishing for decades. Ten years ago the Sunshine Housing Projects were privatized and sold to the highest bidder.

I never understood why any private investor bought the Sunshine. The best you could say was that the entire housing complex could be easily torn down. In less than an afternoon, if need be. Nothing here was worth missing. The current tenants had little inclination now to start paying their rents. New tenants were those who had slipped down the economic flagpole and landed here. The Sunshine was three-story-tall, city-block-long nightmare.

Once inside the courtyard, I noticed the general shabbiness. The gang graffiti was the gang graffiti on the backboard in the playground impressed me the most. There were some shade trees, but they looked as gun-shy as the little children playing with toys beneath them.

I saw some rock hounds lighting up in a doorway of one apartment on the second floor. The look-see boy was the funniest of the lot. He was looking over his shoulders, checking for cops or other strangers, not looking at his buddies. Naw. Naw. No cops around. Then he realized what was going down was what he was missing out on. Hey, that's my pipe you're smoking!

I thought about walking back to my car and getting my gun. I keep a fully-loaded nine-millimeter Browning in a crisp new shoulder holster in my trunk. Unlike Clay Macondray and other paranoids, I don't carry heat on the street. If I carried when I drove, maybe a Beamer Baby or some poor lost tourist would get shot.

I went looking for the apartment manager. The apartment manager was a scrawny guy with refugee eyes and a nervous twitch. He spoke broken English and was eating out of a rice bowl. He told me the cops had been here yesterday and then they had left. He told me the bad news. By dying, Peter Staples, Senior, had lost his apartment, his belongings, his security deposit.

"How does that happen?" I didn't understand modern economics.

"He is dead."

"So you threw him out in the street?"

"Dead men don't pay rent."

"Where are all his belongings? His furnishings? His clothes?"

The manager said, as soon as the cops left, everything was boxed up and taken away.

"So where they are?"

"Ask the management company. His daughter's over there."

"Whose daughter?"

"The management company. That is her father's Mercedes she's driving."

We watched a young white woman walk to a sparkling black Mercedes and disarm its burglar alarm with her remote unit. The license plates read IGM FY.

I swore under my breath. "Who's your management company?"

A Foggy Canyon

A fog advisory had been issued on the Golden Gate Bridge. The fog was yellowish, bile-hued, and rolling across the roadway like a horizontal avalanche. The fog bounced the headlights of other cars back at me, blinding me at times. The gusts of wind and rain-like mist on the bridge were brutal. My wipers were on high. Meanwhile the drops of water came in my car window.

From Doyle Drive down through Tiburon and uphill on Ebbtide Canyon Drive, I drove slowly, living on somebody else's adrenaline. The already-popped airbag was a deflated beach ball that wouldn't go away.

A hundred yards below Danver's house, the night glowed as if a saint were coming for me. Halogen headlights came straight for me!

I wrenched the wheel, hugged the curve on the single-lane road, as four extra-bright halogen high beams blasting through the thick, yellow fog blinded me.

I looked away from the headlights and down at the right edge of the road. While I couldn't see it, I knew a cliff was there, a sheer drop of a hundred feet into San Francisco Bay, and I was on the wrong side of the narrow road.

A truck of some kind roared downhill past me, blaring its horns, and buffeted me with its blast. My eyes refocused quick enough to save a eucalyptus tree from destruction and myself from being pushed off the road. I slid past the tree and into Danvers' driveway and slammed on my brakes.

Once my heart was out of my throat, I noticed there was no car in his drive and his carport was empty. My watch said I was ten minutes early, and I debated whether to go up to the house.

I waited a minute before I made a move. I told myself, don't lose your temper. I told myself, don't punch him in the nose if you don't have to.

I popped my trunk, put my Browning and its holster back inside. I left my gun in the trunk for the same reason I usually leave it there. If I carried a gun inside to see Terry Danvers, I might find a reason to shoot him.

I stood in the damp night and smelled wood smoke in the air. Hard believing we had no rain for two whole months. I checked my watch again. It was a quarter to ten.

I walked to Danvers' house. A lamp on a pole I hadn't noticed in daylight was lit in front of the house. I made the wrought iron gate squeak, and then I walked up the flagstone path. As I reached for the doorbell, I saw the front door was not completely closed.

I heard a gunshot from inside the house, and then a second gunshot sounded. A woman screamed a split second later.

A Quiet Night

It was a long drive back. The fog was still so thick, the Bridge was all I saw, and the only reason I saw it was because I happened to be driving across it. Thank God there was little traffic on this San Francisco summer night.

The clock above the toll booths said it was still earlier than last call. I needed a drink. Everyone hates being nibbled, and today had been a big bite. But I knew better than finding a bar stool. I had already had a drink at Gino and Carlo's. As useless as I felt now, one more drink would lead to another, and too soon I could end up being the target of some CHP trolling operation.

Funny thing about the cops and their much ballyhooed assault on drunk drivers. A blind-ass drunk at four in the afternoon has a far better chance of getting home through rush hour traffic without being stopped than a guy having two beers after midnight, when 95% of the world was asleep. After midnight a guy with two beers under his breath is *guilty, guilty, guilty.*

I didn't want to go home. I am a night owl, a night crawler. There is no elbow room in the daylight, and day people are smug, prejudiced, and colorless. I like my eyes as wide as an owl's. I like the streets to myself.

I was restless, like autumn leaves in the wind. I drove around looking at the street life, hoping my fatigue wasn't far behind me. I told myself that now I was giving it a chance to catch up to me.

The night was cold and nasty, as blustery as the worst wintry night, and there were very few cars and almost no pedestrians out. Fog rattled the bus shelters. The streetlights on the next hill up ahead looked like UFOs floating in the foggy night.

I cut through the Presidio Gate, went up to California Street and rode California toward Market Street. I did have the streets to myself. After Van Ness, the cable car tracks appeared. They were wet and shiny under the yellow streetlights, and they looked like snail tracks crawling over the hills. A daisy chain of Yellow Cabs were catnapping in front of the big hotels on Nob Hill, and no doormen were in sight. Chinatown was still garishly lit, an amusement park caught between the last carouser and the lights turning off. Only garbage trucks and dog-sized rats prowled the vacant streets and back alleys. The Financial District was empty, as it is after nightfall. Grey skyscrapers, silent and spooky, colossi in the fog and night. Hard to know how high a building is with this fog.

If the Almighty Dollar is our god, the intersection of California and Market is one of our open-air cathedrals. I found no solace in that church. A homeless woman was reading a Golden Book to her two tousle-headed children in their raggedy sleeping bags in the doorway of a multi-billion dollar bank. I felt for the kids, for their mom. Hard to sleep when the headlights strike you blind.

I could fire a cannon down Market Street and not hit anyone or anything. The City and County spent millions of dollars freshening Market over the past twenty years. At night it glows golden from the high-powered streetlights. But nobody walks it much at night; the bone-chewers in the shadows keep them away.

I drove up Market to Geary Boulevard, and then down Geary past Union Square and its big hotels, past the legit theatres into Hooker Heaven at Leavenworth. I heard the brassy laughter of whores in the night echoing off the buildings, and I could feel their cold eyes gauging my metal.

Women in the street. Skintight latex dress and black stockings. Hot pink shorts and thigh-high boots. Heels and a short dress. Halter top and skirts split to the crotch. Cowboy boots and a low-cut black dress. Their parkas were unzipped; ya gotta advertise the merchandise, even on the nastiest night.

Welcome to the Night of the Living Dead. Years ago I read a statistic that said hookers are 47 times more likely to commit suicide than the average citizen. A statistic like that had the faces of women and men I knew personally. The ones not suiciding were too busy dying of AIDS.

First Law of Nature: If it's sick, don't touch it.

A young white girl in a slinky red dress came walking down Leavenworth drinking a bottle of beer. She was feminine and dainty, long-bodied and sleek, and in her red sheath dress she was sharp as a knife. She had too much make-up on: too much red lipstick, too much blush (or is it rouge?), too much red nail polish. Her corn---silk hair was carefully curled and teased. She walked like she was very proud of her tits. They were trying desperately to escape from her dress. She was pretty, and she knew that, too. She turned, looked my way, and checked me out with eyes that spoke of ennui. Zombie eyes. She recognized me, did a 180, and was gone faster than a coyote back into the shadows. That she was swallowed by the shadows seemed like a guaranteed prophecy.

But I had recognized her before she had recognized me. She was the crackhead girlfriend of that teenage boy I'd seen being needled at San Francisco General. Seeing her working the streets made me curious enough to look closer at her.

She was fourteen years old and busy looking for tricks. Anyone could tell by her legs she was a kid. Her calves were straight lines, not those rounded muscles women have from years of wearing heels. She was a kid, but she was no innocent. Innocence has a short shelf life on the streets, and she'd been on the streets too long for that. She'd look at you blankly if you asked her if hooking was good or evil. It was how she took somebody's fifty bucks and made it her own. Any dream she had beyond simple survival out here was a luxury she could not afford.

I remembered a runaway kid I had tracked down for his parents. I caught him selling a blowjob to a Muni bus inspector in an alley off Polk Street. I parked the kid in my backseat and took him straight home to his parents. "I make fifty bucks for every blowjob I give," the kid kept bragging. "How much do you make in a day?" he kept asking. His parents called me back three weeks later, asked me if I wanted to track him down again. I said they should get someone else.

I don't ever wonder what happened to him. He's dead now. When I met him, that was 'way back before AIDS cruised these streets looking for a one-shot lover. No, he could not survive that disaster.

This child, too, was headed for the dead. And when she died, there'd be another to take her place. The streets are forever; they never change. They must have their sacrificial lambs.

Mom's Motel on Mission

Annie and I followed Dr. Peter Staples and Gwen Kaufman. Following the red Eldorado was easy. It was the largest car on the road and it had a broken taillight.

Gwen Kaufman went out Lombard to Divisadero to Fulton. She took Fulton west, and then cut through Golden Gate Park. Golden Gate Park was dripping with fog. Fog writhed in the fir trees, like ghosts in a Japanese lithograph. My wipers were on medium. The Eldorado went out Nineteenth Avenue, swooped around San Francisco State, and then jumped onto Interstate 280 South. We trudged along after it and had no problem keeping up with it. The Eldorado took the second Daly City off-ramp, crossed over to Mission Street, and then we drove out to Colma.

Colma, California. Population: 731. The sign was out of date. Colma had nine hundred people according to the last census, and that boost made Colma the fastest growing city in California. Nine hundred. That's the live ones.

Colma is a necropolis. A city of the dead. It has more than twenty cemeteries within its city limits. See, Colma is across the county line from the City and County of San Francisco. Which made it the nearest place to bury the dead from the Big City to the north.

We drove out on Mission Street in Colma to Mom's Motel. Seventy-five years ago liquid stucco was molded into a necklace of a dozen one-bedroom bungalows around a common parking area, and then left here to cool in the shade of a eucalyptus grove. The trees were nice. The bungalows were shit.

Mom's Motel on Mission was set back from the street and surrounded on three sides by cemeteries. It had a swimming pool, but that pool was completely filled in with dirt and was now a victory garden for the current residents. A sunflower a head taller than me peeked over the swimming pool fence and looked for a way out.

"Why are they stopping here?" Annie asked.

The cherry-red Eldorado drove to the rear of the motel cul-de-sac. I didn't follow the Eldorado, but pulled off and parked at the Manager's Office. He too had the basic bungalow, except his had a second bedroom and a carport added.

Peter and Gwen Kaufman parked at the last bungalow. She waited in the car while Peter unlocked the front door. Then she left the car and joined him inside.

Annie and I went inside and spoke with the resident manager of Mom's Motel. "Hi, we're with the guy in the red Eldorado." The three of us watched Peter Staples and Gwen Kaufman disappear into Unit 8.

"I guess I'll go collect some rent," the resident manager said. She was a scrawny woman, middle-aged and very short. She had a GI haircut and a small gold crucifix hung on a rawhide cord around her neck. She also had three earrings per ear and a nose ring in her left nostril. She was dressed as if a naked child had crawled into some adult's dirty laundry and now wore whatever garments had stuck to her in passing.

"How far behind?" Annie asked.

The resident manager gave us a calculating look. "The rent was paid up until yesterday. If the guy living there doesn't come in today with next week's rent, we're ready to move in and take it over. Shampoo the rugs, paint the walls. You know, pretty up the place."

"What was the tenant's name? Peter Staples, Senior?"

The manager was suspicious. "Yeah."

"He's dead," Annie said. "He was the victim of a drive-by shooting Sunday night."

The manager was unruffled by the news. "No wonder he hasn't been around," she mused.

"When was the last time you saw him?" I said.

"Oh, months." The manager gestured at her ledger. "Black Pete paid his rent in cash six months ahead so he wouldn't need to have a credit check."

"So I guess you knew him well," Annie said.

Her smile said she knew him well; it was as old as the hills. "I knew his kind."

"Is all his stuff in there?"

"It's there. Like I said, he's paid up until yesterday."

Annie took out her wallet. "How much to cover another thirty days?" She paid another month's rent. "If you have questions--." She gave the manager her business card. "Frank, give her your card."

The manager read mine, too. "A private eye?"

"Legal services, mostly."

"Call us if you need us," Annie said.

Outside, I was impressed. "You are generous."

"You said it. If Mario Rosales is after him, he needs a safe place to live."

"So you're still acting as his attorney?"

"Black Pete was a very dear friend."

An Afternoon Off

The afternoon was mine to do as I wanted. First I bought a case of pinot noir from the Carneros region and charged it to Ratzinger. I was hoping Mary Noël Wu and I could share a bottle or two. I am a sucker for women who smile at me when they don't need to.

I found Mary Noël had texted me. The final medical report on Jerry Sutton was complete, she said. Oh, he was still in Intensive Care with the other more serious injuries. But she summarized the other injuries. Beyond the expected bruises and laceration, the ambushed chauffeur had a dislocated finger, a chipped elbow bone from where he hit the sidewalk, and of course some unusual cuts and bruises on his face and body. Also a concussion and bruises and cuts. Oh, that gash in his forehead was worth seven stitches. A fractured arm from defending himself. Lastly, he had a black eye. His left eye would still be troubling him when he was released.

Then I went driving along the waterfront. Then through the Marina and up to the Golden Gate Bridge. I went walking alone up there. Even walking beneath the struts of the Bridge to the wildflowers on the other side. In the Outer Sunset I found a quiet coffee shop clad in barn wood. I ordered their tallest Americano and pretended I was diddling my cell phone.

Yesterday I flew into Oakland because it's easier to get in and out of than SFO. Flying in from the southeast was like coming home as a kid.

I flew into and over Golden California. The chaparral and the oak trees, the cypresses and sycamores and the eucalyptus. Oh, the oaks. The great round balls of green on golden grassy hillsides that I loved most of all. Nothing like it in Nevada.

By birth, I am an Angeleno. But California sure has changed since then. When I came home from college, I discovered the river that ran through my neighborhood had vanished. Cemented over, the river was now a supermarket.

My neighborhood was all white stucco buildings with red tile roofs: the Mission style. The Taco Bell style. Come to think about it, most banks, coffee shops, laundromats, carpet stores, and porno theaters in California all look like Taco Bells.

I was horrified when I learned that when the swallows came back to Capistrano, they overflew the Mission and nested at the Bank of America building a half-mile away. I never cared much for swallows, once I found out they were just starlings. And hordes of starlings, all they do is drive you nuts with their noise at sundown and how much they shit on the sidewalks.

I got coffee and sat and stewed. Was it time for me to see my in-laws? Or maybe look up the Atkins woman? She always knew the latest, juiciest gossip.

I mumbled to myself, "What's the story behind the story?"

Emeryville

"My mother was a very beautiful woman. Glamorous. My father bought her jewelry and she would go to nightclubs. She went out at night alone. I remember, when we were still living in Emeryville, often she would take the garbage out at night and be gone for an hour. My father didn't complain, never explained. One night I followed her to the roof of our apartment building. She was looking out at the night lights of San Francisco. She told me the night lights of the city were diamonds cascading over black velvet." But poetry was not enough to anchor this mother to her child. "She was a very hungry woman. She wanted all those diamonds for herself."

Mario's Mom

I drove so fast down the Vallejo Street hill, I got a nosebleed. I roared down and around the Embarcadero, knowing full well what a standstill the 101 Freeway South was. Embarcadero is Spanish for wharf, and on a peninsula surrounded on three sides by salt water, you have mucho embarcadero. Since the last earthquake whacked three freeways off the face of the earth, surface streets are what's left. Once again, the only way to get around was to go around. I left the Embarcadero at Brannan, caught every yellow light, hopped on I-280 at Sixth, and rode it down to Cesar Chavez.

My destination was two blocks over from the housing projects and two blocks down from where the freeway crossed over Cesar Chavez Street. It was a hardworking neighborhood off York and 25th with houses too close together on a narrow street with not enough street parking and too many unemployed young men hanging around the corner mom-n-pop.

This neighborhood was going nowhere, like a hamster wheel. Run like a fool all your days and you end up dying in the same house you were born in and never stopped paying rent for.

I met the SFPD units on York Street. Detectives Curtin and Howard stood beside the Cage. It was a panel truck with a lock and no windows and a zebra paint job. A century ago the mobile cage was called a paddy wagon, but now the cops call it the Cage. The vehicle was dented and banged up, but from the inside out.

Detective Howard, scowling, blamed me. "Your Dr. Staples waylaid Mario Rosales with a gun and tried to shoot him."

He made no sense at all.

"The good doctor shot up the neighborhood," Curtin snitched.

"Peter was here? He knows where Mario Rosales hangs?"

"We think him and the Rosales kid were partners in crime, crack dealers who fell to bickering, who started shooting each other over the profits."

"Hey! Gonna roll the van!"

The Cage was rocking back and forth. The shrieks were muffled, but the language was self-evident. The prisoner within was banging on the sides with fists. Kicking the sides. Hurtling himself against the rear door.

I was surprised. Generally most bravado gets said and done before people see the Cage in all its power and majesty. Once they get thrown inside, the Cage sobers and humbles all.

Howard banged his fist on the back door. "Knock it off in there!" he called.

The curses were directed at him.

Some street person with few teeth and a wandering eye got ballsy and looked in the rear window of the Cage, probably to see if it was somebody she knew. Her eyes went wide, and she called back to her friends, "It's a woman."

"A woman?" I repeated. I had assumed either Mario Rosales or Peter Staples was in the van, that one or the other had run amuck and now was under arrest.

Howard smirked. "It's Mario's mom. She broke parole and now she is going back to jail."

Curtin laughed. "Yeah. She called the police, and we arrested her. She's real upset because Dr. Staples shot up her truck, too."

For the first time I noticed an old Chevy pickup with a windshield star-bursted by a shotgun blast. "He used a shotgun?"

"Yeah. He used a shotgun."

"So where's Peter? Where's Mario?"

"He escaped," Curtin said. "They escaped."

Howard became testy. "Hey, Pasnow, that doc is needed to testify against Mario Rosales."

I shrugged helplessly. "I'm not his mother."

"Don't fuck our case up."

My head tilted. Like you haven't fucked it up already? But I didn't say it. Instead, I went with them to Harrison's office in the Hall.

While there, I dropped off last night's photos with a note asking for any rap sheet that went with the hooker's pictures. Most of my life I have dreaded having the Captain of Detectives at the SFPD as my new best friend. Since my folks got smoked, I have wanted to keep the cops at arm's length from my life. But sometimes a new best friend comes in handy.

Mario's mom was brought upstairs after she was booked. She was a short woman, thick-limbed and pockmarked. She was in her mid-thirties, but she acted like most teenagers when they get busted. She was a lounge lizard with her hands in her white jeans, slouching in a chair, her eyes wandering the floor or glaring at the ceiling, with all the false bravado of the natural-born loser. Her sweatshirt wished the world a Maui Christmas. Bravado all the way to the last steps of Hell.

"Mrs. Rosales, are you HIV-positive?"

"Why? You wanna fuck me?"

"This bitch's done time. Lots of time," Curtin said.

Howard pretended being surprised. "Can you smell it, too?"

"You make me want to puke," she growled.

"Street trash," Curtin said. "Her kind finds trouble in laundromats."

The other detective was more philosophical. "As long as she hasn't bitten anybody recently."

"She said her son Mario's a crack dealer," Curtin confided.

I sighed. "At fourteen he's living off the streets."

Howard snorted and said, "Like runaways his age don't?"

Yo no tengo futuro. I have no future.

"How'd he get tied up with killers?" I asked. "Was it the crack?"

"Crackers." Curtin spat on the pavement. "These rock hounds have cut themselves off from heaven and hell. They've cut themselves off from God. That's the horror. They become animals wearing human faces."

Mario's mom gave me the finger, too. She thought I was one of them. I didn't mind. I've been slapped around by life, too. I recognized the suspicious fear behind the eyes, the false bravado in the timbre of the voice, the weakness in the knees. I had more sympathy for her than anybody else in the room would expect. But I kept my thoughts to myself.

I was supposed to wait for Captain Harrison, but I didn't stay long in Homicide. I get claustrophobic in small rooms filled with detectives with shirt pockets with pens. Like a drowning man I keep seeing my past flash in front of me.

I ran into Captain Harrison in the corridor. He pulled me aside from the pedestrian flow. "The mayor's new personal assistant says the Board of Supervisors is going to fund ten investigator slots for the Office of Citizen Complaints." He punched my shoulder. "I slipped your package in at the top of the list."

For a moment I let myself daydream about regularly arriving paychecks, major medical and dental with lower premiums, vacation pay, even (God help me!) a pension. The daydream vaporized quickly. I do better being my own boss.

The captain ruminated aloud. "I had a very strange phone call from the Public Defender's Office. A young woman called their offices, said Mario Rosales wants protection. She claims he was set up by some Vivisection Valley gang. Probably the same shooters who put him in the hospital. She claims the bangers want to kill him to keep him from testifying against them. And he wants the charges against him dropped."

"Do you think he'll testify?"

"If all the charges against him are dropped."

"Are you buying that, Captain?"

He was noncommittal. "Mario Rosales was a witness to the Vivisection Valley shooting. The DA wants him under wraps. He might be state's evidence against the Valley's shooters."

"But he was the guy who shot Black Pete and his son."

"He's the alleged shooter, Frank. On the plus side, he can identify the Vivisection shooters and we've been trying for years to get them off the streets. Look at it from the DA's point of view. He can try a fourteen year old boy as a gangland shooter, or use him to snitch on a horde of gun-crazed drug dealers. What's the better PR?"

I wasn't convinced. Usually bangers who testify against other gangs' bangers neither live long nor prosper. Since the Federal Witness Protection Program doesn't reach down to street level, snitches die young and they don't leave a beautiful corpse.

Harrison had to leave when his pager went off. I promised him I'd keep in touch. In the main Homicide office, I met Mario Rosales's grandmother. Rosie Alvarez had a round face and saucer eyes, no front teeth, and she spoke limited English. She was a grandmother. Her eyes were all sorrow and doubt. But she was so fat, it was hard to tell how old she was.

"Are you another policeman?"

"No, I am not a cop."

She took my hand and squeezed. "Can you give me a ride home?"

I gave her a ride home. Maybe she would say things to me she'd not say to a cop. Some people get nervous around cops. I get nervous, too, as nervous as that long-tailed cat in the room full of rocking chairs. Maybe that's why I keep resisting applying for a job with the SFPD; I'd make myself so fatally nervous, I'd have a pretext to run myself in.

"May I sit up front?"

Surprised, I said, "Sure."

She opened the door, plopped down on the seat. She lost her posture when she sat. Her shoulders slumped, her boobs flattened and sagged, and her arms flopped about in aimless gestures. But she didn't immediately swing her legs inside.

Instead she hiked her skirt to her kneecap and started fiddling with her left leg above the knee. She noticed me watching. Embarrassed, she said, "Please forgive me, but my leg takes time to undo."

Out of the corner of my eye, I watched as she unscrewed a prosthetic limb, set it between us, and shifted her good leg inside my car. Then she closed the door with a slam and buckled her seat belt.

As we drove away from the Hall, Grandmother Alvarez told me some of the facts of life. The Rosales family had been sliding down the toilet bowl walls for some time now. But the worst of the news was that after Mario's mom had been convicted of receiving stolen property, her children were taken away from her and placed in foster care.

I did not understand one-tenth of the Spanish she gushed out, but apparently Mario's father had been a hick and a whore, a bad husband and a poor provider, a drunk, a womanizer, and in her part of Mexico would have been whipped by her sons for his sins.

We went out Third Street and drove past the shipyards, the metal shops, the factories. Traffic was thick in both directions on Third, with everyone in the know bypassing the freeway's crush. Here at least you could maneuver. On the freeway you could only pout at the bumper ahead of you. We drove on, into the ghetto, its lonesome storefronts and its sorrowful houses. We drove on through a landscape of heartache and hard times.

"Can you tell me where Mario is?"

His grandmother said, "Like a knife thrust into my back."

She had her hands so filled with love and grief, I don't know if she even heard me. Hell, she was on her second generation of heartache.

"Is he staying with anyone you know?"

"Oh, god, not again. I don't know where this child is coming up with this. I don't know what to believe. It's about to turn me and his mother crazy. Our Lady, have mercy on our souls."

"Are there any friends who might know where Mario is?"

"I hope my grandson will purge his soul."

"Have you heard from Mario?"

"I tried talking him to surrender to his lawyer. I'm tired of working against the police, hiding him. I don't know if my heart can take anymore. All this trouble is killing me. I wish he'd quit bringing up trouble I don't know anything about. Troubles like this can't bring anything but hurt."

She lived on the India Basin side of Hunters Point, near the docks at Point Avisadero. Like most San Franciscans, she had a view at the end of her street. Her view was of the City itself, the metallic skyline of San Francisco's downtown, where the flashing knives of skyscrapers were ripping at the dark belly of fog.

"Last night Mario called me. Mario told me his mother sold him for a drug debt. Maybe she did. One day he disappeared, and she had money to keep her house."

"When did he disappear from her home?"

She thought back. "Memorial Day."

"Has he been gone that long? Nobody noticed?"

"By Labor Day the debt would be paid. By then he go back to school."

I watched a seagull fight the wind at the end of the street. "Do you believe she sold him into slavery to pay off a drug deal?"

Grandmother sighed. "I don't know what to believe. She lie to me. He lie to me."

I glared out the windshield until I saw a pattern unfold. "From here, the city's skyline looks like a bed of nails."

She gave me a look that said: It is.

I surveyed the tired clapboard houses and the fenced-in warehouses. A junked car was in every backyard. There were rusted barbecues and barking dogs. An eight month old Christmas tree shared a lawn with an abandoned refrigerator with a missing door. I would hate being here at night. Street lights were further apart down here. Street lights that cast too little light. Shadows that go on forever. Down here you know we're not all in this together. Down here you learn what being left out means.

How you ever gonna get outa here, lady?

She touched my hand again. "Could you wait for me to get inside? I was robbed three times this year."

I watched as she first opened the door and then began reversing the steps to wrench on her prosthetic leg.

"Do you need me to come around and help you out?"

"No, Mr. Pasnow, thank you. You been too kind already." She almost left, but turned back. "Can you pass a message on to somebody for me?"

Embarrassed, I said, "Sure."

She gave me a note with a phone number on it. "That young man my grandson--my daughter say she will go after him and kill him. Maybe somebody can get to him first, warn him my Angela is coming after him."

I sat in my car and watched her toddle towards her side door. A rusty bicycle with two flat tires was chained to her front porch; the porch was ready to collapse. Her lawn needed reseeding. Her house needed a new roof. I watched a teenage boy coming down the street toward us carrying four hubcaps. Two long dark cars came and blocked the boy. Burly men jumped out and took away the hubcaps.

I hit the power locks. As the two dark cars left, as Grandmother Alvarez locked her door, as the boy without hubcaps ran off toward the bed of nails, I was flooring the gas pedal.

One Cold Blonde

Tennessee south and Cesar Chavez, where the long haul truckers sleep off their white line fevers before making their early morning deliveries, has always been one of the gloomier parts of San Francisco. And not because of the constant fog, either. Here, I never see a woman. Not even in daylight. There was no safety here in sunshine. The only light came from the street lights, and the street lights here in this old part of town were further apart.

Tennessee south wasn't a street. It was hardly more than a large gravel driveway between two huge warehouses. Once past them, Tennessee took a dog's leg off to the right. I passed the rear entrance to a fat-rendering plant. More gravel, no street lights, finally a dead-end by some railroad ties another hundred yards back. An eighteen-wheeler was aimed like an arrow at a ravine, and a half-dozen police cruisers with flashing lights but no sirens were perched on the edge of the ravine.

I parked as close as I could and walked towards the cruisers. This far off the beaten track, the freeway noises were still with me, background noise to the City. A few steps further, and they faded off.

I walked through the dark, gravel scrunching under my feet, and I thought about changing my mind, seeing the Captain tomorrow at some more regular time. This trip was pointless, the act of a man too wired and wide-eyed to know what he was doing.

The smell from the fat-rendering plant was palpable, noxious, and almost unbearable. I for one would rather plunge into a lifetime of debt than spend a cold night here in the back of a long-haul cab.

I came upon a homicide inspector talking to some uniforms: "Don't forget to look through that dumpster back there. For all you know, there's a homeless man asleep or a newborn baby abandoned in there. And that junked Chevy over there. Those junked parts there." He saw me; we nodded to each other, and I was accepted as belonging here.

A uniformed officer stood by himself, away from the others, aiming a hand-held spotlight down at some white things in a puddle.

I knelt and squinted. In horror I recognized them.

"Broken teeth," the officer said.

I walked on, my guts churning.

I walked to where the eighteen-wheeler was parked. The big rig's brights were illuminating a handful of men in waders in the watery pond within the ravine. Its big diesel engine was idling, and clouds of hot fumes were billowing from its exhaust. The rig's diesel fumes were noxious and driving me crazy.

I stopped at the edge of the ravine and looked over the crime scene. Aside from the rumble of the diesel rig, this crime scene could have been a silent movie. The world was night-black and spotlight-white, and there were no grays.

Police roof lights were flashing in the night. Cones from flashlights slashed like laser swords through the shadows until the portable lights were in place. Then: hard faces standing in the cold night became even harder in the artificial day. Paperwork being completed. Flash photographs being taken. Crime scene tape being unwound. Latex gloves and latex booties.

Captain Harrison looked tired, and there were pillow creases on his face. We shook hands, and I gave him both the chemise-wrapped shotgun and the skinny on Mario Rosales.

"He's still running," I said. "On foot and ready to steal a car to Mexico."

Harrison said, "Thanks, Frank, I'll add that to his APB." He saw my unease. "This place gets to me, too."

"What happened here?"

"A dead body in the toxic waste," Harrison said.

I saw the corpse floating on the surface of the pond, face-down in the murky waters. Its limbs were outstretched, although the body wasn't that sodden or swollen.

Harrison started down the slope, and I followed him. "Watch your step," he said as we approached the lip of the pond.

I was almost overwhelmed by the stench of a broken urinal. Truckers had been pissing for years into this toxic waste that came from the chemical plants all around us.

We walked to the very edge. Searchlights above us were focused on the paramedics who wore waist-high rubber waders and rubber gloves and now had to wade through thigh-deep goo to pull the corpse out.

I looked at the dozen-odd public employees all around me methodically engaged in the business of tallying all the facts about this death. I marveled at the gyroscopes that kept them on their feet time and again at murder scenes like this.

The corpse was brought ashore. The body of a woman, it wore a pantsuit and tennis shoes. The body was ashen-gray and had started to stiffen from the cold water. At first I thought the clothes looked familiar, but that idea was far-fetched. Nobody I knew would end up dead down here on this dead-end street.

Harrison said, "Any guesses on the murder weapon?"

"She was beaten with a tire iron," the Medical Examiner said. "Classic wound pattern. I may be wrong, but I'd be surprised."

Harrison spoke to a homicide inspector. "Start looking for anything blood-stained like a tire iron." He looked back up at the lip of the ravine. "How did she get here? Where's her car?"

A uniform brought a bottle of clean water and the M. E. poured it slowly over the corpse's face. The water revealed the brutally beaten head, the open mouth, the opened eyes, the blank look of the dead, the blonde hair.

"One cold blonde," Harrison muttered.

She became recognizable with the water. Like a photograph coming into focus, she became someone I knew.

Castle Across The Bay

I went back to my car, and then waited around the Berkeley Marina another thirty minutes for Macondray to finish tossing the boat. When he came out empty-handed, I followed him across the Bay Bridge. Tailing a Rolls is not a snap. They drive very, very slowly. You think you watch out for uninsured motorists?

Even though this was Saturday morning, San Francisco still had left its night lights on, and the foggy morning made the City as magical and mesmerizing as the Emerald City of Oz. To my right, Alcatraz was a faraway castle on an island in the Bay. A hero could swim that magical bay, storm that fortress of stone, and rescue the lady in the tower. I have always wished I was a better person.

Macondray left Interstate 80 at Ninth Street. I followed his Rolls to an alley south of Market off Eleventh Street. He parked well, and then left his car and walked a half-block to a Queen Anne Victorian with curtained windows. Then he climbed the stairs to the Temple of the Sacred Penis.

I turned back to my world. It was a brand-new morning. I went home and back to bed. I was determined to get some sleep. Paradise is where you find it.

Beale Street

I had the cab take us back to the Financial District by way of Brannan Street. "Candy Mac was taken down here," I said.

We were on Beale Street, the 400 block, on the bayside of the San Francisco Bay Bridge, on that thin strip of land beneath the bridge, between the waters of the bay and the anchors of the bridge itself. We were a brisk five minute walk to all of San Francisco's skyscrapers. Even at rush hour's busiest moments, this part of Beale Street was one of the more deserted sections of the downtown. Not much traffic down here after dark, either. Only savvy commuters going for the mostly unknown Bryant on-ramp to the Bridge and what few people who lived in Puppieville itself who might go home this backdoor way.

"You go this way home every night, don't you?"

"Every night," Lucy said promptly.

∞

I had the cab stop. We climbed out on Beale Street. The San Francisco Bay Bridge was three hundred feet overhead, a gray steel-beam Godzilla that blocked out the sky, and once again the constant traffic was an audible waterfall cascading on us.

The west side of the 400 block was a cliff face where the bridge's pylons were anchored in Rincon Hill. The east side of the street was a few warehouses, office buildings, and commuter lots for parking. Then came the Embarcadero, the piers, and the cold waters of the Bay.

The view beyond that eastern side of the street was breathtaking. Spanning the bay itself was the great shadowy Bay Bridge. A black submarine was cruising on the surface of the gray waters of the bay, heading toward the Golden Gateway and the deep blue Pacific depths. In the distance, the glittering lights of Oakland and the East Bay were as exciting and inviting as only skylines can be. But then few cities live up to the promises made by their skylines. Oakland and the East Bay never would.

Pandora Boxx

Pandora Boxx lived in an old red brick warehouse down on Bryant Street near the on-ramp to the Bay Bridge. Her building was waiting for the next Big One to shake it and fling itself apart into a million pieces of rubble.

Bryant Street was a four lane street. Come up Bryant from the west, and it's one-way, a straight climb two long blocks uphill, onto the setting sun, and the commuters drive like their pants were on fire.

Take Bryant Street east from Second Street, and in a half-block, you have your on-ramp to the Bay Bridge. The other side of the street was an unbroken wall of warehouses and lofts that flowed up and over the Bryant Street hill.

Few San Franciscans ever came here; the only goal was the on-ramp to the Bridge. Commuters go too fast to look around at the scenery, too busy eyeing their fellow drivers for road rage or other duplicities. An on-ramp not for beginners.

A notch was between the buildings on the north side of Brannan Street. There, the on-ramp twisted sharply left and sharply right, and commuters immediately joined the eastbound flow of traffic.

To the uninitiated, it must have looked like this lemmings' rush of traffic was being swallowed up by some bottomless warehouse. But no building filled the gap. A few yards later that on-ramp lane dead-ended, and a truck-sized freeway sign said "East Bay," and the lane has a dogleg left onto the on-ramp. And then these lemmings were headed at freeway speeds up and onto the Bay Bridge.

Aside from the constant noise, a lot of solitude was here.

Head east and hug the curb lane and you could avoid the on-ramp, continue past the on-ramp and find yourself on the anchorage beneath the Bay Bridge.

Where do you park? On the median along the on-ramp.

Put your life in your hands at freeway speeds and inches to spare.

That night I discovered where she lived and I broke into Pandora's loft.

When I broke in, a ginger cat in his leather recliner gave me the evil eye.

Her loft celebrated the fin de siècle. A red velvet couch. Forest green velvet drapes. Dark hardwood floors. Very cheery furnishings for a loft. She paid good money to live here alone. Well, maybe not with the freeway outside her living room.

She had great taste. Well, better than me. A waist-high Balinese vase was filled with peacock feathers and those feathery plumes from the hillsides along the freeway. Art deco glassware in an oak cabinet. Posters from Belle Epoch operas at La Scala. A framed vintage Josephine Baker nude, complete with autograph. Signed century-old menus from Maxim's and Café de Paris.

The bedroom was a raised platform overlooking the living area. Upstairs, a king-sized brass bed with a lace canopy. Lubricants filled the backboard of the bed. A lot of colorful and grotesque artwork from some local sculptresses. A photograph of Pandora with her parents. Her BFA diploma in Art History from the University of the Arts in Philadelphia was framed and matted. An enormous, extremely old mirror. Muscle magazines. An exercise bicycle that looked out and down and onto the freeway to Oakland.

In her boudoir I looked through her closets and clothes racks. Pandora's handmade gowns. Her full-length mirrors. Bouffant wigs, low-cut beaded gowns and faux diamond earrings. The usual feminine goodies were plunked down in an antique chest of drawers. Several pairs of crotchless panties, all in lace and in a dozen different tropical colors. Black satin lingerie with gold embroidery.

Frilly and colorful lingerie was drying from every niche in the bathroom. Lubricants filled the medicine chest and gave me a clue to which gender she preferred that particular day. Combined with the scads of make-up and cosmetics scattered mostly in the bedroom and the bathroom, she had no favored gender preference. Who shall I be today?

Then I noticed: the loft was as quiet as a side street in the suburbs. For some reason, the constant freeway sounds didn't burst through the walls. Good insulation, I thought.

I was under the Bridge. Not the GG. But under the San Francisco Bay Bridge. Mind you, it is not the Oakland Bay Bridge. It's not the Oakland Bay out there, beautiful and cold and dreamy. It is San Francisco Bay as far as the eye can see.

A love seat had its back to the living room, faced the full window, and the window looked out at the huge concrete columns of the bridge and the on-ramp that snaked between them, that then merged with on-coming traffic headed east.

Pandora would sit in her love seat and watch the rush hour traffic snarl, tangle, and turn into peanut butter. The love seat also held a love chest. Inside was a very expensive white leather golf bag.

Inside the golf bag was her shotgun.

She had a Mossberg five-shot 12-gauge shotgun. Old, but in loving condition. Family heirloom? Stolen property? A burglar's souvenir?

My cell phone I propped on a shelf midway between me and Pandora.

Colma

I never found out how Trudy Danvers handled the news about the death of Aunt Gwen. By the time Lucy Runyon and I reached the Golden Mountain mortuary, the funeral procession for Trudy's father was lined up and revved up. Some teenage kid came by, told me to turn on my headlights, and slapped a FUNERAL self-stickum on my windshield.

"Lousy turn-out," I muttered.

"More than I had expected," Lucy said.

The funeral procession was shorter than I had expected. The mortuary limos were followed by only a half-dozen cars. Not too many people showed for the funeral for San Francisco's biggest landlord. The funeral procession drove down to Interstate 280, and then headed west to the coastal mountains and the sea. Then we all disappeared into the dense fogs of Colma. Now, the cars in the funeral procession had trouble keeping close together. Other vehicles cut between the funeral cars. But then all California freeways are as indifferent as the cold sea.

We left the freeway at Serramonte Boulevard, and then drove east and halfway up San Bruno Mountain. The cemetery was laid out like a pegboard on a long hillside that sloped down to the freeway and up to the microwave towers; we were quickly enveloped by fog and encircled by a hundred thousand gravestones.

The fog where we stood was thick and damp, and the westerlies off the ocean were cold, constant, and blustery. It felt like years since I had felt the sun on my bones.

Before the gravesite services, there was the usual milling about by the mourners, and a rough sort of pecking order gradually formed around the hole in the ground.

Terry Danvers' funeral had a warm-hearted cast of visitors. I counted heads. There were thirteen of us. Death's favorite number, I thought to myself. The Chinese minister no one knew and who knew no one. Trudy by the minister's side. Clay Macondray off to one side. Lucy and I. There were other people I didn't recognize.

Lucy touched my sleeve. "Trudy needs you."

I went over. Trudy pressed my hand and sighed despondently. She sniffled into a handkerchief. I felt awkward with her. Her father was dead, her aunt was dead, and her stepmother was dead. I realized, by the same token, all her enemies were dead.

After the services, there was the usual milling about of mourners, and a rough sort of reception line formed between the hole in the ground and where the cars were parked. There, we all waited for Trudy Danvers to finish blowing her nose. But then after the mourners approached her, commiserated with her, and then left, the tears disappeared fast. Immediately after the tears disappeared, she got tough.

"Leeches," Trudy said under her breath.

Mini-History Lesson

These two topics--the Gold Rush and how California annexes the USA--are the same story, "about the 20 year period between the Discovery of Gold at Sutter's Fort and the Completion of the Transcontinental Railroad."

The truth of their connection is so much MORE than we're generally told.

The Story of California is unique, and it mythologized one state above all others. That's the underlying root to this course ... as it is reflected both in its unique fictions and in how Americans have viewed this place over the past two hundred years.

Sen. Daniel Webster in 1843 asked his colleagues, "What do you want of that vast and worthless area, that region of savages and wild beasts, of deserts, of shifting sands and whirling winds, of dust, of cactus and prairie dogs?"

Did you know the pioneers were almost all white folks?

Seattle and Portland are STILL at or near the top of the 50 largest U.S. cities for the percentages of their residents who are white.

Portland's population has been and remains predominantly white, as a result of historic policies and trends. In 2009, Portland had the fifth-highest percentage of white residents among the 40 largest U.S. metropolitan areas. A 2007 survey of the 40 largest cities in the U.S. concluded that Portland's urban core is the "whitest big city in the nation".

Some scholars have noted the Pacific Northwest as a whole is "one of the last Caucasian bastions of the United States". While Portland's diversity was historically comparable to metro Seattle and Salt Lake City, those areas grew more diverse in the late 1990s and 2000s.

Portland not only remains white, but migration to Portland is disproportionately white, at least partly because Portland is attractive to young college-educated Americans, a group which is overwhelmingly white.

The Oregon Territory banned African American immigration in 1849. In the 19th century, certain laws allowed the immigration of Chinese laborers but prohibited them from owning property or bringing their families. The early 1920s saw the rapid growth of the Ku Klux Klan, which became very influential in Oregon politics, culminating in the election of Walter M. Pierce as governor.

BTW, many of "the earliest American pioneers" were Irish refugees from the Potato Famine. Land in Oregon? And then Gold was discovered in California.

The Irish gold miners (ah, the 49ers) camped out alongside and intermingled with the Chinese gold miners on Fremont and First Streets in San Francisco.

How do we know the Irish and the Chinese camped alongside? Modern archeologists get called to the scene whenever a new skyscraper construction in downtown San Francisco "discovers" the garbage heaps of the past.

They were even buried together.

Placards carried through San Francisco after the last spike was driven in 1869 read "California Annexes the United States." A lot of truth there, too.

Without the Gold Rush, there would be no America as we know it.

Consider California Dreamin'.

Confined at its birth to the area east of the Mississippi River, by 1853 the continental United States was complete. By 1867 the United States reached all the way to the Bering Strait. Never has a nation grown so large so quickly. The United States is today the third-largest country in the world, behind only Russia and Canada.

Abraham Lincoln was always California dreamin'. He and his wife Mary talked about taking the train there on the night he was assassinated. They were on their way to the theater.

Two years after gold was discovered, California became a state. Two years! No other state became a state so fast! Or was so far away from the United States when it became a state! And it was separated from the rest of the United States by hostile wilderness. It stayed that way for the next twenty (20) years. And we got us a railroad!

How important was that first transcontinental railroad? I mean, how come they had to go all the way across the United States, when they could have, say, picked a shorter route somewhere?

Remember I said you could either walk for six months to America, or take a sailing ship all the way around the tip of South America, or you could walk through the malaria-infested, yellow-fever infested Panama to the Pacific.

Well, easier routes were tried … with disastrous results.

In the 1850s, six thousand workers died during the construction of the Panama railway, the world's first transcontinental line -- 120 dead men for each mile of railway.

A prelude to the Panama Canal, you could say.

Now, before you start going libertarian on us and praising the entrepreneurship of the pioneers and railroad robber barons (i.e., middle-class businessmen from Sacramento,) please know that ….

…. the U.S. government gave very very very large land grants to the Union Pacific & Central Pacific railroads. Between 1850 and 1871 the railroads received more than 175 million acres of public land.

The railroads STILL own most of the best agricultural lands in California.

And remember the old adage about somebody who grew up on the wrong side of the tracks. For most Americans, living next to the railroad meant you lived near the POWER ELITE. The proto-environmentalist John Muir married and lived in Martinez, California; his daughters every day would go out and wave at the railroad crew passing through town. The warehouses and trading centers were on the other side of the tracks.

IGM FY

       With videotape in hand, I went outside. Outside, the songbirds had stopped. I looked out over San Francisco Bay. The fog was so thick that the golden hills around the Golden Gate Bridge were purple bruises. The skyscrapers of San Francisco had a black armband over their towers. I was tired of a summer punched out and slapped around like this. I wanted some sunlight. Sunlight was the best disinfectant, wasn't it?

       I sat again on the crates, rehearsing how I wanted this next scene to go down, knowing it never goes down the way it's rehearsed. Still, like a cat burglar, I circled the target and memorized all the entrances and exits.

       I heard a creaking sound. It came from Terry Danvers' Mercedes. It still sat alone in the carport. All cars make small noises from time to time. Even imported cars with goofy license plates.

IGM FY
I got mine. Fuck you.

The Law Firm at 101 California Street

The high rise at 101 California Street took up a city block in the Financial District and was home base for a dozen hotshot law firms.

I went up to the thirtieth floor and the executive offices for the law firm of Macondray, Macondray and Associates. The entire floor smelled of fresh microwave popcorn. I suppose smelling like a movie house covers up the smell created by lawyers practicing law.

Macondray, Macondray and Associates was one hundred and eighty lawyers who worked like dogs and drove their employees even harder. The law firm was open twenty-four hours a day and three hundred and sixty-five days a year. A pool of underpaid and overworked word processors, couriers, law clerks, proofreaders, paralegals, and legal secretaries kept the partners and associates surfing the global cash flow.

Clay Macondray's great-grandfather had started the firm to help resolve mining claims during the Gold Rush. His integrity was never contested, not even by his enemies. His male issue for the next four generations had devoted their adult lives and most of their clients' money into honoring that man's financial acumen. The Macondray name was held in high esteem for five generations. Until Clay Macondray pushed his father out of the firm.

The receptionist riding shotgun at the gold-and-glass doors sat like a robot on hold. She noticed me out of the corner of her eye, turned herself on, and looked up. I gave her my card, the one from Annie's law firm...

The Girl Made of Silk

"Yesterday, or Centuries before ..."
~ Emily Dickinson, "After Great Pain ... "

At the time, which was several hundred millennia ago, the girl made of silk had no arms. Not that she needed them. She had wings. She was flying over the impossibly green jungle of Borneo, marveling at the trees that had taken two centuries to grow. She was captivated by primordial Borneo on a moonless night. Live among the stars and you desire to know the darkness of the jungle.

She was pausing there and then, randomly, smelling the still-evolving flowers. She too was new to this planet. *Curiosity met delight.*

Borneo: the canopy of trees kept out most sunlight and hid a multitude of dangers. Below the trees in the darkness of the noonday sun, the rainforest had vines that were a foot thick. There were plants that ate bush rats and the other rodents. And the deep shade of the tropical rainforest also hid the malaria that was biding its time.

She was down among the trees, cruising through them like a ship through shallow waters, luxuriating in the primeval vibes, when she realized with a shock that it might instead be Sunday night in San Francisco at the end of the 20th century! That would be a pleasure! And sorrow and grief! Not having any empathy, what a strange trip she might have! Oh, and what she gained? *She would be replenished!*

For an instant she hesitated. Unusual among the angels.

Call her Beatrice, the pure one, if we must name a cosmic force.

The girl of silk could be a ghost with silver hair. Silk swooping through the darkness. If she had eyes, Time was a steel-blue sea.

San Francisco was being "remembered," for girls made of silk never forget anything since they first appeared. They had total recall. But they had accumulated so much knowledge, remembering was itself a distraction. And accessing it took Time and effort.

Why remember a single moment in San Francisco, in the future?

If Time is both a river and a steel-blue sea, then it has a continuous undertow. Therefore Time moves in multiple trajectories. Because each new unexpected event warps Time, and thus the path of Time through the universe tosses and turns like a bad sleeper. Nothing sentient defines it or curtails it. Time itself is also elastic, of course.

But Beatrice's "silkiness" was friction-free. She was water within a stream within a river. Or not. It depends upon where any observer stands.

She flitted through many universes. Imagine surfing atop both spherical and cylindrical energy waves. She was multiple copies of herself.

Where she came out at this place and moment, Time here and now was the bright green of absinthe. But more iridescent. Fluctuating, well, pulsing.

But she wasn't here for more than an instant. Wherever *Here* and *Now* happened, she rebounded. Where she leapt in, a maelstrom formed, a fast-moving frothy whirlpool that left tiny bubbles as the sole trace. Like a dolphin made of silk, she leapt and slid and followed her own whimsy.

Yes, call her Beatrice, if she needs a name. Beatrice and her sisters separately wandered the universe eons before the earliest stellar religions existed, long before dreams of gods or goddesses appeared, at home among thousands of galaxies.

Beatrice and her sisters were beings of pure energy who chose female form for sensuous economy and efficiency, and thus they were evocative of the movement of energy through space and time. In this context, they illustrated the insubstantiality, which is, at the same time, the potentiality for all possible manifestations. They were, in a sense, pure phenomena.

If it helps, we can consider Beatrice a sort of Aeolian harp, but powered by Time and not with the wind. Thus, she oscillated. Or resonated. And how Time moved over her wings, or how her wings moved over Time, either way was both eerie and ethereal.

She was intricately mottled, yet translucent. And when she has them, fingers as delicate and slender and wispy. And she has a long thin vaporous tail you and I could not see.

She could be small enough to stand as high as you or I. Or she could blossom and bloom larger than a planet's orbit. But neither at our beck and call.

Was Beatrice a living being? Well, she wasn't tangible.

Was she less than a random shadow?

She was misty, almost indefinable.

Could we fix our eyes on her...?

Why did she hesitate? Was she intruding...? Her reluctance was natural, a most unnatural phrase to use with our Beatrice.

She had homed in on a speck of sorrow in the universe.

Her reluctance flickered away, faster as a photon.

She was an angel, let's pretend, large and magnificent with white, red and brown plumage. She had moon-silver eyes and roses in her cheeks. And a voice like smoky tequila. That she rarely used except while singing. And she sang in ranges no human ear could discern or imagine, but reverberated in our marrow.

She had a long torso, long arms and legs, when she had arms and not wings. She was remarkably strong. Her arms, her wings, were streaked with scars, yet she could put on a child's voice to speak out. Or to sing in a choir of angels.

Earlier her arms had unfurled into wings. Like tissue paper stretched to the limits had appeared. Swan wings. An eagle's wings. Her arms melted into great white wings that could lift a person effortlessly into the heavens. Into Time itself. If we don't like wings, think vanes. Windmill vanes, okay?

Still undecided, the angel was flying over the coves and gorges of primordial Borneo, relishing the future which was as clear to her as the past. As always, she was curious to learn all things and relive the future.

Yes, call the girl of silk an angel. Angels had elegant forms, women with sinuous bodies that flowed with magic. Their wings were nearly transparent. Huge and powerful.

An angel was a tornado in Time. Time's angels, let's call them that, and they can travel thousands of years in a single flight.

She curled into a ball and tumbled giggling through the night sky of Borneo. Dizzyingly, she tumbled. Such fun! She fell back among the trees and tumbled among them, ricocheting when she struck one, letting random chance spin out her path.

She who remembered everything then remembered *San Francisco* again.

Like a slender white geyser, the girl made of silk whooshed through Time and left the past at phenomenal speeds. At times she was bent like a ray of bright light traveling through water to air. When backlit by a star, she refracted its light, and her body became a long, drawn-out diamond, spitting off red, blue and golden beams in all directions.

She rocketed up beyond the atmosphere.

She would arrive in San Francisco on Time.

She leapt into the future. She made an exquisite and frenzied leap. A moment for her of pure joy. Then the girl made of silk was sinking and sliding down into blurry-eyed Time. She was sluicing through Time to arrive there in Time.

She was neither a girl nor made of silk.

But human vocabularies are woefully inadequate. And unless we all understand strings and things, well, we can't even begin to describe her universes. For all she had, she had her lapses, and empathy was the lone thing she could never treasure. Empathy was a double-edged sword that befuddled her.

She stretched herself out horizontally, or perhaps vertically, depending upon your position and perspective, and she floated into the great ocean of Time, distracted and lulled by its currents.

She was a motion in Time, like silk sliding off our arm.

Time moves in conflicting trajectories. She followed the rip currents, and she torqued in Time. Like a flying fish slimming and gliding, unaware of her own blueish crystalline sheen. She kneaded the continuous undertow of Time, flying like a fist, breaching bulwarks. She was inexorable, gleaming in the light of evolving stars.

She was feminine, but not a warrior. She was younger than her sisters, younger than the oldest stars, but only by a bit. She remembered being clustered, jammed together, and she and her sisters angrily kicking out for more room!

Her kind found it easier to come to our universe than for us to enter hers. That one-sided ease of entry was not a paradox, but an anomaly of the strings and things. And her kind, like us, did not understand the strings, either. They could, however, use them as we use, say, a swimming pool, or skydiving, or a typewriter.

She was a fallen angel, too, although she would have taken umbrage at how we humans meant it. She had no perch ever to have fallen from. She had never known sin or wickedness or even charity. But a fallen angel might be the closest way we humans could describe her. She was more than that, of course.

As she danced and pranced through Time, she had already forgotten San Francisco again. She was easily distracted by pretty things, or shiny things, or, and the universe was awash with both, a giant chest of pretty shiny things. Infinitely long and eternally deep.

Oh, look at this! Oh, look at that!

But we would have taken umbrage, too, at calling her an angel, yet that was what she was. Being humans, we have angels all wrong. We think that angels are ethereal, celestial, cosmic... And each of those words was unconceivable to our limited understanding of the ethereal celestial cosmos.

She kept floating and soaring through Time.

She could swivel and spin, circle and coalesce.

San Francisco, she then remembered.

San Francisco, she reminded herself.

But still she drifted, or floated, or hovered, or... At various times she was falling through Time, and over times pushing through Time, or maybe uncontrollably floating through Time. She was energized, though. She had a purpose, if she could bother remembering. And she was accelerating. Did she hum? Did she sing? Did she vibrate like a string?

She had leapt ten thousand years already with only eternity before her.

If she fell to eternity, the road back was not arduous.

She would know no panic. Only irritation with herself.

At first, she was laughing as she tumbled through Time. Distracted by what amused her, she launched herself and was falling sideways for ten thousand years through galaxies. She needed to slow down. She needed to bounce off someone or something to slow the fall.

Oh, right, San Francisco, I can go there!

She breached... We have no words to describe it.

But gravity wells are not smooth bores. They had scarred tunnels and gouged lanes, long, narrow furrows that empty into niches, fighting each other, pummeled by astonishingly powerful forces. There were jumps, like speed bumps.

The girl made of silk breached and then she braked.

Remember San Francisco!

She soared down and hurtled outward.

When Time played rough, she let herself be lifted on the updrafts of Time. *Take me there*, she told Time Itself, and half-flew there herself. She willed herself there and then. Like all travelers in time, she was never late unless she chose it.

If she were mundane, say, a truck, we could say she skidded into the turn on two wheels, and then fishtailed to a stop. We would also be correct saying she reached backwards and fishtailed to a stop.

She was not alone when she appeared and circled the buildings high above Sansome and Pine Streets. The streets at night glowed yellow gold in all directions, and they were empty of people or vehicles or noise. But a choir of angels already encircled the tallest section of the skyline. She coasted up towards her sisters.

Beatrice moved, she flew, soundless and swift. She came disconcertingly close to some windows of the skyscrapers. She may have seen her reflection on the skyscraper windows. Looking out these windows, anyone would have seen only a blur. A change in the light. A flicker among the fog. A bird seeing its reflection would flee. Much of the light that hit the sidewalks was light bounced down from these empty offices.

A slight tremor in what might be a hand said she had found the Moment. She floated further and searched for purchase within the choir.

This time was long ago, too, although not as long ago as Borneo. Forty years ago, well, about that long ago, on a Sunday night in midsummer before midnight, our angel, the girl made of silk, plowed a path through massive Pacific clouds and joined a choir of angels in San Francisco on a Sunday night. Their numbers were legion.

That night was a touchstone for those too busy to remember. But they had never forgotten that night. The song was too intense. Like swallows, they had returned to their Capistrano. Let us return as often as we remember. Let us feel that alive again.

Her wings softened as she joined them. They may have melted. She hovered. Up here, the fog came in gentle murmurs. It slowed her, and she was like a boat drifting ashore.

A thousand lit windows aglow in the gray fog…

Then the milky-white fog darkened with more whistling wings.

Another band of angels appeared, very old and experienced, with outstretched necks, well-spread wings, and long legs in place of tails directed backwards.

Her sisters shoaled and circled the buildings and then congregated in a circle over Sansome and Pine Streets in the City far below. Oh, their feathers were packed so tightly together that they whistled. They sailed without flapping their wings.

Was this Beatrice alone? Were these other angels all echoes of her through the past and future? Were they reflections rebounding thousands of times from these office buildings? Were they really all her sisters come to meet at this most auspicious time? Can a song be multiplied from a single voice? They sang as one. That was identity enough.

Beatrice opened her eyes, waited, utterly still, utterly quiet. Her unease grew at the silence below. She may have been one of these angels. She may have found she was scowling.

Where was the music?

Every being, sentient or otherwise, has a certain sound she most responds to. A tropism like the sun that she bends to. Why not a note from a saxophone coursing through the night and the fog?

In the daytime the city is a destination, a goal, a journey every individual is on. At night, the city is a presence, alive, a hulk in the dark. It heaves and breathes, itself alone and alive.

Imagine a saxophone player at ground zero for a big city's skyline. She was world famous and commanded audiences wherever she played. Tonight, the woman was alone, anonymous, surrounded by forty, fifty floor skyscrapers, all concrete and glass. It was after midnight, and the buildings glowed like honeycombs lit from inside, encased in blanket-thick fog.

Thirty, forty-odd stories above her, the fog was two thousand feet thick, roiling in, dense and milky-white, lit by the honey-colored lights still on in skyscrapers and by their cleaning crews.

Although at times, the winds up there scream among the buildings like a wounded animal. The airy space between these buildings this high were devoid of lift. If you and I heard the wind, we would shoot it. End its misery.

The lone saxophonist stood bedraggled thirty, forty floors below them, under a streetlight. This was no rehearsal for the big time. Nor was she practicing. She had no playlist, either. She would play *whatever* until she was exhausted. Then, drained, she could go home and re-enter her empty daily life.

She was here alone. She was alone here. She wanted no audience.

She didn't want to be seen.

She was here because nothing happens here at Pine and Sansome on a summer Sunday night after midnight.

She wanted to be cold and alone at midnight in San Francisco.

She wanted her sound swelling up and out and beyond.

She began playing her saxophone. Her music drifted upward, lazy as cigarette smoke. It curled and coiled and doubled back on itself.

Some others might say her music that night was incoherent, or meaningless, a fantasy, or pure delirium brought on by being exhausted by flight.

On the street corner below, the young woman played her saxophone to no one, to everyone, to the very stars in the heavens. But the streets surrounding her were empty, devoid of cars or humans, and the sounds echoed and echoed again off the cold, silent buildings. She played for no one. No one was listening, and in that freedom, she slowly emptied the grief in her soul into the most holy place in the city.

An aching saxophone is unique and intimate. It haunts like memory.

Her music was magnificent. More than that, it was unique to this time and place. It could not be repeated, only renewed

The city is jazz; jazz is the city.

The musician played, relentless in her sorrow. She was alone. Ineffably alone. Devastated, she had lost all. Lord high above, listen...

The universe is awash with loss, any of its denizens will tell us. Grief and sorrow outweigh all the dark matter. Loss permeates. Between the stars, between galaxies.

All sentience knows loss and never stops grieving even now as well as any time within eternity. Here as well as anywhere else, loss makes life numb.

Awareness itself might mean knowing loss.

Grief rips across stars, solar systems, galaxies. It is a primal lament, a shriek. The ineffable sadness that tears us apart. Atonal at some peaks, grief may feel most like the ripping and the shredding of limbs. But then life goes on, a threat that reaches our throat. *How could I have lost you? How can I go on?*

Grief was an eruption against the cold, and the chemical, and the indifferent. As it resonated, it wrenched and twisted, and the heart, like tendons, was ripped apart and shredded. It bled.

Consider the desolate music that a human could create to express her losses: a stillborn and a lost husband. If she could have gone into the grave with her child, she would have. And who would comfort her? The one who could have abandoned her.

Beatrice and her sisters were drifting, wings out-stretched, gliding gracefully between the clouds across the roofs of the buildings. Were some Beatrice merely echoes, were some only her reflections, or were some her siblings from among the stars?

The choir was singing softly. They could have flown anywhere in the universe, for grief and sorrow.

But the angels learn from us of grief and sorrow.

Being immortal, the angels and the devils stand in awe of human sorrow. Being immortal, they never feel it. But they recognize it in others. They treasure it because they can never fully experience it.

Why did Beatrice want San Francisco?

If she even remembered how she felt afterward... The last time she came... Restless, uneasy, itchy... Unfulfilled... Haunted by emptiness... The ache...

She felt less now than before. Deficient again...

Each visit here and now left her feeling ... crippled.

Friendly still, but with a crooked, all-knowing smile.

Grief and sorrow were the backdrop of our universe. A plenitude from the end to its beginnings. As common as stars or black matter.

Perhaps here they resonated stronger.

But grief is magnetic; it drew them here.

Why here? Why now?

The story playing out was common. The clouds around the buildings, the mist were nothing special here and now. And the acoustics were better across the universe. But not out of the ordinary.

It was believed among themselves that angels who cannot absorb grief lacked a moral compass and thus were dangerous to the universe. They lacked principles, the other angels believed.

The angels above absorbed all the sadness and the anger and carried it forever, making them the better angels that we so often speak about.

The acoustics at Pine and Sansome were oddly metaphysically pure.

The music rose to the fog and onward to Heaven, and angels came from all over Time and Space to hear again the nature of grief funneled skyward from one woman's heart.

Unable to fend off her sorrow and grief, she played alone on a Sunday night and thought she was alone.

Her grief was strikingly unique.

And she was no one special.

Grief is a battering ram. It stops the heart. You clutch your chest in shock and sorrow. Your heart is bleeding profusely, spewing out its sorrow. The pain is as pointed as a spike.

Grief is squarely about Time. The past and present and the future were linked and now broken. When someone dies, there was an empty space where that person used to be. An empty space where he used to move within. You still give them room to move in.

He was here. She is here. She is no longer here.

We cannot switch off grief. Grief that only organic beings (i.e., those with a heartbeat) can know. Only organic life can perceive Time.

With grief, we are not processing our world. We are *feeling*.

Thoughts rush from our heads.

We know we are thinking when our thoughts "move."

We experience ourselves. Grief changes the landscapes of our minds.

Grief changes us.

She played until depleted. Her agony then ended the music in mid-note.

Her hand rested on the saxophone. Her fingers fluttered, flickered, found no purchase, and ended.

Motionless, the angels far above could be sucked in.

A maelstrom they barely perceived.

The angels above here and now seemed scared, stock-still, on stiffened wings, their eyes wide and staring bigger and brighter and fearful at the broken woman far below them. Their fear was instinctual, and they could go no closer. They were afraid of her grief.

As she walked exhausted and drained to her car parked a block away, they ruminated over what they had heard and now they knew grief well. The universe at times seems to swell with it. But they had never experienced it. Nor had they learned to wear it.

But now they saw into a world where they had never been.

The choir of angels became a chorus that savored grief. Grief made them uneasy and restless. But it filled the emptiness they felt among the stars.

They sang wordlessly with the saxophonist. They sang of grief and sorrow, unable to find it in themselves. Grief meant once we held something special.

Angels held nothing special.

To lose a child...

There is no greater loss. To be alone with loss dead-ends us.

A grief that only the organic can feel.

In the middle of one empty night, when the angels wept, they were at last one with the world. Beatrice was crying brilliant blue-green tears.

Time is a palimpsest.

Tiburon means Shark

Lucy was a lousy driver. She drove like a tow truck driver. Whatever was troubling her kept her driving too slow and so she missed all the green lights. Once she gave a jackrabbit start when the light turned green. Then she almost took out a jaywalking woman on rollerblades. Soon she was straying into other lanes, tailgating taxicabs, and other foolish things.

She said, "I don't know why you're having me drive your car."

Candy Mac was calm. "It gives you something to do with your hands, Lucy. Try not to hit that cable car."

"Where is Clay Macondray today?" I asked.

His partner and ex-wife never hesitated. "Clay's out suing the Marin School for the Blind for negligence. Some real estate developer stepped in some guide dog's shit and flew ass over keister."

"He's suing the Blind because he didn't see the dog shit?"

Candy Mac said, "The developer is claiming over a million dollars in lost wages, plus punitive damages. And no one has seen his chiropractic bill yet." She estimated the total and smiled. "We should do well on this one."

On the Golden Gate Bridge the fog was blowing in sideways, horizontally like a sandstorm. The Range Rover was buffeted by stiff gusts of wind. Lucy had to flip on the windshield wipers to clear the great drops of mist. Visibility came and went in great white clumps.

"Personally, I love all the fog," Candy Mac said. "I couldn't stand a regular summer. All that bright light for days and days. I couldn't take it."

We drove across the Golden Gate Bridge into Marin County, the most affluent county in California. There was a lot of open space in Marin. For the past thirty years the residents have resisted growth. While they always claimed they were concerned environmentalists, open space kept the property values high. Nowadays, though, their own children couldn't afford to live here. The Marinites loved their property values more than they loved their children.

Candace Macondray was silent until we were leaving the Rainbow Tunnel in Marin. "Try to avoid striking cars that look like they have no insurance," she told Lucy.

A wise move, I thought. I looked at the car next to me. An uninsured vehicle with out-of-state plates with longhairs who were also driving erratically had pulled alongside us. The vehicle had a bumper sticker that said This Car Explodes on Impact. A very wise move, I decided.

Candy Mac looked over at the other car. "I always drive as if the car next to me has no insurance." She stretched and pressed down the power door locks.

We descended into the Sausalito flats and the leeward flank of the coastal range and left the fogbank hovering above us. We left 101 at the Tiburon off-ramp, and then drove east on Tiburon Boulevard. The car was quiet as the boulevard twisted and turned with the hills. Now we had ground fog that squatted on this side of the coastal range. Soon the hills had vanished into the fog, and the black shapes among white fog were just barely oak trees.

"Why don't we call first?" Lucy asked.

"Not if we want Terry to be there," Candace Macondray said. "Slow down ahead, Lucy. The city of Tiburon has a permanent speed trap up ahead."

Lucy slowed, came close to stopping. The Mercedes behind her almost rear-ended her, and then laid on its horn. Absently she gave him the finger. The Mercedes passed her on the next curve.

"This Tiburon speed trap," Candace Macondray continued, "my husband says it's the same officer every time. This one anal retentive gives out 75% of all the tickets in the department. One month he gave out over a hundred tickets. Now, I have heard that he was being reassigned because so many people have protested, but that may be wishful thinking." Her eyes scanned the hedgerows. "Well, he's not here today."

I said, "So you live in Tiburon, too."

"Only my husband does. I live on my boat at Berkeley Marina."

"Who is your husband?"

"Terry Danvers."

I turned and looked over the front seat at her. "Terry Danvers is your husband?"

"He was my first husband and now he is my third one."

"So Dr. Peter Staples is fucked."

"Not like I've been," she said cheerfully. "Don't give up yet," she told me. "Life is still full of surprises."

I couldn't get over it. "You married both Clay Macondray and Terry Danvers?" As far as I was concerned, she was both a glutton for psychic punishment and eligible for electroshock therapy in the Napa State Mental Institution.

Candace Macondray explained the chain of events. She and Terry Danvers were married soon after college. A few years later they were divorced. A few years after that she married Clay Macondray. Sometime after that they were divorced in that highly publicized battle I knew about. A few years later she quietly remarried Terry Danvers.

She gave a horse laugh. "My marriages are simply another example of the Byzantine network of relationships that have often developed from numerous California marriages between friends and / or enemies."

We entered Tiburon and drove past a Mercedes being ticketed by a Tiburon police cruiser. The two most important things I knew about Tiburon were that Tiburon was Spanish for shark and that many of the Big Money Boys from San Francisco lived on its headlands overlooking the Bay. For years I have been content never wanting to find out more about the burg.

Tiburon has the same weather San Francisco has, plus an incomparable view of the skyline of the City. The main highway dead-ends downtown, when it hits the bay. One tributary goes along a block of touristy chandlers and Sunday buffet saloons and seafood restaurants and women's boutiques and bookstores that sell art books and hiking gear, all of which had huge windows that overlooked the bay. Meanwhile the left-handed tributary swings surfside past the municipal parking lot and some bare fields waiting to be condominiums before it goes off to thread itself through the hills. The streets that wound through the hills above the bay seemed waist-wide and made up of curlicues and switchbacks, a maze designed to keep out tourists, the lookie-loos, and any debutante burglars who might be looking for an easy score. More importantly, the Big Money Boys of Tiburon didn't have to share their sunlight with anybody poor.

Where else would the King of the Landlords live?

We left the shoreline road and went uphill on Ebbtide Canyon Road. The asphalt narrowed to one lane, snaked inland, meandered through field and glade; the residents wanted their green space. The road sloped back to the shoreline, and the condos thinned out and manor houses appeared, all set back from the road, and every neighbor had a perfect hedge. This was fire truck hell. I listened to the wind in the trees and prayed no jerk threw a lit cigarette out his car window while I was there.

Candy Mac pointed. "There's his place."

I said, "You don't live there, too?"

"Never have. He bought it after we separated."

Terry Danvers' Tiburon love-nest on Ebbtide Canyon Road was more expensive than an entire street of homes in most Midwest towns. It was beautiful, long and low, a weird house that didn't belong here standing in a field of California poppies. It was Mineshaft Modern: a new home built to look like a pile of old barn wood. As architecture goes, Mineshaft Modern is very dramatic, very theatrical. The house came in sections, all of which were clustered around a single great stone chimney. The sections were not cubes, but irregularly-shaped blocks attached to other irregularly-shaped blocks, and not always the same size, either, as if my youngest son had designed it from his toy chest. Like most Mineshaft Moderns, it stood among the tall grasses like an optical illusion. Studded with glass windows and skylights, it was geometrically designed to crouch and hide among the cypresses and Monterey pines. The roof came and went in different angles. At one point it was flat, at another point it was peaked, another slanted; once the roof swept around in a great arc, and once it sloped in a sharp angle. Bedrooms appeared haphazardly added on like warty growths. In the thick fog, the house looked like a spilled toy chest from the House of Usher.

"How long has your husband had it?"

"Five years. One for each mistress."

Danvers had a circular drive, a rarity along the shoreline of the Bay. Few could afford one; most lots were too small or too narrow. His lawn was forest green and professionally manicured. Here and there stone ornaments gave the lawn a pet cemetery feel. We parked in the drive, and then walked up to his house. On the far left was a two-car carport that dangled over the cliff, empty now except for a huge safe that squatted like a California grizzly bear in the farthest corner of the carport. It was a floor safe, a Mosler, cast iron, and the faded scrollwork on its door said it had once been the property of the Wells Fargo Stagecoach Company of San Francisco, California. While it came with casters, the safe was the largest chunk of metal I'd ever seen outside of an aircraft hangar. It was bigger than a California grizzly, and a refrigerator could fit inside it.

"I love the safe," Lucy said.

"It came around the Horn with the Forty-Niners," Candy Mac related. "Wells Fargo used it to store the first gold dust down from Sutter's Mill."

"Nobody made steel safes in those days," I said.

She gave me a nasty look, as if I had cracked wise about the crows-feet around her eyes. "Terry saw the safe, fell in love with it, and bought it. He thought the pioneer touches lent distinction to the ambiance of the house."

"Why is the safe outside?" I wondered.

"Terry lost the combination," she confessed. "He forgot it, forgot where he wrote it down. Nobody can get in there anymore. Now he has to pay a fortune to have it carted away to the junk pile."

I shrugged. "Hire a locksmith?"

"Nothing in there worth anything. The office Terry bought it from kept their coffee club moneys in there. If you want it, you can take it off his hands."

"Push it over the edge," I said. "Let the fishes have it."

"The state will have you arrested for littering."

We made the wrought iron gate squeak, and then walked up the flagstone path. Lucy grabbed my elbow and held us back. "Can you smell that? Wood smoke."

I inhaled deeply. Everybody in the neighborhood had their fireplace going, and the fog was rich with the thick aroma of wood smoke. I teased Lucy. "August is a great time for hot chocolate and fireplaces."

Lucy didn't laugh. "No, it isn't." She admired the house. "God, it's a beautiful house."

"I wouldn't live here," Candy Mac confided. "He has mice." She remembered more to warn us. "In case you didn't know, Terry Danvers is proud to be the great-great-grandson of a whorehouse madam. His bedroom has been customized to fit around a whorehouse mirror from his great-great-grandmother's Nob Hill bordello. Terry's very proud of it. If you compliment him about it, he'll never stop talking about it, and we'll never discuss your client's needs." She caught my eye. "Yes, I would like to break it into ten thousand pieces."

I rang the doorbell twice before anyone answered.

The housekeeper opened the door. She wore headphones and had an Ipod clipped to her apron. She was a pretty young woman, Chicana, twenty years old at the most, formerly slender and now very pregnant. She had beautiful Spanish eyes, olive skin and a round face. She wore no make-up and had a head of unruly brown hair that was used to being combed by impatient fingers. She had a hunk of pastel crocheting in one hand. She pulled off the headphones, and the sound of norteño music reached us.

Candy Mac dazzled her with a corporate smile. "Hello, Sylvia, is Terry at home?"

The housekeeper glared at her, and then at all of us, and then back at Candy Mac. "Who should I say is calling?" She had a low smoky voice, cautious pronunciation, and a wondrously lyrical Spanish accent. She could curse me to hell and back in slow Spanish, and I would lap up what spilled over.

"Don't you remember me from the Sanctuary last week?"

The housekeeper recognized her and gave her a big, friendly smile. "Si, Ms. Macondray."

"I'm his wife. I'm Mrs. Terry Danvers."

The housekeeper blinked, speechless, immobile.

"Can I see my husband?" Candy Mac repeated.

The housekeeper let us in. Her face was afraid she faced a mad woman.

"Who is it, Sylvia?" a woman called.

"Ms. Cicerone?" The housekeeper backed off. She took a step toward the living room, and then took a step back toward us. "Ms. Cicerone?" She stopped cold, stood her ground and blocked us. "Could you come here please?" she called. Her hands roamed the globe of her belly while she waited.

Ms. Cicerone was young and very short, full-breasted and full-hipped, in her dangerous twenties, and she wore an Oakland Raiders nightshirt. She had some streaks of silver in her overly braided hair. She was young enough that she could tease Fate by having two silver streaks in her hair.

"Hello, Bernie, we've never met, but I swear I know all there is to know about you," Candace Macondray said. "I need to see my husband."

Bernie Cicerone blinked. "What did you say?" She had a little girl's voice and a thick Oakie accent.

"I'm his wife. Mrs. Terry Danvers. It's very urgent."

The young woman was surprised. "Mrs. Macondray?" She had an overbite when relaxed, and a horsy smile that she tried to hide as much as she could. She made an effort to keep her lips closed tight.

She kept us standing in the doorway.

Bernie was disturbed. "I didn't know you were his wife." She couldn't help but sound betrayed.

"Oh, dear. He never told you. I use Macondray for professional reasons. May I see him?"

Bernie was confused, couldn't think fast enough. "Well, he's taking a nap." She gestured vaguely towards a back bedroom. "Please, please come in."

As I entered the foyer, I looked back over my shoulder. The mistress gripped the doorframe as if she could tear off a piece with her bare hand. I saw the suicide scars braceleting across her wrist. Once upon a time she had been emotionally unstable. Once again I was thankful that most people botch their suicide attempts. I wondered if she still was that tormented.

We entered a large living room with a seventeen foot ceiling, a greenhouse skylight and indirect lighting. It was decorated with denim chairs and a denim sofa, Apache rugs, and lots of hanging plants that needed little watering. A grand fireplace had a small redwood tree burning inside. A cup of hot chocolate complete with marshmallows was on a glass-topped coffee table between the sofa and the fireplace, a People magazine opened beside it.

Bernie said, "I'll let him know you're here."

Candy Mac, who had hardly slowed once we entered, dazzled her with her great big smile. "Let's barge in and surprise him." She strode past the younger woman and barged into the master bedroom.

One at a time we all walked into an explosion of glacial-white light that blinded us. The bedroom was huge, and yet it held only one or two pieces of solid, old-fashioned furniture. The entire southern wall was glass and had a magnificent view of sun-bright fog. At the center of the room was a king-size waterbed with American flag pillows and a quilted comforter. A projection television with a screen as tall as a teenage boy took up much of the east wall. The television was on, and the Giants were playing at a fog-shrouded Candlestick Park. There were baby spotlights on the rafters and their bright beams all seemed centered in on the bed itself. An antique mirror in a gilt filigree frame was stretched across the mantelpiece, reclining like a saloon nude. The mirror was huge, fully seven feet long, and must have weighed two hundred pounds. The glass was cracked, and the quicksilver rubbed off or discolored in several places. While recognizing oneself in it was hard, the huge mirror did magnify everything.

"Behold the American male in his splendor."

Terry Danvers was asleep atop the waterbed, snoring with his mouth wide open, completely naked, except for a tropical blue condom on his limp penis. His cellular phone was in his right hand, and the remote control for the television lay atop his beer belly.

Terry Danvers was grayer these days. He was still a big man, stout and broad-shouldered, a strong and fierce-looking man with a sweeping mustache, a grandiloquent beard, close-cropped hair that had receded less than most men his age, and large ears that stood out from his head.

Candace marched in and abruptly woke him up. "Terry! Terry!"

Danvers woke instantly and focused on her alone. He hurriedly grabbed one of his Old Glory pillows and covered himself. That a man covers his nakedness in front of his wife surprised me. He rubbed his face, and then refocused. "It's you," he groaned. "Go away. We made a deal. Leave me alone."

Candy Mac said, "Hello, Papa Smurf."

He rubbed his face as if pulling off cobwebs of sleep.

"Why aren't you out making money?"

Danvers used the remote to turn off his television set. "The only reason anybody wants to get rich is so he can get laid steadily with whomever he chooses."

"Why don't you put some clothes on?"

"What are you doing in my house?"

"I represent Peter Staples, Senior, recently deceased."

"That deadbeat." He barked his disbelieving laughter. "How can that be? You're my wife."

"Pro bono," she said sweetly. "Some things I do for free."

"You are a bitch," he hissed in admiration.

"Get your clothes on," she growled. "We have a security deposit refund to discuss."

The developer slid off the bed and began throwing on clothes. He looked up and saw Lucy and me. "What the fuck are all these people doing in my bedroom?"

"We are here to negotiate for the full and complete refunding of his client's security deposit," she said, indicating me with a flip of her hand.

I smiled like a cop with a warrant.

Danvers glanced at me, caught on that I wanted him dead, and gave me the nervous once-over. "What's your name, pal? Have we met?"

"I'd remember if we had," I lied. "The name is Pasnow."

Our eyes locked. I think he realized the deep wellsprings of loathing I had for him. He didn't believe we had never met.

Danvers scowled over me, still trying to place me. "I know you. I know we met," he insisted. "Years ago, but . . ."

"We never met," I lied.

Bernie Cicerone leaned against the doorframe, half-in and half-out of the bedroom, and watched.

"Let's do this by the numbers," Candy Mac told her husband. "The security deposit."

Danvers barked a laugh. "Nope, he's out of luck and on his own."

I said, "What about his father's stuff?"

Danvers warily eyed me. "That I can do. You should call up the main office. Get a release from my daughter. Tell Trudy I said it was okay." He grabbed his cellular phone and hit redial.

I said, "What about his furniture?"

"It was all shit. We took it to the dump."

I said, "It was his furniture."

"I should charge his kid for what the dump charged me to take it." He waved it off. "It's all long gone." The party at the other end of his cellular phone answered. "Trudy? Listen, some guy's coming by the office tomorrow asking for his property. Peter Staples, Senior. Right. Thanks, Trudy." He hung up. "Good enough, pal?"

I said, "Can he have his father's security deposit?"

Terry Danvers refused. "Nope."

"You won't return his security deposit?" I said.

"I said, no." A vein in his forehead visibly throbbed.

Candy Mac stepped in. "What kind of publicity would you get if the City heard how you treated the victim of a terrible crime?"

"Don't threaten me, Candy."

"Then let's talk about tenant rights and landlord responsibilities," she said.

"I'm not negotiating in my own bedroom with you or anybody for even a dime of that security deposit."

"Your office or mine?"

His grin was more of a snarl. "Candy, you don't want to be my lawyers anymore?"

Candy Mac's face turned scarlet and was made silent. As she looked at me, she noticed Bernie slipped out of view.

She grew very conspiratorial, started wheedling and worming closer. "So, tell me, how are you getting on with her?"

Danvers grew quiet. His face went pale. By nature a braggart, he wanted to boast and lie, but he was afraid to do so, and that was mortifying and shameful.

The housekeeper stuck her head in the room to watch the fireworks. Nobody but me noticed her. I wondered if she were going to call 911. I kept thinking I had seen her somewhere before.

She took off her headphones. "Would you like some coffee?"

"Let's see what happens next," I said, gesturing at the scene still unfolding.

She raked a hand through her hair and waited.

Candy Mac asked her husband about his mistress. "Are you two still in love?"

Terry Danvers made a face. "The word doesn't mean anything. Sex is what you want. And, yes, she's still a good piece." His smirk implied Candy Mac wasn't. He leered at Lucy. "Till someone better comes along."

As he boasted, his mistress slowly walked back into the room. Bernie had gone for a box of tissues, had heard his words spewing from his mouth, and now the truth was sinking in--that this wife of his was visible proof of her boyfriend's essential infidelity. She eyed him carefully, deliberately, as if reconsidering every moment she had ever spent with him.

Danvers realized she had heard his words. "Sylvia, will you get some refreshments?" he asked the housekeeper. "Anybody else want something?"

"Coffee for me," I said. Hell, I was enjoying the show.

"I think not." Candace Macondray looked at her watch, and then at Bernie Cicerone, Lucy, the housekeeper and me. "Would all of you please wait outside?" She was forceful with her husband. "I want to talk to you in private about that letter you sent me at the firm. You make several serious allegations in it."

He was belligerent. "Accusations, not allegations. I mean them, too."

"If they're true," she swore, "I'll fire the son-of-a-bitch myself."

They noticed me being nosey in the doorway.

She said, "Please leave us alone."

They closed the master bedroom door, I wandered through the living room. The sliding door to the back deck was open, and the deck overlooked San Francisco Bay.

I stepped out on the deck. The house was on the edge, on a shelf over a cliff, and the deck was like a fat lip around the face of the house. It ran the length of the house, had some other doors leading out onto it, and at either end an outdoor staircase book-ended it. All of San Francisco Bay lay flat in front of us. The view must have been breathtakingly beautiful. Only a helicopter would have a better view. When the fog was gone, of course.

Today I couldn't see the city, for that layer of fog not only covered the skyline, but everything farther than twenty feet in front of us. I looked over the cliff edge. The cliff went straight down a hundred feet and nose-dived into deep water. Danvers' house even had a pier for a sailboat to anchor off. A long spidery staircase led up from the rocks. A moment of vertigo, and I gave it up.

Danvers' mistress had followed me out. Bernie Cicerone wasn't very attractive, but then men thirty years older than a twenty-something generally weren't too picky. Youth, not looks, was the prize. Or maybe, inexperience was the prize. The less she knew what good performance in bed was just made it easier for the old man to hold his head up.

"You have one fabulous view," I told her, for lack of anything better to say.

She agreed and looked around at the property. "A weird piece of land, but it has the best view. On a clear day you can see . . ." Voices raised in anger back inside cut her next words off. She had lost her train of thought and for a moment was at a loss for words.

"My name's Pasnow. Frank Pasnow."

"Bernie Cicerone. Everybody calls me Bernie."

A brisk sea breeze was blowing, and Bernie hugged herself tightly. It was cold out here, but that wasn't center stage in her mind. My guess: she was always cold. We locked eyes, and she thought she saw sympathy in mine.

"I didn't know she was his wife," Bernie muttered. "She's a dyke. Everybody knows she's a dyke." She thought the implications over. "Her being a dyke explains a lot about him. How he treats women." She looked despairingly at her lot in life.

I gave her my card. Frank Pasnow Investigations. "Never know when you might need to sue the bastard, okay?"

"Are you a lawyer?"

"No, but I can refer you to a good one."

She gave me a slow flirtatious smile. "Might be sooner than later."

I have no idea where the thought came from, but I knew I had found the open wound and she wanted to talk about it. I felt like some Old Testament prophet rising up in righteous anger. "What did he do to you?"

Caught off-guard, she almost told me.

Lucy stuck her head out. "There's trouble, Frank."

We went back inside on the double. The master bedroom was empty. The raised voices came not from the living room, either, but from the closed door on our right. We burst in and found ourselves in the kitchen.

Candy Mac now wielded a wicked butcher's knife, had it aimed at her husband's heart. Her eyes were the eyes of a woman hanging by her fingers above a bottomless abyss, feeling the grip slipping, slipping, *slipping*. "I should kill you!" she hissed, her voice still plagued with uncertainty.

∞

After a fog-blanketed sundown I crossed the Golden Gate Bridge and took 101 North to Tiburon Boulevard. Where the off-ramp met the boulevard, I turned left instead of right and drove west into Mill Valley. On Miller Avenue I slowed for the inevitable speed trap at the lumber yard, successfully passed through that challenge, and then about a mile further on slowed again for some doped-up son of a hippie who was wandering in a daze down the center of the street, shouting incoherently at the fog above his head.

Beyond the downtown stores, I headed downhill and drove deep into a Mill Valley canyon. Like the fog, I infiltrated the redwoods. Twenty minutes later I parked under some redwoods and leaking fog and trekked up the dirt path to his bungalow. I trekked cautiously because I didn't want to trip in the dark on the exposed roots of the redwood trees. The path was rich and thick with wood smoke and barbecued salmon. If barbecue always makes me salivate--which it does--then the aroma of barbecued salmon makes me a prisoner of love.

I heard a saxophone in the fog.

I'm a true city boy. Not much can bring a tear to this cynic's eyes. But then not much sounds quite like a broken hearted saxophone in an empty city after midnight. An aching saxophone echoing off the skyscrapers can be a bullet to pierce my heart. As I have been told, the corner of Pine and Sansome in the Financial District is as acoustically pure as beneath the Bay Bridge at Folsom and Beale.

But this sax man was no musician. He was only going up and down the scales. No tune. No melody. Not much rhythm, either. Just climbing up and down the musical scale like any beginner. In the canyon countryside behind his house a coyote was going through the scales with him. The coyote hit more notes true.

I discovered a gingerbread house set back in the dark forest. I rang the doorbell. No answer. I went around back, followed the saxophone. The saxophonist was waist-deep in a hot tub. He and the tub were encircled by several dozen lit candles and by propane tiki torches. Steam was rising from the hot tub like the smoke that billows from a geyser. A few yards away a barbecue grill was very slowly cooking some very large and thick salmon steaks. I considered snatching a steak and running from the law.

"Kon nichi wa, Pasnow-san."

I was listening to the mouth-watering sizzle of the salmon steaks. "Hello, Chief."

Chief Isamu Kuriura was steaming in his hot tub in his backyard, his saxophone by his side, while giant redwoods surrounded him and dripped fog down upon him.

"Welcome to my home. Will you join me?"

"For supper?"

"And you must soak in the hot tub. It will relax you and increase your appetite, Mr. Pasnow."

"I'll take a rain check on the hot tub, but I will eat with you." I came closer. "So, you play the saxophone."

"Ho, I am terrible." He laughed, didn't care. "I can't do this in Japan. No room." He gestured at the redwoods. "Pity the poor redwoods. A thousand years old, endangered, and they have to listen to my nonsense." He laughed at himself.

Thank God he had set aside the saxophone.

"What brought you to America?"

"Affordable housing, cheap food, parking, Tokyo's humidity." He looked around at the redwoods. "Free air conditioning. Can I bring you something to drink?"

"Sure."

The chief was a very good host. "I will prepare the sake for us," he called. "Thirty seconds in the microwave."

He climbed from his hot tub, and he was both buck-naked and pruney-skinned. He slipped into a thin cotton kimono robe. He grabbed a paper-thin towel, threw it over his shoulder, left the deck, took time to flip the salmon steaks and brush some sauce on each one, and then he headed for his bungalow.

I followed him inside. His house stunk worse than the smoking car of a transcontinental train in winter. He nuked a carafe of sake in the kitchen while I looked around his living room. It was filled with his golf equipment and Old West memorabilia. A minute later he joined me.

"Nice place you got here," I said.

He lit a fresh cigarette. "I am a renter," the chief said sadly.

"We all are," I said dryly, "in the eyes of God."

I followed him back through the kitchen. The chief now had the carafe of warmed sake and two cups the size of shot glasses on a tray. He balanced the tray and two dinner plates in his hands, holding the cigarette between his lips and puffing on it. I pushed open the door to the deck and followed him outside.

The chief went back to his deck and turned the salmon steaks again. God, they were gorgeous. Mouth-watering, too.

I love salmon. I think all the dams and water projects along the West Coast should be ripped out by the roots to make spawning easier for salmon. Salmon is a gift given to us by the gods, whether it's baked, broiled, barbecued, smoked, poached or served as sushi.

Chief Kuriura sucked happily on his smoke. "California is made of landlords and renters," he pontificated. "California is trying very hard to become Japanese. Californians think Japan is the future." He shook his head at such foolishness. "But I could never live this well in Japan." He gestured at the night, the steam, the redwoods, the fog, the salmon steaks and the lonely coyote calls. "The salary man, the office girl, in Japan can never dream of owning this much luxury. He does not own it, she cannot rent it."

He looked like a professor about to give a lecture.

"Do you think the salmon's done?"

Chief Kuriura had mixed soy sauce, sugar and some sake, and then brushed that on the steaks as they grilled. Five minutes on each side was all that they needed.

We ate on a redwood picnic table on his deck. His rice cooker sat by us, tied to an all-weather outdoor electrical outlet. We had barbecued salmon on rice and warm sake. The salmon was exquisite. When the meal was finished, I spoke.

"So where do I come in?"

Fog @ Nite

The Bridge and its yellow lights at night in the fog.

Where the hills vanish into the fog, black shapes of trees among white fog.

Driving creates hypnotic trance in a foggy night. Every street is a fog-filled tunnel.

The streetlights were like runway lights at some fogged-in airport.

Empty skyscrapers shrouded in midnight fog.

Tonight was a cold night in August. The fog hadn't settled in yet, was still writhing eastward and past the bay. Once it settled in, the fog would trap the heat escaping from the city, actually warming up the night. But the winds hadn't died down yet. Inland must still be too warm, or perhaps the ocean still too cold.

The fog goes up to Masonic, filling in the Richmond basin with summer fog. The fog stops above the old Sears store on Masonic and Geary. From the parking lot, it looks like the fog rose to the sun every day.

Because the summer nights in the city were so cold, there are few houseflies in the city.

There are few warm nights in San Francisco's summer. There were even fewer summer sunsets.

The streets looked like they were smoke-filled. But that smoke was cold and damp and drizzled on the streets.

The fogbank looked like a strip of black tape across the peaks of the city's glittering skyline.

Grey skyscrapers, silent and empty, colossi in the fog and night.

Hard to know how high a building is with this fog.

Streetlights in the night fog looking like some connect-the-dots puzzle.

Streetlights disappearing in pairs into the fog.

The lights on the next hill looked like lights suspended, no, *floating!* in the foggy air.

Winter on Jackson Street

For a Thursday night in August Chinatown was unusually quiet. Winter quiet. The restaurants were half-empty. There was no one on the sidewalks. I didn't have to park by a hydrant, in a bus zone, a yellow zone, didn't even have to double-park. Sure, there was only one space on Jackson Street, but nothing is as rare as a parking space in Chinatown.

The Golden Mountain Mortuary was on Jackson Street above Powell, built like a pagoda, a white wood frame building that smelled of beeswax and incense.

I was the earliest arrival at the mortuary. A Chinese hostess with compressed lips and a playful eye twisted her eyebrows and indicated the room to the right where the body lay at the head of a phalanx of folding chairs. The casket was covered with blankets of flowers. The incense was thicker here, almost as heavy as lead. I was surprised by the three security cameras mounted on the rafters above the casket. Shoplifters beware?

∞

I decided to get some air.

Not much is more alive than the smells of Chinatown at night. Seafood, hoisin sauce, cayenne and garlic and ginger root, oyster sauce and sesame oil and the almond smells from the fortune cookie factory on Stockton Street. If there's a heaven I'm allowed in, it smells this sweet.

∞

I stood and left then. Down on the streets, the Friday evening rush still lingered like the smell of a Chinatown cigar. An icy wind was rolling through the concrete canyons. Cold town. Summer in the city.

A Thank You note.

Thank you, San Francisco.
You never loved me as much as I loved you.
But I will forever be in your debt.
Somebody used to say that you have lived too long in San Francisco when the streets get too dirty for your memories. I couldn't tidy it all.

I wanted out of San Francisco. Streets too small, trees too big, and too many people. Too silly-ass expensive. The homeless were getting to me, I must admit. And the entitled had way too much of everything.

I love you, San Francisco. But if I can do one thing and still get out of here alive and not a fugitive, well, what would that be?

I would save my son.

On that note, I called my son and left the same basic message as voicemail. No sense waiting for a chance to talk to my son... And Kitty? Oh, Stevie will surely tell her...

One Last Item

One last item may be worth mentioning. After the bodies of Peter Staples, Senior, and Dr. Peter Staples, Junior, were released by the coroner's office, I used some of the five thousand and paid for both cremations. Because I wasn't next-of-kin, because neither Staples had left a will, it took me four weeks to get their ashes freed from the bureaucrats.

I mingled the ashes of father and son together. I guess I hoped the Staples men would get to know each other that way. God willing, maybe it's never too late.

One sunny Sunday afternoon in late September, Annie Harker and I stood beyond the line on the maps, beyond the margins of my country, on the western slope of the Golden Gate Bridge. The entire continental United States of America was east of us. Only two feet of America lay west, and that was rocky cliffs, and over our shoulders the skyline of San Francisco looked like white stones clustered together, like the tombstones in a Colma cemetery.

The sky was California blue, never-ending blue, and the fresh air off the blue Pacific was as intoxicating as new wine at the vineyards. We were alone, save for a single cloud no bigger than a man's hand over the western horizon.

I poured the ashes into the wind.